"Joyce Ray has brought together an impressive group of library thinkers and data management experts to cover all aspects of research data management now and into the future. This book covers the entire data life cycle—from incentives and mandates for sharing research data, to metadata standards and best practices of describing data for discovery, to preservation and archiving of datasets for use by future generations. Information professionals in the library and archival communities are a natural fit to lead the myriad tasks of research data management, and they will find inspiration in the insights provided in each chapter."

Carol Tenopir
Chancellor's Professor and Board of Visitors Professor
School of Information Sciences
University of Tennessee, Knoxville

"Increasing funder requirements relating to research data, combined with a growing awareness of the value that accessible, citable, reusable data can offer to researchers, mean that every research organisation needs to take research data management seriously as an institutional imperative. This timely book contains contributions on every aspect of the problem from people with practical experience of the solutions. The editor, Joyce Ray, has been closely involved with the community's developing understanding of the challenges for many years; she has drawn together essential guidance and useful case studies that will be of value to all university information and research services."

Kevin Ashley
Director
Digital Curation Centre
University of Edinburgh

"Research data management is becoming a crucial issue for European universities as they tackle the challenges posed by data-driven science. The League of European Research Universities (LERU) is about to publish its 'Roadmap for Research Data,' which will guide universities in their decision making as they tackle the data deluge. This book, therefore, is timely and will provide well-documented guidance on the contributions that the library sector can make. Data-driven research has the potential to revolutionize the way research is conducted, and there is a tremendously important role for libraries to play."

Paul Ayris
Director of UCL Library Services and UCL Copyright Officer
President of LIBER (Association of European Research Libraries)
ir of the LERU Chief Information Officers Community

D1336309

"The variety of approaches and experiences give this book broad appeal for information professionals at different size organizations with different priorities. The details of the process that organizations went through to try and meet data services needs is extremely helpful. This manuscript gets down to the nuts and bolts, and the case studies are its greatest feature."

Stephanie Wright
Data Services Coordinator
University of Washington Libraries

"As a research library-based data management specialist, I have struggled to find robust resources with up-to-date practical information without having to scour the Internet for hours. This book will be a major asset to all professionals who are in a similar position. It is important because it provides relevant, timely, practical information about topics that I deal with every day—repositories, governance, copyright, metadata, data citation, and so forth—and it's all collected in one place. In a more philosophical sense, the book may provide a vehicle for getting everyone in the data services field 'on the same page' with regard to the latest and greatest in research data management, in the sense that the book provides a benchmark for the state of our profession. We all recognize that data services are new to libraries, and many of us are doing a bit of DIY in terms of developing our services. The result of the 'pull yourself up by your bootstraps' approach is that services vary wildly across institutions. The availability of a book like this enables librarians (and other data stewardship professionals) everywhere to seek out a common reference, which fosters dialog and consistency of approach."

Amanda L. Whitmire
Data Management Specialist
Center for Digital Scholarship and Services
Oregon State University Libraries and Press

"This collection of timely articles on the emerging field of librarian support for research data management includes a good selection of topics and well-chosen authors. As a practitioner, I found the case study articles the most useful and interesting parts of the book. They were meaty, blow-by-blow accounts of how an organization, like mine, struggled and succeeded with these uncertain challenges of data management. This is not just a collection of articles written by key players from major grant-funded groups, but also real librarians implementing real services that you can relate to, and best of all, implement yourself."

Lisa Johnston
Research Services Librarian
Co-Director of the University Digital Conservancy
University of Minnesota Libraries

"This book represents a foundational contribution from the guardians of institutional data that will give confidence to those who appreciate the huge potential of data based research in seeking solutions to global and societal challenges in the future."

John Wood
Secretary-General
Association of Commonwealth Universities
and European Chair of the Research Data Alliance

"Research data will drive the next generation of innovation, and the deployment of effective data infrastructure is essential to enable data access and use. The topics in this book are both important and timely, and the contributors and editor read like a Who's Who of key players in the field."

Francine Berman
Chair of Research Data Alliance/US and Co-Chair of the
National Academies Board on Research Data and Information

"A hallmark of every emergent profession is the initial codification of the knowledge that distinguishes it as a specialization. *Research Data Management* serves this function for the cluster of professionals coalescing to support data-intensive science, also known as e-science or cyberinfrastructure. The diverse talents of the contributors to this work reflect the rich intellectual roots undergirding this new data profession. Future generations of data curators, data scientists, data librarians, data managers, and other data specialists will look upon this volume as a seminal work."

Charles Humphrey
Research Data Services Coordinator
University of Alberta Libraries

Research Data Management

Practical Strategies for
Information Professionals

Research Data Management

Practical Strategies for
Information Professionals

Edited by Joyce M. Ray

Charleston Insights in
Library, Archival, and Information Sciences

Purdue University Press
West Lafayette, Indiana

Contents

Introduction to *Research Data Management*

JOYCE M. RAY

Interest in research data has grown substantially over the past decade. The reason for this is evident: the digital revolution has made it far easier to store, share, and reuse data. Scientific research data are now almost universally created and collected in digital form, often in staggering quantities, and all disciplines are making increasing use of digital data. Data sharing increases the return on the large investments being made in research and has the potential to exponentially advance human knowledge, promote economic development, and serve the public good, all while reducing costly data duplication.

The Human Genome Project is a well-known example of the return on public investment resulting from collaborative research and data sharing. The project began in 1990 as an international effort to identify and map the sequence of the more than 20,000 genes of the human genome and to determine the sequence of chemical base pairs that make up DNA. Completed in 2003, the project produced GenBank, a distributed database that stores the sequence of the DNA in various locations around the world. The data are publicly accessible and continue to be mined for research in fields from molecular medicine and biotechnology to evolution. Findings have led to the development of genetic tests for predisposition to some diseases, and ongoing research is investigating potential disease treatments. GenBank now supports a multibillion-dollar genomics research industry to develop DNA-based products.

The success of GenBank and other highly visible research projects has drawn the attention of national governments and international organizations

1

to the potential of data sharing and international collaboration to solve some of the grand challenges facing the world today, from disease prevention and treatment to space exploration and climate change.

But having an interest in data sharing is only the first step in doing it successfully. In order for data to be shared among research teams and maintained for reuse over long periods of time, another grand challenge must be solved—preserving all this digital data and managing it so that it can be stored efficiently, discovered by secondary users, and used with confidence in its authenticity and integrity. When datasets were shared only among colleagues known to each other, trust was implicit. If data are to be made widely available and used by people with no personal knowledge of their creators, and for different purposes than those for which they were created, then trust must derive from how the data are managed and documented.

Required documentation includes not only search terms for future data discovery (descriptive metadata), but also evidence of the data's provenance (how, when, where, why, and by whom it was created), its chain of custody, and information on how it has been managed to mitigate the risk of data loss or corruption. This is true for the "big data" projects that have captured the attention of the news media, and it is just as true and even

Total Grants over $500	12,025 $2,865,388,605	
	20% by number of grants	80% by number of grants
Number Grants	2404	9621
Total Dollars	$1,747,95,7451	$1,117,431,154
Range	$38,131,952- $300,000	$300,000- $579
	20% by total value = $573,077,721	80% by total value = $2,292,310,884
Number of grants	254	11,771
Range	$38,131,952- 1,034,150	1,029,9984- $579

Table 1. NSF 2007 award distribution by award size. Courtesy of Bryan Heidorn.

more challenging for the smaller projects that account for the majority of research grants awarded by the National Science Foundation (NSF).

In Table 1, Bryan L. Heidorn demonstrates that the top 20 percent of NSF grants awarded in 2007 accounted for just over 50 percent of total funds spent, and the top 254 grants (2 percent) received 20 percent of the total. The remaining funds were distributed among 11,771 grants in amounts ranging from just over $500 to more than $1,000,000, with the average award in the range of $200,000 (Heidorn, 2008). Heidorn argues that the data in the top 20 percent of awards are more likely to be well curated than data in the 80 percent generated by smaller grants, and that it is important to improve data management practices in these smaller projects in order to maximize the return on investment.

Data that result from smaller projects often are more difficult to manage than big data because they are highly heterogeneous, require more individual attention per byte, and tend to be less well documented. Academic libraries generally lack the capacity to manage the large volumes associated with big data, but they may be well equipped to assist with managing smaller data projects. For example, they may recommend sustainable file formats and file organization, advise on intellectual property issues for data reuse, assist with determining appropriate metadata and data citation practices, and provide repository services for managing current research data as well as for archiving of data after project completion.

The volume of research data began to accumulate in very large quantities in the 1990s. Recognition that long-term maintenance of digital data requires an investment in human capital and infrastructure has grown over the past 30 years, but at a slower pace than the data itself. Federally funded research on digital libraries began in 1994, with six grants awarded in the NSF's Digital Libraries Initiative I. However, interest in digital preservation and best practices for the long-term management of digital data lagged behind research on digital library development. This was due in part to a false sense of confidence, based on ever-declining data storage costs and the belief that improvements in search algorithms would eliminate the need for concerns about such mundane topics as data organization, descriptive metadata, and file management. Federal funding for the applied research necessary to develop models and protocols for digital preservation and data management has been far more modest than funding for the basic research that is at the heart of the NSF's mission.

Fortunately, the library and archival communities, with their long experience with information organization and documentation, have become deeply involved in the development of principles and best practices for managing digital data for long-term use. These principles and protocols now are being implemented as services, exemplified by the essays and case studies in this volume. While much of the work to develop implementation strategies for curating research data has taken place in research universities, largely in the scientific disciplines, the principles, practices, tools, and services described here have broad implications for all disciplines and all organizations with a preservation mission.

THE ARCHIVAL PERSPECTIVE

Archivists are responsible for preserving *records*, that is, the documentation of activities of the organization within which an archive is located. An organization's records provide evidence of its activities and policies, as well as information resulting from those activities. In order to serve as evidence, or proof, records must have *authenticity*, inferred by documentation of an unbroken chain of physical custody. They must also have *integrity*, showing that they have not been corrupted, and that any alterations have been authorized and documented to show what changes were made, when, why, and by whom.

Digital preservation activities, however, are likely to result in some alteration of the original digital object over time, in the course of migration or other preservation action. For example, even the simple act of opening a digital file automatically changes the "last modified" date and decreases the evidence of its integrity. How much alteration is acceptable? Can documentation about alterations compensate for the inability to preserve the exact form of the original for reuse? If so, what kinds of documentation are needed? Secondary users want access to a wide range of digital content, but in order for that information to have continuing value for scholarly research and to provide evidence for purposes of accountability or legal standing if required, the preserved data must include contextual information not only about the circumstances of its creation, but also about how it has been managed over time. Data repositories that aspire to trustworthiness must include documentation of all "events" that result in any changes to the digital objects they contain in the course of their ongoing preservation activities.

HISTORICAL BACKGROUND: DATA AS EVIDENCE

The science of diplomatics, which has guided the development of archival science, originated in the 17th century from the same need to create trusted documentation about events and transactions that now informs criteria for the management and evaluation of digital repositories to assess their trustworthiness. As government and commerce expanded over larger territories, states and merchants could no longer deal directly with the people they governed and with whom they conducted business. Therefore, they needed to create more documentation of transactions than had previously been required. Diplomatics provides the theoretical framework for a system of recordkeeping to verify and organize information that can be recognized as trustworthy (Gilliland-Swetland, 2000).

One of the fundamental principles of diplomatics is *provenance*, which documents the origin, lineage, or pedigree of an information object. Provenance is central to the ability to validate, verify, and contextualize digital objects, and it provides a large part of the context of meaning of an information object. It is vital for assessing the source, authority, accuracy, and value of the information contained in that object.

Digital preservation aims to ensure the maintenance over time of the value of digital objects. The International Research on Permanent Authentic Records in Electronic Systems (InterPARES) Authenticity Task Force, led by Luciana Duranti at the University of British Columbia, observed that users want to know that digital objects are what they purport to be (they are authentic), and that they are complete and have not been altered or corrupted (they have integrity) (Gilliland-Swetland and Eppard, 2000). Documents that lack authenticity and integrity have limited value as evidence or even as citable sources of information. And because digital objects are more susceptible to alteration and corruption than paper records, extra care must be taken to establish the authenticity and trustworthiness of digital objects.

Most online users begin with a presumption of authenticity, unless some concern arises that causes them to question it, but this may be changing in the digital environment as more challenges to the authenticity of data arise from charges of plagiarism, faulty research methods, and even outright fraud. The only way users who do not have direct knowledge of an object's origin and management can trust its authenticity is for the organization that has taken custody of it to adequately and transparently document the provenance and process of ingest (acquisition or deposit into a digital repository), as well as its management within the repository.

The Research Roadmap Working Group of DigitalPreservationEurope (2007) identified five levels of preservation:

1. Digital object level, associated with issues of migration/emulation, experimentation, and acceptable loss;
2. Collection level, associated with issues of interoperability, metadata, and standardization;
3. Repository level, including policies and procedures;
4. Process level, associated with issues of automation and workflow; and
5. Organizational level, including issues of governance and sustainability.

All of these levels should be considered in designing data services. In order to share datasets across a wide variety of disciplines with different research interests, protocols must be established for describing and documenting data consistently. As repositories move from in-house operations to core services, they become an essential part of the digital infrastructure and must meet high standards of trustworthiness. Decisions made early in the data creation and active management phases of a research project inevitably affect how well the data can later be documented, preserved, and reused, so long-term preservation should be considered early in the planning process.

THE LIBRARY PERSPECTIVE

While it is an oversimplification to say that archives are about preservation and libraries are about access, it is fair to say that the most valuable contribution of archives to the digital infrastructure has been the principle of *context* for future use through data documentation and rules of evidence. The greatest contribution of libraries is most likely their emphasis on *services*, providing the basis not only for future access to digital assets, but also for assistance to data creators in managing their own active data. Attention to current data management ensures not only that data can be preserved and reused by others, but also that creators can find their own data after its initial use. Good management practices ensure that data can be discovered and validated if it is challenged or needs to be reexamined for any reason. Librarians who have worked with researchers on data transfers and documentation have found that recordkeeping practices within research teams are often idiosyncratic and inconsistent, at best. A 2012 survey at the University of Nottingham, for example, asked researchers in science, engineering, medicine and health sciences, and social sciences, "Do you document or record any metadata about your data?" Of the 366 researchers who responded, 24 percent indicated that they did assign metadata, 59 percent said no, and 17 percent did not know (Parsons, Grimshaw, & Williamson, 2013). Based on the results of the survey, the University of Nottingham Libraries are developing services to assist researchers with their needs for managing, publishing, and citing their research data.

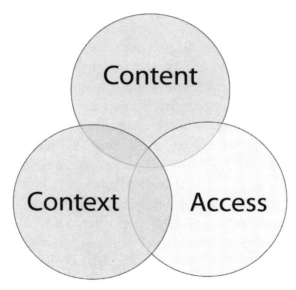

Figure 1. Elements of digital repository services. Courtesy of Lars Meyer.

SCHOLARLY COMMUNICATIONS

Scholarly communications have moved beyond reliance on the published record in academic journals as the preferred way to share information among peers. Research results are now likely to be announced at professional conferences and in the news media, and data are shared through electronic communications among research teams that interact across geographic boundaries and often across disciplines. In response, libraries have adapted and extended their services beyond preserving the published results of research to supporting the communications process throughout the data life cycle. Many research libraries are developing new services, including providing assistance with data management plans, helping with citations to published datasets—which are now beginning to appear in their own right in specialized online data journals—and managing repositories that preserve the datasets referenced in the citations.

Data journals provide quicker access to findings and underlying data in advance of published analyses that appear in "traditional" journals (which, however, are also likely to be issued in electronic form) and which serve the purpose of official documentation of research findings. See, for example, the *Biodiversity Data Journal* (motto: "Making your data count!") at http://biodiversitydatajournal.com as one of these new types of e-journals. Many data journals, like the *Biodiversity Data Journal*, span a range of disciplines, so they have the advantage of presenting in one place datasets that bring together observational and experimental data, as well as analyses, from a variety of disciplines on a global spatial scale. Thus, data journals have particular value for the publication of interdisciplinary research.

In recognition of the growing significance of data publications, Nature Publishing Group (NPG) announced in April 2013 a new peer-reviewed, open-access publication, *Scientific Data*, to be launched in spring 2014. While the initial focus is on experimental datasets from the life, biomedical, and environmental sciences, there are plans to expand to other fields in the natural sciences. *Scientific Data* will introduce what it calls *data descriptors,* a combination of traditional publication content and structured information to be curated in-house, and which may be associated with articles from a broad range of journals. The actual data files will be stored in one or more public, community-recognized systems, or in the absence of a community-recognized system, in a more general repository such as Dryad (http://datadryad.org). An advisory panel including senior scientists, data repository representatives, biocurators, librarians, and funders will guide the policies, standards, and editorial scope of the new data journal (NPG, 2013). All of these professional groups bring specialized expertise to the scholarly communications process and are stakeholders in its successful evolution.

NEW FUNDING REQUIREMENTS FOR DATA MANAGEMENT PLANS

The NSF has had a long-standing policy requiring grant recipients to share their data with other investigators, but it had no policies for how this should be accomplished. Several significant reports published over the past decade have drawn attention to the need for a digital preservation infrastructure (Blue Ribbon Task Force, 2008 and 2010; National Science Board, 2005).

Awareness of the value of data took a leap forward in 2010, when the NSF announced that it would begin requiring data management plans with all grant applications beginning in the 2011 grant cycle. Research universities that depend heavily on NSF grant funding suddenly realized that the game had changed and that they would need to provide resources and assistance to researchers to enable them to compete successfully for grant funding. Other funding agencies in the United States and abroad soon began requiring data management plans also, so the need to act became critical.

Institutions have responded in different ways to the challenge of data management, based on their needs and circumstances. In many cases, libraries have played a critical role in the formulation of data management plans, bringing their knowledge of information standards and organizational skills to the process of setting up file structures, describing data in accordance with established metadata schemas and controlled vocabularies, and raising awareness of copyright, licenses, and other potential data rights issues. Many researchers have expressed willingness to share at least some of their data and have readily accepted assistance in managing their data for their own benefit as well as for sharing with others, as long as their concerns are met that data will not be shared inappropriately and that their work will not be slowed by cumbersome procedural requirements. A good data management plan will not only satisfy grant application requirements, but will also serve as a blueprint for instituting good practices for managing active data and facilitating long-term access. With training, much of this work can be carried out by the people on research teams who already have data management responsibilities, often graduate students and research assistants. It can be expected that many of the graduate students trained in good data management will go on to establish their own research teams and will promote good practices.

THE DATA LIFE CYCLE

Library and archival perspectives have come together in the past 10 years as the need to provide both good documentation and useful access to data and associated software tools has increased. It is now widely recognized that good management practices, in addition to data storage, are essential for successful long-term preservation and sharing. The skills needed to manage data effectively are now seen as spanning the library and archives professions; disciplinary expertise for understanding the specific data at issue is of course also required. This recognition of the need for collaboration across spans of expertise has led to the emergence of a new field known as digital (or data) curation, which can be succinctly defined as the active management of data over its full life cycle. The life cycle concept has helped focus attention on issues of data quality and documentation at the time of creation as critical to data-driven research, as well as for successful data preservation and sharing. The life cycle approach emphasizes the need for involvement of all stakeholders in the scholarly communications process, from those who create the data to those who manage and provide access to it over the long term.

Digital curation became a visible part of the digital knowledge environment in 2004 with the establishment of the Digital Curation Centre (DCC) in the UK (http://www.dcc.ac.uk). The DCC has provided leadership in promoting digital curation standards and best practices. A number of research universities in the United States—particularly research libraries—also have established digital (or data) curation centers and/or data services. These new organizations and service centers have played an important role in developing and supporting a community of data professionals, through such activities as the DCC's International Digital Curation Conference and the *International Journal of Digital Curation*. In the United States, grant funding from the Institute of Museum and Library Services (IMLS), beginning in 2006, has supported the education of a cadre of digital curators by a number of graduate schools of library and information science; it also has provided funding for applied research in digital curation and information science. A study by the National Academy of Sciences Board on Research Data and Information on future career opportunities and educational requirements for digital curation, sponsored by IMLS, NSF, and the Alfred P. Sloan Foundation, is scheduled for release in late 2013 (http://sites.nationalacademies.org/PGA/brdi/index.htm). Digital curators with backgrounds in librarianship, archival science, and related disciplines are contributing to the development of a new set of services that libraries and data service centers are now providing or contemplating.

Developments over the past decade have contributed to research data management in the United States and the roles that librarians and other information professionals are playing. This book provides a snapshot of the current state of the art, both for organizations that are considering such services and those that already provide them and wish to compare their own services with other initiatives. The contributors are all recognized experts in the field who have led the development of the first generation of data curatorship.

THE STRUCTURE OF THE VOLUME

The volume is organized to progress logically from considerations of the policy environment within which research data are created and managed, to the planning and implementation of services to support active data management and sharing, to the provision of archiving and repository services. These sections are followed by two contributions on evaluation planning (which, however, should be considered early in the life of the project or program, once decisions are made about the general goals and objectives and concurrently with the work plan). The last section includes case studies that serve as a link between the "what and why" issues discussed in earlier chapters and the challenge of "how" goals and objectives can be accomplished, presenting accounts of data services implemented at four research universities. The final contribution, by Clifford Lynch, puts the volume in context by considering where the field needs to go from here—not only the challenges that need to be solved in the next few years, but also the next set of challenges that will arise.

PART 1: UNDERSTANDING THE POLICY CONTEXT

This section provides a broad context for understanding how libraries in the United States have arrived at the current juncture between their historical roles and the changing environment of scholarly communications. It also describes innovative service models and strategies for influencing national and international policies to address legal and technological barriers to effective data management.

In "The Policy and Institutional Framework," James Mullins provides an historical overview of the challenges faced by U.S. research libraries in the changing research environment of the past 15 years and how they have responded to evolving needs. He also provides a personal perspective on the Purdue University Libraries' creation of its Distributed Data Curation Center and associated data services. These services are integrated with on-going collaboration with faculty in order to meet their data management needs and to raise awareness of how librarians can support the university's research and scholarly outputs.

MacKenzie Smith discusses the technology and policy context of data governance from a national and international perspective in "Data Governance: Where Technology and Policy Collide." She describes the governance framework—the legal, policy, and regulatory environment—for research data and explains the ways in which it lags behind the established structure for traditional scholarly communications. She also discusses current efforts to resolve the legal, policy, and technical barriers to successful data management, and she offers suggestions for additional community-based tools and resources.

PART 2: PLANNING FOR DATA MANAGEMENT

This section discusses decisions that should be made at the beginning of the research process and the issues that should be considered in making them.

Jake Carlson, in "The Use of Life Cycle Models in Developing and Supporting Data Services," compares the life cycle of data to life cycle models used in the life sciences, that is, identification of the stages that an organism goes through from birth to maturity, reproduction, and the renewal of the life cycle. He suggests that life cycle models provide a framework for understanding the similar stages of data and for identifying what services can be provided, to whom, and at what stage of the cycle. He cautions that gaps that may occur as data is transferred from one custodian to another require particular attention. However, these danger points in the life cycle present opportunities for services to mitigate loss of data or inadequate documentation.

Andrew Sallans and Sherry Lake, in "Data Management Assessment and Planning Tools," discuss their work on the Data Management Planning (DMP) Tool, a community-developed resource maintained by the California Digital Library to help researchers establish a functional approach to managing their research data while fulfilling grant application requirements; its successor, the DMPTool2; and DMVitals, developed by the University of Virginia Libraries. DMVitals combines a data interview with statements developed by the Australian National Data Service to describe best practices in data management. The tool enables researchers to score the "maturity level" of their current data management practices. Librarians can then provide recommendations for improving these practices and offer services to facilitate the process.

Bernard Reilly and Marie Waltz, in "Trustworthy Data Repositories: The Value and Benefits of Auditing and Certification," explain what it means for repositories to be considered trustworthy and how the Trustworthy Repositories Audit and Certification (TRAC) standard and checklist is used in making this determination. This chapter appears in Part 2 because the principles set forth in the TRAC document should be well understood by information professionals and considered early in the research planning process. While decisions about where to deposit research data at the end of their active life cycle may be made later, the TRAC criteria identify decisions that should be made before any data is created—such as assignment of unique identifiers and appropriate metadata—that are important for managing active research data and that also will facilitate deposit and sharing.

PART 3: MANAGING PROJECT DATA

This section presents aspects of project management around which information professionals can design services that build on their traditional areas of expertise to help researchers manage and share their data. These include considerations of copyright and licensing, provision of metadata services, and assistance with data citation. Libraries may consider offering such assistance either as stand-alone services or in combination with repository services.

"Copyright, Open Data, and the Availability-Usability Gap: Challenges, Opportunities, and Approaches for Libraries," by Melissa Levine, discusses copyright in terms of policy, administration, and business choices. She argues that librarians can help researchers achieve academic recognition and protect their data from inappropriate use through licensing (such as the Creative Commons-BY [Attribution] license) as an alternative to copyrighting their data. Levine proposes that assistance with decision making about rights in data is a logical addition to other data services that libraries may offer. Moreover, she cites the White House Office of Science and Technology Policy memorandum issued in February 2013, "Increasing Access to the Results of Federally Funded Scientific Research," as a further incentive to researchers, librarians, and other stakeholders to continue and increase their collaborative efforts. The memo requires federal agencies that award more than $100 million for research and development annually to require data management plans with grant applications and provides for inclusion of appropriate costs to implement the plans. It further requires these agencies to "promote the deposit of data in publicly accessible databases, where appropriate and available" and to "develop approaches for identifying and providing appropriate attribution to scientific datasets that are made available under the plan" (Holdren, 2013, p. 5).

"Metadata Services," by Jenn Riley, points out that metadata is a primary focus of data management plans. While funding agencies do not prescribe any particular metadata schemas, they expect researchers to adhere to the standards adopted by their own research communities and/or that best fit the data they are generating. She notes that metadata, like data, also has a life cycle. In addition to descriptive metadata that describes the content and provenance of the data, metadata will be added by machines or humans at later stages, including during preservation actions taken by repositories to enable access, citation, and reuse. Riley presents survey evidence showing that researchers are aware of the value of metadata yet are not knowledgeable about its proper application. She suggests that libraries can best provide effective metadata assistance by integrating services into the researchers' workflow—thus increasing the benefit to the data creators—rather than waiting until the project's end, when researchers are unlikely to want to spend time documenting data they are no longer using.

"Data Citation: Principles and Practice," by Jan Brase, Yvonne Socha, Sarah Callaghan, Christine Borgman, Paul Uhlir, and Bonnie Carroll, describes the development of and services provided by DataCite, an international consortium of libraries and research partners to encourage and support the preservation of research data as well as the citation of datasets to ensure their accessibility and to promote their use. The authors point out that data have been linked traditionally to the publications that are based on them through tables, graphs, and images embedded in the publications. However, as datasets become larger, it often is no longer possible to publish the data as part of the publication. The datasets referenced in publications frequently are composite data objects with multiple constituent parts, as researchers typically generate many versions of datasets in the course of their research. The purpose of data citation, then, is to provide enough information to locate the referenced dataset as a single, unambiguous object; to serve as evidence for claims made about the data; to verify that the cited dataset is equivalent to the one used to make the claims; and to correctly attribute the dataset. The authors propose a list of 11 elements, ranging from author to a persistent URL from which the dataset is available, as the minimum required for data citation.

PART 4: ARCHIVING AND MANAGING RESEARCH DATA IN REPOSITORIES

This section focuses on the particular issues associated with data repositories. Libraries increasingly are involved as developers, service providers, and customers of such repositories, so they need to be knowledgeable about the range of repository models and services available. Contributors to this section describe a number of repository options, ranging from new roles for institutional repositories (IRs) in hosting active data, to new partnerships between disciplinary and institutional repositories as a means of improving archiving practices and making data more widely available, to emerging repository services offered by nonprofit organizations to accommodate a wide variety of content.

In "Assimilating Digital Repositories into the Active Research Process," Tyler Walters makes the case for IRs as infrastructure to support large research projects. These projects, often involving international teams of researchers from many disciplines, are now typical and require a networked research environment. Walters observes that repositories are being integrated with the communication tools of virtual communities and that social media tools and community networking capabilities are overlaying repositories to link data, people, and web-based resources. He argues that in order to benefit researchers, digital repositories should play a larger role in supporting active research in addition to archiving data.

In "Partnering to Curate and Archive Social Science Data," Jared Lyle, George Alter, and Ann Green discuss the exponential increase in the volume of social science research data in recent years and the potential loss of much of this data through lack of proper archiving. The authors provide evidence that the vast majority of social science research data are currently shared only informally or never shared beyond the original research team. They recognize the valuable role that IRs are playing in capturing inactive research data and suggest that disciplinary repositories such as the Inter-university Consortium for Political and Social Research (ICPSR) at the University of Michigan can improve archiving practices and data sharing by partnering with IRs. They report on the results of an IMLS grant to the ICPSR to investigate the possibilities for partnerships between the ICPSR and IRs, which typically serve as general repositories for a university's scholarly outputs. The project found that many IR managers were receptive to suggestions for improving documentation of social science data and that the ICPSR could successfully obtain relevant datasets from IRs, making them more easily discoverable by social science researchers. The chapter concludes with recommendations for improvements in archiving practices that are relevant not only for IRs, but for all those involved in managing research data, especially information professionals.

In "Managing and Archiving Research Data: Local Repository and Cloud-based Practices," Michele Kimpton and Carol Minton Morris discuss practical considerations for making decisions about what kinds of data to preserve in repositories, for how long, and in what kinds of repositories. They also provide insight into commercial cloud-based storage practices, which are often opaque to users. The first part of the chapter presents an analysis of four recent interviews with research library professionals who use either the DSpace and/or Fedora repository software. The interviews were conducted to better understand the common issues and solutions for preserving and using research data in local repositories. The second part discusses the challenges and benefits of using remote cloud storage for managing and archiving data, including considerations of data security, cost, and monitoring. The authors describe the DuraCloud service provided by DuraSpace as a resource designed to overcome the opacity of commercial cloud-based services.

"Chronopolis Repository Services," by David Minor, Brian Schottlaender, and Ardys Kozbial, describes the repository services provided by the Chronopolis digital preservation network, created and managed by the San Diego Supercomputer Center (SDSC) and the University of California-San Diego Library in collaboration with the National Center for Atmospheric Research in Colorado and the University of Maryland Institute for Advanced Computer Studies. The network takes advantage of its distributed geographical locations to ensure that at least three copies of all datasets deposited with Chronopolis are maintained, one at each of the partner nodes. Data is managed with the iRODS (integrated Rule-Oriented Data System) middleware software developed at the SDSC and is continually monitored through "curatorial audits." Chronopolis is a "dark archive," meaning that it provides no public interface and only makes data available back to the owners; however, it has developed model practices for data packaging and sharing through its ingest and dissemination processes. It promises to become a useful component of digital preservation for a wide variety of content.

PART 5: MEASURING SUCCESS

The contributions here emphasize the need to begin planning for evaluation at the beginning of a new project or program. However, these chapters follow the earlier sections because decisions about what services to provide must be made before evaluation planning can begin. The authors in this section consider evaluation from two perspectives. The first provides an in-depth analysis of the steps involved in developing and implementing an evaluation plan for a large, complex, data-focused project with several goals and many stakeholders. The second takes a high-level view of evaluation as a means of assessing the return on investment of public funds to meet national or international goals.

In "Evaluating a Complex Project: DataOne," Suzie Allard describes the planning and evaluation of DataONE, a multimillion-dollar project funded by NSF's DataNet program. The goal of DataONE is to develop infrastructure, tools, and a community network in support of interdisciplinary, international, data-intensive research spanning the biological, ecological, and environmental sciences. While this project is large and complex, requiring particular care in planning for project evaluation, many of the evaluation components will have relevance for any project that intends to measure outcomes, and particularly for those involving management of research data. Allard emphasizes the importance of developing an evaluation plan in the early stages of the project in order to ensure that relevant data are collected at appropriate times. She also explains how the data life cycle model helped to structure the DataONE evaluation plan, since the ultimate project goal is to improve data management. This framework helped to identify the tools and resources needed at each stage of the life cycle. The evaluation team then developed plans for evaluating existing tools to assess potential improvements and for identifying needs for new tools and services that could be addressed in the work plan. Allard concludes with recommendations for the organizational design and management of the evaluation process.

In "What to Measure: Toward Metrics for Research Data Management," Angus Whyte, Laura Molloy, Neil Beagrie, and John Houghton discuss evaluation metrics from a high conceptual level, asking program and evaluation planners to think carefully about what they are trying to achieve and what metrics they can realistically use to measure results. The authors address the evaluation of research data management at two levels: the services and infrastructure support provided by individual research institutions, and the economic impacts of national or international repositories and data centers. Using cases from the United Kingdom and Australia, they consider methods such as cost-benefit analysis, benchmarking, risk management, contingent valuation, and traditional social science methods including interviews, surveys, and focus groups. However, they observe that the starting point should always be "what can and should be measured." They remind readers that the goal is to identify improvements that have been achieved or are needed to align services with national or international data policies and practices. The authors note that, although data preservation is now perceived as a public good, the public benefit has not yet been proved, presenting particular challenges for evaluation.

PART SIX: BRINGING IT ALL TOGETHER: CASE STUDIES

This section presents case studies that describe how all of the policy, planning, and implementation considerations have come together in new services at four research universities.

Cornell University

In "An Institutional Perspective on Data Curation Services: A View from Cornell University," Gail Steinhart notes the early interest that Cornell took in research data beginning in the 1980s and describes the planning and implementation of new library infrastructure and data services over the past two decades. She discusses important lessons learned from this wealth of experience and makes recommendations for structuring the planning and ongoing monitoring processes that are essential to successful data services.

Purdue University

In "Purdue University Research Repository: Collaborations in Data Management," Scott Brandt extends the observations made by Purdue's Dean of Libraries James Mullins. Brandt provides insight into how Purdue librarians acted within the policy and institutional framework described by Mullins. He emphasizes the value of collaboration with researchers throughout the data life cycle for librarians who are continuously working to improve data services.

Rice University

Geneva Henry's case study, "Data Curation for the Humanities: Perspectives from Rice University," is the only chapter that focuses on humanities research data, an important but often overlooked area in research data management. Scientific data have received the most attention in the development of data services because this area has led the transition to digital research and receives the bulk of research funds. However, the digitization of historical data and the development of data mining and other techniques for analyzing humanities data are now enabling researchers in the humanities to make innovative use of digital tools and to ask research questions that were not possible before.

University of Oregon

Brian Westra, in "Developing Data Management Services for Researchers at the University of Oregon," describes the development of data services, particularly for the sciences and social sciences, at his large, state-supported research university. He provides a detailed description of a needs assessment conducted in 2009–2010 that identified common problems—including lack of file organization, insufficient storage and backup procedures, and inadequate metadata or other documentation—that hindered investigators' ability to find and retrieve their own data. These conditions aligned with gaps in infrastructure, tools, and services that the library then undertook to fill. Westra discusses the use of small pilot studies early in the data life cycle to explore collaborations in the development of data management infrastructure.

CLOSING REFLECTIONS: LOOKING AHEAD

Finally, Clifford Lynch contributes a thoughtful reflection on progress to date in preserving and managing research data. He identifies priorities over the next few years for services to assist researchers with data management, centering on: development of credible data management plans, documentation of datasets to be shared and preserved, and appropriate platforms for data sharing and bit preservation. He further considers what these developments and the current environment suggest for the next set of challenges that will inevitably arise.

CONCLUSION

Institutions have responded differently to the new data environment depending on their own circumstances and needs. Therefore, a variety of approaches are presented in this volume, and information professionals looking to develop strategies for their own institutions will find many examples to choose from and adapt to their own needs. The data infrastructure is still emerging, but there are many more tools and services available now than there were ten or even five years ago. Libraries have played a critical role in developing and managing this infrastructure and are likely to become even more involved as research becomes ever more dependent on digital data. Collectively, the state of the art as described here demonstrates the resilience of libraries and information professionals in responding to the changing needs of their communities.

REFERENCES

Blue Ribbon Task Force on Sustainable Digital Preservation and Access. (2008). *Sustaining the digital investment: Issues and challenges of economically sustainable digital preservation* (Interim Report).

Washington, DC: National Science Foundation. Retrieved from http://brtf.sdsc.edu/biblio/BRTF_Interim_Report.pdf

Blue Ribbon Task Force on Sustainable Digital Preservation and Access. (2010). *Sustainable access for a digital planet: Ensuring long-term access to digital information* (Final Report). Washington, DC: National Science Foundation. Retrieved from http://brtf.sdsc.edu/biblio/BRTF_Final_Report.pdf

DigitalPreservationEurope (DPE). (2007). *Research roadmap.* (Project no. 034762). Retrieved from http://www.digitalpreservationeurope.eu/publications/dpe_research_roadmap_D72.pdf

Gilliland-Swetland, A. J. (2000). *Enduring paradigm: New opportunities, the value of the archival perspective in the digital environment.* Council on Library and Information Resources, 2000. Retrieved from http://www.clir.org/pubs/reports/pub89/pub89.pdf.

Gilliland-Swetland, A. J., & Eppard, P. B. (2000). Preserving the authenticity of contingent digital objects: The InterPARES project. *D-Lib Magazine, 6*(7/8). Retrieved from http://www.dlib.org/dlib/july00/eppard/07eppard.html

Heidorn, B. L. (2008). Shedding light on the dark data in long tail of science. *Library Trends, 57*(2), 280–299. http://dx.doi.org/10.1353/lib.0.0036

Holdren, J. P. (2013, February). *Increasing access to the results of federally funded research* (Memorandum). White House Office of Science and Technology Policy. Retrieved from http://www.whitehouse.gov/sites/default/files/microsites/ostp/ostp_public_access_memo_2013.pdf

National Science Board. (2005). *Long-lived digital data collections: Enabling research in the 21st century.* Washington, DC: National Science Foundation. Retrieved from http://www.nsf.gov/pubs/2005/nsb0540/

Nature Publishing Group (NPG). (2013, April 4). NPG to launch *Scientific Data* to help scientists publish and reuse research data. Retrieved from http://www.nature.com/press_releases/scientificdata.html

Parsons, T., Grimshaw, S., & Williamson, L. (2013). *Research data management survey.* University of Nottingham. Retrieved from http://eprints.nottingham.ac.uk/1893/1/ADMIRe_Survey_Results_and_Analysis_2013.pdf

Part 1

UNDERSTANDING THE POLICY CONTEXT

1 | The Policy and Institutional Framework

JAMES L. MULLINS

INTRODUCTION

This chapter is in two parts. In Part 1, the policy framework on the national level is addressed, including policies of funding agencies to the collective response of research libraries through the Association of Research Libraries (ARL) to position members to be actively engaged in data management planning and services. In Part 2, a general overview of the manner in which Purdue University Libraries responded is provided as a case study to demonstrate how administrative policy within a university and the positioning of one research library meet this changing environment.

PART 1: SCIENTIFIC AND TECHNICAL RESEARCH: THE NEED FOR AND DEVELOPMENT OF POLICIES FOR DATA MANAGEMENT

Setting the stage.

In 1999, John Taylor, director general of the United Kingdom's Office of Science and Technology, coined the phrase e-science to describe projects resulting from major funding undertaken in the many areas of the physical and social sciences, including particle physics, bioinformatics, earth sciences, and social sciences. The term in the United States is not often used as frequently as computational science is to denote a high integration of computer modeling and simulations into the scientific methodologies. During the last several years, scientists and technological researchers tend not to recognize or identify e-science or computational science as unique within research methodology. Computational research is how research is done.

In June 2005, a report was generated by the President's Information Technology Advisory Committee (PITAC), titled *Computational Science: Ensuring America's Competitiveness*, providing then, and still today, a succinct compilation of the development of computational research methods that advanced and facilitated research in areas that were impossible even 30 years ago.

The breakthrough in mapping the human genome would not have been possible without sophisticated algorithms that deduced relationships within the human genome. In order to map the human genome, massive datasets were created that drew upon the research skills of computer scientists, statisticians, and information technologists. It also created a new role, at first not apparent, for an information/data specialist to determine how data could be described, identified, organized, shared, and preserved.

Concurrent with the PITAC report of 2005, Congress was raising questions to federal funding agencies about the high cost of research. Specifically, this was directed to major funding agencies such as the National Science Foundation (NSF), the National Institutes of Health (NIH), and the Department of Energy (DOE). The inquiry from Congress focused on the cost of collecting data in multiple research projects, projects that on the surface appeared to be connected or supportive of each other. If these projects were collaborative or complementary, why would it be necessary to provide funding for a research team to generate new datasets when another dataset already created could answer a question, or provide a dataset that could be mined to test a model or to test an algorithm? Was it really necessary to create a dataset that would be used by one research team for one project and then be discarded? If the dataset were known to the larger research community, couldn't it be reused or mined multiple times, and thereby reduce the cost and possibly speed up the research process?

How did the transition from bench science to computational science take place?

There is an oft-recounted comment made by a biology professor at a major research university that 20 years ago she could tell a new graduate student to, "Spit into that petri dish and research that," requiring little more than a microscope and standard research methodologies and reference sources. Now, the professor opined, a new graduate student arrives, and immediately they need to work with a lab team that would include computer scientists, statisticians, and information technologists. To explore and test a research question generally requires the creation of a dataset. The creation of the dataset requires complicated equipment and the talent of many people, resulting in a very high cost.

Scientists, engineers, and social scientists embraced this new method of gaining insight into their data. By analyzing and determining patterns in massive amounts of data or one large dataset, new hypotheses could be tested. By using data and the proper algorithm, it was no longer necessary to always replicate a bench experiment, rather, by drawing upon standard methodologies and the requisite data, a problem could be researched and a finding could be determined. Each project generated one or more datasets, with variables defined through metadata. The collection of accurate metadata is very important as minor differences here (the way the experiment is done) always impacts the data output. The challenge came when there was no consistent method for describing the process, the storage of the dataset, and the description of the content within the dataset.

Concurrent increase in managing data, or the lack thereof, by the researchers, the transition, and awareness that storage is not archiving.

The work of the researchers generated a massive number of datasets, often stored on an individual researcher's computer, a lab server, or, less often, a university data storage facility or a disciplinary data archive. In the early 2000s it was becoming a greater and greater challenge for scientists and engineers in many different research arenas to know how to share and retrieve datasets, and it was an even greater challenge to retrieve and share datasets that were only a few years old. Research datasets often were lost with the transition of a lab's postdoc or graduate student. When the postdoc or graduate student who developed the methodology for describing, retrieving, and archiving the data from the research of the past three years or so departed, the access to and usability of the research dataset went out the door as well.

Researchers were assuming that the situation in which they found themselves could be managed by their college, school, or central information technology organization. All things considered, that was not an unusual or unlikely scenario. When researchers would meet with information technology specialists, they would be assured that storage would not be a problem, space was inexpensive, and as long as the dataset was in use, storage support would not be an issue. As the researcher continued to explore how best to identify, describe, and share the dataset, it became once again a problem that the researcher had to manage. The information technologist was not prepared to create metadata, or even to advise the researcher on how to create, or what elements should be in the metadata. The storage space used by the researcher typically was not searchable on the web, and was, therefore, hidden and inaccessible until the researcher responded to a request from a colleague to share the dataset, resulting in a file transfer that could be a challenge for the researcher and the colleague to accommodate.

So, the researcher had identified several important collaborators in undertaking computational science: the information technologist to manage storage; the computer scientist to create necessary algorithms to test the data; and the statistician to advise and run tests to determine reliability of the data. An important part of this continuum was missing: how to identify, describe, retrieve, share, archive, and preserve the dataset.

The environment that has created the demand from funding agencies that a data management plan must be included with proposals.

In the early 2000s questions began to be raised by Congress about the inefficiency or duplication of research projects funded by federal agencies, such as the NSF. In response, the NSF held hearings and appointed task forces to assess what the challenges were in data management, specifically data mining, and how could less waste be encouraged. The initial study, *Revolutionizing Science and Engineering through Cyberinfrastructure: Report of the National Science Foundation Blue-Ribbon Advisory Panel on Cyberinfrastructure*, was issued January 2003 (Atkins et al., 2003). Daniel Atkins, dean of the School of Information at the University of Michigan, was chair of the Blue-Ribbon Task Force. The report was groundbreaking, and now over 10 years later, reference is still made to this seminal work, typically referred to as the Atkins Report.

The Atkins Report for the first time brought together the challenges faced by investigators using cyberinfrastructure, large-scale computational facilities coupled with a strong Internet backbone to transfer data to wherever and whoever needed it. However, the Atkins Report identified challenges in fulfilling the potential of the cyberinfrastructure: how to identify, describe, locate, share, and preserve large amounts of data. Who were the players that had to be brought together to work through this dilemma, to ensure that federal research dollars were not being wasted on duplication of research projects across the United States? Among the Atkins Report's findings was an expansion of the Digital Libraries created by the *Defense Advanced Research Projects Agency* (DARPA), the NSF, and the National Library of Medicine (NLM) by an initial allocation of $10 million per year that was increased to $30 million when others, including the Library of Congress, joined the effort. The Atkins Report recommended an increase to $30 million, recognizing the value for provision of access and long-term stewardship.

Following up on the Atkins Report was another report issued by the ARL from a workshop funded by the NSF. *To Stand the Test of Time: Long-term Stewardship of Digital Data Sets in Science and Engineering* was issued in 2006. For the first time, the report detailed the proposed role for academic and research libraries in the management of datasets and as a collaborator in the cyberinfrastructure, computational, or e-science arena. It was not only in the United States that focus had turned to solving the challenge of managing data; in the United Kingdom and elsewhere in Europe, attention was being given to solving or at least understanding the challenges of data management.

In the report *To Stand the Test of Time*, there were three overarching recommendations to the NSF to act upon: "research and development required to understand, model and prototype the technical and organizational capacities needed for data stewardship . . . ; supporting training and educational programs to develop a new workforce in data science . . . ; developing, supporting, and promoting educational efforts to effect change in the research enterprise" (ARL, 2006, p. 12). Any one of these three recommendations could have had an impact upon the role of research libraries in data management. The challenge for research libraries was how to tackle one without the others also being advanced at the same time? How could libraries help effect change in the research enterprise in the use of data, if libraries did not have staff that understood or were interested in the problems of data management? Without staff who understood the challenge, how could the organization—the library—modify its processes or role within the university to facilitate the management of data? Without these two objectives coming together, how could researchers be expected to change the manner in which they did their research?

The two recommendations that particularly resonated with the library community were the management of data and the ability of staff within libraries to collaborate with the researchers on managing data. Librarians had participated in building massive data repositories, albeit of textual data, such as the *Online Computer Library Center*, Inc. (OCLC), or more inclusive of numeric data, the Inter-university Consortium for Political and Social Research (ICPSR). However, these two efforts were accomplished by a cohort of libraries, supported by information technologists and computer science professionals, with a common shared goal and understanding of what the end product was to be. No such common understanding or defined goal existed within the research library community on how to come together to answer the apparent need of the researchers.

Response by the library community by accepting that data management would benefit from the application of library science principles.

The initial response to the challenge being made to the research library community was heard and acted upon by a few universities including Cornell University, Johns Hopkins University, Massachusetts Institute of Technology, Purdue University, University of California-San Diego, and University of Minnesota. For the training of librarians, two library/information schools took the lead to identify curriculum and programs that would prepare library professionals to participate in data management, the University of Illinois at Urbana-Champaign and the University of Michigan.

Where to start was the question raised by many research libraries, or even more elemental, does it really need us, or is it really something with which research libraries should involve themselves? University libraries were and are challenged to define their role among the various players (e.g., the faculty, the office of the vice president for research and information technology). How can these diverse groups and individuals work together? More will be discussed about these relationships below and in succeeding chapters.

There was discussion within the university library community about whether there should be a role for a librarian or the library, since libraries traditionally have been involved in the research process at the end by identifying and preserving the results of research in journals, conference proceedings, and books. Why get involved at the front end of the research process? An awareness did emerge when consideration was given to the role libraries had had for a very long time to preserve manuscripts and records of authors, scholars, and famous individuals. These manuscripts and records were, more or less, raw bits of data until a researcher "mined" them to answer a research question. Therefore, libraries and archives had been partners in data management for a long time. Now it was to be the archive of nontangible data for science and engineering (Mullins, 2009).

Federal funding agencies provide support to study data management challenge.

Soon after the release of *To Stand the Test of Time*, two federal funding agencies responded to the call to look for a better way to steward massive amounts of data: the NSF and the Institute of Museum and Library Services (IMLS). The NSF was looking for the development of the underlying infrastructure that would enable the storage, retrieval, and sharing of data. The IMLS was looking to fund projects and research that would prepare the library community to collaborate on the challenge of data management. These initiatives from the NSF and the IMLS moved to address the first of the two concerns expressed in the report: establish a prototype to manage data, and the education and training of specialists to manage data.

To say this challenge was equal to the old adage about which came first, the chicken or the egg, would not be misapplied. How does the NSF require concrete data management from recipients of grants when there is no infrastructure, standards, or specialists prepared to facilitate data sharing, archiving, and/or preservation?

In the fall of 2007, the NSF issued a call for proposals to prototype an infrastructure for data management that "will integrate library and archival science, cyberinfrastructure, computer and information sciences, and domain science expertise to:

- provide reliable digital preservation, access, integration, and analysis capabilities for science and/or engineering data over a decades-long timeline;

- continuously anticipate and adapt to changes in technologies and in user needs and expectations;
- engage at the frontiers of computer and information science and cyberinfrastructure with research and development to drive the leading edge forward; and
- serve as component elements of an interoperable data preservation and access network." (NSF, 2007)

With an allocated budget by the NSF of $100 million, it was apparent that this was being taken as a serious problem and one that must be addressed. The grants to be made in two rounds would be awarded at a level of $20 million to five projects. For the first time there was a major funding opportunity that required collaboration among a wide range of disciplines: scientific/engineering, computer scientists, social scientists, and library/archival scientists.

This call for proposals was heard throughout the research world, but especially within the research library community. Libraries had been active in receiving grants for collection development and more recently for digitization of unique collections, but no grants had been on this scale or included library and archival sciences as an important partner in scientific research.

Many university libraries were energized by this challenge, one that many had little experience with, unlike the disciplinary faculty and departments on campus. Top universities throughout the country worked to understand the challenge and to identify the players that needed to be brought together to answer and define the answer to the challenge. Among the universities that competed in the first round were: Columbia University, Johns Hopkins University, Massachusetts Institute of Technology, Purdue University, University of California-San Diego, University of Minnesota, University of New Mexico, and University of Washington. Partnerships were formed within each university's team, drawing in investigators with specialties from research labs with a specific disciplinary focus.

In the summer of 2008, two grants were awarded: the Data Observation Network for Earth (DataONE) at the University of New Mexico, and the Data Conservancy (DC) at Johns Hopkins University. The purpose of each, as defined in 2013, follows:

> DataONE provides the distributed framework (comprised of Member Nodes and Coordinating Nodes), sound management, and robust technologies that enable long-term preservation of diverse multi-scale, multi-discipline, and multi-national observational data. This framework would not be possible without extensive partnerships with other institutions, agencies, data repositories, observatories, libraries and sponsors. (DataONE, n.d.)

Initially funded by the NSF's DataNet program, the DC has made significant advances in four major areas (Data Conservancy, n.d.):

1. A focused research program that examined research practices both broadly across multiple disciplines as well as deeply in selected disciplines in order to understand the data curation tools and services needed to support the interdisciplinary research community;
2. An infrastructure development program that developed a cyberinfrastructure base on which these data management and curation services could be layered; and
3. Data curation educational and professional development programs aimed at developing a deeper understanding of data management within the research community as well as workforce development within the library community.
4. Development of Sustainability models for long term data curation.

The IMLS took on the challenge to support the training and provision of professionals who could be data scientists or data managers. Seeing a close relationship between the traditional role of librarians when applying principles of library science to the organization of information, albeit traditionally in tangible formats, a call for proposals went out through the Laura Bush 21st Century Librarian Program. This call spoke to the need to prepare librarians and archivists to work with data, and to collaborate with researchers in solving the challenge of describing the content of the data, establishing metadata schemas that would allow retrieval, and establishing protocols for finding and linking to needed datasets. A major grant funded by the IMLS in 2007 and again in 2010 was the Data Curation Profiles project.

Initially, it was a combined project between the Purdue University Libraries and the Graduate School of Library and Information Science at the University of Illinois at Urbana-Champaign. The major question explored was how do disciplinary researchers view datasets, whether they were shared, and if so, under what conditions? (Data Curation Profiles Toolkit, n.d.)

Through these workshops, librarians were introduced to the Data Curation Profiles Toolkit and its use as a guide to how to approach, discuss, understand, and document data management within a discipline. They also were encouraged to publish completed profiles in the *Data Curation Profiles Directory*, an online, open access publication produced with the support of Purdue University Press (http://docs.lib.purdue.edu/dcp/).

The work undertaken by the NSF with its DataNet call and the work supported by the IMLS was prescient for what also occurred in 2010. In May, the NSF released its Data Sharing Policy that would require, as of January 18, 2011, a supplementary document that would detail the data management of the project (NSF, n.d.). With that announcement, not only were university libraries and the disciplines now challenged to develop acceptable data management plans, but some university research offices realized that NSF funding could be in jeopardy if a sound research data management plan was not established within the university.

Research libraries' response, including the ARL.

In response to the increased interest and role for university and research libraries in e-science and in the management of data specifically, the ARL established a task force on e-science in 2006. Later this was changed to an ongoing working group reporting to all three of ARL steering committees (Influencing Public Policies, Advancing Scholarly Communication, and Transforming Research Libraries) since the issues associated with e-science and data management touched all three areas.

In 2009, the E-Science Working Group conducted a survey of the members of ARL to determine the status of e-science initiative and data management within its members. In 2010, three coauthors expanded upon the survey and its results with case studies at six institutions that had taken leadership roles in data management: Purdue University, University of California-San Diego, Cornell University, Johns Hopkins University, University of Illinois at Chicago, and Massachusetts Institute of Technology (Soehner, Steeves, & Ward, 2010).

In 2010, it was decided by the E-Science Task Force that a concerted effort needed to be made to educate librarians and bring members of the ARL to a level that would provide collaboration throughout the membership. A letter was sent to all ARL members asking for a contribution of $5,000 to support an E-Science Institute that would be held in 2011. Even though it was assumed that there might be interest only in those universities that had a strong science and engineering focus, eventually there were over 70 members who committed to funding the E-Science Institute.

The E-Science Institute was coordinated by a team of librarians experienced in various aspects of e-science. The E-Science Institute was a combination of webinars and conference calls, culminating in a capstone event that occurred in three locations: Atlanta, Dallas, and Phoenix. The experience and knowledge gained by the participants indicated the success of the E-Science Institute, so much so, that a second round was planned, with some modifications, in 2012. To determine whether the E-Science Institute had a significant impact on the integration of e-science and data management among ARL members, a second survey, following up on the 2009 one, is being undertaken in 2013 to assess the impact of the E-Science Institute as well as the growth of data management within ARL member libraries.

The growing awareness of the impact of data and the need for data provenance.

With the proliferation of massive amounts of data, the need was apparent to devise a system to uniquely identify each dataset that would describe the content, the creator, and the variables reported in the dataset. In 2009, an international alliance formed around the need to register and identify datasets. DataCite was chartered by libraries in Europe and North America, incorporated in Germany (DataCite, n.d.). Most were national libraries with a few exceptions, including the United States, where two university libraries were signatories—the California Digital Library of the University of California and the Purdue University Libraries. Each DataCite member is a provider of digital object identifiers (DOIs) that link to the registry at the German National Library of Science and Technology (TIB). DOIs also are used to uniquely identify each published article through Cross-Ref. Finally, with the article and datasets assigned a unique identifier, one is also needed for the author. ORCID is a registry for unique identifiers and a method for linking to the productivity of each individual researcher (ORCID, n.d.).

The proliferation of research articles, datasets, and the introduction of unique identifiers for authors provides a new means to assess impact. Altmetrics uses social media to gather data on the discussion of the research article or dataset (Priem, Taraborelli, Groth, & Neylon, 2011). Eventually, altmetrics could become an alternative or an addition to traditional citation metrics.

PART 2: ONE UNIVERSITY'S RESPONSE: A PERSONAL PERSPECTIVE

Editor's note: The following account of how the Purdue University Libraries responded to the growing need of research universities for data management services was supplied by the author at the editor's request as a first-person perspective on how libraries can transform their services to meet changing needs.

As a university whose signature strengths are in science and engineering, Purdue University was positioned to focus on the need for data management and the necessary role it must play in computational research. The Libraries took the lead in defining this need at Purdue.

In 2004, I arrived as the new Dean of Libraries at Purdue University. Having worked for nearly four years in the Massachusetts Institute of Technology Libraries, I had the experience of seeing firsthand research faculty and librarians working on a project to solve a particular problem—the preservation and archiving of digital textual material, the DSpace initiative. The DSpace project, supported by corporate funding, brought together computer scientists, information technologists, disciplinary researchers, and librarians. Shortly after arriving at Purdue, I undertook a "listening tour" of all academic departments, meeting over lunch with department and research center heads—no easy task, since there are 72 academic departments at Purdue.

At the meeting, each department head would be asked to describe the department's successes, opportunities, and challenges. I listened for areas in which the Libraries could collaborate to develop a solution. For the science and engineering departments and schools, two areas emerged as challenges: interdisciplinary research and data management.

At Purdue University, the librarians have faculty rank and, therefore, have a responsibility for instruction and scholarship. For promotion and tenure, the Libraries faculty must be reviewed and recommended for promotion and tenure by a University Promotion Committee comprised of faculty throughout Purdue University, the deans, and the provost. The reason why this was significant related to the ability of the librarians (Libraries faculty) to engage in the classroom as a colleague and on a research team as a coprincipal investigator. Questions were raised about some members of the Libraries faculty who had an MLS as their highest graduate degree. Research faculty expect the PhD to be the requisite degree, but once it was explained that this was a professional degree, not a disciplinary masters, similar to other professional degrees as in medicine, art, business, or law, they better understood and appreciated the role of Libraries faculty.

The role of library science and the Libraries faculty.

When I would meet with individual faculty members, a question would often arise: "I don't think I know what a librarian is educated to do. What is the philosophy or principles that guide a librarian in his or her work?" This question often would come up concerning the ability of a Libraries faculty member being able to work with a researcher in managing data. The researcher had observed that librarians answered reference questions, cataloged items, and organized collections, making them accessible to the student or faculty member. However, they didn't understand how that could extrapolate or prepare a librarian to work on something as intangible as digital data or massive datasets. It would fall to me to explain the principles of identification and organization of information; that, traditionally, it had been tangible items, such as books and print journals, but the same principles of cataloging or assigning metadata applied to nontangible data. Using terms such as "metadata" seemed to resonate with the researches rather than "cataloging" of the data. Quite often the researcher would have an "aha" moment when realizing that librarians were the specialists for whom they had been searching after expecting computer scientists and information technologists to be their salvation.

At meetings with department and school heads, I would ask if there were faculty in the department or school who would be willing to collaborate with a librarian on working through the process of managing their data. After obtaining a name or two of faculty in a department, I would return to the Libraries and talk this over with the Interdisciplinary Research Librarian (IRL).

Until 2004, Professor Scott Brandt had been working with technology training in the Libraries. With some persuasion, Brandt became the IRL, without really knowing what this involved. One role he had was to follow up with faculty members who had been identified by the department head as likely candidates for collaboration on data management. In a short time, Brandt became adept and knowledgeable in the management of data, even though his background was in the humanities (as was my own).

Definition of the Libraries as a sponsored research partner.
Around this time, in order to emphasize the academic role as opposed to an administrative or support role of the Libraries and its faculty, I recognized that the Libraries' structure needed to reflect that of the colleges and schools. Additionally, since Purdue does not have a school of library or information science, the only faculty on campus to have expertise in library science were the librarians. When the Vice President for Research invited me as the Dean of Libraries to serve on the Research Administration Council, after the first meeting I wondered why I was the only dean serving on the council, while the others were associate deans for research. Surely it should be the IRL. When that was raised, I was told that only those who have the rank of dean (or associate dean) could serve, which was a simple fix: the Libraries now had an Associate Dean for Research. The title Associate Dean for Public Services also was changed at that time to Associate Dean for Learning to reflect its academic role. For further discussion of the role of the Associate Dean for Research in the Purdue Libraries, see Scott Brandt's chapter in this volume.

Challenge to identify data management as a role for librarians and archivists.
Even though librarians had the knowledge to work with data, it wasn't always apparent to the librarians how to do this. And, when researchers were told that librarians could collaborate in managing their data, often their response would be, "But librarians want to share everything and we don't." The solution was to bring archival science into the mix, since archival science has provisions to control access, traditionally to personal papers, to a specific group or for a specific purpose, for a period of time. The researchers were looking for assurance when deciding to collaborate with librarians on

their data that they would have say on when and who saw their data, and working with the archivists provided that assurance.

Librarians also may think they or libraries do not have a role in working within the research process or taking responsibility for managing and preserving data. They often contend that libraries and librarians become involved by organizing and preserving the product of research after publication. However, libraries and archives have been participating in the preservation of data for many years; it just was not as obvious (i.e., the collecting, organizing, and preservation of manuscripts and papers that document a life). Traditionally archived materials have been print materials. Each document or item, more or less, is a tangible bit of data until a researcher uses the document or item to answer a question raised in a research problem.

In 2005, the NSF began to respond to criticism in Congress that federal dollars were being inefficiently used by funding agencies by supporting duplicative research. That is, research was funded that created a massive dataset that was used once and then discarded. The question raised was, couldn't the dataset be mined for more than one research project, thereby reducing the need to create duplicative datasets and reduce cost? With recognition for the work already being done at Purdue, I was invited to participate in an NSF-sponsored workshop to discuss how this could be accomplished, and the result was the publication *To Stand the Test of Time* (ARL, 2006), which called for a requirement that each NSF-sponsored research project would have a data management plan. However, this raised the question, how to do this? When the NSF issued its call for the $100 million DataNet major funding project during the summer of 2007, Purdue Libraries was prepared to respond. It was decided by a group of Purdue administrators and researchers that I, as Dean of Libraries, was the logical person to lead the project as principal investigator to bring together a team of disciplinary and library researchers within Purdue and around the country.

How to position the Purdue Libraries to lead a major research project?

Since it would be unlikely for disciplinary faculty to respond to a request from the Libraries to participate in a grant, we decided to create something that would be similar or analogous to what they are accustomed to, therefore, the Distributed Data Curation Center (D2C2, n.d.) was chartered by Purdue University as an approved research center. A callout was made for faculty to propose how they could contribute to the NSF DataNet proposal being prepared by D2C2. An interesting observation came from these presentations, likely to help librarians in their collaborative work with researchers. When a researcher would present his/her research and how it would inform or be benefited by being included in the DataNet proposal, the librarians took notes and listened intently, while the other researchers paid little or no attention. After the researcher presenting would sit down, he/she would do exactly the same thing—pay no attention to the next researcher's presentation. The librarians were listening carefully and taking notes. Concerned that the Libraries and I, specifically, would not be the right organization and person to lead this University-wide team, I asked a distinguished professor in the College of Engineering, who had just returned from the NSF as a program director, if someone else in one of the colleges should lead the research team. His response was, "No, only the Libraries and you could lead this project, since only the Dean of Libraries can understand the scope and interconnectedness necessary to accomplish this." Purdue did submit a DataNet proposal centered on the HubZero software developed at Purdue. Although the grant was given a positive review, it was not advanced for further consideration. Interestingly, the Purdue University Research Repository (PURR), now nearly completed in 2013 without external funding, is, for the most part, was what was proposed in Purdue's DataNet proposal.

Response of Purdue Libraries.

At Purdue we were aware that it was only a matter of time before there would be a requirement for data management plans for all NSF grants; therefore, we knew that we would have to prepare, since the NSF was the major research sponsor at Purdue University. We took a risk in creating the position of Data Research Scientist (as identified in the report *To Stand the Test of Time*), funded as a two-year pilot with the expectation that the position would be supported by grants. In addition, knowing that the demand on the Libraries faculty time would outstrip available staffing, I informed Purdue University that the time of Libraries faculty would need to be "purchased" if it were needed to serve as a principal investigator on a research project. Basic consulting would be a role consistent with what had been done traditionally as a reference interview or collection development, and it was, therefore, considered to be within the charge of a Libraries faculty member, but anything that demanded more time would have to be purchased as part of a grant. That is, work that required a dedicated commitment of time (i.e., 10 percent over two or three years of the Libraries faculty [librarian's] time) must be bought through the grant. The disciplinary faculty did not find this inconsistent, and as of 2013, Purdue Libraries faculty have or are participating in over 100 funded research projects as coprincipal investigators or senior staff. The salary savings generated have been used to backfill positions with graduate assistants (in 2013, around 25 graduate assistants are employed by Libraries).

With the hiring of the Data Research Scientist, work progressed in studying the needs of the disciplines in data management. An assumption in 2004 that data management would be as easy as applying a standard taxonomy or classification system to the data proved to be naïve. The management of data varied widely between disciplines and even within subdisciplines, often between one lab and another. In addition, the creation of structure to manage data within a discipline was foreign to most disciplinary thinking or even interest. It required the insights of a librarian and the principles of library and archival sciences to bring order to this chaos.

The IMLS—through two of its programs, the National Leadership Grants for Libraries and the Laura Bush 21st Century Librarian Program—focused on projects that assisted libraries and librarians in identifying the problem and solutions as well as preparing librarians to assume new roles in data management. Beginning in 2007, the Purdue Libraries was the recipient of five major grants from the IMLS, both National Leadership and Laura Bush. Total funding through 2013 to the Purdue Libraries reached has $982,295. A major result of this funding has been the development of the Data Curation Profiles. For further discussion of the importance of the Data Curation Profiles, see Chapter 3.

While the Libraries were immersed in learning about data management, participating on grants, collaborating with disciplinary faculty, and raising the issue within the profession, the challenge remained to gain support within Purdue University to build a process to manage data and a digital repository to house the data generated at Purdue. As Dean of Libraries, I raised the need to have a task force formed by the Provost to plan Purdue's data management and preservation program as it was anticipated by the NSF. In 2010, with the announcement that the NSF would require a data management plan for all funded research awarded after October 2010 (later revised to January 2011), the Provost appointed a task force co-chaired by the Chief Information Officer (CIO) and me. Members of the task force were faculty who held NSF grants from each college and school. The charge to the task force was to develop a template that would meet the needs of a researcher in submitting a grant to the NSF. In a short time, it became apparent that trying to look at the challenge from the 30,000-foot level was not possible for researchers, as they were constrained by the particular needs of their own disciplines. Ultimately, a report was issued that included the problems that would need to be addressed by a data repository (e.g., the business model, support for the researcher, etc.). Once the report was submitted to the Provost and the Vice President for Research, it was agreed that the solution had to be generated though a team comprised of Libraries faculty, staff from the Office of Information Technology at Purdue (ITaP), the Office of the Vice President for Research (OVPR), and the Sponsored Programs Pre-Award Services. In 2011, this team was brought together and was given a name, the Purdue University Research Repository (PURR) Team.

The result of the collaborative work at Purdue among the Provost, the OVPR, ITaP, the Sponsored Programs Pre-Award Services, and the Libraries has resulted in not only the development of a working digital research repository in PURR, but an awareness that it must be a collaborative endeavor, that no one unit can, on its own, create a solution to the challenge of data management. A further description of the formation and workings of PURR is given in Chapter 16.

Since I was requested to write this section in the first person, I will end with an observation: the last 10 years of my 40 years as an academic librarian have been the most rewarding and exciting through the work with the disciplinary researchers on data management issues by showing them the critical and crucial role that library and archival sciences must play in research today and in the future.

REFERENCES

Association of Research Libraries (ARL). (2006). *To stand the test of time: Long-term stewardship of digital data sets in science and engineering.* Report from the ARL workshop on New Collaborative Relationships: The Role of Academic Libraries in the Digital Data Universe. Retrieved from http://www.eric.ed.gov/PDFS/ED528649.pdf

Atkins, D. E., Droegemeier, K. K., Feldman, S. I., Garcia-Molina, H., Klein, M. L., Messerschmitt, D. G., . . . Wright, M. H. (2003). *Revolutionizing science and engineering through cyberinfrastructure: Report of the National Science Foundation Blue-Ribbon Advisory Panel on Cyberinfrastructure*. Washington, DC: National Science Foundation. Retrieved from http://www.nsf.gov/cise/sci/reports/atkins.pdf

DataCite. (n.d.). What do we do? Retrieved from http://datacite.org/whatdowedo

Data Conservancy (n.d.). About. Retrieved from http://dataconservancy.org/about/

Data Curation Profiles Toolkit. (n.d.). About. Retrieved from http://datacurationprofiles.org/about

DataONE. (n.d.). Partners. Retrieved from http://www.dataone.org/partners.

Distributed Data Curation Center (D2C2). (n.d.). D2C2: Distributed Data Curation Center. Retrieved from http://d2c2.lib.purdue.edu

Mullins, J. (2009). Bringing librarianship to e-science. *College & Research Libraries, 70*(3), 212–213. Retrieved from http://crl.acrl.org/content/70/3/212.full.pdf+html

National Science Foundation (NSF). (n.d.). *Dissemination and sharing of research results*. Retrieved from http://www.nsf.gov/bfa/dias/policy/dmp.jsp

National Science Foundation (NSF). (2007). *Sustainable digital data preservation and access network partners (DataNet)* (Program Solicitation NSF 07-601). Washington, DC: National Science Foundation. Retrieved from http://www.nsf.gov/pubs/2007/nsf07601/nsf07601.htm

ORCID. (n.d.). About ORCID. Retrieved from http://about.orcid.org/about

President's Information Technology Advisory Committee (PITAC). (2005). *Computational science: Ensuring America's competitiveness*. Washington, DC: Office of the President of the United States. Retrieved from http://www.nitrd.gov/pitac/reports/20050609_computational/computational.pdf

Priem, J., Taraborelli, D., Groth, P., & Neylon, C. (2011). Altmetrics: A manifesto. Retrieved from http://altmetrics.org/manifesto/

Soehner, C., Steeves, C., & Ward, J. (2010). *E-science and data support services: A study of ARL member institutions.* Washington, DC: Association of Research Libraries. Retrieved from http://www.arl.org/storage/documents/publications/escience-report-2010.pdf

2 | Data Governance

Where Technology and Policy Collide

MACKENZIE SMITH

The Internet, web, and related technologies have created new opportunities to advance scientific research, in part by sharing research data sooner and more widely. The ability to locate, get access to, and reuse existing research data has the potential to both improve the reproducibility of research as well as enable new research. Because of this potential there is growing interest from across the research enterprise (researchers, universities, funders, societies, publishers, etc.) in data sharing and reuse in all research disciplines, but particularly in data-intensive disciplines where data is expensive to produce or is not reproducible. The long-term vision is of a truly scalable and interoperable "web of data" that will take scientific progress, social productivity, and cultural understanding to new heights.

Furthermore, reproducible research—a core scientific principle—depends on *effective* sharing of research data that is accompanied by documentation of its production, processing and analysis workflows (i.e., its provenance), and its technical structure and formatting. Without access to all the supporting data, or metadata, as well as the software to interpret and analyze the data, no research is entirely credible or trustworthy.

However, our collective understanding of the legal, regulatory, and policy environment surrounding research data lags behind that of other research outputs like publications or conference proceedings, and this lack of clear understanding is hindering our ability to develop best practices for data sharing and reuse. Data governance is the system of decision rights and responsibilities covering who can take what actions with what data, when, under what circumstances, and using what methods. It includes laws, regulations, and policies associated with data, as well as strategies for data quality control and management in the context of an organization or enterprise. It includes the processes that ensure important data are formally managed throughout an organization, including business processes and risk management. Organizations managing data are both traditional and well-defined (e.g., universities) as well as cultural or virtual (e.g., a scientific disciplines or large, international research collaborations). Data governance ensures that data can be trusted and that people are accountable for actions affecting it. For research data to become a valuable and reliable part of the scholarly communication system, a shared data governance framework is needed. Aspects of data governance to consider include:

- Legal/policy issues (e.g., copyrights, sui generis database rights, confidentiality restrictions, licensing and contracts for data);
- Attribution and/or citation requirements (e.g., as required by legal license or desired by researchers and funders);
- Archives and preservation (e.g., persistence of data and its citability, persistence of identifiers for data and data creators);
- Discovery and provenance metadata, with its own governance issues (e.g., copyright licenses for metadata use);
- Data schema and/or ontology discovery and sharing, including governance (e.g., copyright licenses for ontologies);
- Access to required infrastructure for data interpretation (e.g., software used in its production or analysis).

This chapter attempts to describe the current landscape for data governance and make recommendations for future work to advance a data governance framework for the research community.

LEGAL ISSUES IN DATA GOVERNANCE

Copyright law, while complex and nuanced, is largely harmonized (in the sense that it is structured, interpreted, and enforced in the same way) worldwide, unlike other types of intellectual property law (e.g., sui generis database rights or patent rights). As discussed elsewhere in this book in more detail, U.S. law limits copyright protection for some types of data (e.g., facts and ideas are never protected), and the legal distinction between facts or collections of facts and protected "databases" are murky. Outside the United States, different legal jurisdictions distinguish various types of data—such as "factual" versus creative products—with different protections. For example, a database of automated sensor readings that is automatically in the public domain in one country may fall under intellectual property control in another, making it difficult to combine data produced by researchers in both countries without complex legal negotiation or development of a customized contract to harmonize the different laws for the purposes of the research project. So what is technically tractable becomes politically difficult. Another nuance of research data is the distinction made in many jurisdictions between a database and its contents—the former is often copyrightable, while the latter may or may not be, depending on what it is and its provenance. Finally, research data in some fields, particularly the humanities, consists of original creative works that are clearly under copyright (e.g., visual images, films, fictional works, etc.). The existence of these legal differences across jurisdictions and data types makes it necessary to carefully consider research project data sharing norms.

Copyrights, sui generis database rights, and the public domain[1] are all applicable to various types of research data, and the current legal tools and remedies to protect and share data include contracts, public licenses, and waivers. Where copyright applies, there are straightforward means of sharing data that include the rights holder keeping the copyright or granting rights under a copyright license, such as the Creative Commons license suite, or putting the work into the public domain with a rights waver.[2] For the frequent situation where copyright law does not apply, the data is in the public domain by default and researchers' best recourse is to share it under the terms of a contract (often confusingly referred to as a usage license) described in more detail below.

Privacy and/or confidentiality law is another important part of the legal landscape for data, especially that produced by medical research, and in the social, behavioral, and health sciences. These laws and regulations impose restrictions on storage, dissemination, exchange, and use of data, and they are even more fragmented and diverse than the area of intellectual property. In addition, researchers and institutions often release data under ad hoc, custom contracts (or usage agreements) that can be incompatible with restrictions from other institutions in the same regulatory environment.

Another issue that raises considerable concern among researchers is in the meaning of "open" and some of the terms used in that context, such as "noncommercial" use. While advocacy organizations like the Open Knowledge Foundation have published widely recognized definitions of "open,"[3] these do not allow for limitations on the reuse of data for commercial purposes (e.g., by pharmaceutical companies or software start-ups). Many scientists desire protection from that type of commercial reuse but would agree that imposing legal limitations on reuse of their data might also create a barrier for colleagues interested in using the data for scientific, noncommercial purposes. Since there is no standard or legal definition of "noncommercial,"[4] how such a condition might be enforced is uncertain. For example, if research results that drew from multiple reused datasets generate a patent or are included in a new textbook, is that a violation of the noncommercial terms of the license?

The complexities surrounding research data legalities make it difficult to answer questions like: who can decide which legal approach to use for publishing a given dataset, or is it allowable to combine datasets that were released under completely different contractual terms of use, each requiring that its terms and conditions continue to apply to the data in the resulting derivative dataset? Many researchers rely on scientific norms or conventional wisdom to resolve these questions since they lack resources to help them with any other approach, and this leads to behavior that may or may not be legally defensible and has questionable side effects for research reproducibility and data reuse. Certainly the laws affecting data are not sufficient to ensure that the norms of scientific research are followed. For example, there is an important distinction between releasing data at all (i.e., just making it accessible to other researchers) and making it effectively reusable or repurposable for new research, with only the latter supporting research strategies that require combining multiple existing datasets. So part of data governance that exceeds the reach of law is specifying *how* data is to be shared so that it supports follow-on research and is not merely findable, if sought. Ensuring data reusability requires additional policy to cover data quality and metadata provision, and separate mechanisms for policy enforcement, such as contractual agreement (e.g., as a condition of funding) or dependence on scientific social norms of practice.

Because the laws around data do not enforce scientific norms or researchers' expectations, a typical approach for sharing scientific data is to impose a "terms of use" or "data usage agreement" on a data archive as a condition of searching, viewing, and downloading its data. These are private contracts that apply to the person interacting with the data archive but do not "follow the data" if the person who agreed to the terms subsequently republishes the data, so they can be difficult to enforce. Finally, these agreements are often incompatible with each other, making data integration for new lines of research legally questionable. For these reasons, data usage agreements are extremely problematic for the long-term goals of data sharing, while advancing the short-term goals of researchers in sharing their data.

TECHNOLOGY ISSUES IN DATA GOVERNANCE

The technological landscape for data sharing as it relates to governance is equally confusing. To make data sharing effective at web-scale and thereby enable international e-science or network-scale science, we need a way to support automated, machine-processable information on what can be done with a given dataset or database, as well as the metadata describing its properties and qualities. The technologies involved include media types and formats, metadata (for description and provenance of the data), identifiers, strategies for long-term preservation, and software required to use the data. What is needed to achieve this is nothing less than a new layer of the web architecture to support research and scholarship at the social and legal level, and with minimal process, sometimes referred to as "ungovernance." This layer of web standards would then support the functional needs of data discoverability, accessibility, interpretability, reproducibility, and reusability without human intervention.

The metadata that data governance suggests includes both discovery and provenance information. Discovery requires descriptive metadata to support researchers' ability to learn about and locate data on the web, along with information about its purpose, type, creator, funding source, and so forth. Descriptive metadata will include one or more identifiers that link to the data so that it can be accessed and cited. Provenance metadata includes information about the source of the data and the workflow and methodology used to generate it. This is necessary for the interpretability, reproducibility, and reusability goals of data sharing, as well as determining its quality. There are many challenges associated with metadata for data (sometimes called "paradata"), among which is its transitive nature. Datasets not only evolve over time, but they can be combined, derived from, or built upon. In order to properly manage some types of data, we can imagine using something like the Github[5] software development infrastructure to allow data to transition in multiple directions, while still retaining the original core in a retrievable form. If done properly, having this metadata would be a great boon for scientists, since it would reduce the need to redo experimental and other data-production work. However, producing this metadata can be difficult and time-consuming today, since it is not well-integrated into the research process, and we lack tools to make it easy and the standards to store and share it.

Another type of metadata necessary for data governance and applicable to a governance layer of the web is "rights metadata." Even in cases where the legal metadata has been applied to the data (e.g., a copyright license or rights waiver such as CCo, CC-BY, or ODC[6]), there is no good way to technically communicate that information along with the data today.[7] It is typically published on a webpage connected to the site, or referenced from a separate metadata record describing the dataset. If a common and well-known license or waiver such as one from CC is used, then the researcher can avoid extra effort in determining the eligibility of the data to his or her research, but if a custom contract is used (e.g., a "data usage agreement" or "terms of use"), then the researcher might have to resort to finding a lawyer to interpret the contract for him or her. In practice, few researchers have the time, funding, or access to expertise required for that last step.

Another technological aspect of data governance relates to the software used to generate, process, analyze, or visualize the data (i.e., any software needed to interpret or reproduce the data). All information in digital formats, including research data, requires software to interpret it and is otherwise a meaningless collection of digital bits. So for a researcher to validate research results by recreating or reprocessing data the software used for the original research is usually necessary. Additionally, software that is integral to recreating or reprocessing data should be openly available (e.g., as open-source software and, ideally, technology platform-independent) and publically shared. Therefore, the software must also have metadata (descriptive and provenance, including versioning) so it too can be discovered and its quality assessed, and it must be preserved just as carefully as the data associated with it.

DATA GOVERNANCE IN RESEARCH PRACTICE

A recent survey (Tenopir et al., 2011) of the research community undertaken by the DataONE project showed that 80 percent of scientists are willing to share their data with others in the research and education community; however, the question was never raised with them as to how, legally, they might include a statement in their data about that willingness to share, and under what terms, so that their expectations are clear to others who are interested in using the data. The consensus view was that most researchers have simply never thought about these issues beyond their obligations in relation to human subjects and institutional review board (IRB) regulations.

A research discipline that has already worked through many issues of data sharing and governance is the social sciences, and particularly for census and survey data. They have the legal and technical tools to archive and share data, and well-established behavioral norms. But there are still weaknesses, especially with regard to personal privacy and subject consent agreements, and the legal contracts (terms and conditions) for access can be very complex and incompatible across data repositories.

The main incentives for any research activity are recognition and credit for the work, with a secondary incentive being improved efficiency, quality, and impact of the research (e.g., avoiding replication of effort or ability to better verify results). Compliance with funder, institutional, and publisher mandates also are a consideration but are insufficient by themselves to ensure good behavior unless enforced. Data publishing and citation standards and practices are needed to support better credit allocation and reward mechanisms for good data sharing behavior. And in the short term there are simple measures that would increase awareness and begin to build expectations—proposal questions such as "how has your research data been reused by others in the past" or asking researchers who download datasets to publish their own data and link it back to the source data. Even with proper credit, researchers express uncertainty about what data they should share, when, with whom, in what form, for what purposes, and so forth, and they lack the resources or expertise (or awareness that they lack expertise) to do what is necessary or even get help to find out what options are available to them.

From the publishers' perspective, there is renewed interest in the relationship between data and the publications that capture the research results from the data. Tighter integration of the data and publications is desirable for a variety of reasons, from making it easier to give credit to data providers to enabling "enhanced publications"[8] that simplify the mechanism of locating available data on particular topics. Publishers are increasingly interested in making sure that supporting data is available, often in advance of the article, but they are uncertain of their own role in making that possible. Some are developing archiving solutions, some are partnering with institutions to link data to publications, and some are setting policy but remaining silent on implementation. At a minimum, publications should cite data in a similar manner to related publications, and they could include statements about the data's availability and metadata for where to access it, and terms and conditions.

On the technology side, software used by researchers often makes subsequent data sharing and reuse difficult, since the "one tool per lab"[9] phenomenon is still common and there are few standards for structuring or encoding data to make it useful beyond its creators and the software they used. In other words, even if the data is successfully shared, without the software that produced, processed, analyzed, or visualized it, the data is often not understandable by itself.

Reusing data has its own challenges, since researchers often are uncertain of the provenance of a given dataset and whether it can be trusted, and also often are faced with significant effort to reformat the data for integration with other data or use by a different tool than the original research used. Legal issues play into this, since researchers rarely understand what rights adhere to their data and who holds those rights (i.e., themselves, their institution (the grantee), their funder, or no one, that is, public domain). And even if the determination is made, what contract, license, or waiver to apply to the data is another source of confusion. International, interdisciplinary, and cross-sector collaborations raise further questions, for some of which there may not be clear legal answers.

RESEARCH DATA MANAGEMENT PLANS AND DATA GOVERNANCE

Part of the current interest in data governance comes from the fact that many research disciplines are moving to systematize data archiving, either in large, centralized repositories (e.g., GenBank, DataONE, Dryad, Global Biodiversity Information Facility) or in institutionally supported repositories (e.g., DSpace, EPrints). In a few cases, journals mandate data archiving (e.g., the Journal Data Archiving Policy, or JDAP, imposed by the majority of evolutionary biology journals, or *Nature's* policy on depositing genomic data into GenBank prior to publication[10]). Increasingly, research funding agencies also are requiring data archiving and open sharing as a condition of funding. These range from blanket policies (e.g., the Wellcome Trust) to proposal guidelines from the *National Institutes of Health* (NIH) and the *National Science Foundation* (NSF), among others.[11] While not all agencies mandate sharing in all cases, and could not in some cases (e.g., where privacy laws apply), their intent is to encourage that behavior.

To take a recent example, data management plans for NSF proposals require description of the types of data to be created or used, the standards in which the data will be stored and preserved, and policies for ensuring access to the data and under what terms and conditions. The requirement was created to protect the agency's investment in the research's outputs and to optimize their value. The NSF believes that data management plans and their evaluation by review panels will evolve over time to become a more influential part of both the broader impact and merit review criteria, so adding it as a proposal requirement was just the first step. Review panels currently take direction from program officers and review plans inconsistently, but already there are knowledgeable researchers using their plans for competitive advantage. The NSF is aware that the ultimate success of their plans requires community-driven guidelines, norms, and expectations.

A gap in both the data management plan guidelines and the emerging tools to create them is in the area of policies, and particularly for copyrights, database rights, and other applicable intellectual property policies, related to data sharing. There is a lack of expertise to guide researchers and research administrators, and uncertainty about who controls policy effecting the distribution and archiving of data (which have serious legal aspects and long-term costs). There also are uncertainties about how to create policies that are discipline-agnostic, and how to centralize policy in a time of rapid change. This is exacerbated by a general unwillingness to tackle these issues by all parties concerned.

RECOMMENDATIONS FOR DATA GOVERNANCE

Unless and until researchers have access to appropriate infrastructure—repositories with long-term preservation capability, means of creating identifiers and metadata (or "paradata") for datasets, and so forth—well-intentioned goals and policies for improved sharing of research data will not succeed. Where the infrastructure and support services exist, recruiting data from research to comply with policies and scientific norms is easier, although the infrastructure itself is not sufficient to ensure good compliance.

In order to achieve a good level of appropriate and effective data sharing, several things are needed:

- Clear and consistent statements of policy and enforcement practices by funders, publishers, institutions, societies, and other research stakeholders;
- Easy-to-use and trustworthy infrastructure to accommodate the data and associated metadata;
- Credit mechanisms to reward researchers for the effort of sharing their data;
- Better clarity around the researchers' (and other stakeholders') rights in and responsibilities for the data, including privacy/confidentiality regulations and copyright status;
- Harmonization of data usage agreements, including privacy restrictions.

Many opportunities to improve data governance are achievable in the near-term (i.e., the next few years) with corresponding challenges that must also be addressed. These include common, normative "data usage agreements" that could be proposed to replace the ad hoc and heterogeneous contracts in use today; improved methods for embedding rights and licensing terms into metadata; developing a best practice for the terms and conditions of sharing metadata (as opposed to the primary data); and creating educational modules on data governance for general distribution. Corresponding challenge examples include lack of clarity about the law with regard to research data, or conflicting beliefs about who "owns" and controls data sharing decisions. Beyond issues of access to research data are considerations of possible funding agency policies to avoid unnecessary replication of data that has already been collected (or at least justification of overlap with existing data). Each area of opportunity/challenge is explored briefly below.

Having identified the community of stakeholders involved in governing research data, it would be possible to create a governance process that is community-led and empowered. It could consider all aspects of data governance: necessary standards and best practices, funder mandate recommendations, cost models, and so forth. Such an organization has recently begun—the Research Data Alliance[12]—whose mission is to "accelerate international data-driven innovation and discovery by facilitating research data sharing and exchange, use and re-use, standards harmonization, and discoverability. This will be achieved through the development and adoption of infrastructure, policy, practice, standards, and other deliverables" (RDA, n.d.). The RDA offers a truly international forum to begin discussing and resolving the many data governance issues identified here.

While a community forms around data governance, model practices for policies and legal practices related to research data are needed, as well as clarification of the legalities of ownership of different types of data. Topics for further research include: standardized data sharing licenses, current funding agency policies, and technological challenges of data interoperability under particular governance regimes (e.g., "attribution stacking" caused by certain licenses like CC-BY or ODC-BY, whereby, as datasets are aggregated with additional datasets, attributions become required for many thousands of data producers, each responsible for just a small subset of the resulting data aggregation).

Infrastructure supporting "good behavior" in data sharing and interoperability is also needed and appropriately part of data governance (i.e., ensuring that researchers can act on the stated policy of their funders and institutions). A specific example of that infrastructure is the DMPTool, developed by and available from the California Digital Library in collaboration with the DataONE project, the UK Digital Curation Centre, the Smithsonian Institution, the University of California-Los Angeles Library, the University of California-San Diego Libraries, the University of Illinois at Urbana-Champaign Library, and the University of Virginia Library. DMPTool helps researchers create credible and appropriate data management plans for grant proposals, as mandated by the NSF and NIH. Other examples are long-term archival data repositories, persistent and unique identifiers for published data, standards for descriptive and rights metadata, and so forth.

Just as CrossRef[13] created a large-scale registry of articles with persistent, unique identifiers (i.e., DOIs) and associated metadata to support interlinking, we could consider similar centralized infrastructure to associate datasets with identifiers and related metadata and rights/licensing information. Such a dataset registry or catalog could enable activities like discovering relevant research data that is eligible for reuse or repurposing in a particular manner (e.g., data mining or combining with other datasets). In fact, CrossRef and DataCite already provide this service[14] for datasets and could be further exploited as data discovery services.

Clearer definitions and taxonomies of data types would help the community communicate more clearly about data governance. For example, how should we represent different types of data, their relationship to each other, and the relationship of data to associated metadata or software? A related effort to define metadata standards for describing various data types and their properties (including terms of use) is another priority. A taxonomy of metadata would facilitate discussion and clarify where there are problems and where there is general consensus. Important to this effort is distinguishing practices that are discipline-specific from those that cut across disciplines. The RDA is a natural home to vet and promote these standards in the future, but standards organizations like the World Wide Web Consortium (W3C) and the *National Information Standards Organization* (NISO) also will have a role. Related to metadata standards are the development and promulgation of domain-specific data citation practices, as part of a "code of conduct" or as standalone recommendations from a governance body such as the RDA.

Finally, existing tools can be improved to include policy awareness, such as suggesting specific waivers or licenses available to researchers to share their data. The tools can evolve to include all funding agencies and document their particular policies. This suggests that recommended tools should be open-source software that is community-extensible, having open APIs and open data standards to allow, for example, extensions to data management plan authoring tools that attach a default rights waiver to new plans, with other options available on request.

CONCLUSION

Unlike more familiar research outputs like article publications, primary research data is not yet well understood as a research product or as intellectual property with defined roles and responsibilities for its production, publication, reuse, and preservation. How data should fit into the scholarly record and relate to other research outputs, who has authority and responsibility for it and can set policy for its management, how the research community should think about the relationship between policy and actions by researchers—these are all critical questions we must answer in order to achieve a realistic, credible, and ultimately successful system of large-scale data sharing and reuse. The research community is beginning to recognize the need for progress on these goals if we are to continue to advance scientific and societal progress made possible by the network and the huge advances enabled by data.

NOTES

1. The public domain describes the set of works whose copyrights have expired, were forfeited, or are inapplicable, such as pre-1923 U.S. creative works or works published by the U.S. government.

2. Creative Commons licenses and waivers are described on their website at http://creativecommons.org. In particular, the Creative Commons copyright waiver is known at "CC0" or "CC Zero" and waives all rights for all uses, effectively putting the work into the public domain no matter what rights accrued to the data in the first place.

3. For example, see http://opendefinition.org/.

4. More information on the noncommercial license terms is available from the Creative Commons website at http://wiki.creativecommons.org/Defining_Noncommercial, and in particular, the report "Defining Noncommercial."

5. Github, found at https://github.com/, is a popular online platform for software developers to collaboratively write and manage their code. Such well-tested models for shared software production and management have been suggested for use in other collaborative creative endeavors, including research data generation.

6. See http://creativecommons.org/about/cc0, http://creativecommons.org/licenses/ and http://opendefinition.org/licenses/odc-by/.

7. One possibility for providing this metadata is in a separate "license.txt" file packaged with the data files (similar to the convention for open-source software code), but it would still be difficult to automate discovery processes that incorporate the information in these separate files.

8. For more on this, see http://www.articleofthefuture.com/.

9. This relates to the phenomenon of labs writing their own custom software tools rather than adopting those developed by another lab. While this is sometimes due to perceived or actual lack of documentation and

support for the externally produced tool, it is often unnecessary and leads to a proliferation of tools that do the same (or nearly the same) thing and are unsustainable over time.

10. The JDAP requires deposition to be adopted in a coordinated fashion by Dryad partner journals. The JDAP is distinct from Dryad. However, it is recognized that Dryad is designed in order to make the JDAP easier, and without JDAP there would likely be limited adoption of Dryad; thus, the two efforts are mutually reinforcing. For the text of the policy, see http://datadryad.org/jdap/. *Nature's* policies are detailed on their website at http://www.nature.com/authors/policies/availability.html.

11. The Wellcome Trust's data policies are explained on their website at http://www.wellcome.ac.uk/About-us/Policy/Policy-and-position-statements/WTX035043.htm. The complete NIH grant proposal guidelines are at http://grants.nih.gov/grants/policy/data_sharing/data_sharing_guidance.htm, and the NSF's are at http://www.nsf.gov/bfa/dias/policy/dmp.jsp. Other agencies requiring some degree or form of research data archiving and sharing include the Centers for Disease Control and Prevention, the Department of Defense, the Departments of Energy and Education, NASA, the National Endowment for the Humanities, and the U.S. Department of Agriculture.

12. The RDA (http://rd-alliance.org/) was formed in 2012 as a joint United States, European Union, and Australian initiative to create a new, community-driven organization to promote data sharing and reuse, modeled on the Internet Engineering Task Force (IETF) for web governance. Its first plenary meeting occurred in March 2013.

13. CrossRef (http://crossref.org/) is a nonprofit organization formed by the STM publishing industry to provide persistent, unique identifiers to online journal articles using the digital object identifier (DOI) technical infrastructure. Today, CrossRef DOIs are ubiquitous for scholarly articles and are being applied to other types of research products like datasets, although with challenges for what constitutes the identified "thing."

14. Currently, the CrossRef search interface is available at http://search.crossref.org/, and DataCite's is available at http://search.datacite.org/ui.

REFERENCES

Research Data Alliance (RDA). (n.d.). Get involved. Retrieved from https://rd-alliance.org/get-involved.html

Tenopir, C., Allard, S., Douglass, K., Aydinoglu, A. U., Wu, L., Read, E., . . . Frame, M. (2011). Data sharing by scientists: Practices and perceptions. *PLoS ONE, 6*(6), e21101. http://dx.doi.org/10.1371/journal.pone.0021101

Part 2

PLANNING FOR DATA MANAGEMENT

3 | The Use of Life Cycle Models in Developing and Supporting Data Services

JAKE CARLSON

INTRODUCTION

This chapter will introduce you to the concept and purpose of life cycle models as they apply toward developing and communicating data services in a library. Life cycle models are being adopted by agencies and organizations, such as DataONE (Strasser, Cook, Michener, & Budden, 2012), seeking to develop systems and promote sound practices around managing, organizing, and preserving research data. In the life sciences, life cycle models are used to depict the continuous sequence of stages that an organism will go through from birth to maturity, reproduction, and the renewal of the cycle, usually in a visual fashion. The premise behind the application of life cycle models to research data is that data also progresses through a life cycle of sorts. From its inception to its use and completion, research data will likely undergo multiple transformations in its format, application, use, and perhaps even its purpose. Through identifying and naming the transformations that data will undergo as stages in a larger life cycle, organizations can better target their services toward addressing real-world situations and needs of the communities they seek to serve. The utilization of life cycle models can provide a useful framework to articulate these stages and to contextualize and communicate what kinds of data services could be provided to whom and when.

DATA SERVICES AND LIBRARIES

The increasingly widespread recognition that data could potentially be used to create new products or generate new areas of research is a popular topic in both mainstream and scholarly literature. With this recognition comes increasing pressure for researchers to do more with their data to ensure its availability and utility for purposes outside of the context in which the data were originally generated. However, data tend to be produced and administered "in the wild," meaning that researchers typically devote very little consideration to how the data could be used beyond its initial purpose. The application of "data science"—the planning and actions taken to manage and work with data holistically in ways that give it context, meaning, and longevity beyond its initial purpose—is increasingly of interest to scholarly institutions, research disciplines, and industry (Loukides, 2010).

Although librarians may not take on the full role of data scientists, they can and increasingly are introducing services to their constituencies to support their work in developing datasets that can be shared and used as information resources in their own right. Librarians see themselves as natural partners in this process, as they have a great deal of experience in developing and maintaining systems for bringing together disparate types of information (books, journals, etc.) on a multitude of subjects, organizing them in ways that make them accessible, highlighting connections between them, and ensuring their availability for future generations. Additionally, there is a rich history of librarians acting as service providers for datasets, particularly for social science-based or government datasets.

Traditionally, librarians have focused their attention on serving the needs of their patrons as information consumers. Providing support to researchers in applying data science to their work requires that librarians understand and respond not only to researchers' needs as consumers of data, but as data producers as well. Acquiring this kind of understanding means librarians need to connect with researchers throughout the research process rather than focusing solely on the formal products of research (books, articles, etc.).

From a high-level perspective, there are two types of data services being developed by libraries: data management services and data curation services. Data management services take place during the "active" stages of the data life cycle, when researchers are generating and making use of the data themselves for their own purposes. Oftentimes these services are offered by working closely with the researcher or his or her team. Data management services could include developing data management plans, training graduate students and others to document and organize data, and developing tools or resources to store the data in a secure fashion.

Data curation can be defined as "the active and ongoing management of data through its lifecycle of interest and usefulness to scholarship, science, and education" (GSLIS-UIUC, n.d., para. 1). Services performed to support data curation may take place both during the phase of the data life cycle where data are actively managed by the researcher as well as during the curation phase. In the curation phase, the data are often more widely available to others outside of the original group that created the data and are often stewarded by a third party, such as a repository manager. The data itself is not being developed further; however, data steward(s) frequently take actions to increase the value and utility of the data. Data curation services may include the application of metadata to make the data more accessible, easier to understand, or to contextualize it as a part of a larger collection. Curation services could also include enabling its discovery and citability through assigning permanent identifiers to datasets or developing policies and platforms to ensure the data are preserved for long-term access.

THE USE OF LIFE CYCLE MODELS IN DATA SERVICES

Applying life cycle models to support services for managing and curating research data has several benefits. Managing and curating research data effectively necessitates long-range planning and taking actions at appropriate points. The process is often complex, involving coordination between people, agencies, resources, and events. Life cycle models help to define and illustrate these complex processes visually, making it easier to identify the component parts or distinct stages of the research data. By breaking down the process of how the data comes into being and how it grows and evolves as it is applied toward fulfilling its purpose into interrelated stages, the specific needs of the researcher are more readily identified. Breaking down the data process into component stages also aids in identifying and accounting for the roles, responsibilities, milestones, and other key components in offering data services. Defining these needs and components directly informs the articulation of what data services could be developed to address these needs and when these services could be offered to be of most use.

As life cycle models tend to be progressive and circular in nature, they can be used to demonstrate the connections between the individual stages and the cycle as a whole. In this manner, life cycle models can be used to define the relationships between the data services that are targeted to particular stages and tie them together to form a larger continuum. Being able to view individual services and identify how they fit into a holistic framework can help to identify any potential gaps or address any areas of weakness in services. For example, a data management planning service might be offered at the beginning stages of a data life cycle. However, in order to be effective, the planning service would need to account for activities taking place later in the life cycle. Having a life cycle model in place that depicts data practice would enable the service providers to account for later-stage activities and produce a better service as a result.

Finally, just as life cycle models can provide a useful framework for service providers to identify and develop data services, these models also can help communicate these services to intended consumers. The visual nature of life cycle models can help convey the services in ways that are engaging and easy to understand. They serve as a common point of reference in negotiating what, when, and how the services will be delivered to a particular constituency. They demonstrate the relationships between services and the prerequisites or other requirements needed for consumers to take advantage of the services.

PREVIOUS APPLICATIONS OF LIFE CYCLE MODELS TO ORGANIZE AND DESCRIBE SERVICES

In considering the application of life cycle models toward data services, it is worth taking a moment to explore how libraries and other agencies have made use of life cycle models. One notable example of libraries' use of life cycle models centers on a depiction of the stages and flows of scholarly communication. Volume 26 of the *Encyclopedia of Library and Information Science* contains "Subramanyam's Model," a depiction of "the evolution of scientific information" in the form of a life cycle model. The model conveys how scientific information takes shape in stages, identifies some of the outputs of each stage, and estimates the amount of time required (Subramanyam, 1979). The stages and outputs listed include the following:

- Year One:
  - The "Research & Development" stage produces lab notebooks and/or diaries

- ○ The "Nonformal Communication" stage produces correspondence and/or memoranda
- Year Two
  - ○ The "Conferences" stage produces preprints, proceedings, and/or reprints
  - ○ The "Research Reports" stage produces theses, dissertations, and/or technical reports
  - ○ The "Journal Articles" stage produces preprints, articles, and/or reprints
- Year Three
  - ○ The "Surrogation" stage produces bibliographies and/or abstracting and indexing services
  - ○ The "Compaction" stage produces encyclopedias, handbooks, and/or reviews

Donna Jacobs, a librarian at the College of Wooster in Ohio, took the evolution of scientific information life cycle model, reformatted it to highlight the products of research, and used it on their website as a means to visually connect patrons to the services offered by the library. Clicking on "Primary Sources," "Secondary Sources," or "Tertiary Sources" in the web graphic takes the patron to a description of each type of information source and information about how he or she might access these sources. Jacobs has since retired, but the model she developed was adopted by the Musselman Library at Gettysburg College and is still in use on their website (Jacobs, 2009).

The Loughborough University Library in the United Kingdom provides another library-based example. Loughborough developed its own model of the research life cycle, comprised of: idea/discovery, seeking funding, undertaking research, and dissemination. Services offered by the library to support each stage are listed, and links are provided for additional description and information about these services (Loughborough University, n.d.).

Other organizations make use of life cycle models to organize and describe their services or to convey complex information in ways that make it easier to understand. For example, Microsoft Research developed its own model of a scholarly communication life cycle consisting of four stages: Data Collection, Research and Analysis; Authoring; Publication and Dissemination; and Storage, Archiving, and Preservation. Microsoft products and services that are designed to meet the needs of researchers are listed in

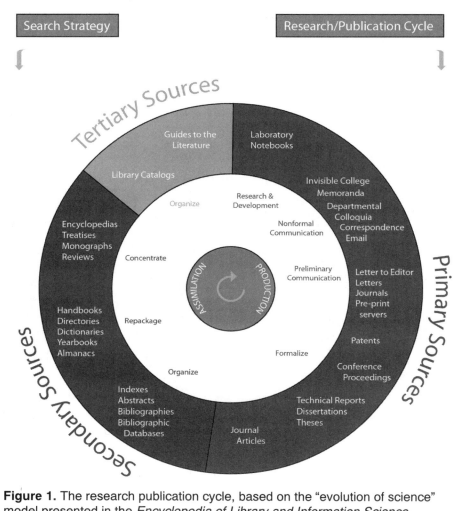

Figure 1. The research publication cycle, based on the "evolution of science" model presented in the *Encyclopedia of Library and Information Science.*

each stage (Knies, 2009). Another example is the Survey Research Center at the University of Michigan, which has developed a life cycle model to illustrate the multiple stages involved in conducting cross-cultural surveys in a way that can be used to depict proper procedures to practitioners (2010).

RESEARCH LIFE CYCLE MODELS

There are different kinds of research life cycle models that are relevant to libraries' considerations of data services. Research life cycle models are de-

signed to illustrate the overall research process, typically from start to fin-
ish. However, research is comprised of an intricate series of interrelated activities that may merit models of their own. These activities may be central
to conducting the research itself, or they may be undertaken to support the
research process or the utility of the outputs. For example, grant funding is
a critical component of research, as many research projects require funding
to carry out or support their activities. Wayne State University's Division of
Research developed a life cycle model to illustrate the stages of acquiring
and servicing a research grant. Their model, shown in Figure 2, is used to
assist researchers in navigating their way through the funding process and
to demonstrate how Wayne State University's Division of Research provides services to help them (Division of Research, n.d.).

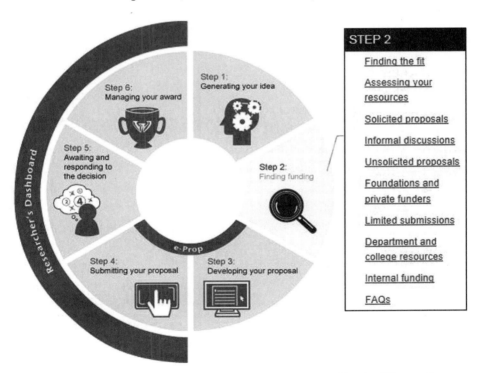

Figure 2. "Learning the Grant Life Cycle" model developed by the Wayne State
University's Office of the Vice President for Research.

Data life cycle models are another subset of research life cycle models,
as they represent a separate aspect of the research process. The activities of

generating, using, and working with data are often important aspects of the research process, but research spans beyond just working with data. Oftentimes data life cycle models will cover the entire research process but will highlight the particular aspects or attributes of the research that pertain to data. An example of a data life cycle model embedded within a research life cycle model is shown in Figure 3.

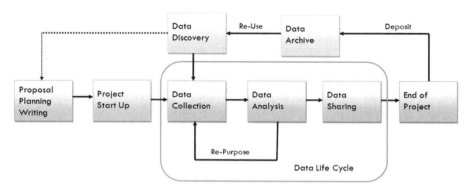

Figure 3. "The Research Life Cycle" model developed by the University of Virginia Library's Scientific Data Consulting Group.

This model was developed by the University of Virginia Library's Data Management Consulting Group. It depicts the first stage of the research process as proposal planning and writing, with a dotted line from data discovery, as data discovery may inform ideas for a proposal. Once the project is defined and approved (and funding is awarded), it moves into the start-up stage. The start-up stage may include activities such as purchasing equipment, hiring personnel, or more detailed planning. Once the project is ready to go, the project will move into the data life cycle phase of the model, which begins with the data collection stage. The nature of the data being collected will vary, of course, depending on the nature of the research conducted, but during this phase, the data needed to conduct the research is generated, gathered, or otherwise acquired in some fashion. Once acquired, the data are then put to use during the data analysis stage to generate the information needed to support the research. Sometimes in the data analysis stage, errors will be discovered and the data will need to be re-collected—an event represented by the repurpose arrow in the model. Once the analysis is complete, the data are shared to varying degrees either indirectly through presentations, publications, and other research products, or directly through individual agreements. The research is then completed and steps are taken to close out the project, such as generating final reports to funding agencies or other stakeholders. Close out activities may also include depositing the data into a data archive of some kind to make it available to a wider audience and to maintain its value beyond the life of the project. The data archive promotes the discovery and reuse of the data, which in turn may spark new ideas for research projects, completing the research life cycle depicted in in this model.

TYPES OF LIFE CYCLE MODELS

There are three types of life cycle models that could be considered in developing and supporting data services: individual-based models, organization-based models, and community-based models.

Individual-Based Life Cycle Models

Individual-based life cycle models are meant to represent the work that comprises a particular research project. Life cycle models can serve as an effective planning or organizational tool for designing and carrying out a research project. By articulating and diagramming the stages of the research project, project personnel can describe and account for the activities that need to take place, when they need to take place, and who will carry out these activities.

As this type of life cycle model is distinctive to the particular research project it represents, it can provide some level of detail about the project and exhibit its complexities. The Data Curation Profiles Toolkit has been used to capture information about a dataset generated through a particular research project and to identify the needs of a researcher in managing and curating this dataset (Witt, Carlson, Brandt, & Cragin, 2009). A key component in developing a Data Curation Profile is determining the life cycle of the dataset under discussion and representing it as a table in the completed profile. The life cycle table includes each of the stages of the life cycle, the output of each stage, the typical file size and number of files produced, the format of the output, and any observations or notes about the stage that would help the reader better understand its purpose. An example of an individual-based life cycle model from a Data Curation Profile is shown in Figure 4.

Data Stage	Output	Typical File Size	Format	Other / Notes
Raw	Field Notebook Entries; Samples		Paper; MS Excel	Plant and soil samples are gathered. Information about the field and observations of the samples are recorded by hand and then entered into a spreadsheet.
Processed	Multiple spreadsheets of data from the samples	100-200kb	MS Excel	Samples are processed in a lab and data are collected in multiple spreadsheets.
Integrated	Master Spreadsheet	1 MB	MS Excel	Data from field observations and processed samples are integrated into a Master Spreadsheet which serves as the official record of the data.
Extraction	Working copies of the data	variable	MS Excel	Data are extracted as needed from the Master Spreadsheet into working copies.
Analysis	Data summaries; Tables and Figures	~50kb	SAS; Minitab	
Qualitative	Gels and Blots	~10 MB	MS Power point	The images of gels and blots are inserted into Power point slides to enable their annotation.
Augmentative Data				
Weather	Weekly / monthly precipitation and temperature ranges		MS Excel	Linking the spreadsheet data to weather data is desirable.

Note: The data specifically designated by the scientist to make publicly available are indicated by the rows shaded in gray. Empty cells represent cases in which information was not collected or the scientist could not provide a response.

Figure 4. The data life cycle table from the "Plant Nutrition and Growth" *Data Curation Profiles Directory* (Carlson & Brown, 2009).

This data life cycle displays the steps taken to generate a dataset from a project conducted by an agronomy professor at Purdue University. His complete process of collecting plant samples, turning them into usable data, working with the data to generate results, and then sharing the important aspects of the data in publications and presentations is represented.

The augmentative data row refers to additional data that was collected to further contextualize the primary dataset. The stages in the life cycle were named by the researcher himself, and they represent his perspective on the stages that his data pass through.

Using the data life cycle developed in this and other Data Curation Profiles that have been generated from others in the same laboratory, the Purdue University Libraries have engaged in multiple collaborations with this lab to help address their needs in managing and curating their data. Currently, librarians are working with a team of information technologists to build a data management system that provides an environment for capturing, describing, and managing the data generated in this lab, with an eye toward its eventual curation. The rich understanding of the data and the lab's specific needs that came from completing the Data Curation Profiles has been instrumental in initiating and carrying out this project.

Organization-Based Life Cycle Models

Organization-based life cycle models often look similar to individual-based life cycle models; however, they serve a different purpose. Organization-based life cycle models are produced by organizations offering services or assistance to researchers. These organizations include libraries, data repositories, scholarly societies, publishers, and others. The different stages of the life cycle model typically serve one of two purposes. First, the stages may serve as touchstones to the services provided by the organization, as demonstrated by the example life cycle models used by Gettysburg College's Musselman Library (Figure 1) and by the Wayne State University's Division of Research (Figure 2). Second, the stages in the life cycle model could be used to instruct researchers about the steps that they should take in preparing to make use of the service.

An example of this approach is the data management life cycle model developed by the Inter-university Consortium for Political and Social Research (ICPSR), as shown in Figure 5. ICPSR provides a suite of services for making social science research data available to researchers and for preserving this data to ensure its utility for future research endeavors. This life cycle model demonstrates how researchers can best prepare their data for submission into ICPSR's data repository and how to avail themselves of their data services. The steps researchers should take to prepare data are

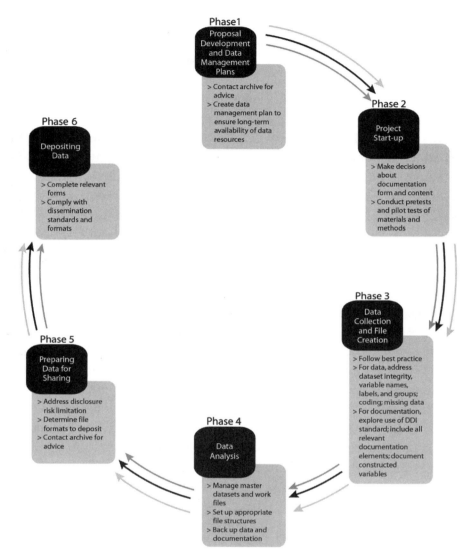

Figure 5. "The Data Lifecycle," a model developed by ICPSR.

broken up and attached to the stages of the research life cycle to convey when they should be done (ICPSR, 2012).

In contrast to individual-based life cycle models, organization-based life cycle models are more general representations of common stages of the data life cycle for a particular field of practice. The ICPSR model represented in Figure 5 is meant to convey the steps a "typical" researcher in the social sciences would undertake to generate, process, analyze, and disseminate his or her dataset. Practitioners of social science research will naturally develop their own processes for their data, which may deviate significantly from the organization-based life cycle model. ICPSR serves more than just a single research project, or even a single field in the social sciences, and the broadly defined stages of their life cycle model reflects this wide scope.

Community-Based Life Cycle Models

Community-based models are those that have been developed to support or address the needs of a particular research community or a community that seeks to address research related needs. A particular aim of the community producing a life cycle model is to convey recommended best practices to interested audiences in a manner that leads to a shared understanding and adoption of these practices. The model serves as a high-level overview representing the components of the best practice and their connections to each other. The model is typically accompanied by a report or other publication that provides a more detailed description of the practices.

An example of a community-based life cycle model is the Curation Lifecycle Model produced by the Digital Curation Centre (DCC) displayed in Figure 6 (DCC, n.d.). The DCC's Curation Lifecycle Model was designed to define and connect the many components and activities that compose curating and preserving data, defined in their model as "digital objects or databases." The article accompanying the model provides a rationale for the model's existence and explains its intended use, helping agencies to plan their activities and ensure that all of the necessary components of curation are done in the correct order (Higgins, 2008). The model is circular in nature, with the outer ring listing the components of curating and preserving data in the particular order in which they are meant to be performed. The boxes and arrows around the outer ring depict places in which data is inserted or extracted from the curation life cycle or where additional actions may need to be performed. The inner circles ("representation information/ description," "preservation planning," and "community watch and participation") represent elements that must be considered across the curation life cycle. Data, the object or materials that are being curated, lie at the center of the model.

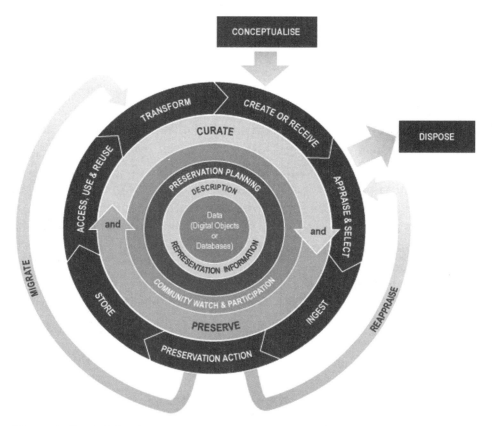

Figure 6. The DCC's Curation Lifecycle Model.

THE LIMITATIONS OF DATA LIFE CYCLE MODELS

"All models are wrong, but some are useful" (Box, 1976). This quote from statistician George E. P. Box also applies to life cycle models as there are limitations to the use of life cycle models that need to be recognized by the service provider. First, models tend to present the ideal rather than reality. In models, the data life cycle is orderly and linear. For example, a life cycle model may begin with a depiction of data being generated, proceeding on toward further development, analysis, and their eventual use. In reality, this process may not flow so smoothly. Data is a product of research, and research is a messy undertaking that entails dealing with the unexpected and responding to errors. Data may reveal unexpected results or contain mistakes that require moving backward in the life cycle to conduct additional processing or even starting over again. Some models, like the one shown in Figure 3, acknowledge this possibility to some degree. Similarly, models often mask the complexity of working with data. Some possible stages within a life cycle model might be "data processing" or "data preservation," both of which may involve multiple processes and activities in and of themselves. Models representing multiple research projects or endeavors tend to overlook the heterogeneity and diversity of approaches and practices that may be present. Finally, models generally reflect the perspectives, interests, and biases of the organizations that created them. This may affect the validity and the utility of the model as applied, especially if the life cycle model was created by one organization and then adopted for use by another. In cases where an organization is planning on adopting the life cycle model generated by another, the adopting organization should take care to ensure that the model and its component parts accurately reflect the research and data practices of the groups they are meant to represent at the adopting organization.

DEVELOPING A LIFE CYCLE MODEL FOR YOUR DATA SERVICES

There are several factors to consider in developing life cycle models to conceptualize and represent the data services you intend to offer.

Scope

In considering developing your own life cycle model, one of the first issues to address is the scope of your data services: at what level do you intend to offer services, and who are your intended audiences?

The previous section covered three different types of life cycle models relevant to providing data services. If the data services you intend to offer researchers are project-based in nature, meaning they are focused on working with a particular research team for a set duration of time, developing individual-based life cycle models is likely the more appropriate option. The level of specificity of an individual-based life cycle model to the project it represents provides a more detailed understanding of the work being performed. This detailed understanding can then be used to generate services that are targeted to address directly the issues that may arise in the management and curation of the data being produced as it progresses through the life cycle. Individual-based life cycle models, and the information needed to understand and respond to in developing data services, can be generated through the Data Curation Profiles Toolkit.

If the data services you intend to offer are more programmatic in nature, meaning they are intended to serve a broader audience than an individual-based research project, then an organization-based life cycle model is more suitable for this purpose. Organization-based life cycle models represent an amalgamation of individual-based data life cycles, and therefore, they provide a broader representation of stages or activities that are common across different research projects. The accuracy and level of detail of the organization-based life cycle model will likely depend on the number and range of research projects, fields, or disciplines that are represented. For example, an organization-based life cycle model that is meant to cover multiple research projects on the behavior of proteins in cells may address similar types of data generated from similar research methodologies in detail, but it may overlook the more specialized or distinctive practices taken by each group. An organization-based model meant to represent the data life cycle in the systems biology field as a whole would reduce the specificity of the stages of the life cycle to common elements across systems biology. The data generated and used in studying the behavior of proteins would be included in this life cycle model, but the more unique characteristics of this line of research would be obscured. Moving the organization-based life cycle model to an even higher level of abstraction, biology, for instance, would further dilute the precision and level of detail of the model as it would have to accommodate additional types of data and research practices. Organization-based life cycle models can be expanded to cover a wide range of data types produced by a variety of research methods. For example, ICPSR's data life cycle model shown in Figure 5 is meant to represent stages that are common across social science research, and the life cycle model developed by the University of Virginia's Library displayed in Figure 3 represents science data in aggregate.

Incorporating Best Practices/Community Standards

No matter what your scope, the life cycle model you develop should be informed by the best practices identified in community-based life cycle models. Naturally, the selection of which community-based life cycle models (the DCC Curation Lifecycle Model, the Open Archival Information Systems [OAIS] Reference Model [OAIS, 2002] for digital preservation, etc.) to incorporate into your model and the degree to which you adopt their specifications will depend upon the types of services (curation, preservation, publishing, etc.) that you intend to offer and your specific areas of focus within these services. Community-based life cycle models can help you identify existing standards, practices, and services to consider, as well as the types of activities that typically compose these services, though additional research is likely to be required to ensure a complete understanding. Community-based models can also inform how components of services or other important elements relate to each other and affect one another. This demonstration of connections can assist in defining the stages of an individual-based life cycle model and as a part of the larger system of data services. It also can inform the sequencing of the stages that compose your model and help to identify requirements or dependencies.

Representation of Real-World Activities

Effective data services depend on an in-depth understanding of the needs of the researchers they are meant to serve. Libraries' initial forays in developing institutional repositories serve as an example of the dangers of launching services without understanding the real-world environments and needs of the targeted users of the services. Although ostensibly designed for use by faculty, many institutional repositories suffered from a lack of contributions when they were first introduced. Studies undertaken at the University of Rochester and Cornell University revealed that the services provided by institutional repositories were not aligned with the research practices and needs of faculty. Without this alignment between practice and service, faculty did not see the value of institutional repositories to their situations, and therefore, they did not make use of the services offered (Davis & Connolly, 2007; Foster & Gibbons, 2005).

In developing data services, libraries must invest time and effort to understand current practices with data; when, how, and why these practices are performed; and the gaps between current and ideal practice from the perspective of the researcher. Without developing an understanding of the research processes and the lab environment, the data services offered by the library may not resonate with the needs of the intended audiences and may go unused. It is acceptable to make use of an existing life cycle model, but your adoption of the model must be led by your knowledge of local issues and needs. Appropriating a life cycle developed by another organization without careful consideration of its relation and fit to your local environment and target audience is a risky endeavor. The services you intend to provide should drive the life cycle model you create to structure and communicate these services to your intended audiences, rather than the other way around.

Mind the Gaps

In his introduction of a life cycle model for research data, Chuck Humphrey (2006) emphasized a need to give attention to the spaces between the stages in addition to the stages themselves. There are some risks to the data that are inherent in moving it from one stage to another. As data progresses from one stage to another, the nature of the work being done with the data or the activities undertaken to manage the data may shift or change completely. In addition, the distinct stages in the life cycle often represent instances where responsibilities for the data are transferred from one person, group, or agency to another. If care and attention are not given to the gaps between the designated stages within a life cycle model, data or needed information about the data may be inadvertently lost.

Perhaps the most critical gap between the stages in a life cycle model is between the stages where the data are actively managed for use by the researcher who developed the data to where the data transition into being curated. In the model produced by the University of Virginia's Library (Figure 3), this juncture is reached when the data move from the "end of the project" stage into the "data archive" stage and is demonstrated by the "deposit" arrow. At this point, data are often transferred from the custody of the original managers to a third party: data repository managers or others assigned responsibility for curating or preserving the data. This is a point where the data life cycle comes to an end for many researchers due to a lack of awareness of curation services or resources (such as data repositories), or due to the perceived time and effort that it would require to complete the transfer successfully. The potential gulf between the parties in understanding the data and its supporting components (documentation, description, etc.) presents a high risk of data loss. If your data services include eventual curation or preservation, you will want to prepare the data for this transition. In doing so you should pay special attention to the transfer process and carefully plan out your services at this juncture to guard against potential loss.

EXAMPLES OF DEVELOPING A LIFE CYCLE MODEL FOR DATA SERVICES

Data Management Rollout at Oxford

The Data Management Rollout at Oxford (DaMaRO) Project is one example of how an organization, Oxford University in this case, has generated a life cycle model to guide the development and communication of its data services (Wilson, 2013a; 2013b). Oxford University has been a past recipient of funding to develop tools and resources to assist researchers in various disciplines with components of working with their data. DaMaRO is an initiative to integrate the findings and products of these efforts into the infrastructure at Oxford University in ways that are holistic and align with researcher and institutional needs. The data life cycle model representing the work of the DaMaRO Project is shown in Figure 7.

The stated principles of the DaMaRO Project are to place researchers at the center of its development and to build sustainable collaborations between the units providing needed support. An understanding of research needs came from a campus-wide survey, which in turn was informed from smaller, more targeted surveys and interviews that had been conducted previously. Questions about the types of data generated, storage, researchers' willingness to share data, the need for training, and long-term preservation were asked. Overall, the results revealed a strong demand for data management services from the research community, but an overall lack of awareness of existing services provided by Oxford University. This survey was intended as a benchmark, and future surveys are planned.

In the data life cycle model produced by DaMaRO, elements of the research data life cycle are listed at the top, and connections between the end and the beginning elements are identified throughout. The tools and services provided to address the needs of researchers in managing their data are listed below these stages, placed in a rough approximation as to when they would be utilized. The tools listed are both "internal" and "external" to Oxford University. Arrows indicate how these tools will feed into two

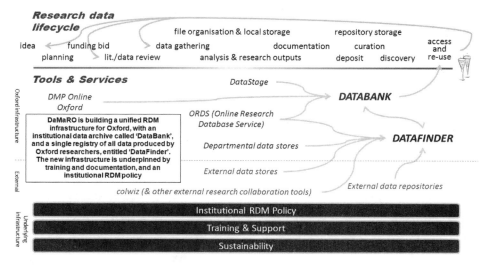

Figure 7. The DaMaRO Research Data Lifecycle Model as presented in a poster at iDCC 2013 (Wilson, 2013).

resources that are currently in development: "Data Bank," a data archive, and "Data Finder," a registry for data produced at Oxford. The foundation of the model, represented by the three bars at the bottom, is provided by Oxford's institutional research data management policy (RDM), training and support materials and programs, and sustainability through developing shared infrastructures and business models.

California Digital Library

A second example of an organization developing a data life cycle model to support data services comes from the California Digital Library (CDL). The CDL was founded by the University of California (UC) system to provide support to UC Libraries through developing services and infrastructure for digital curation, scholarly publishing, archiving, preservation, and other related initiatives. The CDL has been particularly active in crafting responses to the data management and curation needs of researchers in the UC system and in supporting the efforts of UC Libraries in engaging and addressing researcher needs. CDL's efforts, frequently in collaboration with other organizations, have led to the creation of a suite of tools and resources, including EZID to support the citation of datasets and the DMP Tool to help craft data management plans. The goal behind the data life cycle model crafted by the CDL is to demonstrate how their tools and services relate to each other and to a larger continuity of data management. Their model is depicted in Figure 8.

Lifecycle Stage		Service	Functions
PLAN	Grant Application	Data Management Planning (DMP) Tool	Create, edit, share, and save data management plans
COLLECT	Data Collection	Data Up	Open source add in and web application for Microsoft Excel as a data collection tool
		Web Archiving Service	Collect and manage ephemeral web-published content
MANAGE and SHARE	Tracking and Management, Citation	EZID	Create and manage persistent identifiers
	Storage, Management, Sharing	Meritt	Curation repository: store, manage, and share research data
PUBLISH	Scholarly Publication	eScholarship	Open access scholarly publishing services: papers, journals, books, seminars, and more
	Data Publication	Data Publication Platform	An infrastructure to publish and get credit for sharing research data

Figure 8. The CDL's Data Lifecycle Model (Starr et al., 2012).

CONCLUSION

This chapter described the benefits of developing a data life cycle model to support the conceptualization, implementation, and communication of a library's data services. Data life cycle models are increasingly used for these purposes, and when properly conceived and executed, they can be an effective tool. However, crafting a useful life cycle model does require an investment of time and a deep consideration of multiple issues. These include a knowledge of the different levels of coverage and types of life cycle models (individual-based, organization-based, and community-based), and how they could apply to your library's specific goals and objectives. A solid real-world understanding of the research conducted by the audiences you intend to serve is a mandatory precursor in building a life cycle model that successfully represents their data practices and needs. Simply adopting a life cycle model produced by another organization without first acquiring this understanding is not likely to be an effective approach. Although potentially time consuming, the informed perspective that comes from this investment will serve as an effective foundation in employing data life cycle models in ways that promote the growth and advancement of a library's data services.

REFERENCES

Box, G. E. P. (1976). Science and statistics. *Journal of the American Statistical Association, 71*(356), 791–799. http://dx.doi.org/10.1080/01621 459.1976.10480949

Carlson, J., & Brown, N. (2009). Plant nutrition and plant growth—Purdue University. *Data Curation Profiles Directory, 1*(1). http://dx.doi. org/10.5703/1288284315012

Data Management Consulting Group. (n.d.). Research life cycle. *University of Virginia Library*. Retrieved from http://www2.lib.virginia.edu/ brown/data/lifecycle.html

Davis, P. M., & Connolly, M. J. L. (2007). Institutional repositories: Evaluating the reasons for non-use of Cornell University's installation of DSpace. *D-Lib Magazine, 13*(3/4). http://dx.doi.org/10.1045/ march2007-davis

Digital Curation Centre (DCC). (n.d.). DCC curation lifecycle model. Retrieved from http://www.dcc.ac.uk/resources/curation-lifecycle-model

Division of Research. (n.d.). Learning the grant life cycle. *Wayne State University*. Retrieved from http://spa.wayne.edu/grant/

Foster, N. F., & Gibbons, S. (2005). Understanding faculty to improve content recruitment for institutional repositories. *D-Lib Magazine, 11*(1). http://dx.doi.org/10.1045/january2005-foster

Graduate School of Library and Information Science, the University of Illinois Urbana-Champaign (GSLIS-UIUC). (n.d.). Master of science: Specialization in data curation. Retrieved from http://www.lis.illinois. edu/academics/programs/specializations/data_curation

Higgins, S. (2008). The DCC curation lifecycle model. *The International Journal of Digital Curation, 3*(1), 134–140. http://dx.doi.org/10.2218/ ijdc.v3i1.48

Humphrey, C. (2006). E-Science and the life cycle of research. Retrieved from http://datalib.library.ualberta.ca/~humphrey/lifecycle-science060308.doc

Inter-university Consortium for Political and Social Research (ICPSR). (2012). *Guide to social science data preparation and archiving: Best practice throughout the data life cycle* (5th ed.). Ann Arbor, MI: ICPSR. Retrieved from http://www.icpsr.umich.edu/files/ICPSR/access/dataprep.pdf

Jacobs, D. (2009). Research publication lifecycle model. *Musselman Library at Gettysburg College.* Retrieved from http://www.gettysburg.edu/library/research/guides/scientific_information/index.dot

Knies, R. (2009, May 20). Facilitating semantic research [Web log post]. *Microsoft Research.* Retrieved from http://research.microsoft.com/en-us/news/features/zentity-052009.aspx

Loukides, M. (2010, June 2). What is data science? [Web log post]. *O'Reilly Radar.* Retrieved from http://radar.oreilly.com/2010/06/what-is-data-science.html

Reference Model for an Open Archival Information System (OAIS). (2002). CCSDS 650.0-B-1; Consultative Committee for Space Data Systems: Washington, DC.

Starr, J., Willett, P., Federer, L., Horning, C., & Bergstrom, M. L. (2012). A collaborative framework for data management services: The experience of the University of California. *Journal of eScience Librarianship, 1*(2), 109–114. http://dx.doi.org/10.7191/jeslib.2012.1014

Strasser, C., Cook, R., Michener, W., & Budden, A. (2012). Primer on data management: What you always wanted to know. *CDL Staff Publications.* http://dx.doi.org/doi:10.5060/D2251G48

Subramanyam, K. (1979). Scientific literature. In A. Kent & H. Lancour (Eds.), *Encyclopedia of library and information science* (Vol. 26, pp. 375–548). New York: M. Dekker.

Survey Research Center. (2010). *Guidelines for best practice in cross-cultural surveys.* Ann Arbor, MI: Survey Research Center, Institute for Social Research, University of Michigan. Retrieved from http://www.ccsg.isr.umich.edu/

University Library. (n.d.). Research support. *Loughborough University.* Retrieved from http://www.lboro.ac.uk/services/library/research/

Wilson, J. A. J. (2013a, January). *DaMaRO: Data management roll-out at Oxford.* Poster presented at the Eighth International Digital Curation Conference, Amsterdam, Netherlands. Retrieved from http://www.dcc.ac.uk/sites/default/files/documents/idcc13posters/Poster176.pdf

Wilson, J. A. J. (2013b, January). *Towards a unified university infrastructure: The data management roll-out at the University of Oxford*. Paper presented at the Eighth International Digital Curation Conference, Amsterdam, the Netherlands. Retrieved from http://www.dcc.ac.uk/sites/default/files/documents/IDCC13presentations/WilsonIDCC13.pdf

Witt, M., Carlson, J., Brandt, D. S., & Cragin, M. H. (2009). Constructing data curation profiles. *International Journal of Digital Curation, 4*(3), 93–103. http://dx.doi.org/10.2218/ijdc.v4i3.117

4 | Data Management Assessment and Planning Tools

ANDREW SALLANS AND SHERRY LAKE

INTRODUCTION: THE CHALLENGE OF DATA MANAGEMENT

Data is one of the hottest topics in recent years. In the academic world, we see continuous discussion of new initiatives for data-intensive research, of how institutions and disciplines should engage with "big data," and what new data skills are needed to remain competitive in a changing landscape. Much of this change is driven by advances in technology, leading to new opportunities for communicating, collaborating, and rethinking how research is done. Underneath it all, the fundamentals of managing research data become ever so much more important. Although the importance of managing research data is becoming better recognized in the academic environment, the tools and practices are still lagging and generally see slow adoption rates. That said, researchers and sponsors recognize that there is substantial risk due to reduced funding sources, missed opportunities from prior research projects, and the simple issue of insufficient knowledge and attention placed on research data management practices. This chapter will look at some approaches to addressing these issues, from our perspective as service providers in an academic research library.

In our experience, funding agencies provide general information about what the data management plan (DMP) should include, but they often are vague about requirements and provide few resources for researchers to consult when creating their DMPs. Without the proper training or background in data management and digital curation, researchers are apt to continue their current uninformed and incomplete data stewardship practices.

As data management service providers, we often see data management services as being driven by funder requirements, and more specifically, funder requirements for data sharing. As a result, the services that spark up around these requirements are rather limited in nature, often focusing foremost on the language and interests of the given funders, and less so on the idealistic or most pure aspects of data management best practices. This is understandable, given limited resources all around and limited experience, but in our view, this leads to subpar products later on down the line, and in the end, it does not really change behavior or improve practice all that much. In effect, in comparison to a teaching environment, it is much like "teaching to the test." Our data management service team has adopted the philosophy of focusing on best practices first and requirements second, hoping to have a longer-lasting impact upon behavior and skill development. As a result, our services and attitudes around tool development are guided by a long-term view, with a reality check to enable immediate application.

On the side of the researcher, there are similar barriers around improving research data management practices. Time, effort, and resources (both money and staffing) often are noted as reasons for poor management of data, but we also identify a lack of training, poor knowledge of best practices, and insufficient support or guidance as key factors. Most domains in academic research still lack formalized and standardized procedures for managing research data across the life cycle, as well as commitment to training new researchers in proper practices. It is unfortunately often a vicious cycle that keeps practices from improving.

In an effort to develop an understanding of how researchers at the University of Virginia (UVa) manage their research data, UVa Library's Scientific Data Consulting Group (UVa SciDaC Group) began a series of research data interviews. The goals of the data interview process included identifying common research data problems, identifying research support needs, and providing recommendations on improving data management. In practice, however, providing objective suggestions for data management practices proved to be troublesome. It was difficult to make reliable, customized recommendations and be objective in a timely fashion. In response to these challenges, the UVa SciDaC Group developed a system (DMVitals) to easily and objectively rate the current state of the researcher's data management practices.

Our experience with data management planning tools took a different path, and in this chapter, we will primarily discuss the philosophy surrounding the DMPTool (https://dmptool.org). First, however, we must touch on our tool's predecessor, the DMPOnline (https://dmponline.dcc.ac.uk/). DMPOnline was developed by the Digital Curation Centre (DCC) in the United Kingdom following recommendations in the *Dealing with Data* report (Lyon, 2007), an analysis of major UK funding requirements (Jones, 2010), and a period of initial experimentation with development of a "Checklist for a Data Management Plan" (Donnelly & Jones, 2011). As a web-based tool, the DMPOnline offers analysis of funding requirements, support in developing data management plans, and functionality for continued management of research data throughout the entire life of a project. Coverage of funders is mainly for UK agencies and some European Union organizations.

In response to the May 2010 announcement of new United States National Science Foundation (NSF) requirements for data management plans with all new proposals, we began collaborating with several other US research institutions on a US version of the DMPOnline. Although first envisioned as an expansion of the DMPOnline to include US funding agencies, it turned out that funding and research cultures in the United States and United Kingdom are different enough that it made more sense to develop a new tool while still maintaining collaboration between respective teams to share experiences and insights into best practices for data management planning, delivery of services, and anticipating needs in a rapidly evolving environment (Sallans & Donnelly, 2012). In the sections to follow, we offer insights into the development of DMVitals and the DMPTool, how they are employed, and the benefits they may bring to the delivery of research data management services.

DMVITALS TOOL

The DMVitals is a tool designed to take qualitative interview information and use it to systematically assess a researcher's data management practices in direct comparison to institutional and domain standards. Using the DMVitals, a consultant matches a list of evaluated data management practices with responses from an interview and ranks the researcher's current practices by their level of data management "sustainability." The tool then generates customized and actionable recommendations, which a consultant then provides to the researcher as guidance to improve his or her data management practices. By design, the recommendations are far more objective, repeatable, and can be generated rapidly. The use of the DMVitals tool has helped our team expedite and standardize the data management consulting process.

Using best practice statements from UVa sources (Information Security, Policy, and Records Office and SciDaC Group guidelines) and the Australian National Data Service's (ANDS) long-term sustainability scoring model, the system compares the information collected during the data interview process with data management best practice statements. The model then further correlates the researcher's data management practices with the eight data management practice categories developed by the SciDaC Group: file formats and data types; organizing files; security/storage/backups; funding guidelines; copyright and privacy/confidentiality; data documentation and metadata; archiving and sharing; and citing data.

A key part of the tool is the data management (DM) sustainability ratios, which are created for each of the previously mentioned categories using the best practice statements. To provide a framework for defining and improving researchers' data management practices, the DM sustainability ratios are averaged to define a data management maturity level. These levels of maturity are a synthesis of the levels described by Crowston and Qin (2010) and the Australian National Data Service (ANDS, 2011), which are based on the Capability Maturity Model (CMM), typically used in software development (Paulk, Curtis, Chrissis, & Weber, 1993).

The data management maturity level is compared to the maturity levels as defined in the ANDS's *Research Data Management Framework: Capability Maturity Guide* (2011):

- Level 1: Initial (environment is not stable enough to support DM; few individuals have expertise; and infrastructure is disorganized)
- Level 2: Development (the researcher increasingly recognizes the lower level/easier best practices; DM process is under development)
- Level 3: Defined (the researcher is further defining his or her DM practices)
- Level 4: Managed (DM is seen as important at an organizational level and emphasizes coordination between the researcher and other organizational IT units)
- Level 5: Optimizing (the researchers are continually improving their data management practices; DM practices are not static)

The strength of the DMVitals tool is the creation of the DM report, which generates tasks customized to each researcher. These tasks can then easily be grouped into phases, creating a DM implementation plan for each researcher based on his or her personal data interview and subsequent information gathering. Combining this tool with assessment and planning methods helps to expedite the recommendation report process and provide valuable actionable feedback that the researcher can use immediately to improve the sustainability of his or her data.

UVa's Data Interview Initiative

The DMVitals tool evolved out of a need to systematically assess, score, and deliver mostly objective recommendations to a researcher following a start-up consultation interview. When we first began developing our DM services, we recognized that a data interview structure could help us develop a deeper understanding of how UVa's science and engineering researchers manage their research data while also initiating a discussion about how to simplify processes and improve practices. These interviews were constrained to 60 minutes and included the scientific data consultants, the subject librarian, and the researcher. With the data interviews we hoped to:

a. Identify common research data problems and needs,
b. Identify the types of digital data that are being created,
c. Identify communities and individuals who are under the most pressure from emerging grant regulations,
d. Identify potential partnerships for institutional repository data deposit, and
e. Develop opportunities to provide data management recommendations and training.

In creating our interview model we consulted the following models: the Data Audit Framework (DAF) for background reading (Jones, Ball, & Ekmekcioglu, 2008), the University of Oregon for consultation and information on implementation and buy-in (Westra, 2010), the University of Glasgow for interview questions and format (Ward, Freiman, Molloy, Jones, & Snow, 2010), and Purdue's Distributed Data Curation Center (D2C2) Data Curation Profile framework for question refinement (Carlson & Witt, 2007). Our interview protocol was based on the protocol from Wisconsin's Summary Report of the Research Data Management Study Group (Wolf et al., 2009).

Over the first two years of our services, we conducted about 25 data interviews. Through the process, we learned about research data practices at UVa, identified service needs and opportunities, and opened the door to consulting opportunities with researchers. Additionally, we encountered the dilemma of how to manage "unique" conditions of each research environment against common characteristics of DM within domains and institutional frameworks. In terms of support, we were having trouble customizing data recommendation requirements for each researcher.

We recognized a need to reduce the subjectivity and increase the speed at which we produced a report with recommendations. Additionally, we wanted to weigh all assessment factors from our interview, create actionable and repeatable recommendations, and address current DM conditions while showing paths for improvements. These needs are what led to the development of the DMVitals tool.

Development of the DMVitals Tool

The DMVitals tool is built using Microsoft Excel and consists of three types of worksheets: interview questions sheet, data management category sheets, and the data management report sheet. The interview questions sheet (Interview) contains the questions from the data interview. Each of the data management categories, as defined on the SciDaC Group website, are a sheet. In version 1.0 of DMVitals, we use five of the eight categories as sheets: file formats data types (FileFmtsDataTypes), organization of files (OrgFiles), security storage backups (SecStrgBackups), copyright privacy confidentiality (CopyrightPrivConfid), and data documentation metadata (DataDocMetadata). Each category sheet is populated with DM best practice statements for each category from UVa sources (Information Security, Policy, and Records Office (ISPRO), SciDaC Group guidelines) and the ANDS long-term sustainability scoring model. The category sheets also contain the calculated ratio of best practices statements. The third type of sheet, the data management report sheet (Report), is where the DM sustainability index ratios are displayed from the data management category sheets' ratio of best practice statements. This sheet also displays the data management maturity level (the average of the DM sustainability index scores) and the action statements for DM improvement (corresponding to best practices).

Interview Questions Sheet

The questions from the SciDaC Group's Data Interview Protocol are entered on the Interview sheet, one question per column. The current version maps questions from sections 2–5 (see Figure 1). Each question is then associated with one or more DM best practice statements. These DM best practices are listed under each question (or sub-question). Using the answers from the interview, each best practice was coded "yes," "no," or "null." "Yes" meant that the researcher was already doing that action; "no" meant that the researcher was not doing that action and "null" meant that best practice did not apply (for example, the best practice of "data is de-identified" in cases where data need not to be de-identified). "Null" is the default answer.

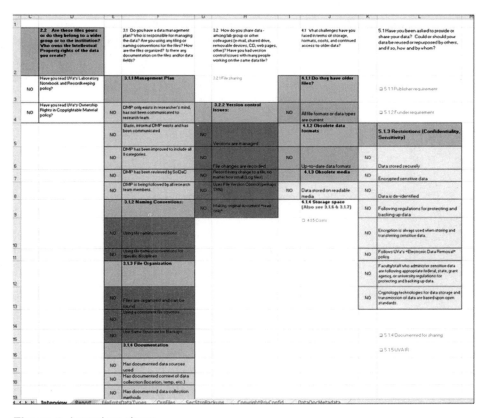

Figure 1. Interview sheet.

Data Management Category Sheets

Each best practice statement from the interview questions sheet is mapped to one of eight data management categories (file formats data types: FileFmtsDataTypes, organization of files: OrgFiles, security storage backups: SecStrgBackups, copyright privacy confidentiality: CopyrightPrivConfid, data documentation metadata: DataDocMetadata, funding guideline: FundingGuide, archiving and sharing data: ArchSharing, citing data: CitingData). Note that in this version, only five of the management categories are being used. The categories funding guidelines, archiving and sharing, and citing data are not used at this time. These will be added in a future version of DMVitals.

Each best practice statement from the interview questions sheet is categorized, given a sustainability level, and is then put in the corresponding column per one of the five sustainability levels (least sustainable, fair, satisfactory, good, and more sustainable). For ease of editing, each best practice statement is linked from its cell on the interview questions sheet to the sustainability level. The actual response to the best practice statement from the interview questions sheet—"yes," "no," or "null"—is also linked. The mapping and linking of each best practice is done for each of the categories on the corresponding category sheet.

To calculate the sustainability index ratio (current best practice to total-possible best practice), each sustainability level was given a "weight": least sustainable (1), fair (2), satisfactory (3), good (4), and more sustainable (5). The total number of "yes" responses (current practice) for each level is multiplied by the sustainability weight. These levels are then totaled and divided by the maximum number of best practices that apply, for that sustainability level, multiplied by the sustainability weight). The ratio for each category is then automatically recorded (via a link) on the data management report sheet as the sustainability ratio. See the screenshot in Figure 2 for the OrgFiles sheet for an example.

Data Management Report Sheet

The data management report sheet is comprised of three distinct sections: sustainability index, data management maturity level and action statements (see Figure 3). The top chart (sustainability index) shows the DM category and the resultant sustainability index (displayed as a percent—a ratio). The

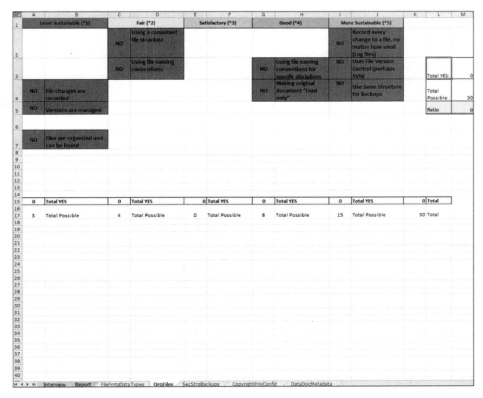

Figure 2. Data management category sheet—organization of files (OrgFiles).

actual ratios are linked from the corresponding data management category sheets. With five levels of sustainability, we divided the ratio values into five groupings—0–20 percent (Level 1), 21–40 percent (Level 2), 41–60 percent (Level3), 61–80 percent (Level 4), and >81 percent (Level 5)—and color-code the values using the colors on the data management maturity level scale (see the colors on Figure 3). This gives a visual view of how the researchers' current DM practices, per category, are ranked, according to the level of "sustainability." The ratios of the categories are averaged for a sustainability index. The average is also color-coded using the above percent groupings.

The bottom of the sheet contains a chart of action statements. The chart includes actionable recommendations targeting improvements for DM. Each best practice statement from the interview questions sheet has a corresponding action statement. The best practice a researcher is not doing is marked with "X." These are the basis for DM improvement recommendations. The phases are customizable and can be moved around as the consultant sees fit. In our consulting approach, we avoid placing too many actions in any phase, which in turn may put researchers more at ease with improving practices.

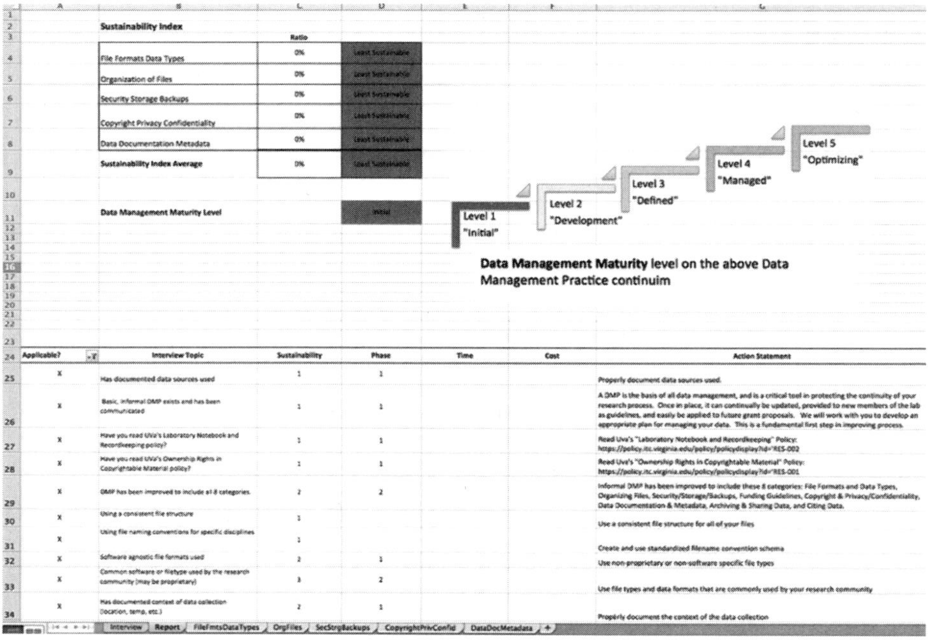

Figure 3. Report sheet.

Use of DMVitals Tool

Recommendations Report

The recommendations report is designed for distribution to researchers (see Figure 4 for an example). It begins with general information on DM and the goals of the report. The DMVitals report sheet provides the rest of the information that goes in the report. The sustainability index chart includes their data management maturity "grade." The chart is copied and pasted from the report sheet. The action statements are grouped into implementation phases (Phase 1: short-term; Phase 2: long-term; and Phase 3: future).

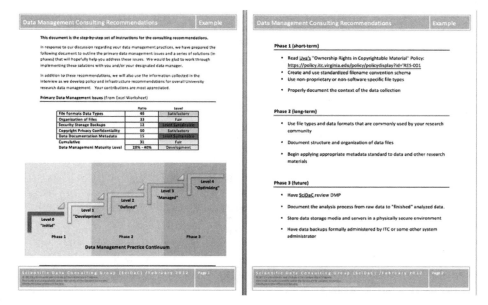

Figure 4. Data management consulting recommendations report.

Data Management Implementation

The next step in UVa's data interview workflow is to distribute the final report, with recommendations, and begin implementation with the researcher. We then sit down with the researcher to go over the recommendations and make adjustments on what actions are done in each phase (see Figure 5). The DMVitals tool is to be used throughout the implementation. As researchers improve their practices, their DMVitals score is recalculated and reflected in their new sustainability index.

The goal of repeating these steps—going back to the DMVitals, updating the best practices, and reevaluating the sustainability index—is for the researcher to obtain a data management maturity score of five "Optimizing," on the ANDS CMM for research DM. But as the model warns, level five is not the "final" level. Level five is labeled "Optimizing." At this level, researchers should be focusing on continually improving their DM practices.

Applying the DMVitals Tool at Your Institution

The DMVitals tool can easily be configured for your institution. It can be used with any data assessment tool. The main interview worksheet can be customized using your assessment questions, local institution policies, and best practices. Ranking of sustainability can be adjusted per discipline or institution. The action statements definitely will require local customizations. These are the actions that your researchers need to do for your institution. Actions might include contacting specific service providers for support. Figure 6 shows the steps in the DMVitals workflow.

The DMVitals tool will continue to undergo improvement to further evaluate whether the scoring accurately represents improved practices. We recognize that the selection of assessment criteria, the calculation

Researcher Interview Response

Data Management Maturity Level

DMVitals

Implementation Plan
Tasks grouped into phases

Figure 5. Data management implementation: DMVitals workflow.

and weighting of scores, and how performance is communicated to the researcher must be done carefully in order to be effective as a communication tool with researchers. We plan for continued refinement of all steps, and we aim to produce a tool that offers value to both DM support providers and the researchers who receive support.

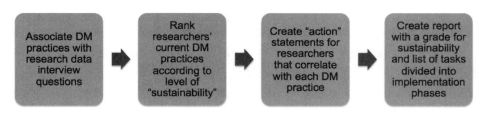

| Associate DM practices with research data interview questions | Rank researchers' current DM practices according to level of "sustainability" | Create "action" statements for researchers that correlate with each DM practice | Create report with a grade for sustainability and list of tasks divided into implementation phases |

Figure 6. DMVitals modification flow.

At the date of writing this chapter, this is still a prototype tool, and we do not yet have metrics to assess the impact or benefit of its use upon effective delivery of services. We are in the early planning phases for an expanded version of the tool, and we likely will integrate it with other broadly used interview models.

DMPTOOL: GUIDANCE AND RESOURCES FOR YOUR DATA MANAGEMENT PLAN

Start Building a Framework

Development of the DMPTool began in early 2011, utilizing in-kind contributions of effort and resources from founding partners (see Acknowledgments), and led to the release of a production version in October 2011. During this first phase, software development was led by partners at the California Digital Library's UC Curation Center (UC3), content/workflow was led by partners at the University of Virginia Library, authentication/integration was led by partners at the University of Illinois at Urbana Champaign, and additional oversight and planning came from partners at Digital Curation Centre (United Kingdom), Smithsonian Institution, University of California-Los Angeles, and University of California-San Diego. Upon initial release, the tool included support for all specified requirements from the NSF, and it has since expanded to include requirements from the National Institutes of Health (NIH), the Institute of Museum and Library Services (IMLS), as well as other funders. The core philosophy behind the DMPTool approach is to: (1) help researchers create a quality and compliant DMP, and (2) inform researchers of resources and local support services available to assist with their data management planning needs.

Embrace a Community Support Model

Following successes in the first year, the team recognized a need to expand and embrace broader community participation. To facilitate the process, the DMPTool Alliance was formed in July 2012, and community building and outreach was placed as a high priority for all future efforts. In January 2013, the DMPTool partners were awarded a grant from the Alfred P. Sloan Foundation to fund further development of the DMPTool. In support of the grant, the DMPTool Alliance will be fully implemented over the course of 2013. This community model draws upon the expertise and resource contributions of original team members and institutions, but also provides structure for participation from the broader community of stakeholders. It includes decision-making processes, roles and responsibilities, terms of participation, and commitments to standards of operation within the alliance, and is a central underpinning to the future strength of the DMPTool and its member community. At this point, the alliance plans to avoid a fee-based service model, and instead continue forward with an open-governance, shared-resource, and grant-funded approach.

From our perspective, the DMPTool offers a way for all information professionals to engage with researchers in the data management planning process. Recognizing that all organizations are at different points in the service development process, a support provider might use the service in the following ways:

1. An organization without staff allocated to data management support services can promote the DMPTool as the main service point, provide links to policies, storage, and other related institutional services and resources, and can begin to foster a discussion and effort at coordinating institutional support providers and services.
2. An organization with a small staff allocated to data management support services can gain some efficiency in repetitive or redundant tasks, allowing for more engagement with researchers.
3. An organization with a larger staff allocated to data management support services can use the DMPTool as a means of scaling and off-loading basic, repetitive tasks, allowing for more focus on high-value interactions, service architecture issues, and support for implementation of data management improvements.

In all cases, individual information professionals, teams, and overall organizations can benefit from approaching broad data management planning issues (i.e., understanding and tracking requirements, coordinating support across institutions, and sharing best practices) as a community, allowing for more time to focus on specialized local research support issues that cannot be initially addressed at scale. Technically speaking, institutions can take full advantage of DMPTool capabilities and community benefits by configuring their campus' single sign-on solution, typically Shibboleth. Institutions can then provide specific information for their researchers to customize their DMPs including help, suggested text, and additional resources.

Lastly, as a commitment to the community aspect of DMPTool, all software created by the project will continue to be made available under open-source licenses on a public code-hosting site, and DMPTool2 will include development of an application programming interface (API) to allow the community opportunities to interface with other software. Following the conclusion of funded project work, ongoing management and governance of the DMPTool will remain community-oriented under the leadership of the DMPTool Alliance.

Approaches for DMPTool2

At the time of writing this chapter, we are nearly halfway through the development of DMPTool2. Through the community approach mentioned above, this new version places emphasis on meeting the needs of main user constituencies (i.e., researchers, librarians, funders, and institutions), with flexibility for expansion and integration of the tool in the future. The team hopes that the tool can serve as a point of convergence for sharing and dissemination of expertise and advice in good DM practices and solutions. For the information professional, this can be a support network for teams of one, and it can help to reduce the burden of individually rediscovering all of the best practices, tools, techniques, and resources that have already been tested elsewhere. For institutions, this approach may offer an enterprise view of successful and failing DM practices, allowing for opportunity to improve and plan resources more effectively.

DMPTool2 is expected to include the functions detailed in Table 1. Although these are the projected functions, they will be revisited throughout the duration of the project via outreach, focus group testing, and evaluation of intermediate prototypes, and are thus subject to change.

Metrics and Impact

Although supporting researchers in data management planning is the core function of the DMPTool, we also recognize that attention to evaluation of the service and ongoing assessment of impact is of equal importance. This is true for operational considerations and use of resources within the information organization, but more importantly as a means of showcasing value to those whom we serve. There are many ways to approach metrics and impact in this case, and we will cover a few here.

Foremost, there are "low-hanging fruit" opportunities. Through Shibboleth authentication and basic database queries of usage, the team has been able to easily track basic web use statistics since the beginning.

New Function	Benefit
Granular modeling of plan templates	Plan templates can be refined with a hierarchical structure, which is important as plan requirements become more comprehensive and complex.
Granular modeling of institutions	Institutions can be represented in any or all of three roles: as a funder, as a researcher's affiliation, and/or as an institution with its own DMP requirements.
Role-based user authorization	Users can hold various roles: plan creators, collaborators, institutional/organizational administrators, and tool administrators, with differing authorizations and capabilities.
DMP life cycle management	Users can track the changes as a plan passes through the major stages of its life cycle, including creation, editing, submission, evaluation and approval or rejection, revision and publication.
Organizational planning activities	Institutions/organizations can define and implement planning activities, with consideration of local resources and needs.
Enhanced search and browse	Users can both perform keyword searches and browse publicly available plans, providing for enhanced discovery.
Institutional branding	Two aspects: (1) hosting neutrality of the DMPTool, that is, removing association of the tool with the California Digital Library via the current domain name dmp.cdlib.org; and (2) increased online institutional branding within the tool's user interface.
Search and reporting for business intelligence	Institutional administrators can mine data on plans, with the ability to filter plans based on their state, users, institutional role and other relevant plan properties.
Advanced administrative interface	Administrators can easily add new funders, requirements, and institutional resources via the enhanced configuration interface.
Collaborative plan creation	Multiple users across institutions can access and/or edit the same plan.
Open API	The tool will be more easily integrated into local automated workflows.

Table 1. Overview of DMPTool2 functions and benefits. Table borrowed from grant proposal and Alfred P. Sloan Foundation grant project documentation.

The team has tracked usage by number of users, number of plans created, and number of institutions represented. During the first 18 months since launching the DMPTool, we saw over 5,000 unique users, over 4,500 plans created, and representations from over 700 institutions. There has been continuous, constant growth of these statistics over the entire course of the service. These use statistics, along with several awards and grants (see Notes), have been helpful for raising awareness amongst particular communities, and for attracting additional resources for growth and continued community building to create a center of mass. While we find these trends encouraging, they do not, however, say much about the qualitative aspects of the service or the impact that data management planning has upon success in research, compliance with requirements, or more openness of research data.

The DMPTool2 project aims to improve what we can learn from use of the service. Current plans aim to look at factors such as adoption of new functionality by existing users, recruitment of new users, and recruitment of new developers contributing to the code base. These elements hopefully will shed light on the best places to focus outreach and educational efforts. Likewise, the project will dig deeper to identify which characteristics may influence higher institutional use rates, and consequently (if possible), better DM practices amongst researchers.

One area that currently looks promising is the institutional adoption demonstrated by integration of DMPTool with local Shibboleth authentication. As one might suspect, taking the step of setting up authentication often also leads to broader promotion at the institutional level, which leads to more opportunities to pull together institutional DM support providers into one service point, which leads to better awareness and informed decision-making by researchers, and lastly, which will hopefully result in better data management plans and practices. DMPTool usage data amongst Association of Research Libraries (ARL) institutions indicates this type of trend, but more thorough analysis will need to be done in future project development before releasing any conclusive results.

Although the factors outlined above are important in evaluating value and impact, we also recognize that there will need to be continued attention to how services and tools like these impact broader issues in data management planning. Some questions might include:

- Does data management planning support provided by the DMPTool lead to improved data management practices and outcomes?
- Does use of the DMPTool correlate with funding proposal acceptance?
- Does the DMPTool actually save the researcher time and effort during proposal writing?

- Does the DMPTool improve the efficiency or effectiveness of institutional data curation service providers?
- Does use of DMPs lead to increased data publication, citation, and sharing, and if so, does that sharing enable avenues of scholarly research and discourse that might not otherwise occur?

Some of these questions may be possible to answer through the planned addition of institutionally oriented business intelligence and mining functions in DMPTool2. For information professionals, this may mean gaining a better understanding of research practices and behaviors, anticipating demands on repositories, or gauging how well researchers understand intellectual property ownership and responsibilities, all gained with little to no interruption of the researcher. Having access to such information may allow for more intelligence, user-oriented design of services, infrastructure, policies, and better anticipation of staffing needs, with minimal cost, effort, and possibly more candid responses. Although these functional needs have been expressed by a number of different institutions, and the team recognizes their value, there are still a variety of policy concerns that will need exploration.

While it may not yet be possible to demonstrate true correlation between the use of the DMPTool and improved data management practices, we believe that use of the DMPTool is a straightforward and easy way for libraries to become more active and engaged in the DM conversation. Our hope is that the structure of the tool facilitates a positive DMP experience for researchers, and leads to learning and insights by librarians and other support providers. It is very easy to get started. Simply visit http://dmptool.org to find more details on setting up an institutional profile to support your researchers.

CONCLUSION

Given the points raised here, we argue that research data management assessment and planning tools can add tremendous value to the services provided by information professionals to the research community today, and can become a true game changer. With this opportunity come expectations for very high-quality products and services, which are tailored to the needs and culture of the academic research community.

Lastly, we believe that it is important to stress that improvement of data management practices must begin somewhere. Going through the process of documenting existing practices affords everyone an opportunity to reflect and determine the best path toward improvement. Along these lines, having an active, operationally focused DMP will enable far easier and better planning for funding proposal data management plans, whether broad in scope or limited to data sharing interests. We hope that additional information professionals can employ the DMVitals and DMPTool to enhance initial data management support services, providing standardization, consistency, and scale.

ACKNOWLEDGMENTS

We would like to acknowledge Susan Borda, a SciDaC Group intern in the summer of 2011 and presently the Digital Curation Librarian at University of California-Merced, for her help on the creation and development of the DMVitals tool. We are most appreciative of our partners in the founding of the DMPTool: California Digital Library (UC3): Patricia Cruse, Perry Willett, Marisa Strong, Tracy Seneca, Scott Fisher, Stephen Abrams, Mark Reyes, Margaret Low, and Carly Strasser; University of Illinois: Michael Grady, Sarah Shreeves, and Howard Ding; DataONE: Amber Budden; Smithsonian Institution: Thornton Staples and Günter Waibel; UCLA: Todd Grappone, Gary Thompson, Sharon Farb, and Darrow Cole; UCSD: Brad Westbook; and UK's Digital Curation Centre: Martin Donnelly.

NOTE

The DMPTool has received a number of awards and grants during the period of development, including (chronologically):

- Library of Congress' Top 10 Digital Preservation Developments of 2011 (January 2012, http://blogs.loc.gov/digitalpreservation/2012/01/top-10-digital-preservation-developments-of-2011/)
- Larry L. Sautter Golden Award for Innovation in Information Technology (January 2012, http://www.cdlib.org/cdlinfo/2012/07/03/dmptool-wins-sautter-award/)
- $149,070 grant from the IMLS National Leadership program (September 2012, http://www.imls.gov/news/national_leadership_grant_announcement_2012.aspx)
- Finalist for Digital Preservation Coalition's Digital Preservation Award for Research and Innovation 2012 (December 2012, http://www.dpconline.

org/advocacy/awards/2012-digital-preservation-awards/928-finalists-2012-research-and-innovation)
- Grant for $590,000 from the Alfred P. Sloan Foundation (January 2013, http://www.cdlib.org/cdlinfo/2013/01/14/cdl-and-partners-receive-sloan-funding-to-enhance-dmptool-features-reach-out-to-community/)

REFERENCES

Australian National Data Service (ANDS). (2011). *Research data management framework: Capability maturity guide.* Retrieved from http://ands.org.au/guides/dmframework/dmf-capability-maturity-guide.html

Carlson, J., & Witt, M. (2007). *Conducting a data interview.* Presented at the 3rd International Digital Curation Conference, Washington DC. Retrieved from http://docs.lib.purdue.edu/lib_research/81

Crowston, K., & Qin, J. (2010). A capability maturity model for scientific data management. *American Society for Information Science and Technology Annual Meeting.* Pittsburg, PA. Working Paper available: http://crowston.syr.edu/content/capability-maturity-model-scientific-data-management-0

Donnelly, M., & Jones, S. (2011). Checklist for a data management plan. *Digital Curation Centre.* Retrieved from http://www.dcc.ac.uk/resources/data-management-plans/checklist

Jones, S. (2010). Summary of UK research funders' expectations for the content of data management and sharing plans. Retrieved from http://hdl.handle.net/1842/3374

Jones, S., Ball, A., & Ekmekcioglu, C. (2008). The data audit framework: A first step in the data management challenge. *International Journal of Digital Curation, 3*(2), 112–120. http://dx.doi.org/10.2218/ijdc.v3i2.62

Lyon, L. (2007). *Dealing with data: Roles, rights, responsibilities and relationships.* Consultancy Report for the JISC. Retrieved from http://www.jisc.ac.uk/media/documents/programmes/digitalrepositories/dealing_with_data_report-final.pdf

Paulk, M. C., Curtis, B., Chrissis, M. B., & Weber, C. V. (1993). *Capability maturity model for software, version 1.1* (CMU/SEI-93-TR-024). Pittsburgh, PA: Software Engineering Institute, Carnegie Mellon University. Retrieved from http://www.sei.cmu.edu/reports/93tr024.pdf

Sallans, A., & Donnelly, M. (2012). DMPOnline and DMPTool: Different strategies towards a shared goal. *International Journal of Digital Curation, 7*(2), 123–129. http://dx.doi.org/10.2218/ijdc.v7i2.235

Ward, C., Freiman, L., Molloy, L., Jones, S., & Snow, K. (2010). *Incremental scoping study and implementation plan.* Project Report. University of Cambridge, Online. Retrieved from http://eprints.gla.ac.uk/54623/

Westra, B. (2010). Data services for the sciences: A needs assessment. *Ariadne, 64.* Retrieved from http://www.ariadne.ac.uk/issue64/westra/

Wolf, A., Simpson, M., Salo, D., Flee, D., Cheetham, J., & Barton, B. (2009). *Summary report of the Research Data Management Study Group.* Madison: University of Wisconsin. Retrieved from http://digital.library.wisc.edu/1793/34859

5 | Trustworthy Data Repositories

The Value and Benefits of Auditing and Certification

BERNARD F. REILLY, JR., AND MARIE E. WALTZ

INTRODUCTION

Within the past decade the digital preservation community has come to embrace a primary set of criteria for assessing the capability of repositories to maintain digital content and information over time. Those criteria are embodied in *Trustworthy Repositories Audit & Certification: Criteria and Checklist*. Since 2007, the Center for Research Libraries (CRL) has used the criteria in audits of several digital repositories. The authors here reflect on the usefulness of the Trustworthy Repositories Audit and Certification (TRAC) criteria in light of the findings and outcomes of those audits.

The authors also aim in this report to suggest the wider application of the TRAC metrics. The criteria developed in 2007 have since provided users of data, including libraries, a powerful lens through which to assess how well a given data repository might serve their needs. TRAC also provides a ready-made set of criteria for data producers to use in creating data management plans. In fact, it is the concept of "designated communities" (i.e., those data producers and users who depend upon digital repositories and services) that forms the core of TRAC and is the key point of reference in the auditing process.

THE ORIGINS OF TRAC

TRAC reflects the knowledge and experience of digital preservation experts representing a range of international communities with interests in digital preservation. These include individual scientists, scholars, and researchers, as well as memory institutions, government agencies, learned societies and organizations, and their funding agencies. The foundations of TRAC can be traced to the beginning of digital preservation. However, the work of four collaborative efforts has had a direct impact on its conception and design.

The first effort was undertaken by a working group supported by the Consultative Committee for Space Data Systems (CCSDS). This group created the Reference Model for an Open Archival Information System (OAIS), which provided the key conceptual framework upon which TRAC is based (CCSDS, 2012). OAIS is a high-level model that describes how digital repositories preserve digital data and content. It provides a common basis for discussion of repository architecture, and a vocabulary for describing in general terms what all digital data repositories do and how they do it. OAIS was approved as ISO standard 14721 in 2003, and it was revised in 2012.

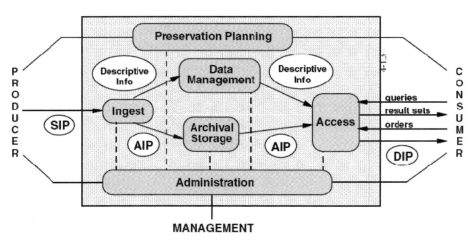

Figure 1. The OAIS reference model. Courtesy of the Consultative Committee for Space Data Systems (2012).

The second effort was the result of a collaboration between the Research Libraries Group (RLG) and the Online Computer Library Center, Inc. (OCLC). RLG and OCLC convened a working group that in 2002 issued the influential report *Trusted Digital Repositories: Attributes and Responsibilities,* which report identified the "characteristics and responsibilities of trusted digital repositories" for large-scale museum, archive, and library collections (Research Libraries Group, 2002, p. i). The characteristics and responsibilities included having in place sound and appropriate tools, practices, and policies with regard to ingest, processing, archiving, and dissemination of digital content.

The RLG-OCLC working group followed the recommendations of the earlier Commission on Preservation and Access/Research Libraries Group Task Force on Archiving of Digital Information, whose 1996 report had called for "deep infrastructure capable of supporting a distributed system of digital archives . . . a critical component of [which] is the existence of a sufficient number of trusted organizations capable of storing, migrating and providing access to digital collections" (Garrett & Waters, 1996, p. 40). Among other things, the RLG-OCLC working group recommended that "RLG, OCLC, and other organizations . . . develop a process for the certification of digital repositories" (Research Libraries Group, 2002, p. i).

To that end, a joint task force was formed by RLG and the National Archives and Records Administration (NARA) to develop a checklist of criteria against which the practices and capabilities of repositories could be measured, to determine their worthiness of the trust and investment of the community. (Research Libraries Group, 2005).

In 2005 and 2006, using the draft criteria developed, Robin L. Dale of the Research Libraries Group and analysts from CRL performed a series of test audits of major repositories. Supported by an Andrew W. Mellon Foundation grant, the CRL team audited three digital repositories: Portico's e-journal preservation service, the Koninklijke Bibliotheek's e-Depot, and the public opinion data repository of the Inter-University Consortium for Political and Social Research (ICPSR). Informed by the experience and findings of the audits, Dale and several others produced the current version of the TRAC checklist, which was published in 2007 by OCLC, the National Archives and Records Administration, and CRL.

Since 2007, a Repository Audit and Certification Working Group, formed by the CCSDS Mission Operations and Information Management Services (MOIMS), and supported in part by CRL, has produced a new set of metrics, based primarily on TRAC, as a standard for auditing and accreditation. That standard, ISO 16363, is also used by CRL in its auditing work. (The discussion of the three TRAC sections or classes of metrics here references the corresponding section of the ISO 16363 as "TDR.")

TRAC AUDITING: APPROACH AND RATIONALE

As published, the TRAC checklist includes 84 criteria for assessing three major aspects of a repository:

1. Section A: Organizational Infrastructure
2. Section B: Digital Object Management and Technologies
3. Section C: Technical Infrastructure and Security

These criteria have formed the basis for CRL audits and certification of a number of digital repositories of interest to its member community: the libraries and researchers at United States and Canadian university, college, and independent research libraries. Since its founding in 1949, CRL has supported major U.S. research library efforts to provide affordable, persistent access to source materials for advanced research. This support is in keeping with CRL's mission to ensure the availability of knowledge resources vital to research and learning in the humanities, sciences, and social sciences. To fulfill this role during the print era, CRL assembled extensive collections of newspapers, journals, government documents, and published archives of interest to its community, and it gathered information about related materials held elsewhere.

Since 2000, however, U.S. and Canadian research libraries have confronted entirely new paradigms of information exchange and access, brought about by digital media and the Internet. With these new paradigms, documentation and the "containers" of information changed from solid, tangible objects, like newspapers, to fugitive signals in magnetic code. Data and information thus went from being enclosed by library walls to being hosted in the Cloud.

Under these circumstances it became clear that insufficient data was available to support the kinds of decisions that North American libraries would have to make to achieve an orderly transition from print to digital collections. Very little was known about how the repositories of digital information would function and how well they would serve academic researchers' long-term interests. Certification became an essential means of helping to answer those questions. Between 2003 and 2013, major support for development of auditing, evaluation, and certification capabilities was provided to CRL by the Andrew W. Mellon Foundation, the John D. and Catherine T. MacArthur Foundation, the Institute of Museum and Library Services (IMLS), and the National Science Foundation (NSF).

The TRAC checklist has been the basis of CRL's audits of several repositories: the Portico and Scholars Portal archives of e-journals, the HathiTrust Digital Library, and Chronopolis. Those audits will serve as case studies in the following discussion of the TRAC criteria. As the case studies show, the certification process has been a means of bringing the repositories audited into compliance with community expectations for persistence. In the process of the audits, the requirements of the designated communities were defined more precisely than they had been previously, and risks that may have been overlooked were identified.

THE "DESIGNATED COMMUNITY": A KEY POINT OF REFERENCE

The underlying thread that runs throughout the TRAC criteria, and indeed throughout the literature of digital preservation, is the notion of a "designated community." This is defined in the OAIS Reference Model as "an identified group of potential Consumers who should be able to understand a particular set of information." The CRL has interpreted the CCSDS definition broadly, to include the community of stakeholders who directly rely upon and interact with the repository, be they the publishers and scientists who contribute the content managed; those who own that content or possess some rights to same; and the populations that use or "consume" the data and content preserved. A designated community can also include the "subjects" of the content: participants in research studies from whom data is obtained (those whose DNA is mapped, for instance); those who give testimony or are described in documents preserved in the repository (victims of human rights abuses in court archives, for example, or interviewees in public opinion polls); and even those who hold creative rights to content and data archived (authors, reporters, and news photographers whose work resides in publisher archives).

It is the needs of these parties that form a fixed point of reference for the TRAC requirements. In short, a "trustworthy" repository must be structured and operated in a way that is likely to serve the needs of the depositors, users, and other stakeholders well. Therefore, the processes and technologies the repository adopts must be so designed as to accommodate both the submission or acquisition of data and content, and the kinds of research and study that will be made of same. While TRAC avoids prescribing explicit standards and specifications for metadata, file formats, database architectures, and so forth, the requirements of the repository's designated community are an absolute.

For this reason identification of a given repository's stakeholder communities figures prominently in CRL's audit and certification methodology. The guiding force of all CRL audits is the certification advisory panel. This is a panel of advisors representing the various sectors of the North American research libraries community, who together bring to the process a deep knowledge of collection development, preservation, library administration, and digital information technology. The panel is constituted in a way that ensures that the certification process addresses the interests of the entire stakeholder population. On the basis of documentation and evidence generated by the audit and panel members' understanding of the interests of the stakeholders, the panel determines whether the repository's practices and services are generally sound and appropriate to both the content being archived and the needs of the stakeholder community.

When appropriate, TRAC auditors interview the users or potential users of the data and content preserved, normally scholars and researchers in the field. Auditors also consider the needs of those producing content for the repository, such as scientific researchers and others who contribute data to repositories, like the ICPSR, Chronopolis, and others. Because of its long history of representing the interests of an international community of researchers in all disciplines and fields, CRL is well positioned to understand the needs of the designated communities of many repositories.

TRAC SECTION A (TDR SECTION 3): ORGANIZATION AND MANAGEMENT OF THE REPOSITORY

Many of the metrics in TRAC Section A are meant to determine how well the organization is structured and positioned to ensure that content with which it is entrusted will continue to exist in a usable form. A fundamental premise of TRAC is that the most important hedge against temporary or permanent events that might result in the repository's failure is the proper organization of repository activities, and informed and capable governance and management of the entity responsible for the repository.

In rare cases are digital repositories freestanding legal entities in and of themselves. Iron Mountain Digital was, until recently, one of those rarities. More often, the repository is a core activity of an organization with legal standing, such as a government agency (the U.S. National Archives and Records Administration, the U.S. Geological Survey), or of a 501c3 corporation (the American Chemical Society, the Associated Press). Most often, however, the repository is a subordinate part of a much larger entity. For example, ICPSR is a service operated by the University of Michigan. Portico is a service maintained under the auspices of the corporation Ithaka Harbors, which also encompasses JSTOR publishing and ITHAKA S+R research.

The first order of business in a TRAC analysis is to "scope" the audit or to define the boundaries of the larger entity's activities that are to be examined. In CRL's audit of Portico, it was decided to examine the funding model and financial situation of JSTOR, the parent organization, as well as Portico itself, because of the latter's dependence upon the former for funding and technology support.

TRAC Section A addresses the organizational infrastructure of the repository. The long-term viability of the repository and its parent institution—and its ability to anticipate and plan for disastrous events—are of paramount importance. Because the repository organization must be stable enough to ensure that the content it commits to preserving will survive for the long term, good administrative oversight and appropriate mechanisms for decision making should enable the repository to make the correct choices regarding the technology to be deployed and the processes implemented. Assessing the basic, underlying administrative framework within the organization includes evaluating the organization's goals, roles, controls, and decision-making mechanisms as they apply to the preservation repository content.

Therefore, TRAC Section A addresses five functional areas that constitute the administrative framework for a trusted digital repository. Those five areas are: governance and organizational viability; organizational structure and staffing; procedural and policy framework; financial sustainability; and contractual obligations.

The checklist begins with a metric (A1.1) pertaining to the relative importance of preservation to the repository organization's mission. The strength of the organization's commitment to preservation can be adduced from how central preservation is to the organization's reason for being. In the case of a government agency, is the long-term maintenance of digital content and data specifically referenced in the statutes or regulations pertinent to the agency? In the case of a corporation, is this role referenced in the organization's bylaws, or is digital preservation an implicit element of activities that are referenced there? Absent this, does the organization's mission statement explicitly express a commitment to long-term retention and maintenance of digital information?

The staffing of the organization is another key administrative function evaluated in a TRAC audit. Competent and adequate staffing ensures that a repository is prepared not only to perform the requisite data management activities, but to anticipate new situations that may threaten the viability of the repository's content. Moreover, responsibilities, roles, and lines of authority must be well-defined. This includes roles related to human resources and financial management, as well as information technology and digital preservation. Auditors look at common organizational documents such as employee resumes, organizational charts, and information about the organization's staff development and continuing education program to assess organizational readiness.

The repository's mechanisms for procedural accountability and its policy framework are also scrutinized. It is important that the policy framework be formalized, well-maintained, and as transparent as possible. Responsibility for making key decisions, and the authority for same, must be clearly assigned and must be understood enterprise-wide. It is important that the repository be able to demonstrate how it carries out its preservation plan through its policies and procedures.

Perhaps most important, TRAC Section A also requires that the repository define some important OAIS concepts, namely, the repository's designated community or communities and their associated knowledge bases. Accountability to the designated communities identified is then ensured by effective mechanisms put in place by the repository for self-assessment, and mechanisms and channels for obtaining feedback from stakeholders, which enable the repository administration to remain sensitive to the needs of its users and supporters.

The financial sustainability of the organization that houses the repository is demonstrated through financial documentation common to most organizations. These include funding plans, financial statements (independently audited statements if the repository is part of a corporation), budgets, balance sheets, and so forth.

Finally, TRAC Section A requires that the repository's commitments and liabilities be reflected in its contracts, licenses, and similar documents. These documents include contracts with key software and hardware providers, as well as those with contributors of content. These documents need to grant—and empower the repository to exercise—the rights necessary for maintaining and, where appropriate, providing access to the intellectual property it holds. It is expected that such rights will be clearly defined and tracked by the repository.

As the concept of a digital repository is relatively new, and many repositories are still forming or evolving, evaluating such entities with TRAC Section A criteria can be a challenge. For this reason, CRL's 2011 audit of the HathiTrust Digital Library was particularly difficult, as HathiTrust was then still an emerging repository. Its governance structure was not yet fully defined or formalized, and its financial model was still in flux. A "distributed" effort, relying heavily on trust among organizations (major U.S. research libraries) with a shared mission (preserving and providing unrestricted access to research materials) and in-kind contributions of labor and technology, the lines of authority for major decisions and acting in critical situations still needed to be established.

It also was difficult to clearly demarcate the boundary between the HathiTrust effort and its host institution, the University of Michigan Libraries, and to sort out the role of the partner organizations in this rapidly evolving entity.

CRL examined the policy infrastructure that was then in place. A number of key documents, such as agreements with content contributors, needed to be reconciled with other key documents. Ownership of certain important repository assets, such as software and code developed for the repository, content, and critical infrastructure was yet to be specified in governance documents and public disclosures. In the course of the audit, improvements in these areas were made, and HathiTrust has since put in place a more formal, well-defined governance structure and financial support model.

TRAC SECTION B (TDR SECTION 4): DIGITAL OBJECT MANAGEMENT

The criteria in TRAC Section B address aspects of how a repository manages or handles digital objects. This involves the workflows and ongoing archiving activities related to the data and content objects preserved in the repository and their critical associated metadata. The OAIS defines much of the workflow surrounding digital object handling, designating three types of digital objects: submission information packages (SIPs), archival information packages (AIPs), and Dissemination Information Packages (DIPs).

Each type of object exists at a different point in the repository's workflow. These points roughly correspond to the six aspects of digital object management scrutinized under the TRAC rubric: ingest or acquisition of content as a SIP; transformation of the content into an AIP; subsequent format migration, annotation, and other processes required to keep the archived content up-to-date in the face of changing technical environments; ongoing monitoring of the characteristics and properties of the archived content and other high-level processes required to ensure the continued integrity of that content and its relevance to stakeholder needs; production of, and/or association of the archived content with, metadata to enable appropriate control by the repository and, in some instances, discoverability; and the "ability to produce and disseminate accurate, authentic versions of the digital object" as needed. (Research Libraries Group, 2007, p. 21).

TRAC Section B provides metrics for assessing whether a repository is preserving the object at a given point in the OAIS digital preservation workflow. In the first stage, data and content are received from a producer in a particular form (SIP) and then ingested into the repository. It is important that the repository specify what type of data or content it is supposed to receive and in what form it is to be received, verify that this is what is received, and then properly store it. TRAC criteria ask how clearly and completely a repository specifies what kind of content it accepts. This is a critical point for repositories accepting content from multiple contributors and in myriad formats, where variation can create enormous costs and disrupt the workflow of a repository.

At the ingest stage in the workflow, data contributors should be provided appropriate feedback so that they know whether the object has or has not been properly ingested by the repository.

Transforming the content into an AIP may involve additional steps, for example, converting or "normalizing" the ingested digital object (perhaps a journal article text in XML) to another file format (like a PDF) better suited to archiving, or creating a wrapper that contains the digital object and its metadata. Most repositories have protocols that automate this process, but it can be quite resource-intensive.

Once the SIP has been processed and is accepted into the archive, it becomes an AIP. The AIP is the object that exists and is preserved by the repository system. It must be constantly monitored and tested by the repository system to ensure it has not degraded or otherwise changed.

Repositories must often produce, obtain, and/or associate with the archived digital content metadata sufficient to enable appropriate control of the content by the repository. This includes descriptive information necessary for the repository operators and systems to uniquely identify the content and to preserve its integrity. In instances where a repository makes its content visible or accessible to a "designated community," the minimal metadata necessary for content discovery, identification, and citation must be present and exposed.

In the case of Chronopolis, a dark archive, the audit determined that the content inventory was visible to the depositors (i.e., ICPSR, Scripps Institution of Oceanography, and others) but not to the general public. Quite differently, the HathiTrust, an open archive and digital library, fulfilled this TRAC requirement by providing an interface adequate to locate and present digitized public domain books in the archive and to identify the presence of nonpublic domain materials in the archive.

In the final stage in the workflow, the AIP is converted to a DIP for service or presentation to the user. Service can entail one-time delivery of content in response to a query, such as a request by a publisher for return of contributed content; or exposure of the content on an ongoing basis through a public interface, like PubMed Central or various Chemical Abstracts Service products. The DIP can take many forms but must in every event be usable and "understandable" by the authorized user. For this reason, auditors must establish that a given repository will be prepared to provide its content to users in a form that is "understandable" using future systems and software. Under some circumstances, repositories can ensure such usability by putting in place processes for migrating content to new formats as old ones become obsolete. In other instances, they can provide interpretive tools, such as code books for statistical data or additional metadata fields that explain the original context of the content.

Throughout this workflow, the repository must exert adequate control over a given digital object and must keep track of the processes that said object undergoes. The importance of the "provenance" of a digital object, documentation of the source and "path" of the object, and of the changes made to it—between ingest and dissemination—is an essential element of digital preservation. In the physical world, conservators of museum and library objects like paintings, rare books, and manuscripts are careful to record all treatments, repairs, and alterations. Similarly, TRAC requires repositories to document any changes made to the digital content ingested and to record the nature of those changes. Digital alterations might include the attachment of new metadata, or conversion of the object from one file format to another.

At the time of the CRL audits, Chronopolis and Portico were "dark archives" (i.e., repositories whose contents are not generally accessible to populations aside from depositors and contributors). Although both were "dark," the two took quite different approaches to managing their digital content. Chronopolis is a distributed digital repository system managed by the San Diego Super Computer Center at the University of California-San Diego. Two other Chronopolis "nodes" are located on the campus of the University of Maryland and at the National Center for Atmospheric Research (NCAR) in Boulder, Colorado (CRL, 2012). The peculiarity of Chronopolis from a preservation standpoint is the nature of its commitment to preserving the content it holds. Specifically, Chronopolis commits only to "bit" preservation of that content. Content and associated metadata that data contributors send for ingestion in Chronopolis are "frozen" or maintained intact at the "bit" level, as they were originally received. The digital content is not migrated or otherwise changed by Chronopolis to adapt to new information environments.

This requires that the depositors play a role in preserving the understandability of content over time (TRAC B2.10) and monitoring digital objects entrusted to Chronopolis for obsolescence of representation information and file formats (B2.7, B3.2).

Nor does Chronopolis create or maintain referential integrity of descriptive metadata for objects archived (B5.2–B5.4). Rather, Chronopolis requires that depositors create the minimal metadata necessary to enable the repository to control and store the digital content they contribute to

Chronopolis, and to maintain necessary external links and other external information.

Despite this fact, CRL determined that Chronopolis did comply with TRAC criteria, because in its agreements with depositors, Chronopolis clearly specified the processes to be performed by the repository, namely, preserving the original object at the bit level. In the course of the audit, CRL auditors determined through consultation with Chronopolis depositors that those processes met the depositors' definition of preservation.

The Portico repository was established in 2005 to preserve e-journal content from scholarly publishers. It has subsequently begun to archive e-book and historical database content. Portico is a community-supported archive, whose clients are largely academic libraries and publishers. Portico obtains journal content directly from scholarly publishers and those who license the content. Like Chronopolis, Portico is a dark archive. It is structured to maintain publisher content offline until the occurrence of any of a defined set of trigger events, such as publisher failure. Unlike Chronopolis, Portico is authorized to make the archived content available to its subscribing libraries, should a trigger event occur.

In auditing the Portico e-journals repository in 2009, CRL encountered one of the conundrums inherent in dark archives: the difficulty of third-party assessment of the repository's systems and processes. In one respect, accessible archives are inherently transparent; their accessibility renders problems and gaps more likely to be detected than those that might affect an inaccessible or dark archive. With Portico, auditors and contributors of content had to go to considerable lengths to determine what journal content was actually present in the archive and to locate the point in the repository workflow at which a particular digital object resided at any given moment (TRAC B1.6). The TRAC requirement (B2.12) that a repository provide an independent mechanism for auditing the integrity of the repository objects is therefore a more onerous requirement for dark archives.[1]

Compliance with TRAC Section B digital object management criteria can be adversely impacted by changes in the types of content archived by a repository. For this reason, CRL specifies in its certification reports the scope of the particular certification. In 2009, CRL certified Portico specifically as an e-journal repository (CRL, 2010). Since that time, Portico has continued to add new types of content to its repository, including e-books and the contents of major humanities databases. Adding such content may impact the workflows, technologies, and data management techniques of a repository, presenting new challenges and complexities to existing digital object management processes. For this reason, auditors must continue to monitor how a repository's services and commitments change in response to new ventures. Certification, therefore, is not a one-time event; CRL requires that the repositories it audits agree to make disclosures periodically after certification to enable CRL to determine whether a new audit and re-certification is called for (CRL, 2010).

TRAC SECTION C (TDR SECTION 5): REPOSITORY INFRASTRUCTURE AND SYSTEMS

Where Section B of the TRAC checklist addresses how well a repository manages the digital objects and metadata entrusted to it, Section C deals with the infrastructure surrounding and enabling that content management activity. TRAC Section C provides metrics for evaluating a repository's core technical systems, networks, hardware, and software. The three parts of Section C look specifically at: the archive's general system infrastructure; the appropriateness of the technologies it employs; and overall system security. Section C criteria align closely with the technical and systems practices required in international management standards like ISO 17799 (Research Libraries Group, 2007.)

While Section C outlines broad requirements for a digital repository's system architecture and configuration, it refrains from specifying particular types of technical systems or system components. This prevents obsolescence of the TRAC criteria with the passage of time. In general, TRAC requires that the system be well supported by both the repository and the outside organizations or entities that create or provide critical components of the system, lest the system be in danger of service degradation or failure due to lack of such support. TRAC requires that there be mechanisms in place for updating critical equipment, software, and other components.

Repository systems should not merely be adequate to the data management demands, but must not require more resources than the repository staffing and finances can support. Demonstrating compliance with Section C criteria is a matter of demonstrating that repository operators have identified and understand the risks involved in the application of its chosen core systems, processes, and software; can anticipate or detect the onset of harm stemming from those risks; and have made adequate and credible provisions for preventing or mitigating such harm.

The second set of TRAC Section C criteria pertains to the repository's choice and implementation of hardware and software. Again, rather than setting specific technical requirements, TRAC's authors reference the needs of the repository's community; a trustworthy repository's software and hardware are adequate to provide the services the repository renders. TRAC's authors acknowledged that maintaining the ability to serve those needs is a moving target, requiring that repositories have in place mechanisms for detecting changes in those needs and in the enabling technical environments for those services over time.

The final part of TRAC Section C pertains to system security. It provides metrics on judging how well a repository's technical infrastructure provides assurances against disaster, failure, and loss of repository content and data. Aside from adequate backup of equipment, provisions include strategies like mirroring, distribution, redundancy of content, and creating a protective physical envelope to protect repository systems and operations from damage caused by natural and human causes. Section C criteria also call for formalized and documented disaster preparedness and recovery plans.

TRAC Section C criteria figured prominently in a recent CRL audit of Scholars Portal. Scholars Portal was created by the University of Toronto in 2002, as a technology platform for hosting and serving digital content licensed, purchased, and otherwise acquired by members of the Ontario Council of University Libraries (OCUL) consortium. The platform provides a common technical infrastructure for delivering digital content and services to support research, teaching, and learning within the Ontario higher education community. Since 2002, Scholars Portal has evolved to include digital preservation, archiving, and repository services.

In CRL's 2012 audit of Scholars Portal's e-journal archive, one area that emerged as a concern was the absence of an online "mirror site" (CRL, 2013). A mirror site is an exact copy of a repository's digital objects hosted at a remote location. Although the repository had adequately backed up its data offline to preserve archived content, and had an adequate recovery plan to bring all archived content back online in the event of a disaster, it did not have a mirror site and thus could not guarantee uninterrupted access to archived e-journal content, should the primary site fail. The backup and recovery provisions put in place by Scholars Portal could, in fact, take weeks or longer to restore the e-journal archive—a significant interruption in access to the content.

Again, the "designated community" provided a point of reference for CRL in determining whether Scholars Portal was in compliance with TRAC Section C criteria. CRL auditors had to determine whether the provisions for restoring access to Scholars Portal archived content met the expectations of the repository's designated community. Confirmation was obtained from the OCUL Executive Committee in the form of the following statement:

> In the view of this committee, Scholars Portal's current recovery planning and service levels fulfill the needs of the OCUL community. While we recognize that an unplanned interruption of service would be an inconvenience to OCUL's user communities, the long-term preservation of the locally loaded materials is of highest importance and as long as the material can be recovered and its integrity and authenticity re-established, the needs of the Designated Community are being met. (qtd. in CRL, 2013, p. 5)

With this statement, Scholars Portal users acknowledged that implementation of an online mirror site would provide an additional layer of security, but that for their purposes, uninterrupted access to the content archived by Scholars Portal was not an imperative.

CONCLUSION

In essence, the purpose of the TRAC metrics and of auditing in accordance with those metrics is to promote transparency in the operations of a repository. The metrics in TRAC Section A encourage the disclosure of repository policies and information about processes and governance. But the thread that runs throughout TRAC is the imperative of the needs and interests of the repository's designated community or communities. These communities can include publishers and libraries (Scholars Portal, Portico, CLOCKSS), scholars and scientists (ICPSR, Chemical Abstracts Service), and even data managers themselves (Chronopolis). Because the interests of the designated communities provide the primary fixed point of reference in TRAC, use of TRAC inherently fosters a dialogue between those operating repositories and the stakeholders the repository serves.

In a sense, then, the certification process is a conversation between the repository and its stakeholders. In many respects, the purpose of the auditing and certification body is, in essence, to mediate that conversation. CRL auditing has found this conversation to be tremendously valuable. Exploring the stakeholders' needs and the process of matching repository operations against those needs has to date never failed to yield new insights into how the repository can better serve its community. The TRAC audit process has thus been beneficial not only for the community, but for the people and institutions building and operating the repositories as well.

NOTE

1. At the time of the audit, Portico was providing library subscribers with an "audit" interface. However, the objects that the interface suggested were contained in the archive were in some instances in the pipeline for ingest but not yet actually preserved. In response to this CRL finding, Portico has since created a new audit interface and system to address these concerns.

REFERENCES

Center for Research Libraries (CRL). (2010). *Portico audit report 2010*. Retrieved from http://www.crl.edu/node/6572

Center for Research Libraries (CRL). (2012). *Chronopolis audit report 2012*. Retrieved from http://www.crl.edu/node/8106

Center for Research Libraries (CRL). (2013). *Scholars Portal audit report 2013*. Retrieved from http://www.crl.edu/archiving-preservation/digital-archives/certification-and-assessment-digital-repositories/scholars_portal

Consultative Committee for Space Data Systems (CCSDS). (2012). Reference Model for an Open Archival Information System (OAIS): Recommended practice (CCSDS 650.0-M-2). Retrieved from http://public.ccsds.org/publications/archive/650x0m2.pdf

Garrett, J., & Waters, D. (1996). *Preserving digital information: Report of the Task Force on Archiving of Digital Information*. Washington, DC: Commission on Preservation and Access, and Mountain View, CA: RLG.

Research Libraries Group. (2002). *Trusted digital repositories: Attributes and responsibilities*. Mountain View, CA: Research Libraries Group.

Retrieved from https://www.oclc.org/resources/research/activities/trustedrep/repositories.pdf

Research Libraries Group. (2005). *An audit checklist for the certification of trusted digital repositories: Draft for public comment.* Mountain View, CA: Research Libraries Group.

Research Libraries Group. (2007). *Trustworthy repositories audit & certification: Criteria and checklist.* OCLC and the Center for Research Libraries. Retrieved from http://www.crl.edu/sites/default/files/attachments/pages/trac_0.pdf

Part 3
MANAGING PROJECT DATA

6 Copyright, Open Data, and the Availability-Usability Gap

Challenges, Opportunities, and Approaches for Libraries

MELISSA LEVINE

THE BIG IDEALS

This chapter is about copyright as one of several significant bodies of law that touches on the creation, preservation, and use of data. And yet, this chapter barely discusses copyright at all, instead approaching copyright as a matter of policy, administration, and business choices that should minimize the complexity of copyright over the life cycle of research data. In doing so, the products of research may more easily be reused and reinvested.

"Data is the new gold," according to Neelie Kroes, vice president of the European Commission responsible for the Digital Agenda (Kroes, 2011). Computing power has increased exponentially at relatively low prices, allowing us to examine the world and detect patterns on a scale never before possible. There is much being written about data, data management, big data, and strategic approaches to managing research data. Interest and commitment have accelerated in response to the combined incentives of increased computing power and the impetus of the demands of research sponsors and funding agencies for data management plans as a condition of funding.

Right now there is a gap between aspiration and reality. Nobody has solved all the complexities of making data available and usable. In fact, nobody has yet even figured out what all the questions are. Complex practical questions abound. For example, most research universities now offer a variety of resources, guides, and planning tools that take the first steps toward providing researchers with the needed infrastructure to meet the formal requirement of having a data plan for grant purposes. It can be daunting simply to navigate all of these resources for researchers trying to write a grant proposal.

Libraries are natural hubs for services that support preparation of data management plans, fulfilling data management obligations, and citing the products that result from research projects. Librarians can help academic researchers to compete for grant funds, protect their data, and receive recognition for it. (See a list of sample guides in "Resources" at the end of this chapter.) Librarians who are considering new data services as an extension of traditional library outreach efforts can benefit from the experiences of libraries that have already established such services and that have been active participants in information access initiatives and by maintaining resolve on key principles.

PRINCIPLES

In addressing copyright—and really most legal questions in the data arena—it is useful to remember that the goal of reliable, efficient access to knowledge is not inherently new. It is foundational for scholarship, and we can tether otherwise complex problem solving by keeping these foundations in mind. Statements like the Denton Declaration maintain focus on essentials in a constructive manner. The Denton Declaration is an aspirational statement for open data that also has practical applications. It is a statement that "bridges the converging interests . . . and promotes collaboration, transparency, and accountability across organizational and disciplinary boundaries" (Open Access @ UNT, 2012). Drafted in 2012 at a meeting at the University of North Texas by stakeholders like librarians, scholars, technology experts, researchers, and university administrators, the Denton Declaration starts with the premise that "open access to research data is critical for advancing science, scholarship, and society" (Open Access @ UNT, 2012). The declarations are:

- Research data, when repurposed, has an accretive value.
- Publicly funded research should be publicly available for public good.
- Transparency in research is essential to sustain the public trust.
- The validation of research data by the peer community is an essential function of the responsible conduct of research.
- Managing research data is the responsibility of a broad community of stakeholders including researchers, funders, institutions, libraries, archivists, and the public.

By keeping these ideas at the forefront in data policy discussions, the Denton Declaration helps to fill the aspiration-usability gap as a mooring point for policy, administrative, and legal strategies (Open Access @ UNT, 2012).

OPEN ACCESS, OPEN DATA, AND FUNDING MANDATES

"Open access" and "open data" differ in complexity, though they have much in common. Open access is now a familiar concept in the research community when it comes to publications. Conceptual familiarity with open access is useful for working through analogous strategic questions for data (in contrast to publications). Open access, for the most part, assumes a text-based expressional artifact with some level of stability (versioning). The technical infrastructure and range of legal concerns is relatively simpler than those associated with data. With data, there is an emphasis on its value as evidence, reproducibility of results for validation, and utility for future research. There is a gap between data that is "available" and data that is "usable," which can be exacerbated in the absence of legal metadata. Mandates from funding agencies are incentivizing the development of needed policies and practice by conditioning funding on meeting open access and data management requirements. In doing so, these mandates are helping to bridge this gap. These mandates reflect a major shift in policy. By directing and requiring openness broadly, and with regard to data specifically here, these mandates dictate that researchers take a new approach to storing, securing, and describing data—including legal information for copyright elements.

Funding Mandates

On February 22, 2013, the White House Office of Science and Technology Policy (OSTP) issued a memo titled "Increasing Access to the Results of Federally Funded Scientific Research." The memo directs federal agencies with more than $100 million in research and development expenditures to prepare policies to make federally funded research results publicly available, free of charge, within 12 months after original publication. The new requirements ensure public access to scientific research data by ensuring that intramural researchers and researchers who receive federal grants and contracts for scientific research have data management plans in place. To support the implementation of data management plans, grant proposals may include "appropriate costs for data management and access in proposals for Federal funding for scientific research" (Holdren, 2013, p. 5). The policies have to "include mechanisms to ensure that intramural and extramural researchers comply with data management plans and policies" (Holdren, 2013, p. 5). Further, they are to "promote the deposit of data in publicly accessible databases, where appropriate and available" and "develop approaches for identifying and providing appropriate attribution to scientific datasets that are made available under the plan" (Stebbins, 2013, p. 5).

This builds on the 2008 National Institutes of Health (NIH) mandate for open access deposit in PubMed Central, which required publications resulting from grant-funded research be open in some way as a condition of receipt of grant funds. The NIH mandate requires that an electronic version of all final peer-reviewed journal articles published as a result of NIH grant funds and accepted for publication on or after April 7, 2008, "be made publicly available no later than 12 months after the official date of publication: Provided, That the NIH shall implement the public access policy in a manner consistent with copyright law" (NIH, n.d.). Similarly, the National Science Foundation (NSF) announced on May 2010 that it would require data management plans for all grant proposals; the mandate became effective on January 18, 2011 (NSF, 2010; NSF, 2011). Other notable examples of influential mandates in this arena were implemented by the World Bank, the Wellcome Trust, and the Australian Research Council (Australian Research Council, 2013; Wellcome Trust, n.d.; World Bank, 2012).

Copyright considerations are among the first items listed to ensure authors have the needed rights to deposit. A condition of funding is that published results must be available open access. In a way, it asserts form of contract; in exchange for funding, research product must be open access. In doing so the mandate trumped copyright restrictions that occur when a researcher signed a publishing contract that transferred copyrights to a publisher. This in turn affected the ability of the general public, taxpayers, to access the product of taxpayer-funded research if the resulting article was available for a fee. The researcher is bound by that open access condition in the grant and can only pass on some subset of rights that he or she has to publishers.

ISSUES AND IDEAS

To master the challenges posed by this new data environment and to take advantage of the opportunities, librarians may wish to consider these ideas and issues as they think about how to navigate the legal implications.

Issues

Technology outpaces law

As is often the case, the pace of technological innovation has outpaced our social and legal frameworks. By analogy, in the scholarly world we are using the tools of the 17th century (that is, linear text). You can move up to the 1980s if you take word processors into account. So we are trying to retrofit the research tools of today into packages that combine technologies that are anywhere from a few decades to a few centuries old. This extends to the legal framework that we work within when it comes to copyright.

Different countries do it differently

Even with international treaties in place, copyright is handled differently in different countries, making interoperable data more challenging. Cross-border privacy norms differ, as do assumptions about contract law. There are inherent differences between public and private sector uses and needs. There are some choices that can be controlled regardless of jurisdiction, however. For example, creators can work toward limiting and reducing complexity through the terms of licenses and contracts associated with data that they generate.

Different disciplines do it differently

Very generally, science research data tends to be expressed as facts, say, numbers and measurements that are not subject to copyright protection under U.S. copyright law. While humanities data may take the form of numbers and measurements, by contrast it is often expressed as clips of sound or video or other modules of information that *are* in and of themselves subject to copyright. Use of those modules in research may indeed be subject to a limit on copyright such as fair use, but it is unclear as to whether a subsequent researcher's use also would be a fair use. Fair use requires a case-by-case consideration of facts each and every time. So in storing research data that includes elements that are subject to someone else's copyrights, it becomes important to document and store legal metadata about the copyright information associated with each module of copyright-eligible element for the resulting body of data to be reusable.

Further, at this moment there are still highly varied comfort levels with the whole notion of research as data, as well as "openness" in concept and practice. The scientific method at its essence is evidence-based. It depends on sharing and requires access to data as evidence of results. Yet many prestigious papers are based on data that is not replicable or even accessible. In the past, it has not been worth the effort and investment to maintain bodies of data once the papers are written—the published papers are the surrogates for the data.

Right now, taxpayer-funded research is probably generating data that is not being fully utilized, functionally missing significant opportunities. As a result, we may waste money on the same research or miss opportunities to reuse existing data for new inquiries. As much as 80 percent of data in science, technology, engineering, and medicine are not replicable (Hartshorne & Schachner, 2012). For economics journals, data practices are in need of reconsideration (Vlaeminck, 2012). Managing copyright and related rights proactively will improve the incentive to maintain data and make it more useable.

Hidden data

Why are researchers hiding their data (Piwowar, 2011; Savage & Vickers, 2009)? Copyright is usually framed as a "problem," but the real impediment seems more diffuse: a disincentive to share, difficulty in credit and attribution, low value in the tenure process, and the essential complexity of managing data are more likely factors. There may not be a single entity that will emerge as responsible for these issues, but there is a growing network of researchers, funding agencies, universities, and corporations engaged in policy and management for research data. With the goal of making research data reusable and open, we have models for copyright management based on established open access frameworks and digital preservation and curation practices.

Citation Standards for Data and the Need for Recognition and Good Data Management

There are real challenges: evolving questions about reliable access, the need for discovery tools and citation standards, and lack of willingness to deposit and cite data that is not stable or reproducible. Some faculty members worry that data in and of itself independently of journal articles will cause them to spend a disproportionate amount of time on data for which they do not get meaningful recognition or credit. This seems to be the case for nonjournal products generally. However, well-managed data will be citable, increasing its relevance for promotion and tenure. Data plan requirements may improve the relevance of generating meaningful data, serving as a catalyst for thinking through the workflow associated with generating and managing data. Library services to assist researchers in developing and implementing data management plans can further the relevance of data to the tenure and promotion process. By providing repository storage and services, librarians can ensure that data is properly documented for citation and reuse.

Data Citation Is Vital for Better Sharing

Standards for data citation are taking form to improve sharing and credit. Since attribution and impact are the lifeblood of scholarship, we need consistent data citation behavior. In doing so, a researcher can be credited not only for his or her direct research, but also for the reuse of the data by someone else. At this moment, the field is working toward the needs of universities and researchers to measure output and impact. For example, the Open Researcher and Contributor ID (ORCID) provides persistent digital identifiers for individual authors and researchers that allow better tracking for credit and valuable information for funders: "ORCID is an open, non-profit, community-based effort to provide a registry of unique researcher identifiers and a transparent method of linking research activities and outputs to these identifiers" (ORCID, n.d.). Basically, it allows researchers to associate unique author identifiers with research products. It is free for individuals—anyone may register for a number. Note that the ORCID identifier is distinct from the digital object identifiers (DOIs) already predominantly used for articles.

What does this have to do with copyright? This kind of citation system enhances the likelihood of having researchers remain connected to their scholarly output—to the extent copyright may exist in some aspect of the data or its structure, the more likely one can trace it back to a particular rightsholder. Currently, it may be difficult to give credit to researchers for their data because the relationship between the data and the researcher is not well documented. By tackling data citation, some elements of the copyright question can be addressed proactively (Mooney & Newton, 2012).

Good Metadata is Expensive

Metadata is as significant as the data itself. Producing meaningful metadata and making it available requires resources and expertise. There is rightly an emphasis on acquisition, preservation, and integrity of content, but without consistent metadata, the data may end up being of variable quality or utility. Data repositories are (happily) not static, but legal metadata (such as rights and access) may or may not be static (not so happily). The ever-changing nature of a repository makes it both valuable and problematic. Partnerships like DataCite are providing an important forum for having meaningful metadata for future utility. Because of their expertise with describing information and awareness of information rights and access issues, librarians are well positioned to extend their activities to include assistance with documentation of legal metadata.

Data Results as Complex Artifacts

What is the legal status of a collection of research data built from a variety of data that is generated by others or that generates other products? The value and emphasis of scholarly output has grown beyond articles. "Publications" might mean products like datasets, software, patents, and other forms of expression or documentation in addition to text-based material. All of these products are eligible for some kind of intellectual property protection; at the same time, the use of licenses can ensure that data products of research are maintained in an open fashion. If datasets are released without licenses, someone else could assert copyright in the dataset or claim credit. If the original dataset includes rich metadata, then subsequent uses can relate back to the source. As long as underlying content is retained as open, is there a reason to prevent commercial use? Intellectual property could be negotiated in a way to maintain usefulness and engage commercial productivity, perhaps with financial support or royalties back to the research endeavor, and provide insulation from liability to researchers and their institutions for subsequent uses.

Different Values, Common Interests:
The False Dichotomy of Public and Private Sector Interests

This chapter focuses on ways to "keep data open," but we could reframe the dichotomy that has developed in the distinctions between public vs. private or commercial vs. noncommercial to think about how these can be complementary. Technology transfer offices are an established feature of research universities with the assumption that the private sector is well suited to bring productive research products to market. If publicly funded data is "open" for further research and is kept open, then perhaps it should be equally available to the private sector for use and investment (provided there is no legal impediment such as privacy concerns). This is a practical and philosophical observation. Businesses can and do gather lots of government data because it is open, and in doing so, they are able to expose other data and develop useful products or services. Investment in editorial staff may be part of the enhancement and value. There is a high level of work involved in taking a content set and developing valuable applications, requiring the right tools, such as subject matter experts. There may be cases where the research agenda does not need or have interest in this kind of enhancement, and where the private sector can make productive use of reliable metadata and rich data generated from publicly funded projects. This is actually a further validation of good data practices and a different kind of enrichment.

Ideas

The copyright questions are a component of the kinds of issues just discussed. Data are not reliable if you do not know where they are located, how to refer to datasets, or if you cannot assess the status of the components that make up the data, which may include elements that are subject to copyright (or indeed some other legal concern, such as privacy). In turn, it is not possible to validate copyrightable outputs based on the data, such as visualizations or articles. Projects and products like DataCite, Data Observation Network for Earth (DataONE), and Databib will help with copyright and other legal matters by providing ways for data to remain associated with metadata.

DataCite (n.d.) explains what the organization does on their website:

> We bring together the datasets community to collaboratively address the challenges of making research data visible and accessible. Members of DataCite meet in person every six months at summer and winter conferences, and collaborate in established working groups. Through collaboration, we support researchers by helping them to find, identify, and cite research datasets with confidence; support data centres by providing

> persistent identifiers for datasets, workflows and standards for data publication; support journal publishers by enabling research articles to be linked to the underlying data. Currently we are working primarily with organizations that host data, such as data centres and libraries.

The website for DataONE (n.d.) describes the organization as: "the foundation of new innovative environmental science through a distributed framework and sustainable cyberinfrastructure that meets the needs of science and society for open, persistent, robust, and secure access to well-described and easily discovered Earth observational data." DataONE provides a substantive example of well-thought-out metadata practices, and provides a "Best Practices Primer" with an explanation of the data life cycle and related tool kit. Thinking through the life cycle will help identify points at which copyright could or should be addressed.

Finally, Databib (n.d.) describes itself as "a tool for helping people identify and locate online repositories of research data. Users and bibliographers create and curate records that describe data repositories that users can search."

Creative Commons and Open Data Commons

Creative Commons licenses may be used to describe rights and permitted uses in an internationally recognized manner, reducing complexity and encouraging global use and reuse. The Creative Commons framework is constructed to work globally. At its most basic:

> Creative Commons is a non-profit organization that created a set of simple, easy-to-understand copyright licenses. These are legally enforceable licenses that allow creators to mark a work with permission to make a variety of uses, with the aim of expanding the range of things available for others to share, quote, adapt, and build upon. Creative Commons licenses do two things: They allow creators to share their work easily, and they allow everyone to find work that is free to use without permission. As long as you obey the terms of the license attached to the work, you can use Creative Commons licensed material without fear of accidentally infringing someone's copyright.

> We encourage the use of Creative Commons licenses because they effectively help communicate information about copyright holders' intentions and thus help everyone know with clarity what may be used and how – and what requires permission. They help authors and creators manage their copyrights and share their creative work without losing control over it. Further, Creative Commons licenses facilitate creators' rights by communicating clearly a contact for permission when appropriate. (University of Michigan Copyright Office, 2013)

Open Data Commons (ODC) provides a Creative Commons-style framework for managing data based on the principle that "open data is data that anyone is free to use, reuse and redistribute without restriction (except, perhaps the requirements to attribute and share alike)" (Open Knowledge Foundation, n.d.a). ODC provides legal solutions for open data. In March 2008, it launched the first open data license: the Public Domain Dedication and License (PDDL). ODC provides licenses tailored to the data environment that are significant tools for expressing research intentions regarding copyright elements of datasets. (These are described succinctly in "Introduction to Intellectual Property Rights in Data Management," in Hirtle, 2011, and Open Knowledge Foundation, n.d.b.)

All Things Open and Commercial Use of Public Domain Data: Rethinking Assumptions

Creative Commons, Open Data Commons, and other open approaches to licenses all provide tools for describing and managing copyright in research data. The Creative Commons model is well established, with a range of standard, easily expressed and understood, legally enforceable licenses (Carroll, 2013). While data as fact is not subject to copyright under U.S. copyright law, datasets and databases may be protected as compilations. With the goal of maintaining an open research framework, one would not want to assert such rights in a way that encumbers the underlying data. One option is to apply a public domain license to bodies of work. The problem with doing this is that the underlying data may not be in the public domain or may be affected by legal duties other than copyright. Assuming all of the elements are in the public domain or are yours to give, placing work in the public domain may actually result in *loss* of control.

The data may become disassociated with the creator and relevant metadata. Another approach: follow the model of open-source-style licenses to data and datasets to facilitate new and flexible uses of the underlying material without risking that it will be functionally removed from the public domain (made proprietary by someone else) or disassociated from citable information.

Getting Legal Advice

Information professionals need the right lawyers, people who understand the different areas of law and the scholarly endeavor. Because copyright is so pervasive, it is treated increasingly as a do-it-yourself subject. Free videos and a plethora of "copyright education" are available from a growing range of sources. Geared for copyright nonspecialists to make them "aware" of copyright basics, many of these resources may emphasize or deemphasize different aspects of the law for any number of reasons. The idea that nonspecialists rolling up their sleeves can address complex copyright or other legal questions is problematic; I did not always have this view. But one would not suggest skimping on the expected training and experience of programmers or other technical expertise. One of the great problems is the way copyright is now ubiquitous and yet not at all intuitive. Ideally, you can or should nurture good relations with your general counsel's office or other legal expertise on your campus. It may be that there are different attorneys in that office with a variety of related expertise from copyright to privacy. Encourage them to join the discussion at your library and make the case on their behalf that it is worth the time for them to develop practical understanding of the issues so they can participate in a real, ongoing conversation with you about data issues. Ideally, they will be in the role of traditional counselors to help you think through options in a legal context and constructively move your work forward. Managing research data and data policy requires a team with sufficient range of expertise and experience; there should be an emphasis on continuous learning and problem solving. An ideal team will include people at staggered levels of experience that reflects a diversity of skills and knowledge. Think of the legal experts as an integral part of the team and assume everyone has something to learn from each other.

NEW LIBRARY SERVICES

A growing number of universities offer resources and expertise for data management support for researchers. These resources often take the form of consulting services through libraries or information provided from grants or sponsored research offices. Grant requirements set baselines for data plans. These plans typically expect the applicant to describe how they will address intellectual property matters, constructively forcing copyright questions to the forefront.

The multiple areas of legal responsibility are a significant issue in managing research data. There are a growing number of librarians stepping into the needs gap to bring together relevant information to assist researchers. The scale and complexity of the legal issues make them difficult to tackle, so in many cases basic checklists are a first step. In discussing this chapter with colleagues, a librarian said, "One of the common problems is that managing research data—in addition to managing one's research—is complicated. Universities in their effort to facilitate new requirements are developing matrices and tools for obligations, say, for storing sensitive data with an emphasis on providing the information and on university legal obligations." This is a reasonable place to start, but individual researchers will need help to follow and implement those resources. Researchers are unlikely to be aware of specific terms of service or security requirements and may need help to ensure that sensitive data is appropriately maintained. Beyond copyright, researchers and universities are responsible for meeting university policies, privacy, and other requirements. For example, a researcher may need to store sensitive data. Librarians can advise on how to store data in a manner that does not compromise security or other applicable policies. (See, generally, Sample Data Management Plan Resources on the following page.)

In trying to make sense of these responsibilities, we also see perceived concerns about the difference between the researcher's responsibility and the legal responsibility of the university. "Tools" that are essentially lists of laws, extraordinarily complex laws at that, fail to help the researcher, the university, or the utility of research data. The advice often comes in the form of web-based lists of information, often from a sponsored research office or an IT department. These kinds of guides are essential steps, but there is a need for human expertise—not just in the area of research—but also in application of law and administrative concerns.

SAMPLE DATA MANAGEMENT PLAN RESOURCES

All sites last visited July 8, 2013.

Best Practices, DataONE: http://www.dataone.org/best-practices

Columbia University Libraries, Information Services: http://scholcomm.columbia.edu/data-management/data-management-plan-templates/

Data Plan Guidance and Examples, Digital Curation Centre: http://www.dcc.ac.uk/resources/data-management-plans/guidance-examples

Data Management Plan Examples, University of Minnesota Libraries: https://www.lib.umn.edu/datamanagement/DMP/example

Data Management Plan Examples, Yale Digital Collections Center: http://ydc2.yale.edu/documentation/data-management-plan-examples

Data Management Plans, Data Management and Publishing, Subject Guides, MIT Libraries: http://libraries.mit.edu/guides/subjects/data-management/plans.html

Data Management Planning, DataONE: http://www.dataone.org/data-management-planning

Data Management Sample Plans, University of North Carolina: http://www.irss.unc.edu/odum/contentSubpage.jsp?nodeid=570

DataONE Example Data Management Plan, NSF BIO: http://www.dataone.org/sites/all/documents/DMP_Copepod_Formatted.pdf

Example Data Management Plans, the University of California-San Diego, Research Cyberinfrastructure: http://rci.ucsd.edu/dmp/examples.html

Generic Data Management Plan Outline and Examples, Digital Data Management, Curation and Archiving, Research Guides at the University of New Mexico: http://libguides.unm.edu/content.php?pid=137795&sid=1422879

NSF Data Management Plan Template, the University of Chicago, Division of the Physical Sciences: http://psd.uchicago.edu/NSF%20Data%20Management%20Plan%20Template.pdf

Preparing Data Management Grant Plans for NSF Grant Applications, the University of California-Berkeley, Science Libraries: http://www.lib.berkeley.edu/CHEM/data/nsf/nsf_dmp.pdf

Research Data Management and Publishing Support, the University of Michigan Library: http://www.lib.umich.edu/research-data-management-and-publishing-support

University of Pittsburgh—NSF Data Management Plan—Example 1: http://www.pitt.edu/~offres/policies/NSF-DMP-Examples.pdf

What Should Be in a Data Management Plan? Research Data Management, the University of Oxford: http://www.admin.ox.ac.uk/rdm/dmp/plans/

Libraries and librarians are stepping in as a natural support for data-related needs. As information specialists, research libraries already are a source for help with data citation standards and metrics. They are extending their outreach to include workflow solutions and data management advice; data storage solutions; and consulting services. There is a growing role for librarians as advisors and liaisons with information on government and business. Librarians also naturally work to complement each other's knowledge so that a single research project may functionally benefit from the collective knowledge of dozens of librarians and their networks.

THE UNIVERSITY OF MICHIGAN LIBRARY

Data management and data curation discussions on the University of Michigan campus have been building for years, and more recently, the University Library has moved toward engaging with data storage, management, and the concept of data curation. The University Library has been involved with discussions on a number of levels, from IT rationalization committees to the creation of resources for reviewing data management plans. Associate University Librarian for Research Elaine Westbrook leads the campus conversations on data management and curation. Today, the University Library offers a range of services for researchers at various stages of their research, from planning studies to the dissemination of their results. A comprehensive set of services that support the full life cycle of research data for faculty and students is at an early stage of development. Director of Research Data Services (RDS) Jen Green also serves as head of Science, Engineering, and the Clark Library. RDS is a network of people and services preparing a roadmap for library services around data and the research life cycle.

As part of developing strategies toward establishing library data services, Council on Library and Information Resources/Digital Library Federation (CLIR/DLF) Data Curation Fellows Natsuko Nicholls and Fe Sferdean are conducting internal and external environmental scans—including a campus data needs assessment—to determine the status of the University of Michigan among academic peers and in the national data conversation. "Data services are increasingly being recognized as a crucial component of library services," says Nicholls. "While researchers are grappling with a deluge of data, libraries are trying to find ways to improve data storage, management, sharing, and preservation. We are looking for ways for researchers and libraries to work together toward the common goals of facilitating innovative, reproducible research and increasing opportunities for data sharing and re-use" (Frick, 2013).

CONCLUSION

Copyright should be considered as part of the information infrastructure at the outset of a research project, along with a data plan as part of the research proposal. Infrastructure is more than storage and computational capacity. Copyright and intellectual property policy is integral to these discussions and resulting analyses. By involving people with expertise in copyright, data, the research process, and data management in those conversations, we can ensure the best possible framework for copyright and research behaviors around data for the research enterprise. The nature of research data and the possibilities for use and reuse globally make it imperative that participants be informed and engaged in the growing body of literature. While resources are limited, it is valuable to have staff attend professional conferences and actively involve themselves in working committees (national and global) because the conversation and problem solving is personal and immediate. Staff members need to report out to their colleagues, and they need to share experiences and observations. Closing the gap between available data and usable data demands painstaking, self-aware discipline; it is a worthwhile effort to ensure that data is truly the new gold rather than fool's gold.

REFERENCES

Australian Research Council. (2013, January 10). ARC open access policy. *Commonwealth of Australia*. Retrieved from http://www.arc.gov.au/applicants/open_access.htm

Carroll, M. W. (2013). Creative Commons and the openness of open access. *New England Journal of Medicine, 368*(9), 789–791. http://dx.doi.org/10.1056/NEJMp1300040

Databib. (n.d.). About Databib. Retrieved from http://databib.org/about.php

DataCite. (n.d.). What do we do? Retrieved from http://www.datacite.org/

DataONE. (n.d.a). Best practices. Retrieved from http://www.dataone.org/best-practices

DataONE. (n.d.b). Data management planning. Retrieved from http://www.dataone.org/data-management-planning

DataONE. (2011). *Example data management plan: NSF bio.* Albuquerque, NM: DataONE. Retrieved from http://www.dataone.org/sites/all/documents/DMP_Copepod_Formatted.pdf

Digital Curation Centre. (n.d.). Data plan guidance and examples. Retrieved from http://www.dcc.ac.uk/resources/data-management-plans/guidance-examples

Frick, R. (2013, January 24). A roadmap for data services [Web log post]. Retrieved from http://connect.clir.org/clir/blogs/blogviewer?BlogKey=d2df07ab-5587-49d0-8805-a9cd5dc83d87

Hartshorne, J. K., & Schachner, A. (2012). Tracking replicability as a method of post-publication open evaluation. *Frontiers in Computational Neuroscience, 6*(8). http://dx.doi.org/10.3389/fncom.2012.00008

Hirtle, P. (2011). Introduction to intellectual property rights in data management. *Cornell University Research Data Management Service Group.* Retrieved from https://confluence.cornell.edu/display/rdmsgweb/introduction-intellectual-property-rights-data-management

Holdren, J. (2013, February 22). Memorandum for the heads of executive departments and agencies. Executive Office of the President, Office of Science and Technology Policy. Retrieved from http://www.whitehouse.gov/blog/2013/02/22/expanding-public-access-results-federally-funded-research

Kroes, N. (2011, December). Data is the new gold. Opening remarks given at the Press Conference on Open Data Strategy, Brussels, Belgium. Retrieved from http://ec.europa.eu/information_society/newsroom/cf//itemdetail.cfm?item_id=7668

MIT Libraries. (n.d.). Data management plans. Retrieved from http://libraries.mit.edu/guides/subjects/data-management/plans.html

Mooney, H., & Newton, M. (2012). The anatomy of a data citation: Discovery, reuse, and credit. *Journal of Librarianship and Scholarly Communication, 1*(1), eP1035. http://dx.doi.org/10.7710/2162-3309.1035

National Institutes of Health. (n.d.). NIH public access policy details. Retrieved from http://publicaccess.nih.gov/policy.htm

National Institutes of Health (NIH). (2013). Frequently asked questions about the NIH public access policy. Retrieved from http://publicaccess.nih.gov/FAQ.htm

National Science Foundation (NSF). (2010). Scientists seeking NSF funding will soon be required to submit data management plans (NSF Press Release 10-077). Retrieved from http://www.nsf.gov/news/news_summ.jsp?cntn_id=116928

National Science Foundation (NSF). (2011). NSF-ENG: COV reports and annual updates. Retrieved from http://www.nsf.gov/eng/general/dmp.jsp

Open Access @ UNT. (n.d.). The Denton Declaration: An open access manifesto. Retrieved from http://openaccess.unt.edu/denton_declaration

Open Knowledge Foundation. (n.d.a). Open Data Commons Open Database License (ODbL). Retrieved from http://www.opendatacommons.org/licenses/odbl/

Open Knowledge Foundation. (n.d.b). Open Data Commons. Retrieved from http://opendatacommons.org/

ORCID. (n.d.). ORCID: Connecting research and researchers. Retrieved from http://orcid.org/

Physical Sciences Division. (n.d.). Template for NSF data management plan. *University of Chicago*. Retrieved from http://psd.uchicago.edu/NSF%20Data%20Management%20Plan%20Template.pdf

Piwowar, H. A. (2011). Who shares? Who doesn't? Factors associated with openly archiving raw research data. *PLOS One, 6*(7), e18657. http://dx.doi.org/10.1371/journal.pone.0018657

Research Cyberinfrastructure. (n.d.). Example data management plans. *UC San Diego*. Retrieved from http://rci.ucsd.edu/dmp/examples.html

Research Data Management. (n.d.). What should be in a data management plan? *University of Oxford*. Retrieved from http://www.admin.ox.ac.uk/rdm/dmp/plans/

Savage, C. J., & Vickers, A. J. (2009). Empirical study of data sharing by authors publishing in PLoS journals. *PLoS ONE, 4*(9), e7078. http://dx.doi.org/10.1371/journal.pone.0007078

Scholarly Communication Program (n.d.). Data management plan templates. *Columbia University Libraries/Information Services*. Retrieved from http://scholcomm.columbia.edu/data-management/data-management-plan-templates/

Science Libraries. (n.d.). *Preparing data management grant plans for NSF grant applications: A guide to the NSF policy for data management plans.* Berkeley: University of California, Berkeley. Retrieved from http://www.lib.berkeley.edu/CHEM/data/nsf/nsf_dmp.pdf

Stebbins, M. (2013, February 22). Expanding public access to the results of federally funded research [Web log post]. Retrieved from http://www. whitehouse.gov/blog/2013/02/22/expanding-public-access-results-federally-funded-research

University of Michigan Copyright Office. (2013, March 13). Creative Commons. *University of Michigan Library.* Retrieved from http://www.lib.umich.edu/copyright/creative-commons

University of Michigan Library. (n.d.). Research data management and publishing support. Retrieved from http://www.lib.umich.edu/research-data-management-and-publishing-support

University of Minnesota Libraries. (n.d.). Data management plan examples. Retrieved from https://www.lib.umn.edu/datamanagement/DMP/example

University of New Mexico Libraries. (n.d.). Generic data management plan outline and examples. Retrieved from http://libguides.unm.edu/content.php?pid=137795&sid=1422879

University of North Carolina. (n.d.). Data management sample plans. Retrieved from http://www.irss.unc.edu/odum/contentSubpage.jsp?nodeid=570

University of Pittsburgh. (n.d.). University of Pittsburgh—NSF data management plan—Example 1. Retrieved from http://www.pitt.edu/~offres/policies/NSF-DMP-Examples.pdf

Vlaeminck, S. (2012, December 12). Research data management in economic journals (Part I) [Web log post]. Retrieved from http://www.edawax. de/2012/12/research-data-management-in-economic-journals-part-i/#more-1245

Wellcome Trust. (n.d.). Open access at the Wellcome Trust. Retrieved from http://www.wellcome.ac.uk/About-us/Policy/Spotlight-issues/Open-access/index.htm

World Bank. (2012, April 10). World Bank announces open access policy for research and knowledge, launches Open Knowledge Repository. Retrieved from http://web.worldbank.org/WBSITE/EXTERNAL/NE WS/0,,contentMDK:23164491~pagePK:64257043~piPK:437376~the SitePK:4607,00.html

Yale Digital Collections Center. (n.d.). Data management plan examples. Retrieved from http://ydc2.yale.edu/documentation/data-management-plan-examples

7 | Metadata Services

JENN RILEY

METADATA IN DATA MANAGEMENT PLANNING

The January 2011 introduction of a data management plan requirement in grant proposals made to the National Science Foundation (NSF) took the academic library world by storm. Many of these libraries quickly mobilized and partnered with sponsored research offices to provide assistance in meeting this requirement, and were prepared when subsequent United States federal granting agencies followed suit in their application procedures. The stakes were further raised in February 2013, when the U.S. White House Office of Science and Technology Policy (OSTP) issued a memorandum directing many federal funding agencies to develop plans for increasing public access to data generated by federally funded research.[1] Metadata about the research data produced is a core part of a data management plan and of public access; indeed, while the NSF is not prescriptive about the contents of data management plans, their examples of the types of information plans present "the standards to be used for data and metadata format" as the second suggestion. A 2013 Educause report on developing data management planning services in institutions expands on this idea, recommending, "Metadata should identify the file formats to be used for the data in question and describe any contextual details dictating metadata to be associated with that data. The ultimate goal is for data formats to be interoperable and mobile across systems . . . to optimize discoverability and accessibility" (Fary & Owen, 2013, p. 5).

The NSF and other agency-mandated data management plans do not specify any particular metadata element set or approach to description. Instead, they rely on researchers to adhere to standards and best practices defined by their communities, and that best fit the data they are generating. Increasingly, software tools that generate or analyze data create metadata about that data that travels with it through additional software and repositories.

Data management plans are constructed to ensure the data can be discovered and used into the future. As a result, the metadata for research data stored in digital repositories serves a number of functions. The Digital Curation Centre's Curation Lifecycle Model[2] includes metadata in its innermost circle, as "description" and "representation information." Metadata drives virtually all of the other steps in the curation life cycle as well, from preservation actions to access and reuse. Discovery metadata, primarily descriptive in nature, typically serves to allow users to search or browse directly within that repository, in aggregated discovery services, or in more generalized search engines, and to adequately cite the data. Preservation metadata, which is more administrative in nature, often describes the provenance of the data (how it came to be in its current state or location) or its structural characteristics, and typically is used to drive preservation actions such as migration and transformation. Despite the differing functions of discovery and preservation for metadata, and their uses at different times in the life cycle of information, there is not a clear distinction between the two, and any given metadata element can frequently serve both purposes.

METADATA IN REPOSITORIES

There are a wide variety of practices for the creation of the metadata that describes research data, and for its ingest into repositories for preservation and access. Within disciplinary repositories, the model most commonly in use is for researchers to create, or provide from preexisting sources, any necessary metadata themselves as part of the deposit process. Yet researchers often are unprepared to create this metadata. In one study, 59.8 percent of researchers indicated that they strongly or somewhat agreed with a statement that they were satisfied with describing their data overall, while 26 percent of respondents were satisfied with tools available for preparing metadata for their research data, and over 32 percent were dissatisfied.

The authors of this study postulate that the large percentage of respondents (42 percent) who did not take a position on this issue might indicate that researchers are unsure what metadata is appropriate. In addition, "More than half of the respondents (56%) reported that they did not use any metadata standard and about 22% of respondents indicated they used their own lab metadata standard. This could be interpreted that over 78% of survey respondents either use no metadata or a local home grown metadata approach" (Tenopir et al., 2011, p. 7).

Disciplinary repositories do often offer help with metadata for deposit, however. The Inter-university Consortium for Political and Social Science Research (ICPSR)'s data preparation guide for its social science data repository includes a section on "best practice in creating metadata," focused heavily on using the Data Documentation Initiative (DDI),[3] within its *Data Preparation Guide*.[4] The Dryad repository for the basic and applied biosciences[5] provides a relatively short set of submission guidelines for researchers, including recommendations to clearly indicate column headings, document symbols indicating missing data, use the ISO8601 date format, and use taxonomic or other standard names when appropriate. Dryad documentation also goes a step further to provide a two-minute YouTube video demonstrating the submission process. The Odum Institute's node of the Dataverse repository[6] for social science data takes a different tactic, simply stating that the preference is for "fully documented" data from data analysis packages with all supporting interpretive information. The Odum Institute provides some tools for collecting information, requiring a five-page deposit form that provides some information about the structure of the data contributed. It also offers assistance to researchers in preparing data that may not yet have adequate documentation.

In libraries, we see a similar trend of assisting researchers with the creation of metadata and its ingest along with research data into a repository for preservation and access. As academic libraries have expanded institutional repositories beyond their original focus on pre- and post-prints into housing research data, metadata practices for papers in the repository have come to apply to research data as well, and the growth of these practices for research articles is closely tied to their implementation for research data. Therefore, metadata for both research data and the articles produced from it will be discussed here.

Institutional repositories housed in academic libraries often began with self-submission forms, as implemented by commonly used software packages, such as DSpace. These forms were designed around metadata standards, such as qualified Dublin Core, commonly used for resource description in libraries. Repository managers quickly realized that this approach was both a barrier to recruiting content and to obtaining useful metadata. Some repositories implemented features designed to speed metadata entry and improve its quality, such as drop-down lists for predefined or previously used subjects, author names, and publisher names in the University of Illinois' DSpace-based IDEALS repository (Chapman, Reynolds, & Shreeves, 2009).

Simply making the process of metadata entry slightly easier was not enough to encourage deposit or to promote better metadata practices at the desired scale, however. Both the conceptual mismatch between high-level, bibliographic-style metadata used in libraries and researchers' conception of metadata as detailed information about the specialized parameters of a dataset and the sheer effort of self-submission continued to present challenges for researchers. As Walters stated in 2007, "Although many universities have operated [institutional repositories] for at least the past two years, their experiences suggest that self-submission has not yet been adopted widely. Libraries need to adjust for this and offer to carry out the submittal process on behalf of faculty and students. . . . As a result, cataloging departments can play this vital role in [institutional repository] development" (p. 219). Yet creating metadata for repository ingest is done by staff throughout many different parts of libraries—"it is just as likely that librarians and library staff outside cataloging departments will create metadata or otherwise catalog and describe the objects contained in these institutional or subject-based repositories" (Babinec & Mercer, 2009, p. 209).

Libraries providing metadata creation support for ingest of papers and research data into institutional repositories quickly grew into a common practice. According to the 2006 Association of Research Libraries (ARL) SPEC Kit survey on institutional repositories, "[n]inety-four percent of implementers and 78% of planners[7] allow depositors to enter simple metadata; many of these same respondents also enter metadata on behalf of depositors (implementers, 60%; planners, 56%) or enhance depositor supplied metadata after the fact depending on the material and source (57% and 72%)" (Bailey et al., 2006, p. 18). This same survey revealed that at the time, research data was beginning to become part of standard repository operations—"Data sets, learning objects, and multimedia materials are the most prevalent non-traditional materials deposited, with over a third of all respondents indicating they include or will include these materials in the IR" (p. 17). Library services for metadata creation and enhancement vary widely, but they can be extensive, as was the case in 2006 for the Cornell University Geospatial Information Repository (CUGIR), for which library staff work with depositors to ensure full *Federal Geographic Data Committee* (FGDC) Content Standard for Digital Geospatial Metadata (CSGDM) is available for use by external geospatial clearinghouses and MARC records are available in the local catalog and in OCLC (Steinhart, 2006).

Libraries appear to have embraced an active facilitation role in creating metadata for research data and the papers derived from it when these materials are collected in a library-hosted institutional repository. A study published in 2007 found that the "inability of contributors to formulate quality metadata" was a bottom-ranked factor inhibiting the implementation of a successful institutional repository (Markey, Rieh, Jean, Kim, & Yakel, 2007, p. 62) This same study found that "better tools for assisting contributors with metadata creation" was rated by 74.2 percent of respondents as an important factor to consider in migrating to a new institutional repository system (p. 41). Together these findings suggest that libraries are comfortable with these metadata enhancement practices.

However, this comfort has only partially translated to consultation with researchers on creating metadata for their own data. An Association of College and Research Libraries (ACRL) survey revealed that only 17.9 percent of responding libraries currently offered a service to the campus consulting on metadata standards, while 58.3 percent do not and have no plans to do so. In addition, approximately 50 percent of respondents had no plans to implement any of the services asked about in the survey, which may indicate that many libraries are waiting to see how data management support on campuses evolves over time (Tenopir, Birch, & Allard, 2012).

WORKING WITH RESEARCHERS

Libraries do not typically create metadata for research data they are incorporating into their collections from scratch. Instead, they typically focus on working closely with researchers to repurpose metadata that was already created as part of the research process. This metadata can be used as the basis for both preservation and access of the research data, and this collaborative process bridges the gap between researchers' conception of metadata as extremely granular information about a dataset and libraries' higher level, more bibliographic approach. This methodology was employed by Purdue University in a data repository prototyping task force in 2008, where librarians with domain expertise worked with researchers to prepare data for repository ingest (Newton, Miller, & Bracke, 2010).

Yet metadata for preservation and access is not foremost on researchers' minds. In a 2012 Council on Library and Information Resources (CLIR) study commissioned by the Alfred P. Sloan Foundation, a series of ethnographic interviews found that "[t]ypically, metadata and documentation are of interest to researchers only if it helps them complete their work and produce publications. After a project ends, the time required to add appropriate metadata often exceeds the researcher's capacity and willingness to edit it, and the demands of publication output overwhelm long-term considerations of data curation" (Jahnke & Asher, 2012, p. 11). This same study provides some recommendations for ways to most effectively leverage the work that is done by researchers in the preservation of their data. These recommendations include "[t]he data preservation step must be fully integrated into a scholar's research workflow" (p. 16) and "reframing data curation within a comprehensive backup and management strategy is potentially valuable (p. 17).

Some attempts have been made to accomplish this deeper integration of data management into research workflows through introducing new tools that researchers might find valuable. Many of these initiatives have struggled with issues of complexity and adoption. One example was the DataStaR project at Cornell University, which originally aimed "to support the needs of researchers during the research process and to provide a flexible and sustainable infrastructure to support library involvement in data curation activities" (Dietrich, 2010, p. 80).[8] This tool's strengths were in exposing metadata that was entered into it in a number of interoperable and semantic web-friendly ways, and as such the project was eventually reframed as a dataset registry that exposes linked data about its contents.[9] The RepoMMan project at the University of Hull took a similar trajectory, performing user studies on the research process, and planning to provide tools for collaborative editing and automatic versioning, and automated generation of descriptive metadata that can then be reviewed by the researcher (Green, Dolphin, Awre, & Sherratt, 2007). This initiative eventually morphed into another project entitled REMAP, which attempted to add a "scholar's workbench" to the Hydra software (Green & Awre, 2009). The REMAP scholar's workbench has not come to pass, though the concept of easy access to tools for researchers remains alive with other initiatives, such as DataONE's Investigator Toolkit,[10] which brings together tools such as the DMPTool, DataUp, and Morpho.

LEVERAGING PREEXISTING METADATA

The researcher-centered approach to collecting metadata about research data as a part of the research activities themselves is an exemplar of leveraging personal information management (PIM) techniques. William Jones (2007) describes PIM as "both the practice and the study of the activities a person performs in order to acquire or create, store, organize, maintain, retrieve, use, and distribute the information needed to complete tasks (work-related or not) and fulfill various roles and responsibilities" (p. 453). Here, a new tool for metadata collection purposes would not be introduced into a researcher's workflow, but rather the library would seek to understand the tools and practices already in use by target researchers, and the organization's staff would look for ways in which those tools and practices already generate metadata that can be used as-is or be repurposed. The advantages of this approach appear straightforward—why spend time to understand and describe data in libraries if this information is already generated earlier in the data's life cycle?

Studies to better understand both personal and group information management techniques in order to better design long-term data management workflows and systems are beginning to emerge. Hollie C. White's (2010) exploratory study of a small number of researchers in evolutionary biology, for example, surfaced wide differences among individuals, yet found some common themes, such as organizing data by research question, or by genus, species, or individual specimen.

The organizational structures in use by researchers are but one aspect of PIM study that can inform library research data management practices. Yet these structures perhaps are underutilized as metadata that can aid in discovery, understanding, and preservation. The organization utilized by content creators is a primary interest of the archives community, and the data management and institutional repository communities can look to archives for inspiration in how to make most effective use of the file and organizational structure of researchers. In archives, the context in which records were created and their original order as evidenced by the creator's practices are key features to understanding the records and their use and purpose. Archival processing involves, among many other things, reviewing any pre-existing arrangement to determine if there are natural series that emerge. In this context, archivists define series as "a group of records based on a file system or maintained as a unit because the records result from the same function or activity, have a particular form, or have some other relationship resulting from their creation, accumulation, or use" (Roe, 2005, p. 61).

The organizational structure a researcher uses for his or her data can be interpreted as an archival series, and it can provide some basic metadata about that data. The Carolina Digital Repository[11] at the University of North Carolina at Chapel Hill takes this approach, with files in a collection organized into a hierarchical structure, which is typically based on the file structure of material as received from the researcher. Archival theory was explicitly brought in when designing this function, "ensuring that the digital objects would be inextricably linked to the context in which they exist within and amongst other records in the collections" (O'Meara & Tuomala, 2012, p. 94). An additional advantage to this approach also comes from the archival community—it does not require item-level description for all files in the repository; names for higher levels in the hierarchy, whether derived from folder names on a file system or provided by either the researcher or library staff on ingest, provide context to the files beneath and allow them to be usable without individual description. If individual description is available, or either feasible or a priority to create, it can then supplement these higher-level descriptions.

More detailed description of data in library-based institutional repositories also can be generated or repurposed from external sources. Chapman, Reynolds, and Shreeves (2009) introduce their article on metadata workflows in their respective repositories by summarizing the situation thusly: "many IRs ingest metadata through multiple workflows and contain a mixed metadata environment. Metadata is mapped and converted from existing systems, elicited from the document creator or manager, or created by library or repository staff" (p. 310). This highly heterogeneous metadata from multiple sources, of unpredictable detail and of varied granularity, is difficult to manage and use as a basis for consistent and high-quality services. Rowan Brownlee (2009) at the University of Sydney Library directly compared alternate structure and workflow designs for incorporating research-generated metadata into their repository. The approach chosen requires the library to map preexisting metadata into the library's format, and it also ingests the native metadata for future reuse. Additionally, it relies on library staff with advanced subject degrees or other domain knowledge in order to most effectively process the metadata received from the researcher.

Metadata that is delivered to the repository ingest process for research data often comes from software that generated or analyzed the data during the research process, or from spreadsheets, databases, or other tracking information used by a researcher. Yet other sources are possible, and these involve ingesting metadata in a batch rather than for one item at a time. The Simple Web-service Offering Repository Deposit (SWORD) protocol[12] is used to automatically ingest research papers from sources such as BioMed Central[13] into local institutional repositories, and this technology can work equally well for exchange of research data between repositories. Among the more innovative recent means of generating metadata about research data is the Dryad repository's examination of the potential for metadata about a published article to serve as a source of metadata for datasets upon which the published research was based (Greenberg, 2009).

EMERGING APPLICATIONS AND USES OF METADATA FOR RESEARCH DATA

Increasingly, online discovery services are making their contents available for reuse, through downloads and programmatic access to their services. One example of these features for research data is the cooperative Data-PASS catalog of social science data, which "provides layered data extraction and analysis services for a selection of publicly distributed data. Users who wish to access this public content can do so directly through the catalog interface, which supports extraction of data subsets, conversion to different statistical formats, and online data analysis" (Altman et al., 2009, p. 178). In addition to discovery through a web interface and manual download of the material, some repositories provide an *application programming interface* (API) by which data can be programmatically accessed, and many also expose metadata via the older Open Archives Initiative Protocol for Metadata Harvesting (OAI-PMH).[14] The linked data[15] movement has hit research data repositories as well, with services such as DataCite,[16] data.gov, data.bnf.fr, and the DataBib[17] registry of research data repositories providing information about materials in the repository in semantic web-friendly formats for others to reuse. The emerging ResourceSync[18] protocol for synchronization of web resources between systems has the potential to further expand the programmatic sharing of metadata about research data. All of these mechanisms for the sharing of metadata and content allow new research to more easily be done based on existing work, encourage replication of research and adequate citation, improve research quality through wider dissemination of results, promote better preservation of data through diversification, and make research data available to users worldwide. The international Research Data Alliance (RDA),[19] officially launched in March 2013, is devoted to this cause of research data sharing and exchange.

By gathering research papers, research data, and metadata about them together into repositories, it starts to become possible to mine the contents of these repositories in order to connect scholars to one another or to provide an institution with analyses of its research output. Two open-source software applications lead in this area of focus.

The first, VIVO,[20] started at Cornell University and scaled up collaboratively, "allows researchers to highlight areas of expertise, display academic credentials, visualize academic and social networks, and display information such as publications, grants, teaching, service, awards, and more" (Albert, Holmes, Börner, & Conlon, 2012, p. 429). VIVO allows administrators to bring in data from many sources, including publication databases, grant databases, and local institutional records. It also focuses heavily on sharing of this data using semantic web technologies: "By storing and exposing data as RDF and using standard ontologies, the information in VIVO can either be displayed in a human-readable webpage or delivered to other systems as RDF, allowing researcher metadata in VIVO to be harvested, aggregated, and integrated into the Linked Open Data cloud" (Albert et al., 2012, p. 429).

The second application, BibApp,[21] was developed by the University of Wisconsin-Madison and the University of Illinois at Urbana-Champaign.

This system serves the same research connection function as does VIVO, and it also focuses heavily on additional data mining to help campuses, libraries, and repository managers to answer institutional questions and plan services. BibApp can help those groups determine whether open access mandates are being met, trends in faculty publishing practices, who is collaborating across campus, which are the most active research areas, and more (Shreeves, 2010). Both systems create new metadata about research outputs that can be added to what already exists and is shared.

Users interacting with research data and the other research products built upon them can also generate metadata. The burgeoning field of "altmetrics"[22] aims to define and promote new, innovative ways of understanding the quality and impact of research as alternatives to traditional means, such as the journal impact factor. This field mines user behaviors—such as bookmarking, sharing via social media, and tagging—to derive information on what material researchers engage with the most and find most useful. These user behaviors generate new metadata that can be incorporated into repositories providing preservation and access, and statistics on action, including downloads, shares, comments, and links, can be used to identify content and researchers for prioritization.

TRAINING FOR METADATA MANAGEMENT OF RESEARCH DATA

Due to libraries' strong focus on making the most of metadata generated through research practices, which vary widely among disciplines, it is difficult for them to provide comprehensive training on how to construct and manage this metadata. Training researchers seems to primarily capitalize on opportunities for researcher interaction at various points in the research process. The DMPTool,[23] for example, does not give prescriptive guidance, but rather asks a few key but generic questions of researchers as they use the tool to create a data management plan. Some data management planning websites run by academic libraries, such as MIT[24] and the University of North Carolina at Chapel Hill[25] go a step further by providing brief tutorials or links to external sites with more metadata guidance based on disciplinary needs. One example of a site that provides guidance by discipline is the Digital Curation Centre,[26] which collects resources for metadata guidance in biology, earth science, general research data, physical sciences, and social science and the humanities. A few more targeted training programs for researchers have been attempted, including a *Joint Information Systems Committee* (JISC)-funded Digital Communication Enhancement (DICE) project, which produced a set of webpages and presentation slides entitled "Sending Your Research Into the Future,"[27] intended for reuse on the web or in training sessions by other organizations.

Training for librarians on data management, including metadata practices, has been a great deal more formal. However, this is still a growing field, and the library community is still learning what the best practices are and how to allow information professionals to gain those skills. For librarians already in the profession, data management is a frequent presentation and discussion topic at conferences devoted to academic librarianship, digital libraries, and librarianship in disciplines where research data is a primary concern. JISC in the United Kingdom has funded the RDMRose project,[28] which is making available open educational resources on data management support, intended for use as continuing education for information professionals. Metadata concepts appear throughout these training modules, including in discussions of the Digital Curation Centre's Lifecycle Model and data management planning. Specialized workshop-style programs, such as those offered by the University of North Carolina at Chapel Hill School of Information and Library Science's DigCCurr project[29] and the Library of Congress' Digital Preservation Outreach and Education (DPOE)[30] events, are also available.

Recent progress has been made in more clearly defining what librarians need to know in order to successfully support research data management. One outcome of the November 2008 Digital Curation Centre's Research Data Management Forum was a set of core skills for data management mapped to roles, including data manager, data librarian, and data scientist (Pryor & Donnelly, 2009), all of which might be fulfilled within libraries. In this framework, metadata is seen as a shared responsibility of the data creator and the data manager. A library-based task force at Purdue University that experimented with subject liaisons working in data management roles defined three core required skills: ability to argue the value of broader access to datasets, fluency in the capability of the repository system, and being research-aware (Newton, Miller, & Bracke, 2010). Research awareness includes a thorough knowledge of metadata practices within individual disciplines, in addition to those used in libraries.

Despite these and other efforts to introduce training for those already in the ranks of professional librarians, fuller adoption is a significant challenge. As one survey shows, "since so few libraries are hiring new positions for [research data services], training of existing staff could be seen to be essential, yet only a quarter of academic libraries currently provide these opportunities" (Tenopir, Birch, & Allard, 2012, p. 35).

Post-masters certificate programs in data curation and data management have begun to emerge as an alternate way of providing training to library professionals. Simmons' Digital Stewardship Certificate[31] is fully online, includes a metadata course as an elective, and offers a version of the program that involves one course taken per semester. With this design, it is possible for a working professional to complete the program. The University of North Carolina at Chapel Hill offers a post-masters Certificate in Digital Curation[32] composed of five in-person courses, none of which has a primary focus on metadata. Additionally, the Library of Congress is offering the National Digital Stewardship Residency (NDSR) program[33] for recent MLS graduates to focus on a one-year, practical project in digital curation or data management.

Library schools are increasingly including data management in their core graduate programs as well. However, according to one report, as of August 2012, "only five LIS schools offer graduate certificates explicitly in data curation"—University of Arizona, University of California at Berkeley, University of Illinois at Urbana-Champaign, University of North Carolina at Chapel Hill, and San Jose State University (Keralis, 2012, p. 33). Of these, San Jose State University's offering appears to be a fairly typical records management program; the University of Arizona focuses more heavily on digital librarianship than data curation and includes metadata in an introduction to a digital collections course; University of California at Berkeley requires an organization of information course; and University of Illinois at Urbana-Champaign requires this, plus offers a metadata course as an elective. Metadata issues tend to pervade many aspects of both these and post-masters curricula as well. Keralis (2012) also describes several other programs in data management at LIS schools in development, at least one of which (Maine) is now available.

LOOKING FORWARD

Training for research data management, like its implementation, is still a nascent activity. With time, we can expect research data management programs, whether library- or discipline-based, to grow. However, given the complex and ever-evolving metadata practices of the disciplines that produce research data and of the technology used to create and share this data and its metadata, we also can expect that metadata services for research data management will be one of the many areas of librarianship that grows and changes over time. Our profession faces many challenges as scholarly communication models undergo radical shifts. Throughout, metadata for research data management can play an important role in libraries' missions to preserve and make available the products of our society.

NOTES

1. http://www.whitehouse.gov/sites/default/files/microsites/ostp/ostp_public_access_memo_2013.pdf

2. http://www.dcc.ac.uk/resources/curation-lifecycle-model

3. http://www.ddialliance.org/

4. http://www.icpsr.umich.edu/icpsrweb/content/deposit/guide/index.html

5. http://datadryad.org/

6. http://arc.irss.unc.edu/dvn/

7. Implementers are defined as institutions that currently have an institutional repository, and planners are defined as those with plans to develop one.

8. For more information, see Gail Steinhart's case study in this volume.

9. https://sites.google.com/site/datastarsite/

10. http://www.dataone.org/investigator-toolkit

11. http://cdr.lib.unc.edu

12. http://swordapp.org/about/

13. http://www.biomedcentral.com/

14. http://www.openarchives.org/pmh/

15. http://www.w3.org/DesignIssues/LinkedData.html

16. http://data.datacite.org/static/index.html

17. http://databib.org/

18. http://www.openarchives.org/rs/resourcesync

19. http://rd-alliance.org/

20. http://vivoweb.org/

21. http://bibapp.org/

22. http://altmetrics.org/manifesto/
23. https://dmp.cdlib.org/
24. http://libraries.mit.edu/guides/subjects/data-management/metadata.html
25. http://guides.lib.unc.edu/content.php?pid=388221
26. http://www.dcc.ac.uk/resources/metadata-standards
27. http://lsedice.wordpress.com/2012/07/25/project-outputs/
28. http://www.shef.ac.uk/is/research/projects/rdmrose
29. http://ils.unc.edu/digccurr/
30. http://www.digitalpreservation.gov/education/
31. http://www.simmons.edu/gslis/academics/programs/post-masters/dsc/index.php
32. http://sils.unc.edu/programs/certificates/digital_curation
33. http://www.digitalpreservation.gov/ndsr/

REFERENCES

Albert, P., Holmes, K. L., Börner, K., & Conlon, M. (2012). Research discovery through linked open data. *Proceedings of the 2012 ACM/IEEE Joint Conference on Digital Libraries,* June 12–14, 2012, Washington, DC (pp. 429–430).

Altman, M., Adams, M. O., Crabtree, J., Donakowski, D., Maynard, M., Pienta, A., & Young, C. H. (2009). Digital preservation through archival collaboration: The Data Preservation Alliance for the Social Sciences. *American Archivist, 72*(1), 170–184.

Babinec, M. S., & Mercer, H. (2009). Introduction: Metadata and open access repositories. *Cataloging & Classification Quarterly, 47*(3/4), 209–212. http://dx.doi.org/10.1080/01639370902740301

Bailey, Jr., C. W., Coombs, K., Emery, J., Mitchell, A., Morris, C., Simons, S., & Wright, R. (2006). *Institutional repositories. SPEC Kit 292.* Washington, DC: Association of Research Libraries.

Brownlee, R. (2009). Research data and repository metadata: Policy and technical issues at the University of Sydney Library. *Cataloging & Classification Quarterly, 47*(3/4), 370–379. http://dx.doi.org/10.1080/01639370802714182

Chapman, J. W., Reynolds, D., & Shreeves, S. (2009). Repository metadata: Approaches and challenges. *Cataloging & Classification Quarterly, 47*(3/4), 309–325. http://dx.doi.org/10.1080/01639370902735020

Dietrich, D. (2010). Metadata management in a data staging repository. *Journal of Library Metadata, 10*(2/3), 79–98. http://dx.doi.org/10.1080/19386389.2010.506376

Fary, M., & Owen, K. (2013). Developing an institutional research data management plan service. Retrieved from http://net.educause.edu/ir/library/pdf/ACTI1301.pdf

Green, R., & Awre, C. (2009). Towards a repository-enabled scholar's workbench: RepoMMan, REMAP and Hydra. *D-Lib Magazine, 15*(5/6). Retrieved from http://www.dlib.org/dlib/may09/green/05green.html

Green, R., Dolphin, I., Awre, C., & Sherratt, R. (2007). The RepoMMan project: Automating workflow and metadata for an institutional repository. *OCLC Systems & Services*, 23(2), 210–215. http://dx.doi.org/10.1108/10650750710748513

Greenberg, J. (2009). Theoretical considerations of lifecycle modeling: An analysis of the Dryad repository demonstrating automatic metadata propagation, inheritance, and value system adoption. *Cataloging & Classification Quarterly, 47*(3/4), 380–402. http://dx.doi.org/10.1080/01639370902737547

Jahnke, L., & Asher, A. (2012). *The problem of data*. Washington, DC: Council on Library and Information Resources. Retrieved from http://www.clir.org/pubs/reports/pub154/pub154.pdf

Jones, W. (2007). Personal information management. *Annual Review of Information Science and Technology, 41*(1), 453–504. http://dx.doi.org/10.1002/aris.2007.1440410117

Keralis, S. D. C. (2012). Data curation education: A snapshot. In L. Jahnke & A. Asher (Eds.), *The problem of data* (32–43). Washington, DC: Council on Library and Information Resources. Retrieved from http://www.clir.org/pubs/reports/pub154/pub154.pdf

Markey, K., Rieh, S. Y., Jean, B. S., Kim, J., & Yakel, E. (2007). *Census of institutional repositories in the United States: MIRACLE project research findings*. Retrieved from http://www.clir.org/pubs/reports/pub140/reports/pub140/pub140.pdf

Newton, M. P., Miller, C. C., & Bracke, M. S. (2010). Librarian roles in institutional repository data set collecting: Outcomes of a research library task force. *Collection Management, 36*(1), 53–67. http://dx.doi.org/10.1080/01462679.2011.530546

O'Meara, E., & Tuomala, M. (2012). Finding balance between archival principles and real-life practices in an institutional repository. *Archivaria, 73*, 81–103.

Pryor, G., & Donnelly, M. (2009). Skilling up to do data: Whose role, whose responsibility, whose career? *The International Journal of Digital Curation, 4*(2), 158–170. Retrieved from http://www.ijdc.net/index.php/ijdc/article/view/126

Roe, K. (2005). The Practice of arrangement and description. *Arranging and Describing Archives and Manuscripts* (pp. 45–70). Chicago: Society of American Archivists.

Shreeves, S. (2010). BibApp: Campus research gateway and expert finder. Presentation for 2010 EDUCAUSE Midwest Regional Conference in Chicago, IL. Retrieved from http://hdl.handle.net/2142/16541

Steinhart, G. (2006). Libraries as distributors of geospatial data: Data management policies as tools for managing partnerships. *Library Trends, 55*(2), 264–284. http://dx.doi.org/10.1353/lib.2006.0063

Tenopir, C., Allard, S., Douglass, K. L., Aydinoglu, A. U., Wu, L., Read, E., Manoff, M., & Frame, M. (2011). Data sharing by scientists: Practices and perceptions. *PLoS ONE, 6*(6), 1–21. Retrieved from http://works.bepress.com/kimberly_douglass/2

Tenopir, C., Birch, B., & Allard, S. (2012, June). *Academic libraries and research data services: Current practices and plans for the future.* Association of College & Research Libraries. Retrieved from http://www.ala.org/acrl/sites/ala.org.acrl/files/content/publications/white papers/Tenopir_Birch_Allard.pdf

Walters, T. O. (2007). Reinventing the library: How repositories are causing librarians to rethink their professional roles. *portal: Libraries and the Academy, 7*(2), 213–225. http://dx.doi.org/10.1353/pla.2007.0023

White, H. C. (2010). Considering personal organization: Metadata practices of scientists. *Journal of Library Metadata, 10*(2–3), 156–172. http://dx.doi.org/10.1080/19386389.2010.506396

8 | Data Citation

Principles and Practice

JAN BRASE, YVONNE SOCHA, SARAH CALLAGHAN,
CHRISTINE L. BORGMAN, PAUL F. UHLIR,[1]
AND BONNIE CARROLL

INTRODUCTION

In the last decade, the amount of data created by large scientific facilities, sensors, new observation instruments, and supercomputing has outpaced our ability to process, store, and analyze the data. As technological factors—such as faster processors, better storage, and increased bandwidth—have enabled the much greater production and capture of data, the creation of standards to manage these data has not kept pace. Nor are data management issues solely limited to the data produced by high-performance computing (HPC) and scientific computing (SC); in fact, the aggregated data produced by individual researchers or small research groups may well dwarf that created by HPC or SC. By its nature, these "long tail" data are hard to find, standardize, and account for, but they still deserve proper data management.

While some organizations have recognized the need for policies regarding data management (Helly, 1998) and have implemented policies that begin to address the issues (Helly, Elvins, Sutton, & Martinez, 1999; Helly et al., 2002; Staudigel et al., 2003), there is still a lack of overall consensus regarding the treatment of data, especially in ways to reference datasets and maintain the scholarly record.

Traditionally, scientific findings are shared by a mechanism of publication and citation, in which papers are published, read, and critiqued, while the links between papers are made through a formal process of citation. So well established is this practice that well-defined instructions to authors provide the details of what information should be provided and how the

167

citations should be structured for almost every journal. As datasets have become larger and more complex, however, it often is no longer possible to publish them as part of a paper, although the ability of scientific assertions in the paper to withstand scrutiny demands that the link between the data and the publication be maintained.

Data and citations to them are critical to verify research conclusions and enable reuse of data. The relatively new practice of the citation to datasets solves important parts of long-standing problems limiting our collective ability to locate data and use them effectively in advancing science. Citations support a research infrastructure to provide the necessary recognition and reward of data work, in addition to providing attribution detail, facilitating future access, and fostering cross-collaboration and investigation (Berns, Bond, & Manning, 1996; Committee on the Preservation of Geoscience Data and Collections, Committee on Earth Resources, & National Research Council, 2002; Committee on Responsibilities of Authorship in the Biological Sciences & National Research Council, 2003; Fienberg, Martin, & Straf, 1985; Sieber, 1991; Towne, Wise, & Winters, 2004; Uhlir & Schröder, 2007).[2] It is for these and many other reasons that the more pervasive use of data citation is beneficial to the scientific community.

When data are captured as part of the publication, in the form of a graph, table, or image, for example, they are cited as a part of that article. Datasets have been included to some degree as supplementary materials related to published manuscripts. The data themselves reside on servers maintained by the publishers, accessible only to those with subscriptions.

More recently, most federal funding agencies have required that publicly funded research data be deposited with national data centers. As these practices become better established, the ability to detect, locate, obtain, and understand the data from prior research becomes limited by our ability to have a sufficient description of those data: a citation. This is the link between the data and the published research results needed to maintain the integrity of the scientific method.

THE ROLE OF DATA IN THE RESEARCH LIFE CYCLE

Data are essential products resulting from and useful to basic scientific tenets, such as reproducibility and transparency. Data should be labeled in ways that allow them to be reused; the new mode of data-intensive science makes the use of existing data a central asset of future science (Hey, Tansley, & Tolle, 2009). Data have always been the cornerstone of science, as it is not possible to replicate experimental findings, perform observational research, or test assertions without them. Because data often have a longer life cycle than the research projects that create them, understanding the role of data in the research life cycle is vital. However, it is important to note that research life cycles are as varied as the types of research performed.

Data are integral to the modern practice of research. When data are not included as part of the dissemination of scientific research, the link from the published research results back to them is broken, and the provenance and trustworthiness of the results may be in question. In a research cycle, data undergoes several changes and processes; it is derived, continued, combined, or divided. Not all these versions of the data are recorded in the same database or repository. The dataset is therefore a composite object. The identifying descriptors of that object must include enough specificity about its constituent parts so that the citation can refer to one and only one unambiguous, clearly defined dataset. This requires versioning of records and identification of entities that have contributed to or changed them, such as original data author or additional authors that interpret existing data for new scientific work. However, this is not simply a problem of assigning identifiers or metadata. For the purposes of aggregation, computation, verification, reproducibility, and replicability, the dataset must be defined so that it can be referenced in a way that yields a concrete search result (Wynholds, 2011).

Currently, datasets exist mostly in the prepublication phase and are only infrequently part of the scholarly dissemination process for research publications. Furthermore, data associated with manuscripts in the current nodes of dissemination are usually in highly reduced forms, such as tables or graphs. In order to fully realize the potential offered though data mining, discovery, collaboration, and reuse, data citation is a necessary endeavor, though it is important to remember that data can and will be cited without it being made open to all users. Much work is being done by data centers and research funders to encourage researchers to include data curation and data management into their research practice, including identifying community needs for supportive facilities, such as data repository services, metadata services, data discovery and data-mining services, and data preservation services.

EMERGING PRINCIPLES FOR DATA CITATION

Data citation principles have evolved considerably since early efforts in the 1990s to preserve digital scientific data. Increased awareness of the need for improved practices and methods for data publications have spurred such efforts as the standardization of the digital object identifier (DOI) syntax in 2000 through the National Information Standards Organization (NISO) and its subsequent approval as an ISO standard in 2010.[3] Many individual and collective efforts have led to the current recognition of the need for data citation standards and procedures, as well as for something equivalent to "instructions to authors" guidelines used by publications to ensure standardized manuscript and citation preparation.

The primary purpose of citation has been to support an argument with evidence, though over the years it also has become a mechanism for attribution, discovery, quality assurance, and provenance. Altman and King (2007) state that data citations should contain information sufficient to locate the dataset that is referred to as evidence for the claims made in the citing publication, to verify that the dataset the user has located is semantically equivalent to the dataset used by the original authors of the citing publication, and to correctly attribute the dataset.

Based on observation of emerging practices and analysis in existing literature on citation practices, we have identified a set of 10 "first principles" for data citation: status, attribution, persistence, access, discovery, provenance, granularity, verifiability, standards, and flexibility.

I. The Status Principle

Data citations should be accorded the same importance in the scholarly record as the citation of other objects.

The scholarly record comprises the relationships among scholarly works and evidence. Traditional citations most often signify the relationship between statements in the article and statements in other published works to which the former are related.

The relationship between a statement in the article and the supporting data is neither less important nor representative of a different intellectual relation than the traditional citation of other published works. Thus, data citations would be treated in a similar manner as citations to other works.

Citations to data would be presented along with citations to other works, typically in a references or "literature cited" section (Altman, 2012; Callaghan et al., 2012). The former stated the principle that data citations should be first-class objects for bibliographic purposes, and the latter made the argument that data itself should be a first-class object for scientific purposes. In other words, publishers would not impose additional requirements for citing data, nor would they accept citations to data that do not meet the core requirements for citing other works (Altman, 2012).

II. The Attribution Principle

Citations should facilitate giving scholarly credit and legal attribution to all parties responsible for those data.

Credit is the universally recognized currency for both quality and quantity of scientific activity. Citing data allows the use of metrics to evaluate use and impact factor of datasets, potentially encouraging data creators to make their data available for use by others. This fosters transparency and enables recognition of scholarly effort.

Current legal attribution requirements do not necessarily match expectations for receiving credit, nor do they perfectly map to accepted standards of citation. To avoid the problems of attribution stacking and the need to inject legal text into research publications, licenses should be used that recognize citations as legal attribution, such as the forthcoming version 4.0 of the Creative Commons licenses. Where additional information is required to satisfy legal attribution, it should, if at all possible, be obtainable via the persistent identifier that is included in the citation, as per principle three.

Citations may function to provide credit directly through the text of the citation, or indirectly through well-known and reliable linkages to other resources that provide more detailed credit and attribution; it is not necessary to embed all contributors within the citation itself.

Tracking each contributor's data and providing credit to the contributor's effort is a necessary task, as with a manuscript. If many contributors contributed to a work, it may be more practical to list them elsewhere; this is acceptable as long as there is a reliable and systematic (ideally programmatic) way of looking up the full list of contributors based on the citation. The full list of contributors may be indexed in the metadata associated with the DOI, for example, rather than embedded in the citation. In other words, data citation must support unambiguous assignment of credit to all contributors, possibly through the citation ecosystem.

III. The Persistence Principle

Citations should be as durable as the cited objects.

The citations themselves have to be persistent and must be linked in some manner to the identity of the curator currently responsible for the referent dataset (whether the curator is an institution or a named individual). Based on the findings of the 2011 "Data Citations Principles Workshop" (http://projects.iq.harvard.edu/datacitation_workshop), citations should persist and enable resolution to the version of the data cited, at least as long as the cited work persists. If possible, data publishers should use some form of persistent resource identifier such as DOIs, persistent URLs (PURL), or others (Altman & King, 2007; Green, 2009; Lawrence et al., 2007; Star & Gastl, 2011). It is strongly recommended that these persistent identifiers be in URL form or directly resolvable to URLs.

A persistent digital identifier enables unambiguous referencing, cross-referencing, authentication, and validation. It also provides a basis for practices such as citation counting in career merit reviews. Furthermore, as noted in the provenance and attribution principles, registries or related services are needed to guarantee the persistence of metadata associated with the citation, such as fixity information or the full list of contributors.

A central resolver and registry require maintenance and must be sufficiently robust. For example, resolver databases could be mirrored and updated in multiple locations around the world in a timely manner, given our current Internet architecture. To ensure reliability and availability, there should be redundant access points without single-point failures.

IV. The Access Principle

Citations should facilitate access both to the data themselves and to such associated metadata and documentation as are necessary for both humans and machines to make informed use of the referenced data.

Access to data citations facilitates attribution, verification, reuse, and collaboration. Anyone who has an interest in data will benefit from access—data centers, data creators, data scientists, publishers, funding organizations, and the wider scientific community as a whole.

The remaining six principles embody functional requirements to enable meaningful access:

V. The Discovery Principle

Citations should support the discovery of data and their documentation.

Discovery of data enabled by citations makes it easier to validate and build upon previous work. Facilitation of discovery through data citation ensures proper attribution and provides information about related methodology that allows the data to be put into context.

Data should include metadata that aid in their discovery. Part of such metadata should be the citations of all publications related to the data. In effect, this means bidirectional linking from datasets to publications and from publications to datasets (Borgman, 2007).

While data are discoverable only if they are archived, any embargo period specified for the data can influence their discovery. Consideration also will vary by the discipline and type of data, such as raw data, observations, models, samples, and the like (Borgman, 2012). Descriptive titles and content tagging in the metadata can also be aides to discovery.

VI. The Provenance Principle

Citations should facilitate the establishment of the provenance of data.

Citations should include sufficient fixity and other *administrative* provenance metadata to verify that a data object later accessed is equivalent to the data object originally cited. Provenance information related to data processing, including, for example, data versions and fixity checks, are used for a variety of purposes, such as understanding the process and auditing, as well as for reproducibility (Tilmes, Yesha, & Halem, 2011). Accurate provenance facilitates accurate comparison of data and enables reproducibility and the chain-of-custody.

Additionally, *methodological* provenance is challenging to include in the citation itself, but it often is required for a full understanding of the data. Many datasets are frequently derived from measurements, simulations, or other datasets in ways that are not obvious from reading the paper. The metadata associated with a dataset should include sufficient methodological provenance to evaluate the dataset and to link it to other datasets. For derived or aggregated data, such metadata will generally include citations to the parent or aggregated datasets.

VII. The Granularity Principle

Citations should support the finest-grained description necessary to identify the data.

Where a more finely grained data subset is used to support a specific evidentiary claim (such as statement, figure, or analysis), that subset should be described in the text reference, preferably as part of a structured "deep citation" or as an unstructured note, if necessary. Note that this rule does not require that separate persistent identifiers (such as DOI names) are created for fine-grained citation, merely that there be some way of unambiguously identifying the portion used within the data cited.

A dataset may form part of a collection and be made up of several files, with each containing several tables and many data points. Abstract subsets, such as features and parameters, may also be used. It is not always obvious what would constitute a whole dataset (Ball & Duke, 2012). For authors, the pragmatic solution is to list datasets at the finest level of granularity provided by the repository or institution and to clearly identify the subset of the data that underlies each figure and analysis. This is analogous to using the Library of Congress citation to refer to a book, but including page numbers in the in-text reference.

Providing explicit granularity minimizes additional information needed to find the source. The optimum level and nature of granularity, however, would vary with the kind of data.

VIII. The Verifiability Principle

Citations should contain information sufficient to identify the data unambiguously.

Citations are used to associate published claims with the evidence supporting them and to verify that the evidence has not been altered. Thus, there must be sufficient fixity information embedded in or associated to verify that the data used matches data originally cited.

For scientific literature, persistent identifiers, such as DOI names, often have resolved to a landing page containing at least bibliographic metadata. This practice arose partly because publishers had different views on how much of their content they were actually prepared to expose to a DOI lookup, but also because there is reasonable homogeneity of type across the scientific literature. Datasets are more heterogeneous in terms of size, file type, and intended purpose.

Resolution of persistent identifiers consistent with the verifiability principle may be achieved by bringing the user to a landing page (data surrogate) where additional metadata, such as the data form, provenance, fixity, and content, are given explicitly. It also is permissible to link directly to a dataset, provided that the combination of citation and dataset together contains adequate metadata to verify that it is what is being sought, including fixity information in the citation. If at all possible, open protocols, such as Content Negotiation (http://www.w3.org/Protocols/rfc2616/rfc2616-sec12.html) and Resource Description Framework in Attributes (RDFa, http://www.w3.org/TR/xhtml-rdfa-primer), should be used so that computational agents are given direct access to the metadata and data in machine-readable form when resolving identifiers such as DOI names, rather than forcing a detour to a human-readable HTML page.

IX. The Metadata Standards Principle

Citations should employ widely accepted metadata standards.

Some scientific disciplines have invested decades of effort in developing community metadata standards. Implementing metadata standards alleviates both redundancy and ambiguity that can diminish interoperability. Additionally, standards also provide legal clarity and certainty concerning the permitted uses of the data.

Unlike narrative publications, data are designed to be processed directly. Standardized metadata for data publications would explicitly enhance current and future automation for data ingestion, authentication, and quality control needed for reliable reuse of the data, both in verification of published results and repurposing of data.

It is important that interoperability requirements distinguish semantics from presentation, and provide the necessary and sufficient information about the data independently of any presentation layer, format, or style. New metadata standards continue to be developed, and some will be appropriate for data citation. Notwithstanding, metadata design used in citation must be open, platform-independent, and well-recognized by the community. There must always be a means of exporting and importing metadata across systems that are used within and between disciplines.

X. The Flexibility Principle

Citation methods should be sufficiently flexible to accommodate the variant practices among communities, but these should not differ so much that they comprise interoperability of data across communities.

Widespread adoption of data citation practices requires that these practices serve the needs of a broad range of constituencies. The nature of data used in different disciplines varies in size, complexity, useful level of granularity, and other characteristics. This principle addresses the commonly stated maxim that one size does not fit all.

While broad acceptance requires that citation practices accommodate the needs of a diverse array of disciplines and communities of practice, there should be a minimum baseline set of elements upon which the different disciplines and communities can build in order to meet their specific needs.

STANDARDS FOR DATA CITATION

Although the underlying caveat that "one size does not fit all" is true at many levels of data citation, there are elements underlying data citation for which disciplinary or community of practice (CoP) guidelines are emerging. Objectives include discovering, describing, sharing, and preserving the data, and also making them interoperable. While some of the elements in more traditional citations of literature can be transferred to the citations of datasets, upon which a standard citation system can be built, others need more formulation, implementation, and adoption.

Data citations derive from metadata elements, or components, that are selected as a way to uniquely identify a dataset and make it discoverable. These elements may also vary by CoP guidelines. Core elements of a traditional publication citation, such as author or contributor, title, source or publisher, and access date are generally transferrable from long-established norms. However, there are less obvious elements that are in need of review and consensus development.

In addition to standardizing a "citation" as the proxy for a dataset, the content of some metadata elements that will compose the citation also should be standardized. The disambiguation of a dataset, its granularity, the control of versions, and the identification of data are aspects that need to be considered in light of the unique properties of datasets. Initiatives to develop interdisciplinary standardized authority files for those elements are currently underway. Through such standardization, ambiguity regarding the dataset can be reduced. Other metadata elements, such as those describing provenance, privacy controls, and reuse rights, are potential but novel parts of a data citation that should be standardized as well.

In recent years, a growing number of repositories and publishers have developed good, consistent practices in data citation (Ball & Duke, 2012). The elements that would make up a complete citation are still a matter of some debate. The following list is taken from the Digital Curation Centre (http://www.dcc.ac.uk) and combines tenets of several research papers (Altman & King, 2007; Green, 2009; Lawrence et al., 2007; Starr & Gastl, 2011.) See also the next section, which focuses on the citation structure rather than the metadata elements selected as core for a citation.

As evidenced from consensus via previously cited research, the required components that should be present in any citation are the creator or author, title, date, and location. These components, respectively, give due credit, allow the reader to judge the relevance of the data, and permit access to the data. In theory, these elements should uniquely identify the dataset; in practice, a formal identifier is often needed. The most efficient solution is to give a location that consists of a resolver service and an identifier.

Author	The creator of the dataset.
Title	As well as the name of the cited resource itself, this also may include the name of a facility and the titles of the top collection and main parent subcollection (if any) of which the dataset is a part.
Publisher	The organization either hosting the data or performing quality assurance.
Publication date	Whichever is the latter: the date the dataset was made available, the date all quality assurance procedures were completed, and the date the embargo period (if applicable) expired. In other standards, an "access date" field is used to document the date the dataset was accessed.
Resource type	Examples: database, dataset.
Edition	The level or stage of processing of the data, indicating how raw or refined the dataset is.
Version	A number increased when the data changes, as the result of adding more data points or rerunning a derivation process, for example.
Feature name and URL	The name of an ISO 19101:2002 "feature" (e.g., GridSeries, ProfileSeries) and the URI identifying its standard definition, used to pick out a subset of the data.
Verifier	Information to verify the identity and integrity of the content like a checksum.
Identifier	An identifier for the data, according to a persistent scheme. There are several types of persistent identifiers, but the scheme that is gaining the most traction is the digital object identifier (DOI).
Location	A persistent URL from which the dataset is available. Some identifier schemes provide these via an identifier resolver service.

Table 1. Data citation elements (Digital Curation Centre).

DATA CITATION IN PRACTICE: DATACITE

The German National Library of Science and Technology (TIB) developed and promotes the use of DOI names for datasets. A DOI name is used to cite and link to electronic resources (text as well as research data and other types of content). The DOI system differs from other reference systems commonly used on the Internet, such as the URL, since it is permanently linked to the object itself, not just to the place in which the object is located. As a major advantage, the use of the DOI system for registration permits the scientists and the publishers to use the same syntax and technical infrastructure for the referencing of datasets that are already established for the referencing of articles. The DOI system offers persistent links as stable references to scientific content and an easy way to connect the article with the underlying data. For example:

The dataset:

> Storz, D., et al. (2009). Planktic foraminiferal flux and faunal composition of sediment trap L1_K276 in the northeastern Atlantic. PANGAEA. http://dx.doi.org/10.1594/PANGAEA.724325

is a supplement to the article:

> Storz, D., Schulz, H., Waniek, J. J., Schulz-Bull, D. E., & Kucera, M. (2009). Seasonal and interannual variability of the planktic foraminiferal flux in the vicinity of the Azores Current. *Deep Sea Research Part I: Oceanographic Research Papers, 56*(1), 107–124, http://dx.doi.org/10.1016/j.dsr.2008.08.009

Since 2005, TIB has been an official DOI Registration Agency with a focus on the registration of research data. The role of TIB is that of the actual DOI registration and the storage of the relevant metadata of the dataset. The research data themselves are not stored at TIB. The registration always takes place in cooperation with data centers or other trustworthy institutions that are responsible for quality assurance, storage and accessibility of the research data, and the creation of metadata.

Access to research data is nowadays defined as part of the national responsibilities, and in recent years, most national science organizations have addressed the need to increase the awareness of, and the accessibility to, research data.

Nevertheless, science itself is international. Scientists are involved in global unions and projects; they share their scientific information with colleagues all over the world; and they use national as well as foreign information providers.

When facing the challenge of increasing access to research data, a possible approach should be global cooperation for data access via national representatives; A global cooperation, because scientist work globally, scientific data are created and accessed globally. National representatives are needed, because most scientists are embedded in their national funding structures and research organizations (Brase et al., 2009).

The key point of this approach is the establishment of a Global DOI Registration Agency for scientific content that will offer dataset registration and cataloguing services to all researchers. DataCite was officially launched on December 1, 2009, in London, to offer worldwide DOI registration of scientific data to actively offer scientists the possibility to publish their data as an independent, citable object. Currently, DataCite has 17 members from 12 countries, including the German National Library of Science and Technology (TIB); the German National Library of Medicine (ZB MED); the German National Library of Economics (ZBW); and the German GESIS—Leibniz-Institute for the Social Sciences. Additional European members include: the Library of the ETH Zürich in Switzerland; the TU Delft Library in the Netherlands; the L'Institut de l'Information Scientifique et Technique (INIST) in France; the Technical Information Center of Denmark; the British Library; the Swedish National Data Service (SND); and the Conferenza dei Rettori delle Università Italiane (CRUI) in Italy. North America is represented through: the California Digital Library; the U.S. Department of Energy's Office of Scientific and Technical Information (OSTI); Purdue University; and the Canada Institute for Scientific and Technical Information (CISTI). Furthermore, the Australian National Data Service (ANDS) and the National Research Council of Thailand (NRCT) are members.

DataCite offers through its members DOI registration for data centers. Currently, over 2 million objects have been registered with a DOI name and are available through a central search portal at http://search.datacite.org.

Based on the DOI registration, DataCite offers a variety of services, such as a detailed statistic portal of the number of DOI names registered and resolved (http://stats.datacite.org).

In cooperation with CrossRef, the major DOI registration agency for scholarly articles, a content negotiation service has been established that allows persistent resolution of all DOI names directly to their metadata in XML or RDF format (http://www.crosscite.org/cn).

In June 2012, DataCite and the International Association of Scientific, Technical and Medical Publishers (http://www.stm-assoc.org) signed a joint statement to encourage publishers and data centers to link articles and underlying data (http://www.datacite.org/node/65).

CONCLUSION

As Clay Shirky (2010) observes: "The problem with alchemy wasn't that the alchemists had failed to turn lead into gold—no one could do that. The problem, rather, was that the alchemists had failed informatively" (p. 138). A robust infrastructure for data citation promises to substantially increase the frequency with which previously collected scientific evidence informs current research and future policy.

While data citation offers broad potential benefits for domain research, interdisciplinary research, and generally improving our understanding of science, achieving a robust and effective data citation infrastructure requires enabling research, coordination, and resources. Effort is required to build broad and coherent theoretical models, and to translate and apply these to enable evaluation of the semantic equivalence of data; to strengthen theoretical and practical applications of data provenance; and to enable standardized approaches to managing the legal rights and responsibilities that adhere to research data. Evaluation research will be needed to assess the effectiveness and impact of the implementation of the data citation, and to guide development of the infrastructure.

A robust data citation infrastructure, complemented by wider and more uniform data access, including free global access to bibliographic and data citations by means of open citation corpora, would catalyze domain research. Analysis that requires evidence from multiple measurement domains, scales, populations, or that requires extensive longitudinal data collection, is challenging to fund and implement within the scope of a single research project. Uniform citation and access to research data would lower the barriers to this type of research. Similarly, data citation and sharing would make research that combines information across disciplines substantially easier to conduct. Furthermore, reviews of published work, such as Cochrane reviews and other systematic evidential reviews that synthesize the findings of previous studies, would be easier to conduct, and these would yield more informative results.

Moreover, while work within each specific discipline is vital, creating a robust data infrastructure cannot be accomplished within a single discipline or by relying solely on the skills and perspectives of a single discipline. Data citation and access infrastructure requires research and implementation at the intersections of several disciplines: law, computer science and informatics, and policy and systems research. Figure 1 summarizes this.

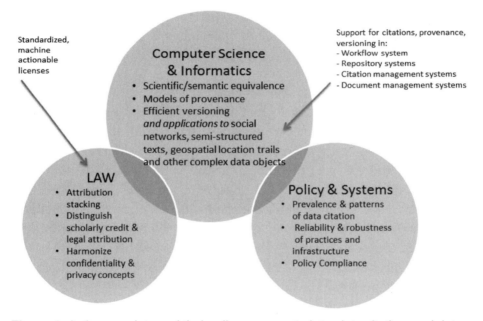

Figure 1. Actions on data and their reliance on metadata, data citation, and data management (adapted from Altman, 2012).

In the last decade, substantial effort has been made and insights achieved in the "science of science" and in the "science of science policy." Much of this work is based upon analysis of scientific outputs and collaborations, and it uses bibliographic data describing research publications as its primary evidence base. It is primarily from bibliographic data (and secondarily from analysis of the texts of the publications themselves) that we have been able to map the universe of scientific practice and results. If publications are the stars and planets of the scientific universe, data are the "dark matter"—influential but largely unobserved in our mapping process. A robust and open data citation infrastructure would render visible this dark matter, improving our understanding of the practice of science and improving science policy.

ACKNOWLEDGMENTS

This chapter is a summary of the two-year report from the CODATA-ICSTI Task Group on Data Citation Standards and Practices entitled "Out of Cite, Out of Mind" that was released in summer 2013 through the *CODATA Data Science Journal* (CODATA-ICSTI, 2013). In addition to the topics covered in this chapter, that report has an extensive discussion of many organizations playing different roles in developing policies and practices for data citation through different communities of scientific practice. It also contains an extensive bibliography on the topic of data citation.

The CODATA-ICSTI Task Group was first organized in 2010 jointly by the international and interdisciplinary Committee on Data for Science and Technology (CODATA) and International Council for Scientific and Technical Information (ICSTI). Both CODATA and ICSTI adhere to the International Council for Science (ICSU), a nongovernmental umbrella scientific organization headquartered in Paris, France. Additional information about all three groups is available at: www.codata.org, www.icsti.org, and www.icsu.org, respectively.

The CODATA-ICSTI Task Group members besides the authors are (in alphabetical order): Micah Altman, Elizabeth Arnaud, Todd Carpenter, Vishwas Chavan, Mark Hahnel, John Helly, Puneet Kishor, Jianhui Li, Franciel Azpurua Linares, Brian McMahon, Karen Morgenroth, Yasuhiro Murayama, Fiona Murphy, Giri Palanisami, Mark Parsons, Soren Roug, Helge Sagen, Eefke Smit, Martie J. van Deventer, Michael Witt, and Koji Zettsu.

Consultants to the Task Group are: William L. Anderson, Daniel Cohen, Yvonne Socha, Melissa L. Turcios, and Lili Zhang. The Task Group Project Director is Paul Uhlir, and the CODATA Executive Committee Liaison is Niv Ahituv (until April 2013) and Bonnie Carroll (since April 2013).

NOTES

1. The views expressed here are those of the co-author and not necessarily those of the National Research Council or the National Academy of Sciences.

2. Note that, though matters such as integrity and provenance are relevant for determining if data are suitable for use in new research, these cannot be determined from the citation alone, as they cannot be embedded in the citation itself. Instead, discovery of provenance and integrity information can be facilitated by citation through providing links to other relevant information.

3. It is important, however, not to conflate the DOI, which is a persistent ID and *part* of the citation, with the citation itself. DOIs do not by themselves address provenance, fixity, nor granularity, among other things.

REFERENCES

Altman, M. (2012). Data citation in the Dataverse Network. In P. F. Uhlir (Ed.), *For attribution: Developing scientific data attribution and citation practices and standards: Summary of an international workshop* (pp. 99–106). Washington, DC: National Academies Press. Retrieved from http://www.nap.edu/catalog.php?record_id=13564

Altman, M., & King, G. (2007). A proposed standard for the scholarly citation of quantitative data. *D-Lib Magazine, 13*(3/4). Retrieved from http://www.dlib.org/dlib/march07/altman/03altman.html

Ball, A., & Duke, M. (2012). *How to cite datasets and link to publications.* DCC How-to Guides. Edinburgh, Scotland: Digital Curation Centre. Retrieved from http://www.dcc.ac.uk/resources/how-guides

Berns, K. I., Bond, E. C., & Manning, F. J. (Eds.). (1996). *Resource sharing in biomedical research.* Washington, DC: National Academies Press. Retrieved from http://www.nap.edu/catalog.php?record_id=5429

Borgman, C. L. (2007). *Scholarship in the digital age: Information, infrastructure, and the Internet.* Boston, MA: MIT Press.

Borgman, C. L. (2012). The conundrum of sharing research data. *Journal of the American Society for Information Science and Technology, 63*(6), 1059–1078. http://dx.doi.org/10.1002/asi.22634

Brase, J., Farquhar, A., Gastl, A., Gruttemeier, H., Heijne, M., Heller, A., . . . Sens, I. (2009). Approach for a joint global registration agency for research data. *Information Services and Use, 29*(1), 13–27. http://dx.doi.org/10.3233/ISU-2009-0595

Callaghan, S., Donegan, S., Pepler, S., Thorley, M., Cunningham, N., Kirsch, P., . . . Wright, D. (2012). Making data a first class scientific output: Data citation and publication by NERC's environmental data centres. *International Journal of Digital Curation, 7*(1), 107–113. http://dx. doi.org/10.2218/ijdc.v7i1.218

CODATA-ICSTI Task Group on Data Citation Standards and Practices. (2013). Out of cite, out of mind: The current state of practice, policy, and technology for the citation of data. *CODATA Data Science Journal, 12.*

Committee on the Preservation of Geoscience Data and Collections, Committee on Earth Resources, & National Research Council. (2002). *Geoscience data and collections: National resources in peril.* Washington, DC: National Academies Press. Retrieved from http://www.nap.edu/ catalog.php?record_id=10348

Committee on Responsibilities of Authorship in the Biological Sciences & National Research Council. (2003). *Sharing publication-related data and materials: Responsibilities of authorship in the life sciences.* Washington, DC: National Academies Press. Retrieved from http:// www.nap.edu/catalog.php?record_id=10613

Fienberg, S. E., Martin, M. E., & Straf, M. L. (Eds.). (1985). *Sharing research data.* Washington, DC: National Academies Press. Retrieved from http://www.nap.edu/catalog.php?record_id=2033

Green, T. (2009). We need publishing standards for data sets and data tables. *OECD Publishing White Papers*, OECD Publishing. http://dx.doi. org/10.1787/787355886123

Helly, J. (1998). New concepts of publication. *Nature, 393*, 107. http:// dx.doi.org/10.1038/30086

Helly, J., Elvins, T., Sutton, D., & Martinez, D. (1999). A method for interoperable digital libraries and data repositories. *Future Generation Computer Systems, 16*(1), 21–28. Retrieved from http://www.sdsc. edu/~hellyj/papers/FGCS_jjh01.pdf

Helly, J., Elvins, T. T., Sutton, D., Martinez, D., Miller, S. E., Pickett, S., & Ellison, A. M. (2002). Controlled publication of digital scientific data. *Communications of the ACM, 45*(5), 97–101. Retrieved from http:// www.sdsc.edu/~hellyj/papers/CACM2002.pdf

Lawrence, B., Pepler, S., Jones, C., Matthews, B., McGarva, G., Coles, S., & Hey, J. (Eds.). (2007, May). *Linking data and publications in the environmental sciences: CLADDIER project workshop.* Southampton, UK: CLADDIER project. Retrieved from http://eprints.soton.ac.uk/46207/

Shirky, C. (2010). *Cognitive surplus: How technology makes consumers into collaborators.* New York: Penguin.

Sieber, J. (1991). *Sharing social science data.* Newbury Park, CA: Sage Publications.

Starr, J., & Gastl, A. (2011). IsCitedBy: A metadata scheme for Datacite. *D-Lib Magazine, 17*(1/2). http://dx.doi.org/10.1045/january2011-starr

Staudigel, H., Helly, J., Koppers, A., Shaw, H. F., McDonough, W. F., Hofmann, A. W., . . . Zindler, A. (2003). Electronic data publication in geochemistry. *Geochemistry, Geophysics, Geoscience, 4*(3). http://dx.doi.org/10.1029/2002GC000314

Tilmes, C., Yesha, Y., & Halem, M. (2011). Distinguishing provenance equivalence of earth science data. *Procedia Computer Science, 4,* 548–557. http://dx.doi.org/10.1016/j.procs.2011.04.0057

Towne, L., Wise, L. L., & Winters, T. M. (Eds.). (2004). *Advancing scientific research in education.* Washington, DC: National Academies Press. Retrieved from http://www.nap.edu/catalog.php?record_id=11112

Uhlir, P. F., & Schröder, P. (2007). Open data for global science. *Data Science Journal, 6,* 36–53. Retrieved from https://www.jstage.jst.go.jp/article/dsj/6/0/6_0_OD36/_pdf

Wynholds, L. (2011). Linking to scientific data: Identity problems of unruly and poorly bounded digital objects. *International Journal of Digital Curation, 6*(1), 214–225. http://dx.doi.org/10.2218/ijdc.v6i1.183

Part 4

ARCHIVING AND MANAGING RESEARCH DATA IN REPOSITORIES

9 | Assimilating Digital Repositories Into the Active Research Process

TYLER WALTERS

INTRODUCTION

Digital repositories, including institutional repositories (IRs), are being integrated into emerging systems of e-research and associated virtual sites. These repositories are evolving to support large interdisciplinary research communities throughout the entire life cycle of the research process. Several factors are driving this development. Sponsored research, particularly in the science and engineering domains, is becoming increasingly multi-institutional. National research agendas, such as those funded by the National Science Foundation and the National Institutes of Health, often necessitate inter-institutional collaboration in the form of "Big Science" projects. Many of these projects are interdisciplinary in nature, involving scientists and humanists from many fields (e.g., computer/information scientists and engineers working with epidemiologists, historians, sociologists, and psychologists). Thus, professionals from numerous institutions and countries may be involved. Given this evolving system of collaboration, virtual systems and environments are changing rapidly to provide the information technology and communications infrastructure necessary for open networked research.

In recent years, developers of digital repositories have begun addressing earlier stages of the research life cycle. Researchers are using repositories to deposit data generated in the first stages of a research project. In these cases, repositories become platforms where research team members can review datasets, annotate them, and share commentaries, assessments, and interpretations within the research group. Repository platforms also increasingly are becoming modular, and some systems are evolving to facilitate virtual collaboration during project planning. Stages supported often include research project conception, grant proposal development, project scheduling and milestone setting, note-taking, meeting support, and synchronous and asynchronous communications required by research teams and other involved university units. Digital repositories are maturing into content and asset management components of broader ecosystems, ones that support communication and documentation, in addition to the research process itself and its associated results.

Repositories also are being integrated into the middle of research projects by providing interfacing with software tools necessary for e-research. These tools are used to discover, analyze, and visualize datasets. Many researchers rely upon digital tools for mining text, images, graphics, and numeric and geospatial data. These tools need to be discoverable within a research community. They must be stored and preserved as applications and at the code level. As a result, researchers are using digital repositories to preserve as well as interface with these software tools. Repositories are also being integrated with the communication tools of virtual communities. Social media tools and community networking capabilities are overlaying repositories to link data, people, and a myriad of web-based resources.

IRs and other types of digital repositories are evolving to help manage not only the research data, but also the secondary information generated as researchers share data and methodologies and communicate about results. They are becoming part of the research community infrastructure as content stores, providing access to vast amounts of research data and additional information that researchers and other interested people use, both after research projects are completed and during earlier, active research phases. The quickly expanding roles and capabilities of digital repositories reflect the researchers' desires to emulate and extend their *physical worlds* into their virtual, online realms.

Existing IR platforms, such as DSpace and Fedora, are being used in managing research data and are beginning to form the core of a technology stack that provides for some of the other aforementioned tools and services. For instance, universities such as the University of Illinois at Urbana-Champaign, the Massachusetts Institute of Technology, and several others are using their DSpace IRs for repositing files of research data. Others, such as the multi-institutional Dryad organization (http://datadryad.org), which holds datasets referenced in many bioscience journals, has built data repositories on the DSpace platform with many customizations to meet data depositors' and users' needs. Other institutions are customizing their Fedora-based repositories for data management. The University of Virginia's IR, Libra (http://libra.virginia.edu), is an example of a Fedora-based repository taking in research data. The University of Virginia with Stanford University and the University of Hull (United Kingdom) have advanced the Fedora platform through the Hydra project (http://projecthydra.org). Hydra is a stack of technology components comprised of a central repository with multiple "heads" that provide for specific workflows and user interfaces; it is based on the Fedora repository software, Solr, Ruby on Rails, and Blacklight. Penn State's ScholarSphere (https://scholarsphere.psu.edu) is a recent example of a Hydra/Fedora repository. A similar Fedora-based technology stack is Islandora (http://www.islandora.ca), which is built on Fedora, Drupal, and Solr, created by the University of Prince Edward Island University Robertson Library (Canada) and subsequently supported by the company Discovery Garden (http://www.discoverygarden.ca). Islandora is being used by many universities and government research facilities, primarily in North America and Europe. Repository systems are becoming part of a more complex and robust technology environment, serving researchers in their information management, data management, and virtual community needs.

SERVING EMERGING VIRTUAL RESEARCH "ECOSYSTEMS"

Repositories exist to serve research, and research is becoming more inter-institutional, interdisciplinary, and international. Consequently, it is being conducted within virtual platforms. In this virtual realm, research instru-mentation, data and information, and communication are digital. A new *virtual research ecosystem* is on the rise, involving all research stages, from project conception, proposal, and implementation to communication, data capture, and publishing.

Protein crystallography research (Figure 1) taking place in Australia provides an example of how this emerging ecosystem is supported by digital repositories. This is a national-level research program with international ties. Australian protein crystallographers use the Australian Synchrotron (a particle accelerator) to conduct their experiments. The crystallographic data produced by the synchrotron is initially stored in a local research data store while the metadata is automatically extracted and stored in a local instance of MyTARDIS. The synchrotron's data store is limited in size, so raw data is only retained for a few months. If the researcher's institution has a local instance of MyTARDIS, then the raw data and its metadata are immediately transferred from the synchrotron to the researcher's local instance (Androulakis et al., 2009). The researcher's local MyTARDIS platform is then used to review, process, share, and prepare datasets for publication. To enhance the use, reuse, and discovery of publicly available protein crystallographic data, collection-level metadata is disseminated in a variety of ways:

- TARDIS, or The Australian Repositories for Diffraction ImageS, is a national registry of protein crystallographic data. It federates Australian crystallographic data collections by harvesting publically available, discipline-rich, collection-level metadata from each of the instances of MyTARDIS.
- Research Data Australia, operated by the Australian National Data Service, is a national registry of research data. It federates Australian research data collections by harvesting generic, collection-level metadata from each of the Australian research data repositories (including MyTARDIS).
- MyTARDIS can also facilitate the publication of its data and metadata with the Protein Data Bank in the United States.

The Australian example is but one national-level scheme that illustrates the emergence of a virtual ecosystem of research and the incorporation of digital repositories (Androulakis et al., 2008).

SUPPORTING EARLY-STAGE DEPOSIT AND RELATED RESEARCH ACTIVITIES

Increasingly, researchers are utilizing digital repositories in the early phases of research. In particular, early-stage deposit is becoming a popular approach in e-research settings because it facilitates early analysis of digital data. Once raw and lightly processed data are deposited, tools embedded within or alongside repositories are used to share this data with other researchers. These researchers then can annotate and comment on the data and share early interpretations. Cyberinfrastructure projects like the Sustainable Environment Actionable Data initiative (SEAD, http://

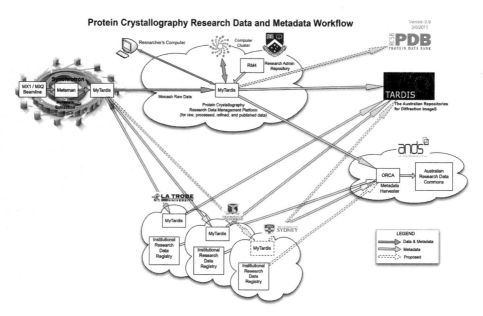

Figure 1. The Australian protein crystallography research data and metadata workflow. Courtesy of Anthony Beitz and Steve Androulakis, Monash University, TARDIS.

sead-data.net) are incorporating social media tools to support early data sharing as well as ensuing communications (Plale et al., 2013). Tools also can be used to automatically capture metadata and make it available in the repository. The Data Conservancy at Johns Hopkins University (http://dataconservancy.org) uses tools to automate metadata capture (Choudhury & Hanisch, 2009). The targeted metadata is defined by the data producers (i.e., individuals working at the institutions with which the Data Conservancy collaborates). Then the Data Conservancy uses tools to aggregate the metadata and share it with other portals and repositories, such as with the National Snow and Ice Data Center (NSIDC, http://nsidc.org) via its data search systems and access tools (Scharfen et al., 2000). The NSIDC's system, known as Reverb, allows researchers to search, discover, and order data from repositories managed by the NSIDC and other related data centers. It supports data subsetting, FTP distribution of datasets, and image browsing. NSIDC also operates the new IceBridge Portal, which provides access to all Operation IceBridge reports and visualizations of the NSIDC's flights over Greenland. Additionally, the NSIDC provides researchers with its own suite of tools for data analysis and imaging (http://nsidc.org/data/tools). These are shared among several national-level scientific data centers. The tools and services being leveraged by data management programs like SEAD, the Data Conservancy, and the NSIDC illustrate that digital data curation is evolving to facilitate data storage and sharing during earlier stages of the data/information life cycle.

PROVIDING ACCESS TO SOFTWARE TOOLS

Researchers are beginning to rely on digital repositories for access to tools and toolkits they need for discovery, analysis, visualization, and mining (e.g., text, image, spatial, and numeric) of datasets. Various types of software tools are being used today, including open source, proprietary, community-built, custom-built, and discipline-specific. Currently, there is much focus on creating new tools and toolkits and expanding capabilities to allow access to existing ones. The DataONE project, a global data network focusing on environmental science (Michener et al., 2012), is a leading example. DataONE's Investigator Toolkit incorporates many existing tools such as MyExperiment, MATLAB, Kepler, Medeley, the Data Management Planning Tool (DMPTool), and many others (Sallans & Donnelly, 2012). As DataONE focuses on expanding its already robust toolkit, the DataONE Users Group is identifying and prioritizing new tool additions. Other repository programs, such as the Oak Ridge National Laboratory's Distributed Active Archive Center for Biogeochemical Dynamics (DAAC), host and link to many software tools that allow users to search for data by type, address visualization and analytical needs, perform data subsetting, and use other web-based querying and discovery services. This linking of tools and services by the DataONE project and DAAC illustrates the large-scale cooperation and collaboration taking place among research communities and the significant role repositories play.

While repository developers are improving the usefulness and usability of software tools, researchers and repository managers must be able to sustain the tools themselves. Given this need, digital repositories are becoming repositories for tools as well, describing, preserving, and organizing access to them. One example is the HathiTrust Research Center (HTRC) and its digital repository (Plale, Poole, McDonald, & Unsworth, 2012). The HTRC maintains a repository of text mining algorithms and retrieval tools available online for discovery. These tools "cover a wide variety of functions ranging from simple statistical analysis of words to complex algorithms relating concepts and meaning" (http://www.hathitrust.org/htrc_collections_tools). The HTRC is working with the Software Environment for the Advancement of Scholarly Research (SEASR), which is an Andrew W. Mellon Foundation-funded project providing "a research and development environment capable of powering leading-edge digital humanities initiatives," that "fosters collaboration by empowering scholars to share data and research in virtual work environments" (http://seasr.org). They have collaborated on tools development such as Author Search, which integrates the two organizations' infrastructures to support textual analysis and visualization with analytical processing capabilities. They also have worked together to integrate the use of Zotero in SEASR services and to use HTRC collections to generate visualizations, including social network relationships. The HTRC also registers any derived datasets, indexes, and versions in their registry repository. The HTRC identifies and hosts existing data analyses from the corpus of the HathiTrust Digital Library as well as other text mining, retrieval, and analytical tools that are of interest to their community. Digital repositories are managing scholarship and data, but they also are managing all manner of software, digital tools, and other related source codes to serve and sustain the new virtual research ecosystem.

CONNECTING VIRTUAL COMMUNITIES AND LINKING DATA

Today, some of the more important changes in digital repository development are occurring as a result of increased dependence on community networks. Researchers and others involved in the research process are communicating virtually throughout the research project (Walters & Skinner, 2001). Repository developers with the SEAD initiative are recognizing and responding to this (Plale et al., 2013). They are utilizing cyberinfrastructure to build and support and ever-expanding research community. SEAD uses software platforms such as the VIVO researcher network software (http://vivoweb.org) to connect researchers with one another and their research outputs (Krafft et al., 2010). VIVO is the platform used by the SEAD group to support virtual collaboration and discovery among scientists and scholars. SEAD uses other tools as well, such as Medici, which was developed at the University of Illinois at Urbana-Champaign. Medici (http://medici.ncsa.illinois.edu) is used for data processing and previewing, and it is incorporated into the VIVO network (McHenry, Ondrejcek, Marini, Kooper, & Bajcsy, 2011). The SEAD group is developing a robust platform for what they call the *social curation* of data within a virtual community platform. The SEAD virtual environment supports activities such as coauthorship, shared tagging, microcitation, threaded discussions, and reviewing and commenting on data and research projects. It offers shared project repositories, workflow support for cofunded projects, and an array of data visualization capabilities.

Other repository teams have taken related but different directions with their platforms and services. The Purdue University Research Repository (PURR, https://purr.purdue.edu) focuses on workflow support for research teams involved in the pre-award phase (Witt, 2012). A host of capabilities support team collaboration, such as virtual workspaces and tools for research proposal writing, to-do lists, calendaring, forums, project notes, file-sharing, tagging, blogs, and wikis. While emphasis is on the proposal phase, PURR supports ongoing communication and information sharing via these tools throughout the research process, and it provides support for other important research steps as well. It connects with other tools, such as the DMPTool, for data management planning and the California Digital Library's DOI-provisioning service to publish data with unique identifiers (Starr, Willett, Federer, Horning, & Bergstrom, 2012). These services help to integrate the repository platform into the early, active phases of a research project. PURR's capabilities also are integrated into Purdue's HUBzero software (http://hubzero.org/), which forms the foundation of the repository architecture in PURR (McLennan & Kennell, 2010). The SEAD and PURR examples demonstrate how repositories are being thought of more holistically, tying them to virtual spaces where researchers collaborate, communicate, and use data.

ENHANCING INSTITUTIONAL REPOSITORIES

While data use and curation drive many of the new developments in repository design and architecture, traditional institutional repositories and *papers* still have a place in the virtual research ecosystem. From a technological perspective, IRs can be more effective if they have services over an active content layer that is backed up by and harvested into a federated archive infrastructure, one which draws from institutional resources such as the

IR (Figure 2). Through such an architecture, scholarly documents, along with data, websites, and personal web profiles (e.g., a researcher's VIVO profile) can be published as structured data, interlinked, and queried on the web as linked data elements (http://www.w3.org/standards/semanticweb/data). In this linked data environment, researchers can tag and annotate data, overlay it with other data sources, organize it using domain-based terminology (e.g., ontology), and link it with online conversations between researchers.

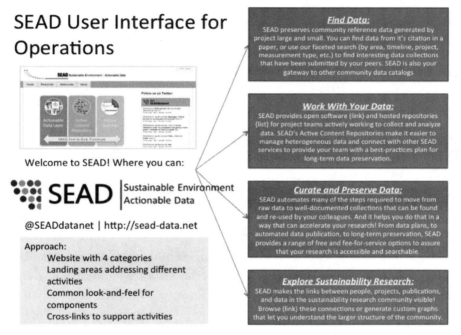

Figure 2. Image taken from the Sustainable Environment Actionable Data (SEAD) DataNet Project Prototype. SEAD is funded by the National Science Foundation under cooperative agreement #OCI0940824 (http://sead-data.net).

In the example of the SEAD project, they approach the described architecture in three components: the SEAD Active Content Repository (ACR), SEAD VIVO (their social networking platform), and the SEAD Virtual Archive (VA). Researchers using SEAD can submit data, use and annotate it, as well as search for other datasets in the ACR. The ACR leverages tools such as Dropbox for deposit and provides web interfaces and mapping tools to view and interact with the data. Data submitters control the data in the ACR, specifically, who can access and view it before publishing or moving it to another more open repository. SEAD's VIVO layer provides researcher profiles that include links to the person's citations, publications, and datasets. Researchers will use SEAD VIVO to search for other researchers of interest and reach out to them, thus promoting communication and collaboration between researchers. The VA is a component that supports the researcher's movement of datasets from the ACR to other long-term preservation and access systems, such as IRs. Current VA work has tested moving datasets from the VA to DSpace-based institutional repositories at Indiana University Bloomington and the University of Illinois at Urbana-Champaign. Enhancing IRs through technology stacks as SEAD has done will become more prevalent.

CONCLUSION

In the ten or so years of the IR's existence, it has evolved to become a mainstay in the virtual research ecosystem. Through web services, repositories can enhance their usefulness and capabilities by offering access to tools for data and scholarship use, visualization, and analysis. They also can provide access to applications and middleware used to assign unique identifiers and format identifiers and registries. However, the nature of the digital repository itself is changing far beyond these capabilities due to the influence of research data repositories and the research communities that use them. They are becoming workspaces, holding content of myriad types during the course of a research project. A researcher's ability to deposit early forms of research data—be they numeric data from a scientific experiment, or survey and interview data from a social science project—and review, annotate, comment, tag, and share it is becoming essential to a repository's usefulness. The repository is now a part of the *social curation phase*, which has been articulated by the SEAD project and in other virtual research communities.

Preserving and providing access to data and scholarship in repositories is no longer enough. People want to *do things* with that data and scholarship. The offering of tools within the repository as well as outside it (through web services, for example) is just one area of repository growth and development. Repository-human interfaces and repository-software application interfaces also are changing the way researchers interact with digital repositories. Even the very use of research data is altering due to new, emerging tools, as is being witnessed with the independently developed and codeveloped tools of the HTRC and SEASR. New platforms for collaboration, discovery, and communication, such as VIVO, as well as semantic web standards, such as linked data, provide new ways to interact with, utilize, and represent research data, scholarship, communications, and virtual representations of researchers. Institutional repositories can be leveraged in these ecosystems with all of these robust tools and standards as researchers come to rely upon them to retain and publish datasets, scholarship, and other forms of research information. In addition, with proper associated tools, they become platforms to serve research design and conception, grant proposal development, and collaborative efforts to formalize research projects. They are now virtual environments where research teams review, analyze, vet, comment on, and tag data and information. While continuing to evolve, repositories are proving to be a cornerstone in the emerging and highly active virtual research ecosystem.

ACKNOWLEDGMENTS

This chapter is based on a paper presented at the SPARC Open Access meeting, Kansas City, MO, March 12, 2012.

The author would like to acknowledge the conversations, advice, and input from the following colleagues in the production of the paper: Suzie Allard, University of Tennessee-Knoxville; Anthony Beitz and Steve Androulakis, Monash University and TARDIS; Robert McDonald, Indiana University and SEAD; William Michener, University of New Mexico and DataONE; and Sayeed Choudhury, Johns Hopkins University and the Data Conservancy.

REFERENCES

Androulakis, S., Buckle, A. M., Atkinson, I., Groenewegen, D., Nicholas, N., Treloar, A., & Beitz, A. (2009). ARCHER—E-research tools for research data management. *International Journal of Digital Curation*, *4*(1), 22–33. http://dx.doi.org/10.2218/ijdc.v4i1.75

Androulakis, S., Schmidberger, J., Bate, M. A., DeGori, R., Beitz, A., Keong, C., . . . Buckle, A. M. (2008). Federated repositories of X-ray diffraction images. *Acta Crystallographica*, *D64*(7), 810–814. http://dx.doi.org/10.1107/S0907444908015540

Choudhury, S., & Hanisch, R. (2009, December). *The data conservancy: Building a sustainable system for interdisciplinary scientific data curation and preservation.* Paper presented at the European Space Agency's PV 2009, Madrid, Spain. Retrieved from http://www.sciops.esa.int/SYS/CONFERENCE/include/pv2009/papers/47_Choudhury_DataConservancy.pdf

Krafft, D. B., Cappadona, N. A., Caruso, B., Corson-Rikert, J., Devare, M., Lowe, B. J., & VIVO Collaboration. (2010, April). VIVO: Enabling national networking of scientists. Paper presented at the Web Science Conference 2010, Raleigh, NC. Retrieved from http://vivoweb.org/files/websci10_submission_82.pdf

McHenry, K., Ondrejcek, M., Marini, L., Kooper, R., & Bajcsy, P. (2011). Towards a universal viewer for digital content. *Procedia Computer Science, 4,* 732–739. http://dx.doi.org/10.1016/j.procs.2011.04.077

McLennan, M., & Kennell, R. (2010). HUBzero: A platform for dissemination and collaboration in computational science and engineering. *Computing in Science & Engineering, 12*(2), 48–53. http://dx.doi.org/10.1109/MCSE.2010.41

Michener, W. K., Allard, S., Budden, A., Cook, R. B., Douglass, K., Frame, M., . . . Vieglais, D. A. (2012). Participatory design of DataONE—Enabling cyberinfrastructure for the biological and environmental sciences. *Ecological Informatics, 11,* 5–15. http://dx.doi.org/10.1016/j.ecoinf.2011.08.007

Plale, B., McDonald, R. H., Chandrasekar, K., Kouper, I., Konkiel, S., Hedstrom, M. L., . . . Kumar, P. (2013, January). *SEAD Virtual Archive: Building a federation of institutional repositories for long-term data preservation in sustainability science.* Practice paper presented at the 8th International Digital Curation Conference, Amsterdam, Netherlands. Retrieved from http://hdl.handle.net/2022/15247

Plale, B. A., Poole, M. S., McDonald, R., & Unsworth, J. (2012). *HathiTrust Research Center: Computational research on the HathiTrust repository.* IU ScholarWorks Repository. Retrieved from http://hdl.handle.net/2022/14133

Sallans, A., & Donnelly, M. (2012). DMP Online and DMPTool: Different strategies towards a shared goal. *International Journal of Digital Curation, 7*(2), 123–129. http://dx.doi.org/10.2218/ijdc.v7i2.235

Scharfen, G. R., Hall, D. K., Khalsa, S. J. S., Khalsa, S., Wolfe, J. D., Marquis, M. C., . . . McLean, B. (2000). Accessing the MODIS snow and ice products at the NSIDC DAAC. In *Geoscience and Remote Sensing Symposium, 2000. Proceedings. IGARSS 2000. IEEE 2000 International* (Vol. 5, pp. 2059–2061).

Starr, J., Willett, P., Federer, L., Horning, C., & Bergstrom, M. L. (2012). A collaborative framework for data management services: The experience of the University of California. *Journal of eScience Librarianship, 1*(2), 7. http://dx.doi.org/10.7191/jeslib.2012.1014

Walters, T., & Skinner, K. (2011). *New roles for new times: Digital curation for preservation.* Washington, DC: Association of Research Libraries. Retrieved from http://www.arl.org/bm~doc/nrnt_digital_curation17mar11

Witt, M. (2012, April). *Curation service models: Purdue University Research Repository.* Paper presented at the ASIS&T Research Data Access & Preservation Summit, New Orleans, LA. Retrieved from http://docs.lib.purdue.edu/lib_fspres/3/

10 | Partnering to Curate and Archive Social Science Data

JARED LYLE, GEORGE ALTER, AND ANN GREEN

OVERVIEW

Improvements in data processing and storage technology are resulting in an increase in research data on a variety of social, economic, and political subjects. Many datasets could be profitably reanalyzed, but they are at danger of being lost since they are never properly archived. Institutional repositories (IRs) are charged to preserve the scholarly products of their faculty or institution and are increasingly tapped to add data services, but not all feel prepared to curate and archive data. In some cases, IRs work closely with local experts who have a history of supporting data on their campuses (for example, data specialists who serve as Inter-university Consortium for Political and Social Research (ICPSR) official representatives (ORs) or statistical computing consultants), but in many cases we have found that IR managers would welcome additional support for their data curation efforts.

ICPSR, a research center in the Institute for Social Research at the University of Michigan and the world's largest archive of social science data, led an Institute of Museum and Library Services (IMLS)-funded project exploring how specialized domain repositories can partner with IRs to curate and preserve data. In this chapter, we describe why partnerships are important, explore guidelines we developed to help IRs and others partner to curate and archive data, and discuss the resulting services and tools we propose repositories will find most helpful when working with data. While our project was directed at IRs, we emphasize the relevance of the guidance and proposed tools and services to anyone who works with data, especially information professionals.

WHY PARTNERSHIPS

Although ICPSR has more than 50 years of experience archiving social science data, we know that a large number of valuable, unarchived datasets exist. As part of the Data Preservation Alliance for the Social Sciences (Data-PASS), a partnership of social science data archives sponsored by the Library of Congress, ICPSR identified more than 11,000 National Science Foundation (NSF) and National Institutes of Health (NIH) grants for social science research that may have produced data. ICPSR then contacted 6,500 grantees, and the organization found that more than 800 have data that are at risk of being lost. Overall, the Data-PASS project found that less than a quarter of all datasets have been archived, but the vast majority of researchers report that the data are still available in some form (Pienta, Gutmann, Hoelter, Lyle, & Donakowski, 2008). More recently, ICPSR conducted a survey of NSF and NIH researchers and found that just 12 percent of data produced by research awards have been formally archived. The vast majority of awards are either shared informally (45 percent) or never shared beyond the research team (44 percent) (Pienta, Alter, & Lyle, 2010).

The spread of institutional digital repositories offers hope that many of these valuable data collections can be saved. Institutional repositories can draw upon institutional loyalties and personal contacts to encourage faculty to reveal and deposit their research materials. As more and more faculty members learn that depositing in an IR preserves and enhances their scholarship, it is possible that even more materials will be revealed. Although ICPSR and other specialized domain repositories are intensely dedicated to the preservation of data, our resources are limited, and we cannot afford to discover, much less curate, all of the worthwhile data produced by researchers.

As Lynch has suggested, an IR can "act as an entry point for redistributing works to systems of disciplinary repositories" (2003, p. 6). Further, Green and Gutmann highlight the importance and benefits of collaboration throughout the entire data life cycle, not just at the redistribution point:

> Early partnerships that match the skills and knowledge of the data producer (data production) with those of the repository (data life cycle management expertise and long-term curation planning) can have significant impacts: efforts made in

the data production stages will reap long-term benefits in the publishing, reuse, and archiving stages. Informed selection of file formats and metadata standards at the creation of digital resources can increase both short- and long-term benefits. It is necessary to provide tools and processes that make best practices attractive and cost effective at the design and production phases of the data life cycle. (2007, p. 43)

NEED FOR SUPPORT

While we are encouraged by the possibilities of the IR movement to inform and disseminate data, we also are concerned that lack of experience in curating and archiving data will pose a serious problem. Most IRs have grown out of initiatives to archive and share digital texts, and they have limited experience dealing with quantitative or qualitative data. Social science data, in particular, such as surveys and vital statistics stored in statistical analysis software, pose special problems for selection, preservation, and documentation.

Thus, there is a need for guidelines to inform IRs about best practices in archiving social science data and specialized services for unusual or complex curatorial tasks. The ICPSR *Guide to Social Science Data Preparation and Archiving* (2012b) and similar guides from the United Kingdom Data Archive (Van den Eynden, Corti, Woollard, Bishop, & Horton, 2011) and MIT Libraries (2013) are written to help data creators and depositors. The Joint Information Systems Committee (JISC)-funded DISC-UK DataShare project (2007–2009) created a compilation of issues and resources that repositories can use as a decision-making and policy-planning tool if they are contemplating taking data into their repository collections (Green, McDonald, & Rice, 2009). However, none of these guides and documents cover the full range of issues faced by IRs as they take on the challenges of curating research data.

GUIDELINES

Through partnerships with librarians and repository managers, we have developed guidelines to help IRs find, curate, and archive data.[1] In many instances, it is advantageous for IRs to partner with specialized repositories to conduct each task. We focus here on working with data once a project is complete, acknowledging that in an ideal world a data producer would consult with a data curator, specialized archive, or IR about proper data standards and collaboration from the start of the project, when best practices can be built into the workflows to generate well-formed and fully curated data collections.

We selected social science history data as our pilot projects to inform the guidelines since these data pose a broader range of problems than most social science data, and since they are highly endangered. Some of the leaders in the field, such as Robert Fogel, Charles Tilly, and Alice Hanson Jones, made their social science history data available to other researchers almost immediately through ICPSR. Unfortunately, though, many important datasets are not presently available. As Allan G. Bogue, second president of the Social Science History Association, pointed out, the practice of sharing and reusing data was not (and still is not) strongly established in some disciplines (1979). Most disciplines and information professionals face similar challenges of finding, curating, and archiving data, and can draw from the guidelines shared below.

Find

Once a project is completed—data collection long-finished and analysis finalized—the first step of curating data is finding it. Many data producers move quickly to the next project, taking little time to organize, label, and describe data and documentation. If the project had not built in good data management practices from the beginning, the data are likely shaped, organized, and distributed according to the idiosyncrasies of the project staff. For projects with multiple data files and formats, these can be especially challenging to find and select relevant material essential to understanding the study. Research projects typically generate multiple versions of data and documentation.

To help find relevant data and documentation files, consider these questions:

- Where are all files located? An inventory can help catalog available data and documentation.
- Which of these files were used for the final analysis?
- Which of the final versions are the data files? Which are the documentation files?

- Which of the final versions are needed to make the data collection complete and self-explanatory for future users?

Speaking directly with the primary investigators and research staff is the ideal way to find answers. Researchers often rely on graduate students or research assistants to handle data management. These people are excellent additional sources for both information about the data collection and copies of the data and documentation. That said, it can be challenging to find original staff from older studies; even if found, memories are likely to have faded.

Great secondary sources for piecing together the context of a data collection include grant applications, study descriptions, abstracts, publications, or other documents that describe the project as a whole or the research questions addressed by the study. File names and other information embedded within the files, such as date of last modification, are also useful clues.

Institutional repository staff, whether on their own or working closely with their local data librarians and subject specialists, are among the best poised to make the direct connections with researchers to comb memories and are usually closest to search for the physical sources of information. Domain repositories can consult, where needed, on the media, formats, and data structures typically used for the specified data collection.

Case Studies: Find

In our case studies, finding the relevant data and documentation turned out to be one of the most challenging and frustrating issues. One investigator, for instance, provided his partner IR with over 80 distinct pieces of removable media and very general instructions on what to find. From these media, more than 30,000 files (11.5 gigabytes) were identified. Finding the relevant files felt somewhat like searching for a needle in a digital haystack. Many, if not most, of the retrieved files appeared irrelevant, such as the Internet shortcut file named "David's Favourite Captain Haddock Curses." But how to find the relevant files, and which of those were essential?

The repository began by creating an inventory of files, names, sizes, dates of last change, and types. Using the names and file types as filters, the repository teamed with ICPSR to search for what looked like relevant data. ICPSR had familiarity with the data types and could point out which files to target. We knew we were looking for Census data from the 1800s that were created and saved in the 1980s or 1990s. Figure 1 shows a potential "find": ED1870.DBF. The file name includes reference to year and, possibly, subject, with the file extension showing a likely data file.

1	Name		Size		Last Change		File Type		Path
10920	ED1870.DBF		1024.5 KB		8/29/1986 4:20 AM		.DBF (OpenOffice.org 1.1 Spreadsheet)		E:\SCX\2012\
10921	EDAW Career Opportunities.url		0.1 KB		10/20/1999 8:58 AM		.url (Internet Shortcut)		E:\SCX\2012\
10922	EDAW ISG Home.url		0.1 KB		10/20/1999 8:58 AM		.url (Internet Shortcut)		E:\SCX\2012\
10923	EDAW Main Frame.url		0.1 KB		10/20/1999 8:58 AM		.url (Internet Shortcut)		E:\SCX\2012\

Figure 1. File inventory (sorted alphabetically).

Next, we sorted the same inventory of files by date of last change (Figure 2). This yielded the most promising results, with many of the oldest files appearing to contain relevant data based on the file name and file type. These were presented to the investigator and his former graduate student for review.

1	Name		Size		Last Change		File Type		Path
114	AGE.LIS		9.1 KB		6/22/1989 4:27 PM		.LIS (LIS File)		E:\SCX\2012\
115	1850.MSP		5.7 KB		6/25/1989 7:52 AM		.MSP (Windows Installer Patch)		E:\SCX\2012\
116	1870WHAGE.LOG		0.2 KB		6/30/1989 10:20 AM		.LOG (Text Document)		E:\SCX\2012\
117	70WHAGE.XLS		1.2 KB		6/30/1989 4:32 PM		.XLS (Microsoft Excel 97-2003 Worksheet		E:\SCX\2012\
118	70WHAGE.XLC		1.0 KB		6/30/1989 4:35 PM		.XLC (XLC File)		E:\SCX\2012\
119	1850AGE.XLS		1.6 KB		7/3/1989 6:38 AM		.XLS (Microsoft Excel 97-2003 Worksheet		E:\SCX\2012\
120	1850AGE.XLC		1.3 KB		7/3/1989 6:49 AM		.XLC (XLC File)		E:\SCX\2012\
121	1850AGE.DOC		1.5 KB		7/7/1989 6:10 AM		.DOC (Microsoft Word 97 - 2003 Documer		E:\SCX\2012\

Figure 2. File inventory (sorted by date of last change).

For another investigator, the data were fairly easy to identify since they were saved on just a few 9-track tapes. More difficult was figuring out which of the hundred or so files on the tapes were the final version of the data. The investigator ended up spending considerable time sifting through his basement for hard-copy documentation files, ultimately finding the original notes his assistant used to create the final analysis file (Figure 3). Thirty-seven detailed pages document how the files were created, merged, and sorted. Tape location and file names are stated also.

Using the notes, and with an ICPSR staff member talking with him through the phases of data collection and file transformations, the investigator was able to pinpoint which file likely was the final analytic file to target for curation.

In a third example, all data from a collection were located in a former graduate student's records. ICPSR consulted on identifying all files necessary

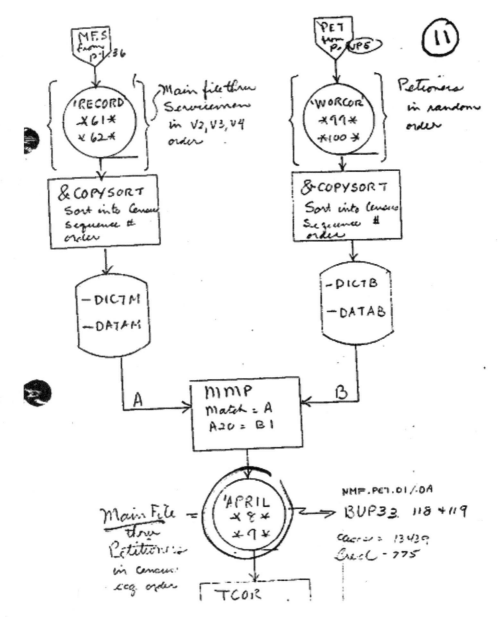

Figure 3. Original notes. Courtesy of Maris A. Vinovskis.

for extraction. However, to interpret key geographic information stored in the files, the original map from the 1970s was needed. Working with the university map librarian, the IR sifted through storage closets to locate the original map.

Recover

After data and documentation are located, organized, and prioritized, the next step is to read and recover the information. Data often are stored on computerized or digitized media. Specialized hardware and software is often necessary to read the data. Old data might need to be converted to a modern format. Note that recovery applies to hard-copy materials as well, such as codebooks, manuscripts, or supplementary documentation. Paper materials might need to be stabilized or pieced together.

Questions to consider when reading and recovering materials include:

- On what media are the relevant, final versions of the files stored (e.g., floppy disk, hard drive)?
- In what formats were they saved (e.g., Excel, SAS, proprietary database, text analysis system)?
- Can files be read using a modern computer?
- Is specialized software or hardware needed to read the files?
- What is the amount of technical effort needed to read the files?

Recovery can be expensive or full of failure. In those cases, staff will need to reevaluate the final goals of archiving the data collection. Perhaps just a partial collection will be made available, especially if recovery is cost-prohibitive.

Institutional repositories vary in their access to machinery and statistical software needed to recover and check the quality of data. Some IRs can draw upon the expertise of on-campus statistical consultancies and data librarians to read and process data, although many others cannot or simply do not feel capable or comfortable doing the work themselves. Domain repositories can recommend trustworthy vendors to convert the challenging cases or do the conversion work themselves for more standard formats and hardware.

Case Studies: Recover

All of the data from our case studies were from fairly old data collections that were created in the 1970s to 1980s. This posed unique, although generalizable, challenges. In the most straightforward case, the investigator simply e-mailed ICPSR the data and documentation files. The data were in a modern statistical format and opened just fine using current software. Documentation files opened acceptably, as well, although there were slight formatting adjustments that were needed.

For other studies, the IRs required assistance to read obsolete media and outdated file formats. For instance, one study's files were stored on four 9-track tapes. After recommending a data recovery company to retrieve the information from the tapes, ICPSR used software (Stat/Transfer) to convert the retrieved obsolete statistical file, OSIRIS (Figure 4), to a modern, readily used format (SPSS) (Figure 5). The repository did not have the expertise to handle the files, so it was happy to partner with ICPSR to make the conversion.

Figure 4. Original OSIRIS file.

Name	Type	Width	Decimals	Label
V16	Numeric	1	0	WIDOW/WIDOWER
V17	Numeric	1	0	SOCIAL CLASS
V18	Numeric	1	0	RACE
V19	Numeric	1	0	ELDERLY CHAR HEALTHY?

Figure 5. OSIRIS file converted into SPSS.

Review and Clean

As data and documentation are recovered and organized, they are ready for review. At this point, they are inspected for adequate description and completeness. To be usable, they will need to be accurate and self-explanatory.

Questions to ask about the data include:

- Are variables and values labeled?
- Are there wild or undocumented codes? For example, if a variable that records the sex of a respondent has documented codes of "0" for female and "1" for male, an undocumented code of "7" would be a wild code.
- Are there out-of-range codes? For example, a value of "387" would be out-of-range for a variable that records the age of a respondent.

- Are codes in the data reasonable? For example, if date variables contain long string text responses instead of dates, the data would not seem reasonable.
- Do the number of cases and variables in the data match what is defined in the documentation?
- Do codes in the data match what is listed in the documentation?

Questions to ask about the documentation include:

- Is there a codebook or user guide that describes the data collection, especially how variables and cases are coded, and helps users interpret the data?
- Are there relevant supplementary documentation files, such as a questionnaire or data collection instrument for survey research?
- Are all other resources included that are needed to interpret the data? For example, geographic locations may be coded according to a specific map.
- Do all documentation files match the information contained in the data files?

We want to emphasize the importance of the review and clean stage in curating data. The role the IR will take in regard to making modifications to data and documentation varies. Some IRs will not prepare enhanced materials, while others will have accepted the curatorial role of verifying and cleaning incoming files. The partnerships outlined in this chapter can support this very important step in the curation life cycle.

When making corrections to data and documentation, keep track of what is updated and retain the original files. For data files, especially, create a syntax or log file to track changes, such as changing value labels or making data recodes. This will help when reviewing files to ensure that the intended changes were made and the data files run properly. Managing this information about what changes were made to the original data file is important for tracking the versioning and provenance of data.

For data containing human subjects research, repositories should take special care. Data repositories are obligated to protect individuals' privacy. Multilevel studies (e.g., studies that include data about patients, doctors, clinics, and treatments), studies with precise dates or geocodes, and qualitative studies all pose confidentiality challenges. The same holds true for data with direct identifiers, such as social security numbers, and even combinations of indirect identifiers, such as detailed geography paired with occupations held. Confidential data require intense review and, where needed, recoding or deletion of variables and cases.

With access to proper software, IRs oftentimes can perform the basic review (described in preceding paragraphs) of data and documentation themselves, especially knowing the common errors and misplacements to seek out. Domain repositories or others familiar with statistical files can do the review on behalf of the IR or simply retrieve the basic descriptive statistics about the data, which can be enough for the IR to conduct the substantive checks for completeness and accuracy themselves.

Case Studies: Review and Clean

Like all well-used (and well-loved) data collections, our case studies required some level of cleaning to be accurate and self-explanatory. One investigator, for instance, provided 100 data and documentation files. The data were in pristine shape, with full labels and no apparent out-of-range codes. The same was true for the documentation. It was only when the repository compared the codebook against the data that one of the primary data files was discovered missing. When asked, the investigator replied that the file was never fully completed due to an unforeseen accident with his research assistant. The repository added a basic but important note in the documentation alerting users about the missing file.

Other data collections required more intensive curation. In one, for instance, codes were missing in the data file, and no further explanation could be found in the documentation (Figure 6). A variable like state/country of birth, for instance, can be near-impossible to interpret without labels for raw numeric codes.

The investigator was sought out for further information about labels for the state/country of birth codes.

Preserve

Preservation is making content available in usable and meaningful formats to current and future users. Materials, especially digital files, are susceptible to obsolescence, deterioration, corruption, and loss, although advance action can do a great deal to prevent loss and ensure long-term preservation.[2] Long-term preservation also mitigates both technological and physical threats. Preservation is not as simple as storing the files to disk or uploading to an IR system.

STATE/COUNTRY OF BIRTH

		Frequency	Percent	Valid Percent	Cumulative Percent
Valid	1	13	.1	.1	.1
	2	872	6.5	6.5	6.6
	3	9223	68.6	68.8	75.4
	4	805	6.0	6.0	81.4
	5	29	.2	.2	81.7
	6	76	.6	.6	82.2
	7	12	.1	.1	82.3
	8	48	.4	.4	82.7

Figure 6. Missing labels.

Preservation is best considered from the beginning of a research project, but many of the significant actions are implemented toward the end of a project (or perhaps long after) when correcting and making final versions of data and documentation to share. Questions to consider when preserving the data collection include:

- Are the files stored in proprietary formats? Proprietary formats can be challenging to read over time, especially if the company supporting the format goes out of business or discontinues the product line. It also means that future users will need the proprietary software to open the file. To avoid this, make a preservation copy of the proprietary format using an open format. Many data files, such as SAS, SPSS, or Excel, can be saved as ASCII text files with a supporting, descriptive file.
- Are the final files replicated and stored in distributed locations, in case of disaster or accidental loss?

Most IRs are established with preservation in mind. Persistent identifiers are assigned to the original files and to those created during the recovery process, and some form of preservation commitment guarantees, at minimum, as-is, bit-level storage. That said, as-is preservation of proprietary statistical files, such as SPSS or Stata, does not guarantee usability 5 or 50 years down the road. Domain repositories can boost preservation efforts by normalizing files to open formats that are proven to be long-lived. They also have the capability and capacity to migrate older, obsolete versions to newer, workable files.

Case Studies: Preserve

Preserving our case studies involved ICPSR normalizing to an accepted preservation format. For the social sciences, this usually involves converting a SAS, SPSS, or Stata data file into two outputs: a raw data file (Figure 7) and a DDI XML descriptive file (Figure 8). The XML can be used to read and interpret the raw data. This enabled the IR to store a normalized, long-lived version in the IR, alongside the original statistical file.

```
5 795 862 1MARTIN     H CAWLES      531 PHYSICIAN          3500 3000 13
5 795 862 2SILVINE    S CAWLES      502                            13
5 795 862 3GEORGE     DHCAWLES      181  FARMER                    13
5 795 862 4ANN          SMITH       172 DOMESTIC                   23
5 796 863 1FRAZIER      HEANIS      691 CARPENTERJOINER   1200  300 13
5 796 863 2FRONELLA     HEANIS      422                            13
5 797 864 1WILLIAM    W SAUNDERS    271 MERCHANT           800  500 13
5 797 864 2LOUISA       SAUNDERS    222                            13
5 797 864 3EVA        L SAUNDERS     62                            23 1
5 798 865 1ELIZABETH  A WOLAER      432                   1000  100 13
5 799 866 1WILLIAM      FISHER      471 PRINTER               1000  2
5 799 866 2ELIZABETH  R FISHER      382                             3
5 799 866 3WILLIAM    H FISHER      191 LABORER                    13
5 799 866 4FRANK      A FISHER      151                            13 1
5 799 866 5DAVID      J FISHER       91                            13 1
5 799 866 6KATE       C FISHER       52                            13 1
5 800 867 1PATRICK      DONEVAN     521 MERCHANT           3000 1000153
5 800 867 2CATHERINE    DONEVAN     522                           153
5 800 867 3JOHN         DONEVAN     191                            13
5 800 867 4JAMES        DONEVAN     171                            13
5 800 867 5WILLIAM      DONEVAN     141                            23 1
5 800 867 6MARGARET     DONEVAN     122                            23 1
5 800 867 7CORNELIUS    DONEVAN      91                            23 1
5 800 867 8DANIEL       DONEVAN      71                            23 1
5 800 867 9EDWARD       DONEVAN      51                            23 1
5 800 86710GEORGE       DONEVAN      21                            23
5 801 868 1GEORGE       HEANE       671 FOUNDRY            1000  500150
5 801 868 2MARY         HEANE       672                           150
```

Figure 7. Raw data file.

```
<dataDscr>

    <var name="v1" ID="v1" dcml="0" nature="interval">
        <location RecSegNo="1" StartPos="1" width="1"/>
        <labl level="variable">
            WARD NUMBER
        </labl>
        <catgry missing="N">
            <catValu>
                1
            </catValu>
            <catStat type="freq">
                1366
            </catStat>
            <catStat type="percent">
                14.9
            </catStat>
        </catgry>
```

Figure 8. DDI descriptive file.

Not all data, though, could be normalized without loss of fidelity or information. Old database files, for instance, required migration by ICPSR from old versions of software to newer versions. Other files were simply left as-is, with the understanding that the IR would commit to preserving just the bits.

Describe

The final step in the curation and archiving process is to describe the data collection. In addition to original documentation, study-level metadata is crucial to provide an overview of the entire data collection. These metadata populate search results and are where users will turn to for general but essential information, such as reading about the study description or methodology.

Some disciplines have formalized metadata specifications for documenting information about a dataset. The Data Documentation Initiative (DDI), for example, provides guidelines and recommendations for social science metadata. These greatly enhance the basic metadata fields offered in standard IR configurations.

It is tempting to include metadata as additional readme text files. While this is a step in the right direction, readme files can be cumbersome or ignored. Data stored in spreadsheets often are not fully documented either, and by themselves do not provide enough information for reuse. It is optimal to add new fields to existing IR metadata for both findability and ease of use. Considering the social sciences, suggestions for basic core metadata enhancements include[3]:

Title
Investigator(s)
Abstract
Version
Funding Agency
Date of Collection
Source of Data
Mode of Data Collection (e.g., mail questionnaire, web-based survey)
Type of Data (e.g., quantitative, mixed-mode)
Universe (i.e., the group of persons or objects to which the study results refer)
Unit of Analysis (e.g., individual, household)

Geographic Coverage

Sampling Description

Weighting Description

Not all repository managers will have access to the metadata schema or will be able to add metadata fields. Additionally, if fields are added, they can be challenging to migrate when updating to a new version of repository software. Domain repositories can consult on which additional metadata fields to include. They also can cross-list studies, linking to the source data and including rich, domain-specific metadata in the catalog.

TOOLS AND SERVICES

These guidelines serve as reference points for curating and archiving data and documentation—from finding to recovering to reviewing and cleaning, preserving, and describing. Through our experiences working with IRs and through surveying the community (ICPSR, 2012a), we consistently heard that practical examples of working with and presenting data would be especially useful. "To begin with, we just need some firsthand experience in order to answer questions we have," one IR staff member told us. Another wrote, "Guidance from a 'larger,' more experienced institution [is needed to help us overcome challenges to working with data]. A working model."

Beyond general guidance, we also heard that repositories would consult and accept external help via tools and services. In our survey, which had 109 responses from repository managers and affiliates, nearly all respondents said they would (72 percent) or might (27 percent) consult external help when working with data.

What might these tools and services look like? We propose some ideas and discuss how these can be fulfilled by ICPSR.

1. *Community wayfinder.* Repositories need help connecting with trusted vendors and tools to convert, curate, and preserve their data. A domain repository can play community go-between to match requests with providers. For instance, where can an IR turn to for help reading 9-track tapes? What local and regional statistical support is available to help open and read a data file for review? Who are my local representatives to ICPSR?

    ICPSR already receives similar requests from its member institutions. For questions about local resources, ICPSR can tap into its network of ORs, who are familiar with our data holdings and have community ties to data resources. We can expand the OR connections to the IR community. For questions about trusted tools and vendors, we are creating an online resource (http://www.icpsr.umich.edu/icpsrweb/content/datamanagement/tools.html) and are available to field specific questions.

2. *Access to processing tools for data recovery, review, format migration, and curation.* With a modest amount of training and experience, repository managers can readily learn the skills needed to curate data. What is often more challenging is accessing the software or hardware needed to read the data, particularly by institutions lacking financial or human resources.

   ICPSR has taken steps to create a virtual, online environment for social science data curation that can be used by remote desktop. Since 2012, we have been leading a virtual data curation working group where participants curate data using ICPSR's secure processing environment (Lyle, Vardigan, Carlson, & Nakao, 2013). Participants use virtual machines loaded with statistical and data conversion software to read, review, and transform files. They also have access to the normalization tools used to create preservation copies of datasets, as well as metadata tools to create DDI documentation and standards-based study descriptions. When they are finished, users can retrieve a copy of the fully curated data collection from the virtual processing environment. While this working group is still a trial run, we look forward to opening additional access to the processing tools used by ICPSR staff.

3. *Confidentiality review and treatment.* As we noted in a recent position paper, "Research designs in the social sciences are more likely to include elements that make it easier to identify human subjects, such as longitudinal data, geospatial locations, and multi-level data (e.g. student, teacher, school). Analyzing data for disclosure risks has become more complex, and measures to mitigate those risks are costly" (Lyle, Alter, & Vardigan, 2013, p. 2). Even repositories in institutions with nonhuman subject research report concern about disclosure risks.

   ICPSR is available to review and make recommendations on issues of data confidentiality. We have a human research protections officer on staff who can consult on individual data collections. Recently, for example, she worked with a research team that was concerned about small cell sizes (responses with less than 10) that might breach the privacy of research subjects. The team wanted to know how to maintain the privacy of these respondents while keeping the potentially sensitive information in the public use data. Our human research protections officer suggested collapsing response codes and provided examples of similar actions ICPSR had taken with other data collections.

ICPSR also hosts QualAnon (https://www.icpsr.umich.edu//icpsrweb/DSDR/tools/anonymize.jsp), a free web-based program to anonymize qualitative data. QualAnon uses a name key created by the user to change identified names to specified pseudonyms.

CONCLUSION

The relationship between data archives and IRs is maturing, particularly as both parties identify roles and develop guidelines, tools, and services to complement each other. To be sure, there remain significant challenges to partnering to curate: time, money, resources, commitment.

The engagement of IRs has much to offer in the curation of research data and might be carried out in different ways, depending upon the local situation. For example, repository managers and information professionals at a particular institution might focus upon gathering primary source materials on-site to enrich the study metadata. Others might be able to work on reviewing and preparing sharable versions of data files sooner given the close and direct proximity to the original investigator, rather than the time-delayed correspondence that often occurs when data are processed off-site. As roles emerge and skill sets are coordinated, partnerships will enhance the steps of providing stewardship and will enable a brighter prospect for the reuse of valuable digital assets over time.

Repositories, information professionals, and the institutions they support have increasing opportunities to curate and archive data, and can receive support from numerous sources. ICPSR looks forward to continuing to partner with IRs and others in the development of a network of distributed digital archives.

ACKNOWLEDGMENTS

This project was supported by IMLS National Leadership Grant LG-05-09-0084-09. We would like to acknowledge our partners at the IRs who contributed time, effort, and ideas: Tracy Popp, Sarah Shreeves, James

Ottaviani, Shawn Martin, and Jani Little. We also would like to acknowledge the project advisory committee members: Jake Carlson, Jennifer Darragh, Sarah Shreeves, Libbie Stephenson, and Ryan Womack.

NOTES

1. The full guidelines are described in our "Guide to Archiving Social Science Data for Institutional Repositories" (http://www.icpsr.umich.edu/icpsrweb/content/IR/guide.html).

2. For an introduction to digital preservation concepts and strategies, see the *Digital Preservation Management: Implementing Short-Term Strategies for Long-Term Solutions* online tutorial (http://www.dpworkshop.org/dpm-eng/eng_index.html).

3. The JISC-funded Research Data @Essex project, based at the United Kingdom Data Archive, developed a basic metadata profile "suited to describing the huge variety of research data generated at institutions with disciplinary diversity." See http://www.data-archive.ac.uk/media/398085/rde_metadataprofile_public_02_00.pdf (original quote was at http://researchdataessex.posterous.com/repository-beta-metadata-profile-released). Another excellent resource is the "DSpace Metadata Schema for *Edinburgh DataShare*, Ver. 1 (3.7.2008)". See http://www.disc-uk.org/docs/Edinburgh_DataShare_DC-schema1.pdf.

REFERENCES

Bogue, A. G. (1979). Data dilemmas: Quantitative data and the Social Science History Association. *Social Science History, 3*(3/4), 204–226. http://dx.doi.org/10.2307/1170962

Green, A. G., & Gutmann, M. P. (2007). Building partnerships among social science researchers, institution-based repositories and domain specific data archives. *OCLC Systems and Services, 23*(1), 35–53. Retrieved from http://deepblue.lib.umich.edu/handle/2027.42/41214

Green, A., McDonald, S., & Rice, R. (2009). *Policy-making for research data in repositories: A guide.* DISC-UK Datashare Project. Retrieved from http://www.disc-uk.org/docs/guide.pdf

Inter-university Consortium for Political and Social Research (ICPSR). (2012a). *Survey of data curation services for repositories, 2012* (ICPSR 34302). Ann Arbor, MI: ICPSR. http://dx.doi.org/10.3886/ICPSR34302.v1

Inter-university Consortium for Political and Social Research (ICPSR). (2012b). *Guide to social science data preparation and archiving: Best practice throughout the data life cycle* (5th ed.). Ann Arbor, MI: ICPSR. Retrieved from http://www.icpsr.umich.edu/files/ICPSR/access/dataprep.pdf

Lyle, J., Alter, G., & Vardigan, M. (2013, January). *"The Price of Keeping Knowledge" workshop: ICPSR position paper.* Presentation at "The Price of Keeping Knowledge: Financial Streams for Digital Preservation" workshop, Amsterdam, the Netherlands. Retrieved from http://www.knowledge-exchange.info/Admin/Public/DWSDownload.aspx?File=%2fFiles%2fFiler%2fdownloads%2fPrimary+Research+Data%2fWorkshop+Price+of+Keeping+Knowledge%2fJared+Lyle+ICPSR_Position+Paper_Price+workshop_public.pdf

Lyle, J., Vardigan, M., Carlson, J., & Nakao, R. (2013, May). *An applied approach to data curation training at the Inter-university Consortium for Political and Social Research (ICPSR).* Paper presented at the Framing the Digital Curation Curriculum conference, Florence, Italy. Retrieved from http://www.digcur-education.org/eng/International-Conference/Programme

Lynch, C. A. (2003). Institutional repositories: Essential infrastructure for scholarship in the digital age. *ARL*, 226, 1–7. Retrieved from http://www.arl.org/resources/pubs/br/br226/br226ir.shtml

MIT Libraries. (2013). *Data management and publishing.* Retrieved from http://libraries.mit.edu/guides/subjects/data-management/index.html

Pienta, A., Alter, G., & Lyle, J. (2010, April). *The enduring value of social science research: The use and reuse of primary research data.* Paper presented at "The Organisation, Economics and Policy of Scientific Research" workshop, Torino, Italy. Retrieved from http://hdl.handle.net/2027.42/78307

Pienta, A. M., Gutmann, M., Hoelter, L., Lyle, J., & Donakowski, D. (2008, August). The LEADS database at lCPSR: Identifying important "at risk" social science data. *Paper presented at the Quantitative Methodology Open Refereed Roundtable session at the 2008 American Sociological Association Annual Meeting*, Boston, MA.

Van den Eynden, V., Corti, L., Woollard, M., Bishop, L., & Horton, L. (2011). *Managing and sharing data: Best practices for researchers* (3rd ed.). Colchester, England: United Kingdom Data Archive. Retrieved from http://data-archive.ac.uk/media/2894/managingsharing.pdf

11 | Managing and Archiving Research Data

Local Repository and Cloud-Based Practices

MICHELE KIMPTON AND CAROL MINTON MORRIS

PART 1: MANAGING RESEARCH DATA IN DSPACE AND FEDORA REPOSITORIES

When King Richard III of England died in the 1485 Battle of Bosworth Field ("Richard III of England," n.d.), the words "research" and "data" were unknown. King Richard would not have believed that in 500 years his bones would be discovered under a parking lot, providing scholars with a wealth of information about his life and death (McRobbie, 2013). The world changed and we learned how to extract DNA from bone tissue using scientific methods that were unheard of when that long-ago "data" was preserved in a hasty grave (Jones, 2013). King Richard's unheralded and unrecorded burial could be an analogy to modern-day flat file data dumps that become inaccessible dark archives that are indecipherable using current technologies.

Advancing knowledge in all fields of research now requires the curation, collection, management, access, and long-term preservation of digital datasets that go far beyond burying a flat file on a hard drive. Research libraries are planning and experimenting with how to put digital data policies, workflows, and economic models in place to ensure that data will persist to serve researchers and institutions far into the future.

To accomplish this task, librarians and repository managers are grappling with how to define research data within the context of their libraries, as well as figuring out how to decide which data to preserve in repositories, the cloud, or other types of storage media, and for how long. Along with those questions are issues around what kinds of systems to use, what services to provide, and what kinds of contextual information to attach to data objects and datasets that can include metadata, use policies, and access tools. Finally, it is being left to research libraries to manage spiraling preservation costs as more and more institutional scholarship is born digital. The Richard III example highlights the importance of finding answers to these questions even though we cannot see over the rim of the future to what scholars will be able to extract and demystify from contents of long-ago digital repositories.

Aspects of recent discussions with the following library staff members who use DSpace or Fedora to operate repositories are presented in part one: Dean Krafft, Chief Technology Strategist and Director of IT, Cornell University Library; Jill Sexton, Information Infrastructure Architect, University of North Carolina at Chapel Hill; Geneva Henry, Executive Director, Rice University's Center for Digital Scholarship; and Sarah Shreeves, Coordinator, Illinois Digital Environment for Access to Learning and Scholarship (IDEALS) at the University of Illinois at Urbana-Champaign.

The interviews were conducted to gain an understanding of common issues and solutions around the preservation and use of digital research data in DSpace and Fedora repositories.

What is research data?

Librarians often define research data beyond what is found in a spreadsheet or in a dataset.

Some institutions rely on libraries to provide persistent and secure access to financial, enrollment, administrative, and even medical records. Others are required to ensure that the intellectual output of the university is preserved in electronic theses and dissertations along with associated files across all disciplines. Others preserve historic scholarly journals that have been purchased over time. Data formats vary and can include library-generated digital content and special collections from the humanities and scientific disciplines. The common thread here is that institutions have made a conscious decision to define what constitutes research data.

DSpace repository software is used by 41.3 percent of institutions (OpenDOAR, 2013) worldwide to provide open access and discovery across a wide range of materials and collections that can include data objects. Fedora is seen as a solution for institutions that need to archive, scale, and provide use policies and authorization for access to materials. Both types of repositories currently house and provide access to some amount of research data.

Institution	Current description of research data in repository	Future
Cornell University	Small open access data objects deposited in a DSpace (DuraSpace, n.d.) repository; not a lot of data	CULAR Fedora repository to contain administrative record data; only available for restricted access; Hydra-based implementation that would specifically support research data deposit
University of North Carolina at Chapel Hill	Library-generated digital content, special collections, and electronic theses and dissertations; datasets are attached to other types of content as supporting documents in Fedora repository	Academic Preservation Trust (n.d.) partner—looking to expand replication infrastructure
Rice University	Mostly humanities, not much scientific—one or two spreadsheets in DSpace	Islandora (n.d.)/Fedora repository implementation to allow for scaling
University of Illinois	Steady stream of datasets into IDEALS (n.d.) DSpace repository, but not high quantities that often are supplemental files attached to theses and dissertations; datasets coming in as a result of being part of funding agency-required data management plans	Looking into a Fedora preservation repository; will move some content from IDEALS DSpace repository for preservation purposes

Table 1. Libraries currently capture some amount of research data that is primarily associated with documents.

How is it to be packaged for preservation?

Institutions require provenance information to archive data. Though some libraries are accepting deposits without intervention, most try to review data as it is added to make sure that it includes appropriate identifying information.

Policies and procedures for archiving research data are currently being written, updated, and implemented.

Institution	Current processes and workflow for research data ingest	Future
Cornell University	Institutional Repository Deposit Policy (eCommons@Cornell, n.d.): suggested file formats, no descriptive/preservation metadata suggestion	Staff working on data curation profiles in order to develop a set of services and best practices
University of North Carolina at Chapel Hill	Institutional Repository Deposit Policy (Carolina Digital Repository, n.d.): no specific file format recommendations, no descriptive/preservation metadata suggestion	Working on a more comprehensive preservation policy; how to get scientific data into the workflow
Rice University	Digital Curation Profile (Digital Projects for Fondren Library, n.d.): not specifically developed for research data	In one year, anticipate working with datasets
University of Illinois	Require a read-me file (Digital Projects for Fondren Library, n.d.) that outlines what it is, how it was generated, was it analyzed; deposits come in without intervention that do not necessarily indicate when a dataset is added	Set up policies for thesis and dissertations to capture as much of read-me file information as possible

Table 2. Libraries use various tools and policies to add data to institutional repositories.

How long will it be saved?

Most research libraries plan to persist research data for the life of their institution, and in many cases, this already adds up to well over 100 years. Forever is a period of time that cannot be defined or understood. The "long haul" is different for each institution, but there is agreement over libraries' key role in ensuring that digital scholarship moves into the future.

Institution	How long is long?	Future
Cornell University	At the least, it is necessary to be able to preserve the outputs that went into print back in the day; interesting issue around the degree of ownership the Cornell University Library should have for the entire scholarly output of the university	Ongoing policy refinement discussions
University of North Carolina at Chapel Hill	Forever. It is brave to promise, but it becomes more difficult as finances get tighter; starting to look at ways to create balance; branching out with other departments to fulfill demand that is acceptable to legal counsel and the university	Ongoing policy refinement discussions
Rice University	NA	
University of Illinois	NA	

Table 3. "How long is forever?" and "What data merit longevity?" are being discussed.

Who will pay for it?

The length of time that research data can be preserved depends on the amount of funding available to pay for it. Though archival data storage costs are becoming more affordable, this is just one part of a typical institutional strategic preservation budget. Curatorial, technology, administrative, and other staff costs are fixed or increasing. Business models for research data preservation have been identified as a missing piece of the puzzle. As libraries begin to see what they do and who they serve through a different lens, the question of who pays for long-term data preservation becomes more important. One idea is to divide known disciplines among research universities with particular specialties in particular areas with the responsibility to oversee a field. Smaller universities with valuable knowledge collections might be left out of this equation.

Institution	Business models for research data stewardship	Future
Cornell University	Good business models are missing; for small data, it is possible to piggyback on institutional repository; for medium and larger datasets, there needs to be some sort of business model (perhaps one-time payment models, the Unidata/National Center for Atmospheric Research model, membership, or pay per use)	Work with other university libraries to flesh out business models
University of North Carolina at Chapel Hill	Great interest in partnerships within the university to work on business models	Interested in looking toward interuniversity solutions
Rice University	Look to direct partnerships with research computing to be part of research grants; first sale has to happen with the head of research computing; librarians should be totally engaged in the research process. Researcher could care less about rights and collection policies—they just want to do their research	Strengthen library ties to research computing
University of Illinois	NA	

Table 4. Business models and internal/external partnerships form the basis for future sustainability strategies.

How useful is the data for validation or regeneration of experiments?

None of the library staff members who were interviewed had direct experience with regeneration of experiments based on data that had been stored in a repository. Social sciences (e.g., the Cornell Institute for Social and Economic Research and the Inter-university Consortium for Political and Social Research) and other discipline-specific repositories have experience in this area. One librarian commented that because digital replicas of field data are now available for archeologists on campus, their processes for analysis are now more efficient.

What opportunities does it present?

Librarians feel that there is a good research data business model going forward that depends on building relationships with campus IT departments and others beyond their universities. Libraries traditionally have not been direct partners in research. As funding agencies require data access, management, and preservation as part of grant funding, libraries now have the opportunity to be an integral part of this work. As Geneva Henry says:

> There is a huge barrier to overcome with regard to culture and perception about what libraries do. It is critical to be walking hand-in-hand with campus research computing. They don't go to the library with research requirements like compute cycles— to get support for their HP computer cluster from a grant, for example. Librarians know how to handle research outputs— what comes out of the compute cycle—and that is where they can be a vital part of the research data management process.

What challenges does managing research data present, and what technology improvements would be helpful going forward?

Libraries will continue to investigate issues and opportunities around making research data accessible for the long term through their institutional repositories. The solutions they will implement will help to provide future scholars with insights into long ago culture, heritage, and scientific discovery.

PART 2: MANAGING AND PRESERVING DATA IN THE CLOUD

Academic libraries are being tasked with providing persistent access to digital data that may accompany a final publication, as well as other complementary research objects that will allow the reuse and regeneration of the results for future researchers. Archiving and providing long-term access to data presents new and different challenges for librarians, such as the following:

Institution	Challenges to managing research data in repository	Future
Cornell University	Workflow—how to take in research data and make it useful for future researchers; representing the data at the level that you could do anything useful with it is a big challenge, and it varies widely across disciplines; access issues, IP issues, privacy, and confidentiality	Collaborative policy and services development within and external to the university
University of North Carolina at Chapel Hill	How to choose—curation; capacity guesstimates—hard to develop capacity until you need the capacity and don't know when that will be or how much will be required; finding time and connections to build the reputation of the library as a serious player in the data management arena	Collaborative policy and services development within and external to the university
Rice University	Totally engaging librarians in the research process	Changing the culture of librarianship to include research data management
University of Illinois	Hard to track citations within the repository; nice if it was easier; difficult to describe research data; hard for any repo that is multidiscipline; can we have a DSpace workflow for datasets? Showing use and impact for a scholars—Open Researcher and Contributor ID (ORCID) integration; ability to communicate more with external systems	Looking at an architecture that has several pieces; dark archive plus open access; sensitive data is not such an issue because no medical data; storage arch for management side; cataloging datasets on and off campus

Table 5. Workflow, curation, capacity, and technology are all part of challenges and new opportunities for leveraging research data in institutional repositories.

- describing the data so that it may be useful and identifiable to others
- linking the data to the research output effectively so that the research output and data streams make a coherent object
- ensuring one can regenerate or reuse the dataset if they have the appropriate tools
- developing and applying policies that specify the appropriate preservation and access policies for keeping the data

For smaller institutions, it can be challenging to even implement a basic data archiving and preservation strategy, as they lack the appropriate tools and infrastructure to manage more data in their current systems. In this section we will discuss some of the challenges and benefits of using remote cloud storage for managing and archiving data.

Benefits and limitations of remote cloud storage.

Where institutions have needed to look beyond their own campuses for data management support, a small but growing number have begun to investigate and experiment with cloud-based solutions for digital archiving and access. Over the last several years, cloud computing and storage, provided as a service, has become a commercially viable option and is offered competitively by many large IT companies around the world. There are also several academic institutions that have begun to offer cloud-based services to constituents outside of their own campuses, such as San Diego Supercomputer Center Cloud Storage (SDSC Cloud, n.d.) and the Open Cloud Consortium (n.d.). We anticipate many more institutional or consortial cloud data centers will evolve that are controlled and operated by the academic sector.

At the time of writing this chapter, the largest commercial cloud service provider is Amazon (Amazon.com, n.d.), offering compute and storage at three locations in the United States, and an additional five locations worldwide. The pricing model for most cloud providers is to pay for the storage and compute as you need it, and you do not provision any capital upfront. This exchange is similar to how you might pay your electricity bill. You pay for what you use each month, and you are not charged for the electrical poles, wires, grids, or infrastructure. Smaller institutions have become intrigued with cloud services, mainly storage, as it can provide an easy and flexible way to provision additional storage without an upfront capital investment. In the case where libraries are being asked to steward increasing amounts of digital content, even being able to provision storage securely and easily in the short term can be attractive when compared to the alternative of storing on portable media, such as CDs, or worse, having no options to secure the data.

Although the ability to store and manage your data in the cloud has appeal, there are several barriers that can prevent institutions from enabling cloud storage, such as:

- lack of clarity about what security protocols are in place if the data is breeched
- unclear and unpublished policies regarding offshoring of data and data privacy
- ability to monitor the health of the data over time
- ability to negotiate agreements that are specific to the needs of the university

It is difficult to get complete answers to many of these questions due to a lack of understanding on the cloud providers' part about what the requirements are from the academic sector. Also, many of the larger commercial companies do not have the staff or processes in place to address the direct needs of the academic market, and therefore, it is difficult for institutions to build the level of trust required for these institutions to hand over data. That being said, many of the commercial providers do have robust processes and internal policies in place to ensure the data is secure, that unauthorized personal cannot access the data, and that there are continual processes in place to check and monitor the data. However, many times these policies and procedures are not reflected in the documentation and are not represented on the standard service-level agreements. Therefore, without a special contract or direct communication with the cloud provider, there is a layer of opaqueness that blocks the universities from understanding what really is occurring.

Data security requirements imposed by university IT.

Many of the larger universities have made it almost impossible to use commercial cloud providers because of data protection and security agreements they have put in place. These typically are umbrella agreements, meaning one agreement is put in place regardless of what type of data is being managed. Universities require vendors handling any type of data to sign these umbrella agreements. The agreements typically do not distinguish data type, such as personal information with privacy concerns requiring HIPAA (United States Department of Health and Human Services, n.d.) compliance, or sensitive administrative records produced by the university compared to open data produced by government-funded research. Additionally, these types of agreements are modeled after the use case where a university gives its sensitive data over to a third party vendor, paying some large annual fee, and the university has no access to the data or control over how the data is managed. The data is put in a dark archive, without Internet access and off-site. Some of the unique features of using a commercial cloud provider to archive data, compared to the traditional archiving solutions, make several requirements of these agreements obsolete. Having data in the cloud allows universities to do the following actions, not possible with traditional archival solutions:

- the university has 24/7 access to their data and can get a copy at any time.
- the university decides how it would like to package the data, and moves the data into the cloud with its own process and tools.
- the university chooses where the data will be stored, and it can typically specify a particular data center and geography.
- the university can choose to delete any or all data whenever it wishes.

The DuraCloud service for managing and archiving data.

DuraSpace (n.d.) is a nonprofit organization providing services to the academic community to support the management of long-term access to digital data, developed the DuraCloud (n.d.) software to address the unmet need for digital preservation storage and services in the cloud. DuraCloud is an open-source software project and managed service that provides organizations with an easy pathway to the cloud while mitigating some of the risks of adopting cloud technologies. Uniquely, DuraCloud secures data by placing copies of information on multiple providers, insulating organizations from single provider incidents, as well as enabling the easy transition from one cloud storage provider to another.

Specifically, DuraCloud provides the following unique features that address many of the initial risks of adopting the cloud for digital preservation use cases:

- Integration with multiple cloud service providers: DuraCloud integrates with no less than two cloud vendors at all times. Currently, DuraCloud is integrated with Amazon Web Services, Rackspace Cloud Files, and the SDSC Cloud Storage Services.
- Ability to backup and synchronize across multiple cloud service providers: DuraCloud manages all cloud content through one unified web interface, with multiple copies of digital content being synchronized seamlessly. In addition, these copies can reside in multiple geographies, removing the possibility of data loss through regional catastrophe.
- Ease of migration between cloud providers: DuraCloud easily enables moving content seamlessly from one cloud vendor to another through one unified web interface.
- Transparent/open software: DuraCloud is an open-source software project, and therefore, it leverages a coordinated and collaborative effort of transparent software development of an open-source codebase with no proprietary lock in.
- Straightforward pathway to the cloud: DuraCloud provides access to all cloud content through one web accessible interface with all stored content possessing unique storage URLs.
- Easy access to and visibility of data: Instead of "dark" archives that content is submitted to, relying and trusting a vendor to keep safe, cloud preservation through DuraCloud provides a transparent means of access, visibility, and control of content.
- Continual health checking of content: As soon as data is stored in DuraCloud, a health checking service is run on a continual basis, which monitors all content's health as it is stored in the cloud. Detailed health reports are provided through the web interface.

The DuraSpace organization has been able, on behalf of its academic customers, to open conversations with the cloud providers to begin to communicate the needs and requirements that are important for the academic market. In many cases the needs of the institutions are being met, but they are not documented legally. DuraSpace has been able to provide a higher level of transparency and communication to academic users regarding what policies and procedures are in place to safeguard their data, and it has built redundancy systems in the DuraCloud software to ensure data integrity and improved security. These improvements are possible because DuraCloud provides access to more than just a single cloud provider. These enhanced requirements are reflected in the Duracloud service agreement. At the time of writing this chapter, many of the cloud vendors had still not achieved HIPAA compliance for cloud storage. Several were moving in this direction, so they could better serve the medical and academic community. If successful, this will put in place a layer of security and policy that will match what is currently in place at several large university IT centers, and potentially remove some of the barriers today for using cloud storage.

Data management and archiving use cases.

Many organizations have found a variety of uses for DuraCloud in order to preserve and/or make digital content accessible. Because of DuraCloud's flexibility, both preservation and access use cases can be achieved through the use of the software. The following are just several ways in which Dura-Cloud is currently being employed:

- Geographic distribution of data: For one organization, maintaining multiple copies of content in different geographical locations is a core piece of their preservation policy. Before using DuraCloud, a system administrator would set up accounts at multiple cloud vendors, create manifests for the content, and store content at two cloud providers. The administrator would manually pull down and audit the content periodically to check the health. However, there was no easy or automated way to do this at both providers. Now using DuraCloud the administrator can manage the content in both cloud stores through one web-based dashboard and can monitor the health of the content in both places through the automated reporting. For this use case, one copy of content was originally uploaded to DuraCloud and stored in the Amazon US East region, while a secondary copy was created simultaneously by DuraCloud and stored in the SDSC Cloud Storage location on the West Coast. As content continues to be added to DuraCloud, all copies are kept synchronized and their health is checked by ongoing DuraCloud services.
- Collaborative access: For another institution, cloud backup was supplemented by shared access to portions of the content stored in the cloud. With DuraCloud, content permissions were granted to a subset of users, thus allowing for collaborative access to content for research groups, departments, or even partner institutions.

- Repository backup and restoration: For organizations running local repositories, backup and restoration that is reliable and quick is crucial. When traditional backups are stored offsite on tape drives, performing partial or full system restores can take days, if not weeks. Because of this, one institution turned to DuraCloud to store critical DSpace backups. Using the DSpace Replication Task Suite (2013a), DSpace backups and restores are simple and can be executed directly from the DSpace administrative interface. This includes backup of data that is part of the DSpace repository. Within DuraCloud, the user can pull out a single file, single collection, or single community. These are different hierarchal layers within the DSpace application, so for partial restore and recovery, the total transaction time is much simpler and faster.

Although many of the current users of DuraCloud are backing up and preserving all types of digital content, preserving data is at the beginning stages. Currently, data is handled in the same manner as any other raw digital file that is stored in DuraCloud, and this may not be good enough in order to make the data identifiable and reusable for future generations. Therefore, it will be important to develop process and metadata for long-term data management, which will lead to more effective archiving practices. However, for many users, DuraCloud is providing an easy way for them to store and save their data in the interim until these processes are more fully developed; they know their data will be safe.

Future developments.

The DuraSpace organization continues to develop and provide additional features and functionality to DuraCloud to make it easier for managing research data. Some of the latest developments include integration with Box (Box, n.d.), a cloud application based on the "freemium" business model where researchers can share, annotate, and develop their work using free basic software. Other projects include enhanced metadata and workflow for organizing data within DuraCloud, such as integration of the tools like the University of North Carolina Library's Curator's Workbench (Carolina Digital Repository Blog, n.d.) and Archivematica (n.d.). For example, a DuraCloud Archive-It pilot program designed to provide Archive-It partner organizations with additional backup options is currently underway (DuraSpace, 2013b).

DuraSpace's vision for academic cloud services is to be able to build a layer of services for managing data as part of the Internet (Internet2, n.d.) backbone, which provides secure, fast data transfer and connects academic institutions and research organizations as well as commercial cloud providers. We are currently working with Internet2 as a NET+ service provider (Internet2, 2012), key universities that are Internet2 members, as well as several of the current cloud providers to be able to realize this vision.

REFERENCES

Academic Preservation Trust. (n.d.). *APTrust*. Retrieved from http://academicpreservationtrust.org/

Amazon.com. (n.d.). Amazon web services [Web site]. Retrieved from https://aws.amazon.com/products/

Archivematica. (n.d.). Wiki main page [Web site]. Retrieved from https://www.archivematica.org/wiki/Main_Page

Box. (n.d.). Box [Web site]. Retrieved from https://www.box.com/home/

Carolina Digital Repository. (n.d.). Policies and guidelines. *UNC.edu*. Retrieved from https://cdr.lib.unc.edu/scontent/aboutPages/policies Guidelines.xml

Carolina Digital Repository Blog. (n.d.). Archive for "Curator's Workbench" tag [Web site]. Retrieved from http://www.lib.unc.edu/blogs/cdr/index.php/tag/curators-workbench/

Digital Projects for Fondren Library. (n.d.). Digital curation profile template. *Rice University*. Retrieved from https://digitalriceprojects.pbworks.com/w/page/50366573/Digital Curation Profile Template

DuraCloud. (n.d.). DuraCloud [Web site]. Retrieved from http://duracloud.org/

DuraSpace. (n.d.). *Dspace*. Retrieved from http://dspace.org/

DuraSpace. (2013a). Replication task suite [Wiki]. Retrieved from https://wiki.duraspace.org/display/DSPACE/ReplicationTaskSuite

DuraSpace. (2013b). New pilot program: Universities join DuraCloud/Archive-it collection back-up test. Retrieved from http://duraspace.org/new-pilot-program-universities-join-duracloudarchive-it-collection-back-test

eCommons@Cornell. (n.d.). eCommons policies. *Cornell.edu*. Retrieved from http://ecommons.library.cornell.edu/policy.html

Illinois Digital Environment for Access to Learning and Scholarship (IDEALS). (n.d.). Welcome to IDEALS. Retrieved from https://ideals.illinois.edu/

Internet2. (n.d.). Internet2 [Web site]. Retrieved from http://www.internet2.edu/

Internet2. (2012). Internet2, 16 major technology companies announce cloud service partnerships to benefit the nation's universities. Retrieved from http://www.internet2.edu/news/pr/2012.04.24.cloud-services-partnerships.html

Islandora. (n.d.). *Islandora*. Retrieved from http://islandora.ca/

Jones, B. (2013, February 5). Body found under parking lot is King Richard III, scientists prove. *CNN.com*. Retrieved from http://www.cnn.com/2013/02/03/world/europe/richard-iii-search-announcement

McRobbie, L. R. (2013, February 8). The battle over Richard III's bones . . . and his reputation. *Smithsonian.com*. Retrieved from http://www.smithsonianmag.com/history-archaeology/The-Battle-Over-Richard-IIIs-BonesAnd-His-Reputation-190400171.html

Open Cloud Consortium. (n.d.). Open Cloud Consortium [Web site]. Retrieved from http://opencloudconsortium.org/

OpenDOAR. (2013). Use of open access repository software—Worldwide. *University of Nottingham, UK*. Retrieved from http://www.opendoar.org/onechart.php?cID=&ctID=&rtID=&clID=&lID=&potID=&rSoftWareName=&search=&groupby=r.rSoftWareName&orderby=Tally%20DESC&charttype=pie&width=600&height=300&caption=Usage of Open Access Repository Software - Worldwide

Richard III of England. (n.d.). *Wikipedia*. Retrieved from http://en.wikipedia.org/wiki/King_Richard_III

San Diego Supercomputer Center (SDSC) Cloud. (n.d.). SDSC cloud storage services [Web site]. Retrieved from https://cloud.sdsc.edu/hp/index.php

United States Department of Health and Human Services. (n.d.). Health information privacy: The security rule [Web site]. Retrieved from http://www.hhs.gov/ocr/privacy/hipaa/administrative/securityrule/

12 | Chronopolis Repository Services

DAVID MINOR, BRIAN E. C. SCHOTTLAENDER, AND ARDYS KOZBIAL

The National Science Foundation (NSF) requirement that researchers create a data management plan for each NSF proposal submitted after January 2011 reinforced to its constituency the need for long-term stewardship of data and research output. Other funding agencies already had other requirements in place (for example, the National Institutes of Health [NIH] data sharing requirement of 2003). These requirements make clear the importance of having infrastructure in place that enables the long-term preservation of digital objects.

While researchers familiar with the language of the data life cycle might have had a solid enough understanding of phases comprising that life cycle—like "plan," "collect," "process," and "analyze"—they were largely unfamiliar with "discovery" and "reuse," and had little to no comprehension of "preservation." From their perspective, data preservation meant going to the nearest electronics store and buying a 1 TB external hard drive to keep in their bottom desk drawer.

Long-term preservation of digital data is a fundamental component of contemporary research. The amount of data being created increases exponentially every year, while the complexity of data types, sizes, tools, and services is on a similar arc. Preservation of basic research data is essential to future data use and reuse—and, one could say, to the future development of the scholarly and scientific record.

Around the turn of the century, several major digital preservation initiatives were launched, initiatives intended to address a variety of preservation needs and concerns. Many of these initiatives had their start in the Library of Congress' National Digital Information Infrastructure and Preservation Program (NDIIPP) (Library of Congress, n.d.b). Tasked by Congress to address digital preservation on a national (and often international) scale, NDIIPP funded a number of efforts: some targeted at specific communities or disciplines; others intended to create more general, and more generally applicable, solutions. All of the NDIIPP-funded initiatives were generally tasked with exploring various aspects of the digital preservation problem space. Some tackled shared governance and business models (e.g., the MetaArchive Cooperative [Educopia Institute, 2013]), while others designed and implemented technical infrastructure to support digital preservation. Chronopolis was one of the latter sorts of initiatives, focused on the development of a digital preservation infrastructure that spanned the country, providing a backbone that could accept a wide variety of data types.

Since 2007, the Chronopolis program has been building and refining an environment for digital preservation that now offers a professionally managed, constantly monitored service in which data can be housed. Chronopolis does not care about data format or quantity, and it is suitable for any kind of data provider, from an individual researcher to an institution.

This chapter describes what digital preservation is, what Chronopolis' solutions to the problems of digital preservation are, and how Chronopolis relates to other digital preservation efforts in the United States.

CHRONOPOLIS: FEDERATED DIGITAL PRESERVATION ACROSS SPACE AND TIME

Because digital information, by its very nature, is always at risk of loss or damage, it has become increasingly important to preserve the digital assets that are society's intellectual capital—the work on which future research and education will be built.

The San Diego Supercomputer Center (SDSC) and the University of California-San Diego (UCSD) Library, working with the National Center for Atmospheric Research (NCAR) in Colorado and the University of Maryland Institute for Advanced Computer Studies (UMIACS), have created Chronopolis to address this critical need.

The Chronopolis digital preservation network provides services for the long-term, federated preservation and curation of digital materials. Chronopolis services are designed to ensure data preservation for decades into the future and across a wide variety of disciplines. Data within Chronopolis are considered "dark." That is, once data have been ingested, there are no access services provided directly to the data. Instead, Chronopolis carries out all needed preservation actions, and any dissemination of data is mediated. Chronopolis' fundamental premise is that data will be maintained in such a way that they can be handed back to data owners in exactly the same form in which they were provided.

Chronopolis provides active preservation management for objects at the "bit level." This means that all of the infrastructure, services, and management of data is directed at guaranteeing that stored objects are in the exact state expected. Chronopolis does not provide services such as file format normalization or migration, either upon data ingest or at any time during storage. This is intentional—the Chronopolis philosophy is that only the owners of the data should be able to make changes to it. It is not the responsibility of the preservation system to decide when and how files should be changed. If data owners want to change the nature of their content, they upload new versions of it to Chronopolis as appropriate.

Chronopolis can preserve hundreds of terabytes of digital materials, of any type or size, with minimal requirements imposed upon the data provider. Using high-speed networks, mass-scale storage capabilities, and the expertise of its partners, it provides a geographically distributed, heterogeneous, and highly redundant preservation system.

The core services of Chronopolis are:

- Geographically distributed copies of all data;
- Constant curatorial audit reporting; and
- Use and development of best practices for data packaging and sharing.

Chronopolis is part of a new breed of distributed digital preservation programs, programs that use a virtual organizational structure in order to assemble the best expertise and framework to provide data longevity, durability, and access well into the next century (SDSC, 2011).

THE CHRONOPOLIS DIGITAL PRESERVATION NETWORK IN DEPTH

The Chronopolis digital preservation network leverages the data storage capabilities of its partner institutions to create a preservation data grid built on heterogeneous and highly redundant data storage systems. Each Chronopolis partner node operates a storage instance containing at least 250 TB of storage capacity. The network provides a minimum of three geographically distributed copies of all data stored. At each node, curatorial audits are run constantly, reporting key information. The underlying technology for managing data within Chronopolis is the "integrated Rule-Oriented Data System" (iRODS), a preservation middleware software package that allows for robust management of data (iRODS Consortium, n.d.). The Chronopolis team also develops best practices for the worldwide preservation community for data packaging and transmission among heterogeneous digital archive systems.

Chronopolis has concentrated on housing a wide range of content that is not tied to a single community. Some of the significant collections housed in Chronopolis include:

- Data from the North Carolina Geospatial Data Archiving Project, a joint initiative of the North Carolina State University Libraries and the North Carolina Center for Geographic Information and Analysis. It is focused on collection and preservation of digital geospatial data resources from state and local government agencies in North Carolina.
- Cruise data from UCSD's Scripps Institution of Oceanography academic research fleet, one of the largest such fleets in the world.
- Collections from the California Digital Library's "Web-at-Risk" project, an initiative to develop tools that enable librarians and archivists to capture, curate, preserve, and provide access to web-based government and political information.
- The complete digital library holdings of the UCSD Library, representing many decades of cultural artifacts.
- 50 TB of research datasets from UCSD's Research Cyberinfrastructure Curation Program. These data have been determined to be scientifically important, and part of the intellectual fabric and future of the university.

As Chronopolis focuses on bringing data into the network from other institutions and individuals, it is anticipated that the amount of data under active preservation will grow at a rapid pace.

CONTENT PRESERVATION PROCESSES

For all of the data in its network, Chronopolis provides a suite of replication and preservation services. These services—the very mechanics of the digital life cycle—span ingest to audit and include what follows.

Data Ingest

The Chronopolis ingest process comprises several steps, including negotiation with data providers, data transfer, registration into Chronopolis, and quality assurance/quality control (QAQC) at various stages. The initial process starts with human negotiations between Chronopolis and data provider personnel. During this discussion, issues such as the number of collections, the size of collections, naming conventions, and transfer methods are discussed. While packaging and transfer processes vary somewhat according to the data provider, for the most part "BagIt" has been used during data collection transfer to SDSC storage devices. BagIt, a format for packaging files for exchange (California Digital Library, 2012), originated from work led by the Library of Congress and the California Digital Library, and it is targeted to the digital preservation community.

Starting with a BagIt file name that is accessible from the data provider, the collection must be retrieved, usually via the Secure Shell (ssh) or Wget transfer protocols. Once onto an SDSC storage device, a QAQC process is run against the authoritative collection manifest file provided by the data provider. This process includes checking inventory and individual data object checksums. The collection is transferred to a storage device that is a registered iRODS resource, so that the actual iRODS ingest is merely a registration of the collection into the iRODS catalog, iCAT. The iCAT is the iRODS CATalog, a database-driven tool that tracks where data lives within iRODS. Once ingested, read permissions are granted from SDSC to the NCAR and UMIACS iRODS zones so that the replication process can proceed. The final step includes registration of the collection into the ACE monitoring system (see "Data Auditing" below).

Data Replication

Replication from SDSC to UMIACS and NCAR is monitored using iRODS at each site. Prior to replication, each replica site designates an account local to its zone that will host the data. Using a local account ensures that accessing a partner's data is not dependent on any services running at a remote partner site. After this account has been established, the master site grants read-only access to this new account. This account will be used to pull data from the master site to remote peers.

The collection is then registered to iRODS. After all data have been ingested and access permissions set on the master site, replica synchronization is started. This synchronization will compare the files in the master collection with each registered partner. Any data that are different or nonexistent on a partner site will be copied to the remote site. Resulting replicas at peer sites are under the custody of local peer iRODS accounts.

As new data are added to collections on the master site, replication may be triggered multiple times to ensure that all partner sites have copies of the complete collection. The replication process pulls data only from the master site to partner sites. Any data that exist on partner sites that do not exist on the master site are not automatically removed: manual deletion is required. During the ingest of collections into Chronopolis, only one situation has thus far been encountered wherein the manual removal of files from a partner site has been necessary.

Data Auditing

An Audit Control Environment (ACE) Audit Manager has been installed at all three partner sites to monitor the integrity of replicated files. Each of the three partner sites administer their ACE installations independent of the other sites. After replication to a partner site finishes, that site registers the new collection into ACE for monitoring. During registration, collections are grouped by data provider, an audit policy is assigned to them, and connection information for iRODS is gathered. Each collection is assigned a unique audit policy that determines when the Audit Manager will scan collections for changes. The current default policy in Chronopolis is to audit collections approximately every 30 days.

During the initial audit, SHA-256 digests (Wikipedia, n.d.a) are registered for all files in the collection. These digests are secured and used to validate the contents of a collection during subsequent audits. After the collection has been registered, auditing will occur as dictated by the collection's audit policy, or manually as triggered by an administrator. After each audit, a report is generated summarizing what activity occurred during the audit.

After a collection has been fully registered, an administrator may compare the collection to either a supplied manifest or to a peer site. After replication, partner sites that recently received data compare their new, replicated collections to the master collection in order to detect any files that may have not been properly replicated. In Chronopolis, both partners at UMIACS and NCAR compare their collections against SDSC to ensure they have been replicated properly.

Performance testing of the Audit Manager installation at UMIACS has shown that the entire Chronopolis holdings can be audited in less than one week.

Best Practices Investigations

As already noted, Chronopolis also investigates and recommends digital preservation best practices. This has been, and is being, done through several avenues, including the TRAC certification process (CRL, 2007). As part of their work on TRAC (discussed in detail below), Chronopolis team members developed a set of recommendations for transfer and ingest methods. These eventually became a major part of the Chronopolis "Submission Requirements," but are in many ways generic enough that they could be applied to a wide range of preservation environments. Important components of these "Submission Requirements" include:

- Object Packaging: the BagIt format is strongly recommended.
- Authoritative Manifest: a manifest with checksums is required. Organization of objects is unrestricted.
- Naming of Objects, Object Packages, and Collection Uniqueness: required.
- Metadata Requirements: data provider information required, collection information optional.
- Transfer Process: flexible.
- Ingest Confirmation: formal confirmation provided.

Object Packaging

It is strongly recommended that a collection of objects be packaged using the BagIt format prior to transfer into Chronopolis. The BagIt format is simple and flexible, and tools exist to automate its creation from a collection of files in a directory structure within a file system. BagIt is simply a .tar file with the addition of a few metadata files, in particular a manifest file, and the content objects in a /data directory. Holey BagIts are also accepted. (Holey bags have the normal bag structure, but instead of including actual objects, the /data directory is empty and a fetch.txt file is provided with URL pointers to objects [Library of Congress, n.d.a].) This requires server access to the objects on the data provider end.)

Chronopolis is quite comfortable ingesting BagIts up to 2 TB in size. While in general the fewer the number of BagIts the better, Chronopolis has no restrictions on the number of BagIts used to package a collection of objects.

Authoritative Manifest

Chronopolis requires a manifest file generated by the data provider to accompany all object transfers. This manifest should be in a standardized format and should include, at a minimum, a listing of pathnames and checksums for all objects in the transfer package. The BagIt manifest format is strongly recommended. Tools exist to generate this manifest as well as the BagIt package.

Validated manifests generated by the data provider are designated as authoritative, incorporated into a Chronopolis hierarchical manifest system, and used in many Chronopolis processing steps.

Organization of Objects

Chronopolis has no restrictions on how objects are organized. In general, the organizational structure, content, and name of a collection or grouping of objects are determined by the data provider. A collection can be packaged into one or more Bags. In the simplest case, a complete collection in its native directory structure can be put into a single BagIt/data directory. Or, if desired, a collection can be divided into several BagIt packages.

Naming of Objects, Object Packages, and Collections

Chronopolis has no restrictions on object names except that their characters must come from en_US.UTF-8 (special characters such as #, !, <, >, etc., are not recommended) (Wikipedia, n.d.b). Also the "/" character will signify a directory branching. Collection names must be unique within a data provider's archive, and object package names must be unique within a data provider's collection.

Metadata Requirements

The data provider is required to fill out a one-time data provider description metadata form that includes data provider name, contact information, and so forth. At the package level, at a minimum, content metadata must include a manifest file, as described above. It is recommended that a supplementary metadata file at the package level include collection information pertinent to the package. For the BagIt format, this can be included in the bag-info.txt file. Chronopolis can provide examples of this file demonstrating acceptable formats.

Transfer Process

Chronopolis is flexible in the transfer method data providers use to make packages available to SDSC. Methods that can be used include http-wget, ssh, FTP, e-mail, and the iRODS client.

Ingest Confirmation

Once a package has been transferred, validated against the manifest, and ingested into Chronopolis, the data provider will receive a confirmation of that particular package manifest and an updated manifest of its complete Chronopolis archive.

The recommendations above are current as of mid-2013 and are being studied and refined through various lenses, including grant-funded work with other preservation networks.

Chronopolis Data Portal

Chronopolis staff have developed and maintained a web-based data portal to provide information about collections held in the network. This portal brings together statistics from several sources, including ACE and iRODS. The purpose of the data portal is to provide a place that is easy to access and understand. It assumes no specific technical knowledge or understanding on the part of the data provider. The portal not only functions as a specific tool for the Chronopolis network, but also as an example of a standard data portal that will be of interest to the library community in general as it moves forward with large-scale digital preservation of content from multiple data providers.

The ACE Audit Manager provides JavaScript Object Notation (JSON) access to most functions. Among these are collection status, state of an individual collection, event log browsing, and item-level browsing. Access permission to the JSON services requires an ACE account. Within Chronopolis, a common read-only account has been created at all partner sites so that various harvesting software tools may automatically retrieve data from audit managers for display in a portal. Specifically, the following access is required at all three sites: overall collection status, item-level browsing, log retrieval, error report retrieval, activity report viewing, download collection digests, duplicate detection, and token downloading. This access allows remote sites to pull enough information to determine what differences may exist among their collections and their peers' collections, and to show overall collection health.

Figure 1 is a sample screenshot of the data portal, showing details about one of the collections stored within Chronopolis.

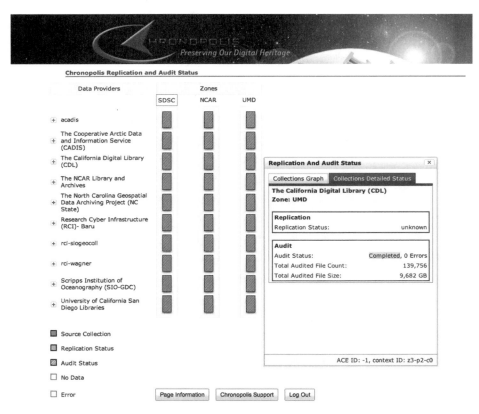

Figure 1. Sample screenshot of Chronopolis portal, circa 2013.

In this screenshot, the portal shows both the size of data in the network as well as the number of files stored.

TRUSTWORTHY REPOSITORIES AUDIT CERTIFICATION (TRAC)

The Chronopolis team spent 18 months working with the Center for Research Libraries (CRL) to complete a full TRAC audit. Chronopolis was the first general purpose preservation archive to undergo a TRAC audit, and thus, the first to be certified as a trustworthy digital repository that meets accepted best practices in the management of digital repositories.

The primary metrics used by CRL in its assessment are derived from *Trustworthy Repositories Audit & Certification: Criteria and Checklist* (2007). The TRAC criteria focus on organizational infrastructure, digital object management, technologies, technical infrastructure, and security. These criteria are targeted at best current practices and thinking about the organizational and technological needs of trustworthy digital repositories.

The TRAC process for Chronopolis occurred in three broad steps:

1. The Chronopolis team completed a "self-audit," answering all of the questions posed in the TRAC document. This self-audit was sent to CRL, which used it as the basis for their work. The Chronopolis self-audit is available for public viewing at http://chronopolis.sdsc.edu/trac/chronopolis_TRAC_self_audit.pdf.

2. CRL then analyzed the Chronopolis network and the self-audit, conducted a site visit to interview Chronopolis staff, and a held number of interviews with Chronopolis users and other stakeholders. Based on input, the audit team and Chronopolis began an interactive phase, discussing changes and recommendations.

3. CRL released the final audit report. This report is available on the CRL site at http://www.crl.edu/archiving-preservation/digital-archives/certification-and-assessment-digital-repositories/Chronopolis.

The TRAC audit "scores" on three categories: (1) organizational infrastructure, (2) digital object management, and (3) technologies, technical infrastructure, and security. Each of these categories is scored from 1 to 5 (wherein 1 is low and 5 is high). Chronopolis scored a 3 in organizational infrastructure and a 4 in the other two categories. These scores were seen as quite high and encouraged future targeted work in several areas.

FUTURE WORK

Chronopolis is involved in several major initiatives in 2013 that are anticipated to fundamentally change future work for the network, both in terms of scale and services. Two examples of this work are as follows.

DuraCloud and Chronopolis Integration

The DuraCloud service, an offering of DuraSpace, is a suite of cloud-based storage and data services, served up via an advanced, but easy to use, front end. While DuraCloud's data services are provided by a variety of discrete cloud providers, DuraCloud's users receive but a single invoice for these services, as well as a single point of contact.

Throughout 2012, Chronopolis and DuraCloud integrated services in such a way that a DuraCloud user would be able to "click a button" and have a snapshot of his or her data added to Chronopolis. This would provide an easy way to integrate a preservation archive into his or her more active data management needs. As noted at the beginning of this chapter, Chronopolis explicitly does not provide active access to data within the network. Working with DuraCloud allows for Chronopolis to be a part of a full data life cycle portfolio.

The Digital Preservation Network (DPN)

Chronopolis is one of the initial technical partners and replicating nodes for the Digital Preservation Network (2013). DPN is being designed to ensure that the scholarly record is preserved for future needs. It will be a preservation solution shared collectively across the academy that is intended to support existing preservation efforts and existing service providers.

The initial DPN replicating nodes are Chronopolis, the Stanford Digital Repository, HathiTrust, the Texas Digital Library, and the Academic Preservation Trust.

For Chronopolis, DPN will represent a significant driver for future preservation work. It is anticipated that DPN could quickly generate several petabytes of data that need to be preserved. In addition, the DPN technical team is defining the processes necessary for data to be shared between the partners as well as the services needed for preservation to take place.

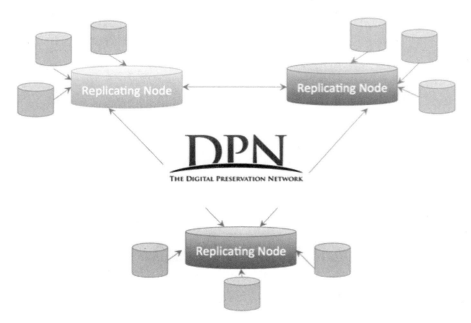

Figure 2. Conceptual diagram for DPN node infrastructure.

CONCLUSION

A pioneer in its approach to digital preservation, Chronopolis is neither a demonstration nor a theoretical project. The focus through all phases of development has been on the creation of a working, production-level digital archive that can accept large varieties and quantities of data. This is clear from its initial development as an NDIIPP project, through its transition to a fee-for-service offering, to, finally, its emergence as a critical component in an emerging suite of services of which the preservation community can take advantage. Now, Chronopolis is poised to join other nascent data stewardship efforts, bringing its considerable experience into the mix to create a coherent national digital preservation ecosystem.

REFERENCES

California Digital Library. (2012). BagIt file packaging format [Wiki entry]. Retrieved from https://wiki.ucop.edu/display/Curation/BagIt

Center for Research Libraries (CRL). (2007). *Trustworthy Repositories Audit & Certification: Criteria and Checklist.* Retrieved from http://www.crl.edu/sites/default/files/attachments/pages/trac_0.pdf

Digital Preservation Network (DPN). (2013). The Digital Preservation Network. Retrieved from http://www.dpn.org

Educopia Institute. (2013). MetaArchive Cooperative. Retrieved from http://www.metaarchive.org

iRODS Consortium. (n.d.). iRODS: Data grids, digital libraries, persistent archives, and real-time data systems. Retrieved from https://www.irods.org

Library of Congress. (n.d.a). Digital content transfer tools. Retrieved from http://www.digitalpreservation.gov/series/challenge/data-transfer-tools.html

Library of Congress. (n.d.b). Digital preservation. Retrieved from http://www.digitalpreservation.gov

San Diego Supercomputer Center (SDSC). (2011). Chronopolis. Retrieved from http://chronopolis.sdsc.edu

Wikipedia. (n.d.a). SHA-2. Retrieved from http://en.wikipedia.org/wiki/SHA-2

Wikipedia. (n.d.b). UTF-8. Retrieved from http://en.wikipedia.org/wiki/UTF-8

Part 5

MEASURING SUCCESS

13 | Evaluating a Complex Project

DataONE

SUZIE ALLARD

Project evaluation is conducted to determine a project's level of success as well as to help manage an ongoing project more efficiently. Using a systematic approach to evaluation allows for the identification of the project's merit or significance (Scriven, 1999). Developing a systematic evaluation approach for a complex project in a data-intensive environment can be challenging. This chapter discusses the experience of creating and implementing an evaluation plan for the Data Observation Network for Earth (DataONE), an interdisciplinary, multi-institutional, multinational project that supports the data life cycle in the biological, ecological, and environmental sciences. DataONE is funded by the United States' National Science Foundation (NSF). DataONE's principal investigator is Dr. William Michener, who is a professor and director of eScience Initiatives at the University of New Mexico Libraries. This chapter begins with a brief introduction to the DataONE project and the evaluation environment that helped to shape the DataONE evaluation plan. The next section of the chapter outlines how the evaluation was designed and implemented. The final section of the chapter reviews the quality of the evaluation and then discusses lessons learned from the experience, noting how the data-intensive challenges were addressed.

THE PROJECT: DATAONE

For this discussion, the inception of DataONE is defined as occurring in the fall of 2007, when a team was put together to answer the NSF's call for proposals, "Sustainable Digital Data Preservation and Access Network

Partners" or DataNet (NSF, 2007). Although the primary DataONE investigators had been developing the foundation for this project well before this time, 2007 is the year when the specifics for DataONE were outlined and submitted for funding. The DataNet call noted that proposed projects should address four dimensions: (1) providing reliable services for science and engineering data over the long term, (2) developing and adapting technologies to meet user needs and expectations, (3) engaging in computer and information science research and development, and (4) participating in building an interoperable data access and preservation network. DataONE's cyberinfrastructure (thoroughly described in Michener et al., 2012) was designed to address these dimensions by providing distributed management at existing and new repositories, facilitating software that meets the needs of scientists and data providers, and using existing community software that may be free or open source. This meant that the cyberinfrastructure (CI) had three main components: Coordinating Nodes that catalog content, manage replication of content, and provide search and discovery mechanisms; Member Nodes that are existing or new data repositories; and the Investigator Toolkit, which allows scientists to interact with the DataONE infrastructure using common analysis and data management tools. While DataONE's community engagement (CE) activities provide support for CI development and implementation, it was important that evaluation activities be designed to assess each of the CI's three components.

One measure of the complexity of DataONE is that even at the inception of the project, members were from 11 institutions spread across the United States. These institutions included Cornell University, the National Evolutionary Synthesis Center at Duke University, Oak Ridge National Laboratory, the University of New Mexico, the California Digital Library at the University of California, the National Center for Ecological Analysis and Synthesis at the University of California-Santa Barbara, the University of Illinois-Chicago, the University of Tennessee-Knoxville, the University of Kansas, the U.S. Geological Survey, and Utah State University. As the project has matured, institutional participation has grown and some assessment activities needed to be redesigned to reach all of these participants for input in order to remain transparent.

Today, DataONE is described as "the foundation of new innovative environmental science through a distributed framework and sustainable CI that meets the needs of science and society for open, persistent, robust, and secure access to well-described and easily discovered Earth observational data" (DataONE, 2013a). The complexity of the organization is evident on several fronts: it crosses scientific domains and includes disciplines outside of science; it includes a large number of institutions distributed across the world; it is engaged in building technological capabilities and also is addressing sociocultural issues related to data management and data sharing; and it has a large, diverse stakeholder network.

DataONE's objectives revolve around the need for accessible, secure, and robust data. These objectives, which also demonstrate the complex scope of the project, paraphrased from Allard (2012), are:

> (1) to provide access to current databases (such as the Ecological Society of America, the National Biological Information Infrastructure, the Long Term Ecological Research Network, and others);
>
> (2) to create a global CI that contains both biological and environmental data coming from different sources (research networks, environmental observatories, individual scientists, and citizen scientists);
>
> (3) to facilitate a new culture in science that includes establishing new CI practices and building global communities of practice.

DataONE is working to meet these objectives by developing a toolkit that facilitates data discovery, analysis, visualization, and decision making, by providing a means to assure persistent data access through the promotion of easy and secure storage, and by building the community of environmental data stakeholders. The outcome of addressing the four dimensions outlined in the original DataNet call was a very complex undertaking. This meant that evaluation of the project and its effects was a challenge that could only be addressed if the evaluation process was a part of the very fabric of the project. As a result, when the DataONE organizational structure was being developed, finding a way to incorporate assessment activities into the organization itself was an important consideration.

RELEVANT EVALUATION APPROACHES

From the start, the DataONE team knew that project evaluation was vital in order to report progress to the project's funding agency, the NSF. The project evaluation results also were considered key for internal project management. In most cases, agencies that provide funding require projects to engage in evaluations so that the effectiveness of the project can be measured and reported. The NSF and another U.S. agency, the Centers for Disease Control and Prevention (CDC), offer valuable guidance for project assessment. The DataONE team used a combination of these approaches in its evaluation design. The brief review that follows outlines the CDC (2013) and NSF (Westat, 2010) evaluation approaches, illustrating that evaluations require planning and commitment over the long term. It also is interesting to note that these agencies do not offer explicit guidance for evaluation of the characteristics of a complex, data-intensive project.

The CDC's evaluation process (CDC, 2013) is useful because it helps to set the project evaluation in the context of the ecosystem within which the project exists. This six-step process begins with engaging the stakeholders. Stakeholders include those people who run the project, those who are served by the project, and those who will be using the evaluation. The second step is to describe the program. This is the point when the project activities, resources, and other characteristics are identified. The third step is focusing the evaluation design. For this step, stakeholder concerns are prioritized so it is clear what are the most important characteristics to be measured. The fourth step is to gather credible evidence. This requires identifying metrics that may serve as indicators and may measure the quantity and quality of the project's activities. The fifth step is to use this evidence to come to conclusions using the following five elements: standards, analysis/synthesis, interpretation, judgment, and recommendations. The final step is to present the evaluation, so that others may benefit from lessons learned. Concerns about conducting evaluations include the cost of the activities, the timing of the evaluation activities so the results are meaningful, and any technical problems that are encountered. An additional area of concern is the possibility that evaluation activities may not engage all stakeholders and, therefore may not accurately reflect the situation.

The NSF also provides extensive project evaluation guidance (Westat, 2010). Although this guidance is specific to planning and conducting evaluations for education programs, NSF guidelines are still useful for assessing any kind of scientific project. The NSF approach is built around two kinds of evaluations—formative and summative. A formative evaluation assesses the project while it is in operation and over the course of the project's life. A summative evaluation reviews the project's success in reaching its goals. The NSF project evaluation focuses on a project development cycle, so that evaluation data includes performance indicators as well as data for formative and summative evaluations. The NSF evaluation process is a six-phase process that begins with the project's conceptualization and the identification of key evaluation points. In the second phase, evaluation questions are designed and operational definitions are developed for key outcomes. Next, the evaluation plan is designed. After this, the data are collected and analyzed. The final phase is that the information is made accessible to others. The NSF recognizes that this six-phase approach requires significant resources and suggests that 5 to 10 percent of project costs be used for project evaluation.

A key premise for the DataONE team was that the project evaluation method must be of a high quality. Therefore, the evaluation planning process began at the inception of the project. In the United States, the Joint Commission on Standards for Educational Evaluation (JCSEE) has addressed how to best assure the quality of assessments (JCSEE, 2013). JCSEE membership is made up of representatives from major professional associations, so that many viewpoints are represented. Although these standards were specifically created to address the evaluation of educational programs, the principles can be applied to the assessment of projects such as DataONE that have technology, research, and education components. JCSEE created an American National Standard that identifies five areas that are essential for a quality evaluation (JCSEE, 2013). Evaluations must have *utility;* that is, they must provide relevant stakeholders, such as funding agencies and principal investigators, with appropriate information. The evaluation also must be *feasible,* meaning that it must be practical to implement and efficient in its use of resources. Evaluations should meet *proprietary* standards, including meeting legal, ethical, and moral requirements. All evaluations should be *accurate* and should depend on sound design and analysis, as well as reliable information. Finally, the evaluation must be *accountable,* which means the evaluation process and its implementation should be transparent. How the DataONE assessment design aligns well with these five areas will be reviewed later in this chapter.

Evaluating any project requires planning and careful implementation. However, two factors can intensify the difficulty of this process: the need to evaluate a complex project and the need to include assessment of data-related activities associated with data-intensive science. Data-intensive science is becoming more prevalent, as advances in computational simulation and modeling, automated data acquisition, and communication technologies have supported the amount of data collected, analyzed, reanalyzed, and stored (Committee on Ensuring the Utility and Integrity of Research Data in a Digital Age, 2009). As a complement to the data-intensive activities, science is operating in more complex environments in which scientific inquiry is no longer based in one or two disciplines, but instead reflects an increasing interconnectedness as science crosses many scientific domains (Hannay, 2009). Climate change is one example of an area of scientific inquiry that engages many different disciplines, and it is characterized by a wide range of scholarly interests (Dozier & Gaile, 2009; Hunt, Baldocchi, & van Ingen, 2009). Scientists engaged in examining questions related to climate change come from a wide range of domains including, but not limited to, climatologists, biologists, oceanographers, ecologists, and zoologists. These scientific inquiries produce large volumes of data that scientists may want to share and integrate across domains. To do this, efficient and consistent data management practices are essential (Hampton, Tewksbury, & Strasser, 2012). Additionally, in order to study complex data-intensive questions, scientific CIs are being developed, and their accompanying organizational structure is likely emergent and complex. DataONE is one such project, and examining the assessment experience can be helpful to other complex scientific projects.

FOUNDATION FOR EVALUATION: THE DATAONE ORGANIZATION

The DataONE organizational structure has been a key factor in shaping the evaluation design and empowering evaluation activities. Cyberinfrastructure development is a driving force for DataONE; however, CI must be supported by vibrant CE activities in order to assure that scientists' concerns are met and to encourage participation in DataONE. The question is how the organization can support evaluation activities that provide meaningful input throughout the organization and across the life of the project. A quick overview of the DataONE organization is helpful for understanding how the project operates and how evaluation activities are integrated into the structure.

Key management functions are handled by a small team comprised of the principal investigator, executive director, and the directors for CI and CE. This Management Team is advised on issues related to project planning and implementation by the Leadership Team, which is comprised of people representing each of the key CI and CE areas. The complexity of DataONE is further illustrated by the fact that the 14 Leadership Team members represent 10 institutions and a range of domains, including scientists, librarians, information scientists, and computer scientists. Two external bodies also are a part of the DataONE organization: the External Advisory Board, comprised of leading thinkers in the scientific and data management worlds, and the DataONE Users Group, comprised of people who use or are interested in using DataONE services. The DataONE organizational chart specifically notes the relationship with the NSF, the requirements of which include complying with a disciplined reporting schedule (Allard, 2012).

While CI development is undertaken by the Core Cyberinfrastructure Team, many DataONE activities are guided and carried out by working groups. The DataONE working group structure is important, because the working groups facilitate the conduct of targeted research and education activities with a broad group of scientists and users. In order to assure a sufficient focus on evaluation, one working group was initiated solely to address usability and assessment activities. While most working groups are designated as being either related to CI or to CE, the Usability & Assessment Working Group (U&AWG) is one of only two working groups that is placed in the organizational structure as a bridge between CI and CE activities.

The U&AWG focuses on assessment work for both internal decision making and external audiences, such as the funding agency. The working group addresses assessment from two perspectives—the assessment of DataONE stakeholders both internal and external to the project, and the assessment of the tools that can be used by scientists in the data-intensive environment.

The U&AWG charter (DataONE, 2013b) notes that the working group focuses on "the research, development, and implementation of the necessary

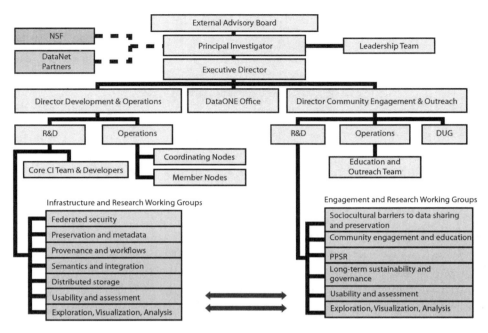

Figure 1. DataONE organizational chart (source: DataONE).

processes, systems, and methods to insure DataONE products and services meet network goals, include appropriate community involvement, and demonstrate progress and achievements of DataONE." The charter also notes that the scope of the U&AWG is "defined as many activities necessary to establish network performance indicators, measure performance, and adopt usability analysis principles and methods to insure high quality, community-driven products and services result from DataONE activities. In addition, the scope includes baseline and ongoing assessment of data practices of any DataONE stakeholders."

The U&AWG was one of the first working groups to be formally chartered; however, before it was fully commissioned, assessment activities had to begin in order to record important evaluative data, such as the attitudes and practices of stakeholders, so that a baseline could be established for the measurement of summative outcomes. To meet this need, an ad hoc assessment team was formed immediately after DataONE was funded, in order to begin these early assessment activities. When the U&AWG was constituted, the leaders of the ad hoc team served as working group leaders in order to maintain continuity.

Please note that many of the evaluation activities began concurrently, and the order in which they are discussed in this chapter should not be taken as a chronological sequence.

ENGAGING THE STAKEHOLDERS

As mentioned at the start of this chapter, an important part of evaluation activities is engaging stakeholders. In order to do this, a project must identify the stakeholders and understand the relationship between the project and each of the stakeholders. Therefore, one early assessment activity was to identify the stakeholders in the DataONE ecosystem and create a graphical representation of this network. The impetus for doing this activity came from three groups within DataONE—the U&AWG, the Management Team, and the Sociocultural Working Group (SCWG). The SCWG created the drafts for this network depiction, which were then shared with the rest of the DataONE organization for review and refinement. Opening up evaluation activities for review by DataONE CI and CE team members meant that evaluation was not merely developing in an isolated part of this complex organization, and that evaluation was a transparent and participatory process (Michener et al., 2012).

The stakeholders are viewed from two perspectives—those who are within the DataONE team as represented by the organizational structure and those with whom DataONE may interact. After carefully examining the environment in which data-intensive environmental science takes place, the stakeholder network diagram was created. The primary stakeholders in the network are scientists, who are viewed as being heterogeneous. Scientists are not represented by disciplinary boundaries since environmental research is highly interdisciplinary, and many scientists are practicing integrative science. Instead, the stakeholder community was organized by how scientists "do" science. This led to the identification of five *science research environments*: academia, government, private industry, nonprofit, and community (Allard, 2012; Michener et al., 2012).

DataONE also has a strong group of secondary stakeholders that were prioritized in the following order, so that assessment activities could be more focused:

> (1) Libraries and librarians exist in four of the five science research environments. The term "libraries" is meant to include

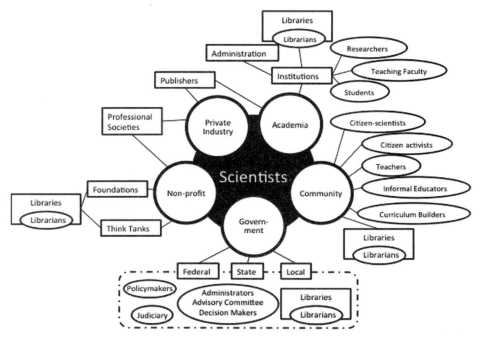

Figure 2. DataONE stakeholders network. The primary stakeholder is the scientist who may work in one of five science research environments. Secondary stakeholders are associated with each of these environments. Boxes represent organizations, and ovals represent individuals. Each level of government is represented by dashed boxes (source: Michener et al., 2012).

the full range of information-centric agencies and services that exist to serve environmental scientists and other stakeholders in the environmental science ecosystem.

(2) Administrators and policymakers at the federal, state, and local level.

(3) Publishers and professional societies.

(4) Think tanks, because they develop evidence-based position papers or policy suggestions.

(5) Citizen scientists, citizen activists, K-12 teachers, informal educators, and curriculum builders.

Identifying and prioritizing the stakeholders provided the U&AWG with a framework for scheduling baseline and follow-up assessments with the different groups. It also provided the U&AWG with a means to identify the different stakeholders who might be using tools for data-intensive science. It should be noted that for project management purposes, an assessment was designed to gather information about the attitudes and satisfaction of people participating on DataONE teams.

DESCRIBING THE PROJECT: STRUCTURING THE EVALUATION OF THE DATA-INTENSIVE ORGANIZATION

Another important assessment activity is describing the project so that the assessment can measure the key concepts. DataONE presented some unique challenges because of its focus on data-intensive science. Therefore, it was important to find a way to describe the diverse data-related activities in which DataONE was engaged over the full life of the project. Ultimately, the focus of DataONE is data, so a foundational concept for this organization was the data life cycle. The Leadership Team, with input from the working groups, developed a life cycle model that reflected the focus on the data-intensive environment. This life cycle is centered on "the data" and the different stages through which *data* pass, rather than following the actions of one person who engages the data. Data may not move through each stage, and it is most likely that different people will interact with the data over the eight stages in the life cycle.

The data life cycle begins when scientists plan their research. Next is the data collection stage that may occur in the field or laboratory. The data are then reviewed to assure the quality and described using metadata. The well-described data are then ready to be deposited into a trusted repository and preserved. At this point, data are discoverable and can be found by others. Data may then be accessed and integrated into multiple datasets for analysis.

The data life cycle is important for assessment since it provides a means for structuring questions to stakeholders about their current attitudes toward data and data practices. It also provides a way to group the tools that scientists need, and to catalog the tools that already exist that are helpful for both usability testing and assessments such as surveys.

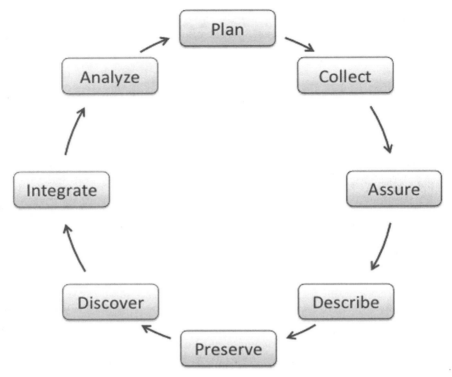

Figure 3. The DataONE data life cycle focuses on the eight stages for the "life" of data (source: DataONE).

KEY CONCEPTS AND METRICS

The complexity of the project made it a challenge to identify a manageable number of key concepts that should be measured. This identification process began with the three DataONE objectives and the activities that were being undertaken to accomplish these objectives. Addressing each of these objectives required a different assessment design. Below each objective is listed with the focus of the associated evaluation activities. This includes an example of the metrics that were identified for the evaluation. In each case, the evaluation was designed to provide formative information for project management, as well as establish a basis for summative evaluation at predetermined points over the life of the project.

Objective 1: Providing Access to Current Databases

Evaluation for this objective focused on CI operational elements. Metrics were identified for logging and monitoring of instrumentation services, since these describe how the CI made items accessible to potential users. Other metrics focused on the content and use of the current databases by recording the number of users and the volume of data distributed and made available. The process to capture and record these metrics was implemented. Addressing this objective also required evaluation of the tools that scientists use to find data, in terms of their usability and effectiveness.

Objective 2: Creating a Global CI of Biological and Environmental Data from Different Resources

Evaluation for this objective focused on the emerging DataONE network. Metrics included counting the number and diversity of the participating member nodes, the volume of their holdings, and the diversity of these data sources.

Objective 3: Facilitating a New Culture in Science

Evaluation of this objective was focused on planning for measuring summative outcomes, and it required an understanding of the existing data attitudes and practices among stakeholders, so it would be possible to measure any change that occurred. Therefore, a series of "baseline" studies were planned early in the project, with follow-ups scheduled thereafter to allow for a longitudinal comparison. A schedule was created for the primary stakeholder group—scientists (for full baseline results, see Tenopir et al., 2011; for other analyses from the baseline, see Sayogo & Pardo, 2012; Tenopir, Allard, & Davis, 2011)—and for several of the secondary stakeholder groups, including libraries and librarians, both academic and federal (for academic library baseline results, see Tenopir, Birch, & Allard, 2012), and educators. Data managers also were part of the evaluation plan, as they often are prominent in the government research science environment. While a change between the baseline and follow-up survey could not be causally tied to DataONE activities, it could capture a change in the environment. Some key questions in the survey do allow for the DataONE team to measure awareness of DataONE and participation in DataONE events.

Another important part of assessing this objective relates to the tools used to work with data across the data life cycle. The evaluation design included doing an assessment of existing tools that are available and are being used at each point in the data life cycle. The tool assessment also includes doing usability tests on tools that are designed specifically for DataONE. These formative assessments directly queried stakeholders who use or would use the tools, and results were immediately shared with the Core Cyberinfrastructure Team so they could be utilized to refine and improve the tools in the Investigator Toolkit.

LOOKING AT THE QUALITY OF THE EVALUATION

Substantial effort has gone into the DataONE evaluation process, from the early stages of project development and throughout the life of the project. Now it is time to assess the quality of the evaluation itself, by comparing the DataONE evaluation to the items listed in the JCSEE American National Standard (JCSEE, 2013). It is important to note that this chapter's author is a member of the DataONE Leadership Team and has been closely involved in several evaluation activities; therefore, this analysis does not represent a review by an independent evaluator. However, this kind of analysis conducted by an evaluation team member still holds value because it provides an overview of strengths and identifies areas that would benefit from improvement.

Utility refers to whether the evaluation process and results are useful to the project's stakeholders. There are many dimensions that are applied to assess the level of utility. The DataONE evaluation program exhibited quality in several dimensions, including: (1) the evaluations are primarily overseen by the U&AWG, whose members are well-qualified to design, implement, and analyze usability and assessment studies. Each member was specifically invited to be in the group for these skills. (2) The evaluation has devoted attention to the internal stakeholders, such as surveying DataONE team members about their satisfaction with working in the organization. Additionally, the evaluation has provided the Core Cyberinfrastructure Team with results to aid in their work. (3) Communication about the evaluation has been timely. A utility dimension that could benefit from more attention is including the full range of stakeholders. Because of the complexity of the project, the evaluation focus was narrowed to only the primary stakeholders, and the highest-priority secondary stakeholder. If there were sufficient resources available, the evaluation would benefit from being able to devote more attention to other stakeholders.

Feasibility refers to increasing the evaluation's effectiveness and efficiency. The DataONE evaluation has done a good job of using project management strategies to drive the evaluation. In addition, the evaluation has been implemented in a manner that is responsive to the project. For example, the data mangers' assessment was added after it became clear that this was an important stakeholder subgroup that had not been identified in the initial stakeholder network. Finally, because the evaluation design was embedded in the fabric of the organizational design, it has been able to make good use of limited resources.

Proprietary standards refer to doing what is legal and ethical. The Data-ONE evaluation strategy has focused on learning from the stakeholders, and all surveys have been conducted under review from the institutional review board of the investigator's university. This assured that the rights of the participants were protected. In addition, the surveys and usability tests clearly identified the fact that this was a DataONE activity. Whenever possible, results have been published to share with the broader community of stakeholders.

Accuracy refers to the truthfulness and dependability of the evaluation's results. Published results have been peer reviewed, which suggests that reviewers felt the findings were well-supported by a valid research design, by the data collected, and by evidence presented. Most of the usability work has been used internally rather than submitted for publication. However, care has always been taken to follow the best practices for usability research implementation and analysis.

Evaluation accountability refers to creating adequate documentation of the evaluations and to working to improve the evaluation processes. The DataONE evaluation program has produced documentation both for internal use and external publication. However, it would be useful to more fully study the accountability of the evaluation design and procedures and to conduct external assessment of the evaluation program.

LESSONS LEARNED

The evaluation of DataONE does offer some important lessons for other complex, data-oriented organizations seeking to develop an effective evaluation program.

Planning is essential.

If possible, evaluation activities should be considered at the inception of the project. In DataONE's case, this allowed for evaluation to be built into the organizational structure of the project, which resulted in the most effective use of limited resources and also provided a formal communication conduit between the many parts of the organization. Planning also meant that there were sufficient resources in place to allow assessment to begin as soon as the project was funded, although the initial planning was done by an ad hoc committee.

Complexity must be simplified.

When dealing with a complex project, it is important to find ways to identify key concepts and to depict complex relationships in other ways, such as with diagrams. For example, focusing on the organizational objectives helped to clarify what needed to be measured. Examples of diagrammatic simplicity are the stakeholder network and the data life cycle. Each of these provided direct ways to talk about important aspects of the project in direct terms.

The evaluation team is key.

DataONE's evaluation activities did include many members of the DataONE community. However, the design and implementation of the overall program was the responsibility of a small team that had extensive skills in assessment-related research. The team leaders were experienced in facilitating team participation in assessment activities, and they were also highly qualified to lead this kind of work.

Evaluation needs to be supported by sufficient resources.

Creating a working group that focused on usability and assessment guaranteed that there would be a team devoted to these activities. Integrating this group into the organizational structure also helped assure that resources would be allocated to evaluation activities.

Organizational communication is important.

With a complex organization, it is very easy for activities to be isolated in one area, meaning that communication across the organization needs to be purposely nurtured. Evaluation activities must engage all of the stakeholders, including those within the organization. Therefore, creating and maintaining strong communication channels is a core value. DataONE accomplished this by placing the U&AWG in a position to address both the CI and CE aspects of the project. Additionally, evaluation team leaders were members of the Leadership Team, which promoted conversation across all the working groups, the Management Team, and the Core Cyberinfrastructure Team.

Data should be specifically addressed.

DataONE recognized that in a data-intensive organization, there needs to be a special focus on data. Therefore, a data life cycle was adopted and used as a guide during evaluation design. Additionally, specific metrics should be developed to assess the data in the environment.

A complex project characterized by a distributed organization focused on data-intensive science offers challenges for effective and efficient project evaluation. However, careful planning and disciplined implementation can result in assessments that yield useful information for both project management and external agencies.

SIX BEST PRACTICES

The lessons learned can be condensed into six best practices for evaluation of data management programs.

Plan, plan, plan.

Evaluation usually does not start until the project is underway, but before the data management project begins, it is essential to identify how accomplishment and change will be evaluated. Evaluation planning takes time and effort that does not reap immediate rewards, but as the project progresses, planning will make the evaluation process smoother and the results more meaningful.

Simple is good.

Two common sayings provide helpful guidance when planning and conducting evaluations for data management programs—"simplicity is elegance" and "a picture speaks a thousand words." It is useful to find ways to state the project goals simply and then share these goals visually. For example, a diagram can quickly convey key concepts that are important to measure and the relationships that exist between the many concepts related to the project.

Leadership is key; teamwork is required.

Evaluations require planning to design and commitment to implement. Leadership from a very small core group of project members is needed to accomplish this. However, regardless of the size of the data management program, the people involved represent a wide range of expertise and skills. Input is needed from many of these people in order to assess all aspects of the program. This happens more smoothly if the leaders cultivate respect for evaluations and build a sense of team around the activities required for collecting the evaluation data.

Evaluation requires resources.

During the planning process, it is important to allocate sufficient resources to evaluation activities. It can be tempting to use these resources in other aspects of the data management program. However, evaluation is important for the sustainability of the project in terms of demonstrating the project's progress and ability to meet the project's goals.

Develop strong communication channels.

Evaluation activities involve many members of the data management project's team. Having established pathways for communication helps assure that evaluation activities can be accomplished smoothly. Communication processes should be identified during the evaluation planning stage so the framework is in place before the evaluation begins.

Focus on data.

Remember that this evaluation is about the data rather than simply about the team or the organization. Be sure to identify metrics to assess the data.

ACKNOWLEDGMENTS

Data Observation Network for Earth (DataONE) is supported by NSF award #0830944 under a Cooperative Agreement. The author wishes to acknowledge all the team members of the DataONE Usability & Assessment Working Group, who are leading the assessments, and the team members of the Sociocultural Working Group, who are providing support.

REFERENCES

Allard, S. (2012). DataONE: Facilitating eScience through collaboration. *Journal of eScience Librarianship, 1*(1), 4–17. http://dx.doi.org/10.7191/jeslib.2012.1004

Center for Disease Control and Prevention (CDC). (2013). A framework for program evaluation. Retrieved from http://www.cdc.gov/eval/framework/index.htm

Committee on Ensuring the Utility and Integrity of Research Data in a Digital Age. (2009). Ensuring the integrity, accessibility, and stewardship of research data in the digital age. Washington, DC: National Academies of Science. Retrieved from http://www.nap.edu/catalog.php?record_id=12615

DataONE. (2013a). What is DataONE? Retrieved from https://www.dataone.org/what-dataone

DataONE. (2013b). Usability & Assessment Working Group charter. Retrieved from https://www.dataone.org/sites/all/documents/U&A_Charter.pdf

Dozier, J., and Gail, W. B. (2009). The emerging science of environmental applications. In T. Hey, S. Tansley, & K. Tole (Eds.), *The fourth paradigm: Data-intensive scientific discovery* (13–19). Redmond, WA: Microsoft Research. Retrieved from http://research.microsoft.com/en-us/collaboration/fourthparadigm/4th_paradigm_book_complete_lr.pdf

Hampton, S. E., Tewksbury, J. J., & Strasser, C. A. (2012). Ecological data in the Information Age. *Frontiers in Ecology and the Environment, 10*(2), 59. http://dx.doi.org/10.1890/1540-9295-10.2.59

Hannay, T. (2009). From Web 2.0 to the global database. In T. Hey, S. Tansley, & K. Tole (Eds.), *The fourth paradigm: Data-intensive scientific discovery* (215–220). Redmond, WA: Microsoft Research. Retrieved from http://research.microsoft.com/en-us/collaboration/fourthparadigm/4th_paradigm_book_complete_lr.pdf

Hunt, J. R., Baldocchi, D., and van Ingen, C. (2009). Redefining ecological science using data. In T. Hey, S. Tansley, & K. Tole (Eds.), *The fourth paradigm: Data-intensive scientific discovery* (21–26). Redmond, WA: Microsoft Research. Retreived from http://research.microsoft.com/en-us/collaboration/fourthparadigm/4th_paradigm_book_complete_lr.pdf

Joint Committee on Standards for Educational Evaluation (JCSEE). (2013). Program evaluation standards. Retrieved from http://www.jcsee.org/program-evaluation-standards

Michener, W. K., Allard, S., Budden, A., Cook, R., Douglass,K., Frame, M. . . . Vieglais, D. A. (2012). Participatory design of DataONE—Enabling cyberinfrastructure for the biological and environmental sciences. *Ecological Informatics, 11*, 5–15. http://dx.doi.org/10.1016/j.ecoinf.2011.08.007

National Science Foundation (NSF). (2007). Sustainable digital data preservation and access-network partners (DataNet) (NSF 07-601). Retrieved from http://www.nsf.gov/pubs/2007/nsf07601/nsf07601.htm

Sayogo, D. S., & Pardo, T. A. (2012). Exploring the determinants of scientific data sharing: Understanding the motivation to publish research data. *Government Information Quarterly, 30*(Supplement 1), S19–S31. http://dx.doi.org/10.1016/j.giq.2012.06.011

Scriven, M. (1999). The nature of evaluation: Part I. Relation to psychology. *Practical Assessment, Research and Evaluation, 6*(11). Retrieved from http://pareonline.net/getvn.asp?v=6&n=11

Tenopir, C., Allard, S., & Davis, M. (2011). Understanding the data management needs and data sharing challenges of environmental scientists. In M. B. Jones & C. Gries (Eds.), *Proceedings of the Environmental Information Management Conference 2011 (EIM 2011)* (138–144). Santa Barbara, CA. Retrieved from https://eim.ecoinformatics.org/eim2011/eim-proceedings-2011/view

Tenopir, C., Allard, S., Douglass, K. Aydinoglu, A. U., Wu, L. Read, E., & Manoff, M. (2011). Data sharing by scientists: Practices and perceptions. *PLoS ONE, 6*(6), e21101. http://dx.doi.org/10.1371/journal.pone.0021101

Tenopir, C., Birch, B., and Allard, S. (2012). Academic libraries and research data services: Current practices and plans for the future. Chicago, IL: Association of College Research Libraries.

Westat, J. F. (2010). *The 2010 user-friendly handbook for project evaluation.* Washington, DC: National Science Foundation.

14 | What to Measure?

Toward Metrics for
Research Data Management

ANGUS WHYTE, LAURA MOLLOY, NEIL BEAGRIE,
AND JOHN HOUGHTON

INTRODUCTION: WHY MEASURE, WHAT TO MEASURE, AND HOW?

The importance of metrics for evaluating research data management (RDM) seems almost too obvious to state. Yet as the quotes below suggest, choosing metrics or indicators requires careful planning and consensus on what to measure and how. In RDM, that consensus has yet to be achieved. So while some of the metrics we refer to in this chapter employ readily countable things, such as downloads, most employ metrics that are not truly numeric, such as rating scales or categories of variables.[1]

> "If you cannot measure something, your understanding of it is meagre." Lord Kelvin

> "The most important things cannot be measured." W. Edwards Demming

> "Not everything that counts can be counted, and not everything that can be counted counts." Albert Einstein

Choosing an appropriate framework is a challenge for information professionals involved in evaluating changes brought about by developing and using RDM infrastructure and services. In this chapter, we review relevant approaches applied in several contexts in the United Kingdom and Australia. These employ methods from economics, management, and information science, and they include cost-benefit analysis, benchmarking, risk management, contingent valuation, and traditional social science methods, such as interviews, surveys, and focus groups.

In this section, we introduce key evaluation aims and concepts. Our starting point is that the main questions will be "what can and should be measured?" as much as "what criteria and metrics should be used?" The chapter focuses on two evaluation contexts: (1) developing research institutions' support services and infrastructure for RDM, and (2) assessing economic impacts of national or international repositories and data centres.

In each evaluation context, we assume the aim will be to identify improvements achieved or required, considering how a project or programme's aims, activities, and outputs relate to their wider context of data policy and practices.

The final section offers conclusions and suggests factors that will affect evaluation in coming years, including growing opportunities to track impacts of data sharing and publication.

Evaluation Aims and Key Concepts

Measurement is a tool for bringing about improvement in any activity that needs to be managed. It is as essential to evaluation as it is to research, enabling information, understanding, and knowledge to be derived from data. Evaluation enables everyone involved in RDM and its governance to decide where to invest their time and public money. As well as assessing what worked and why, evaluation can feed into learning and decision making. It can help in planning the deployment of resources toward new outputs that will produce desired outcomes.

Evaluation also can serve other aims: It can help communicate requirements for more effective change; it can alert people to unforeseen risks; and it can aid reflection on their assumptions and uncertainties about problems still to be addressed. Figure 1 summarises common evaluation types according to the questions they consider.

Evaluation needs data, and data management planning, just like other forms of research. The main parameters will come from an evaluation plan. This will set out criteria to match the expected benefits, costs, or other outcomes of the intervention being evaluated, and metrics or indicators that provide the evidence of whether or not these have been met.

Evaluation Type	Suggested questions
Process including Product and Needs	Does it work?
	Is resource use minimized?
	Does it attain longer-term goals?
	Is it pleasing to use?
	Are there any ethical/legal/safety issues for those who are involved?
	To what extent are the desired changes occurring? For whom?
	What are the potential barriers/facilitators?
	What is most appropriate development activity?
Outcome	What are the desired changes in behavior or state?
	To what extent are desired changes occurring? For whom?
	Are the changes effective?
Impact	What are the unintended outcomes?
	To what extent have the intended benefits been achieved?
	What is the overall effect of the development activity?
	What are the cost benefits?
	What is the cost effectiveness of the development activity?

Figure 1. Source: Glenaffric Ltd. (2007).

An evaluation framework guides the planning and conduct of an evaluation. The framework should help establish and track how those involved have framed the situation they are trying to improve and its context. Evaluation frameworks are ways of conceptualising why actors and others with an interest saw the need to act, and with what resources and expectations. For example, on what basis has repository X been funded? Has policy Y been framed with the right expectations, considering the intended outcomes and resourcing for its implementation?

Evaluation frameworks can be expressed in terms of a "logic model." This is a flow diagram expressing principles and outcomes the project or programme outputs should satisfy, to justify deploying the capabilities believed necessary to provide a range of activities and outputs, with the expected short-term outcomes or longer-term impacts. Figure 2 introduces a logic model for RDM evaluation that presents common elements of these.

Working with a logic model should help identify what criteria and metrics will best fit the aims and scope of the project or programme. Evaluation also should be based on an appreciation of the context, to understand

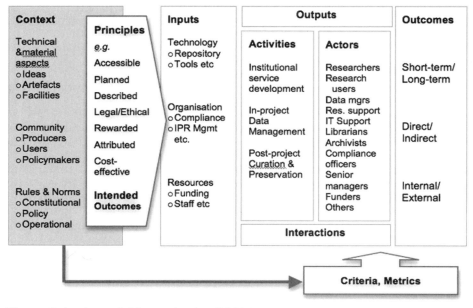

Figure 2. Logic model for evaluating RDM in context.

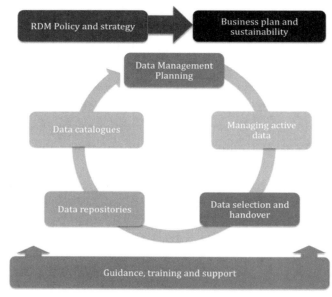

Figure 3. Outputs of institutional RDM development: support service components.

implicit assumptions that have been made in the intervention, or factors that may explain any unforeseen outcomes. These contextual factors do not need to be explicitly stated in a logic model as shown in Figure 2, but they will be implicit in it.

Contextual factors are summarised in the rest of this introduction. In the three main sections, we look at methods and approaches suited to different contexts, which highlight different parts of Figure 2 as follows:

- Benchmarking to identify gaps in the support capabilities needed as inputs to further development;
- Developing criteria and metrics indicating the outcomes from service development; and
- Evaluating the economic impacts of data centre activities to curate and preserve research data.

The outputs will typically be support services and infrastructure for RDM. One view of the "components" of these is shown in Figure 3, reflecting the authors' involvement in the Digital Curation Centre's Institutional Engagement programme and the United Kingdom's Managing Research Data programme.[2]

EVALUATION IN CONTEXT

Developing new RDM policies and systems requires appreciation of those already in place. One way to appreciate the dynamics of data management in context is through case studies of disciplinary practices (e.g., Hartswood et al., 2012; Whyte, Job, Giles, & Lawrie, 2008). Nevertheless crossdisciplinary RDM infrastructure development is relatively new, and there are few frameworks offering the information professional comprehensive and well-established metrics.

The Institutional Analysis and Development (IAD) framework is used in this chapter to relate contextual factors to RDM principles, capabilities, service components, and their outcomes. The main factors are included in Figure 2 under "context." This economic framework was developed to analyse how organizations and communities make decisions and rules in order to sustain a resource or achieve a desired outcome (Hess & Ostrom, 2005).

The IAD framework has been applied to a wide range of infrastructure and resource types. These include analysing how open access repositories of research outputs contribute to a shared pool of knowledge (Hess & Ostrom, 2005). The approach focuses on "common-pool resources." These are resources with two key economic characteristics: firstly, it is difficult to effectively exclude people from consuming the resource, and secondly, one person's consumption subtracts from the resource available to others. A "public good" also has the first characteristic, but it can be consumed by any number of people without diminishing the resource (Hess & Ostrom, 2003).

The economic definition of research data as a "public good" is important because it has been the cornerstone of funding body policy on research data management, stemming from a 2007 OECD report. However, systems such as digital libraries and data repositories that provide infrastructure for distributing data are common-pool resources (Hess & Ostrom, 2005). Accordingly, we define RDM infrastructure as common-pool resources that provide and sustain the public-good qualities of research data.

There are types of economic good, apart from private goods. A "club good" is only available to members of closed circles, although sharing more widely would not result in there being less of it. Recent surveys and case studies have illustrated the barriers to openly sharing research data (e.g., PARSE Insight, 2010). The picture emerging from these is that research data producers treat much research data as a club good. Some data legitimately stays in this category, such as sensitive personal data that may only be shared with researchers who are subject to ethical oversight.

The IAD framework analyses "patterns of interaction," such as those involved in developing digital repositories for research materials. An evaluation might, for example, examine the interactions between research groups and service providers involved in developing workflows for depositing data, or how a data centre consults its depositor community on changes to its collection policy. The value of the IAD framework here is in pointing out the external variables relevant to the evaluation.

Technical and Material Aspects of Data as a Resource: Ideas, Artefacts, and Facilities

Research data begin as traces or impressions that result from the expression of ideas, leading to further ideas being expressed: "data is the primary building block of information, comprising the lowest level of abstraction in any field of knowledge, where it is identifiable as collections of numbers, characters, images or other symbols that when contextualised in a certain way represent facts, figures or ideas as communicable information" (Pryor, 2011, p. 3).

The process of turning research data into an economic "good" starts with the claim that it signifies something relevant to a research question. As research progresses through stages of cleaning, analysis, and transformation into outputs, the data accumulates a network of relationships to models and other information, asserting how the data describes properties of whatever phenomena are being investigated (Edwards, 2010). Data gains in value if the researchers' peers and others who use the research outputs can access and understand this contextual information sufficiently to make use of it. If it has that value, a formally governed archive or repository will be more likely to want to support further exchanges between producers (the originating researchers) and consumers.

This process and the RDM infrastructure to support it is, in effect, about turning data into a commodity. Until it is contextualised and packaged, its potential consumers are excluded, and sharing it may lower its value if doing so diminishes the producer's ability to describe what it relates to and how it was produced. Some data will resist attempts to turn it into a commodity (e.g., because it depends on nontransferable technology or on material aspects of the context; because it depends on the tacit knowledge of its producers to understand it; or because no consensus has been established on how it should be packaged to translate its meaning between contexts).

Research facilities, instruments, and analysis platforms shape data production and management. Their location, capacity, and capabilities will set boundaries on what more can be achieved by developing new RDM infrastructure to support the institution as a whole, as well as offering examples of good practice. These need to be considered in any evaluation of (say) institutional backup solutions. Users' requirements for data retrieval will vary across different instruments (e.g., in file quantities, sizes, complexity, and overall volumes). It is important to recognise limits on the feasibility of one-size-fits-all approaches.

Data archives have been around for decades in some disciplines, notably in areas such as astronomy, geosciences, genomics, and particle physics, where there are strong drivers toward sharing access to large, expensive instruments and facilities. These have been the focus of insightful studies on the development of cyberinfrastructure facilities to support collaborative research (e.g., Cragin & Shankar, 2006). Smaller science and scholarship communities also increasingly are using data-intensive methods, such as analysis of digital images or large public datasets (Wilson, Martinez-Uribe, Fraser, & Jeffreys, 2011).

The "artefacts" that embody data and relate it to its producers' expressed ideas also will limit the possibilities for harvesting and pooling data. Moving to digital research artefacts requires careful attention to the relative risks and affordances of physical and digital artefacts, such as workflows and notebooks (Hartswood et al., 2012). De Roure, Bechhofer, Goble, and Newman (2011) identify dimensions of "digital research objects" that could be used in evaluating how these support RDM. These are the extent to which objects need to be reusable, repurposeable, repeatable, reproducible, replayable, referenceable, revealable, and respectful.

Research objects may be managed in a formal and collaborative manner, in a similar way to software code used for data analysis, but standardised "enterprise" solutions will not necessarily meet the needs of research to explore novel ways of working with data. Information professionals need to codesign with research communities (e.g., to build on the platforms they already use) and minimise the effort to share data (e.g., by extracting metadata automatically) (Beitz, 2013).

Communities: Producers, Users, and Policymakers

Data producers may be anyone involved in producing outputs, including those working on the supporting infrastructure, as well as researchers and "citizen scientists." In most research fields, there will be a range of stakeholders involved in data production (e.g., companies, policymakers, nongovernmental organisations, and individual citizens). They may be participating as representative users interested in testing the results, or more directly involved in project design and data gathering.

Stakeholder analysis is an important early step in evaluation. The information professional will need to establish the range of actors involved. In an institutional context, they are likely to include, for example, library, IT, research support, and governance representatives. For a subject-based data repository, the stakeholders will likely include representatives of funding bodies and the user community. It is as important to ask questions about who the client of the evaluation is and who "owns" the outcomes or process as it will be to ask the same questions of the project being evaluated.

To evaluate an RDM project, increasingly we need to ask how its provision will interoperate with other actors. The landscape that repositories operate in is becoming more complex, with a diverse range of organisations involved in providing infrastructure. Infrastructures for RDM can be thought of in terms of layers; at the bottom, we have networked computing and storage providers, including commercial providers of cloud services as well as public National Research and Education Networks (NRENS). On top of this, we see "cyberinfrastructure," such as DataONE emerging in the United States, and "research infrastructures," like OpenAire in Europe, providing increasingly standardised services that are federated across national borders (Whyte, 2011)

Policymaking bodies are well established in some communities, bringing self-governance of data practices and curation resources. Committees comprised of scientists and research users plan large particle physics experiments and astronomical studies, for example. This is likely to become more common across all disciplines with the trend toward larger and more interdisciplinary research teams (Wuchty, Jones, & Uzzi, 2007).

Rules and Norms: Constitutional, Policy, and Operational

In recent years, "top-down" data governance through public funders and regulatory bodies has become more pronounced, reflecting the need to address technology changes in science, and broader public interest in research transparency and integrity (Smith, this volume).

Common principles are being adopted across national boundaries and funding bodies. Australian institutions, for example, are governed by principles of responsible research conduct (NHMRC, 2007). Research councils in the UK jointly expressed a set a data policy framework in 2011. Their "common data principles" set out institutions' and researchers' shared roles and responsibilities. In summary, the principles are that data management should (Research Councils UK, 2011):

1. Share data as a public good: Publicly funded research data are produced in the public interest and should be made openly available with few restrictions.

2. Plan for preservation: Institutional and project-specific data management policies and plans needed to ensure valued data remains usable.

3. Make data discoverable: Metadata should be available and discoverable; published results should indicate how to access supporting data.

4. Ensure confidentiality: Research organisation policies and practices should ensure legal, ethical, and commercial constraints are assessed, and that the research process is not damaged by inappropriate release.

5. Support first use: Provision for a period of exclusive use, to enable research teams to publish results.

6. Give recognition: Data users should acknowledge data sources and terms as well as conditions of access.

7. Use public funding well: Investment is appropriate and must be efficient and cost-effective.

Principles such as these help identify capabilities an institution needs in order to contribute to a research data commons. The IAD framework makes an analytic distinction between "constitutional rules," which are principles such as these that define broad roles and responsibilities, and "collective choice" policies, such as those formed by individuals in research councils and institutions that constrain rules at an operational level. Operational rules include, for example, who may submit research data to a repository and access it.

Sustaining common-pool resources like repositories demands "nested levels of governance," according to the IAD framework. This is most effective when higher-level authorities set parameters that allow self-determination by relatively smaller communities of providers and decision makers, each "unified as to the purpose and goals of the information resource or knowledge commons at hand" (Hess & Ostrom, 2005, p. 54). This implies distinctive approaches should be allowed to evolve to meet broad principles. Government, public, and commercial funding bodies, institutions, learned societies, and journals define policy principles, for example, on data licensing and privacy. These provide broad criteria for evaluation purposes, but research groups and stakeholders with shared research goals need to determine how metrics should be applied consistently with their research goals.

Examples of this "nested" governance include repository certification and data appraisal. Criteria in use for both of these are similar across disciplinary data repositories (see chapter by Reilly & Waltz, and the criteria listed in Whyte & Wilson, 2010). Yet they vary enough in their detail to accommodate differences between, for example, the kinds of contextual information needed for reuse and quality assurance measures. Compare, for example, the criteria used by the UK's environmental and social science data centres (NERC, 2012; Van den Eynden, 2013).

EVALUATING RESEARCH INSTITUTIONS' CAPABILITIES FOR SERVICE DEVELOPMENT

A range of capabilities is needed to set up RDM services and infrastructure. The "inputs" to development activities are human and technical capabilities, as well as the financial resources to deploy them. How well deployed are these currently, and are they enough for the institution to implement its own policies or to comply with others? Information professionals may be called on to help answer this question by conducting a review and gap analysis. Benchmarking approaches can be used to support this type of formative evaluation, drawing their criteria from a capability model for the service concerned.

The Collaborative Assessment of Research Data Infrastructures and Objectives tool (CARDIO, 2011) aims to help establish consensus on RDM capabilities and identify gaps in current provision. Institutional preparedness is assessed using a capability model adapted from Cornell University's digital preservation programme (Kenney & McGovern, 2005). CARDIO users rate existing provision on 30 criteria covering 3 areas—organisation, technology, and resources—and come together to agree on their ratings and to prioritise action. The tool can be used online, in person, or in a combination of these.

Requirements gathering and gap analysis complement one another. Many institutions have begun the process by consulting with academic staff in two or three research groups or departments in different schools or faculties. It helps to involve researchers whose experience spans a range of funders, career stages, and research disciplines and data types. A workshop that brings academics who have participated in requirements gathering together with the relevant service providers can offer a forum to consolidate the findings and put together a plan for further action.

A challenge for RDM is to measure the financial input required to sustain RDM services and assess whether these resources have been appropriately spent. The costs may cut across a university's established functions (e.g., IT, library, research support), and a large proportion will arise from academic activities that have not traditionally been accounted for in grant applications.

Life cycle models for RDM can address this by providing standard activity categories, so that time spent on each activity can be counted or estimated. Two examples are the Keeping Research Data Safe (KRDS) project activity model and the California Digital Library Total Cost of Preservation (TCP) framework (Abrams Cruse, Kunze, & Mundrane, 2012).

WHAT DIFFERENCE HAS IT MADE? IDENTIFYING OUTCOMES

Measuring benefits is often quite challenging, especially when these benefits do not easily lend themselves to expression in quantitative terms. Often a mixture of approaches will be required to analyse both qualitative and quantitative outcomes and present the differences made. To assist institutions, the KRDS project created a Benefits Framework and a Value-Chain and Benefit Impact Analysis Toolkit (Charles Beagrie Ltd., 2011a). These aim to help institutions identify the full scope of benefits (e.g., management and preservation of research data) and to present them in a succinct way to a range of different stakeholders (e.g., when developing business cases or advocacy).

The KRDS Benefits Framework uses three dimensions to illuminate the advantages that investments potentially generate. These dimensions serve as a high-level framework within which thinking about benefits can be organised and then sharpened into more focused value propositions. The framework is shown in Figure 4.

Each tool—the KRDS Benefits Framework and the Value-Chain and Benefit Impact Analysis tool—contains a more detailed guide and worksheet(s). Both provide a series of common examples of generic benefits that have been revealed by their application to frequently arise from the management and preservation of research data.

The first dimension is "What is the Outcome?" which may consist of direct or indirect benefits. Direct benefits are positive statements about the value created by the outputs of RDM development (e.g., those in Figure 3). For example, we might say that preservation of a certain corpus of digital materials permits future scholars to undertake particular forms of schol-

WHO BENEFITS?

Figure 4. The KRDS Benefits Framework (source: Charles Beagrie Ltd., 2011a).

arship. In general, direct benefits take the form of a value proposition along the lines of, "If this activity occurs, an outcome will occur, which is of value to some groups of stakeholders."

Indirect benefits are another form of benefit that can potentially emerge and are best understood as "costs and/or risks avoided." For example, investing now in the preservation of a particular research dataset might be justified on the basis that if the data were allowed to disappear, recreating it at a later time might be extremely (or even prohibitively) expensive. In this sense, investment in preservation now avoids a larger cost sometime in the future. The indirect benefits of RDM can be as compelling as the direct benefits, and these should not be overlooked.

The Benefits Framework can be customised and extended as needed to visualise and present benefits in different ways. For example, "Who Benefits (Internal/External) in the Framework?" could be further subdivided by more specific groups of stakeholders, if desired. It is a powerful tool for stakeholder analysis. An illustration of this, populated with some examples of common benefits, is provided in Figure 5.

Dimension 3 (Who Benefits) Sub-divided by a University's Stakeholders					
Internal Benefits			**External Benefits**		
Researcher	**Research Group**	**Institution**	**Research Funder**	**Discipline**	**Others** (e.g. NHS, etc)
Increased visibility/ citation	No data lost from Post Doc turnover	Fulfilling organisational mandate(s)	Increasing research productivity	Scholarly communication /access to data	Knowledge transfer to other sectors

Figure 5. Example of dimension three of the KRDS Benefits Framework, expanded for a selection of a university's stakeholders (source: Charles Beagrie Ltd., 2011b).

The University of Bath recently published a more detailed example (Beagrie & Pink, 2012). This illustrates benefits for internal stakeholders (academic staff and researchers, students, professional services, and the institution) and external partners (industry and commerce, public and voluntary sectors, government, and society).

UK institutions taking part in the Jisc Managing Research Data programme (Jisc, 2013) have provided a useful context to apply the KRDS framework. The programme aimed to improve RDM practice in UK universities in two phases: 2009–2011 and 2011–2013. One aim was to establish activities that institutions could justify sustaining beyond the projects, against a background of reduced public funding. This demanded clearly articulated evidence of the benefits achieved by project and programme activity.

Eight projects in the first iteration of the programme (2009–2011) each produced a benefits case study using the KRDS framework to identify potential advantages and metrics (Charles Beagrie Ltd., 2011a), and their input was used to develop lists of common benefits in the KRDS Toolkit (Charles Beagrie Ltd., 2011c). This was a first step to building an evidence base for the programme.

Overall, the first iteration of the programme emphasised the relative newness of impact and benefit assessment for RDM, and corresponding challenges arising from that such as:

- The importance of providing templates and guidance on best practice to assist projects;
- The implications in terms of resources and time for undertaking different levels of impact and cost/benefit analysis; and
- The need to further explore metrics that could be applied to measure many of the benefits identified.

The programme's second phase of activity ran from October 2011 to July 2013 and centred around seventeen projects to design and implement RDM infrastructure in their host institutions. Each aimed to provide a range of the outputs shown in Figure 3 and also to enable a more formative "evidence-gathering," programme-wide activity.

This activity gathered and synthesised evidence for beneficial change as the evidence emerged. The emphasis in this second phase of the programme was on encouraging regular blogging as a reporting platform and means of dialogue, and on building up a narrative from emerging themes and challenges.

Each of the projects in the Jisc programme had to produce a report at the end of the project detailing the benefits achieved, with specific evidence supporting each benefit. It was recognised that some measures could relatively easily be tracked numerically (such as website visits, usage statistics of web resources, number of enquiries for support received, number of data management plans created and approved, or attendance at RDM training events), but some benefits would not be so quantifiable.

A team of three "evidence gatherers" led this work, negotiating with projects to identify benefits that could be demonstrated and to clarify the evidence available to support their claims. This context demanded a model that was lightweight, simple, and clearly defined, yet capable of producing compelling and comprehensive evidence of benefits delivered by the programme as a whole. It also would need to be applied within relatively short timescales and tight resource limits.

Guidance was provided to help projects discriminate between an output, the benefit achieved by that output, and the evidence available for each benefit claimed. A benefit was described as something that could be determined by asking, "What does this output help us (the institution/researchers) to do better?" The guidance described the evidence that would be sought as "specific, clear metrics (quantitative measures) and specific, clear qualitative evidence such as narratives and short case studies, all of which support or prove the benefit" (Jisc, 2012). Projects were then encouraged to select and focus on three to five benefits each and produce a statement outlining these. The evidence gatherers scrutinized these statements and, after analysis across the programme, anticipated benefits were categorised as shown in Figure 6.

Four types of benefits were identified through this activity, each with its concomitant evidence. The first type corresponded to benefits emerging from the projects that were considered to have the required level of evidence. These were considered "components" of a refined list categorizing the direct benefits arising from project interventions or outputs (type #2 in Figure 6). Each type #2 benefit is comprised of several individual type #1 benefits. The following examples illustrate these.

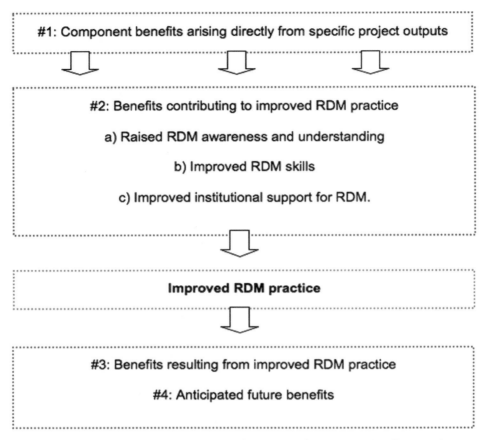

Figure 6. Typology of benefits emerging from the JISC's Managing Research Data programme.

Output example 1: Development and promotion of RDM training course.
Benefit: Increased number of staff receiving RDM training.
Evidence: Figures tracking increased attendance at RDM training.
Contributes to: Type #2a, raised understanding and awareness of RDM.

Output example 2: Production and promotion of data management plan, tailored for institution.
Benefit: Improved data management planning.
Evidence: Improvement in quality of data management plans, using scoring methodology originally developed by the UK Data Archive.
Contributes to: Type #2b, improved RDM skills.

Output example 3: Formation and approval of data policy.

Benefit: Structured approach across campus, encouraging sustainable RDM and use of the institutional data repository/metadata catalogue; easier compliance with funder requirements.

Evidence: Quantitative: increased number of references to the data policy within research proposals. Qualitative: Case study with a researcher showing how the policy helped a successful bid for funding.

Contributes to: Type #2c, improved institutional support for RDM.

All type #2 benefits contribute to improved RDM practice, the overall goal of the entire programme. In this way, projects provided rich information that could be interrogated to different levels of detail, but all of which supported the programme's claims to have achieved progress toward its overarching goal.

Projects also provided evidence of further achievement—benefits arising *from* improved RDM practice. These were named type #3 benefits (i.e., indirect benefits), including greater visibility and/or use of an institution's research data, improved compliance with funder requirements, time or costs saved by improved RDM infrastructure, and improved uptake of the institution's infrastructure.

Type #4 benefits were those that could be reasonably anticipated to result from type #1–3 benefits, based on the projects' evidence. They include, for example, improved metrics for research assessment activities, such as the UK Research Excellence Framework, enhanced institutional reputation, higher funding bid success rate, improved productivity or effectiveness, enhanced motivation for further improved RDM practice, more cohesive practice across the institution, and minimised risk of data loss. These are in addition to enhanced potential for new knowledge creation, which surely can be considered the overarching goal of research activity in general.

Further relationships may be articulated (e.g., the likelihood of raised RDM awareness contributing toward improved RDM skills). Relationships may become complex where an output engenders multiple benefits, or where multiple outputs contribute to a single benefit. The purpose of the framework needs to be borne in mind—to produce compelling, irrefutable, and easily interpretable evidence without absorbing more effort than necessary. At the same time, it should be specific enough to inform third-party evaluation of the successes of the projects and of the overall value of pro-gramme activity.

ECONOMIC IMPACT OF DATA CENTRES

A challenge for the RDM field is to identify long-term impacts. Eco-nomic impacts are especially relevant, as evidence will be needed of whether investments in infrastructure can be justified. A recent review of studies of economic value and impacts of research publications and research data, public sector information, and library and information services suggested that the field is relatively new and that no single approach has dominated across these related fields. Consequently, in recent studies we (Beagrie, Houghton, Palaiologk, & Williams, 2012) adopted a number of approaches to explore the value and impacts of research data services and the data sharing and archiving that they have enabled. These include approaches that enable us to estimate minimum values and approaches that help us measure some of the wider value and impacts.

In selecting these approaches, we took account of the practical limita-tions of collecting the necessary data through interview and survey tech-niques, and we sought to maximize economy in data collection through commonality (i.e., the same data can be used to inform more than one of the approaches). Data collection has involved focused user and depositor surveys, and data centre financial and operational data (e.g., user registra-tions, dataset deposits, and downloads), supplemented by in-depth inter-views. Not all impacts can be captured and quantified; therefore, we have used these economic approaches with others, such as the KRDS Benefits Framework, to illustrate wider benefits.

Methods and Approaches

The most direct indicators of economic value are investment value (i.e., the amount of resources spent on the production of the good or service) and use value (i.e., the amount of resources spent by users in obtaining the good or service). These offer measures of the investment in providing access, and they suggest the minimum amount that the good or service is worth to the consumers. Both investment and use value can be established from user and depositor interviews and surveys, through questions about the time and costs involved in the creation of the data, preparation and deposit of the data, and its discovery, access, and use.

Contingent valuation involves assigning monetary values to nonmarket goods and services based on preferences (Pearce & Özdemiroglu, 2002). If a good or service contributes to human welfare, it has economic value, and whether something contributes to an individual's welfare is determined by whether or not it satisfies that individual's preferences. An individual's welfare is higher in situation A than situation B, if the individual prefers A to B.

Preferences are revealed by what an individual is willing to pay for a good or service and/or by the amount of time and other resources spent obtaining the preferred good or service. Where preferences are not revealed in the market (as is the case for research data shared through most data centres), individuals can be asked what they would be willing to pay or to accept in return for the good or service in a hypothetical market situation (i.e., stated preference). For a public good, the value is the sum of "willingnesses," as consumption is nonrivalrous (i.e., the same information can be consumed many times).

The key difference between willingness to pay and willingness to accept is that the former is constrained by the person's ability to pay (e.g., by disposable income), whereas the latter is not. In the case of some research data services where many users expect institutional support and where there is a relatively large number of student users, willingness to pay may be severely constrained and willingness to accept can be the better indicator of value.

Where there is a bundle of different goods and services, these can be treated in the aggregate, or disaggregated and reaggregated in a way that reflects the bundling and/or use, thus weighting by the structure of the bundle and its use. This can be particularly important where most users of a data service use just some parts of the services, not all, and so the value that they express (i.e., would be willing to accept or pay) relates to just some parts of the service, not all. In such cases, weighting the user survey responses by the totality of uses is crucial.

The benefit or welfare impact of a good or service for a consumer is measured by the consumer surplus. In a market situation, willingness to pay is made up of what is actually paid and any excess willingness to pay over and above the price paid (i.e., consumer surplus). Hence, consumer surplus is the net gain derived by the consumer from the purchase of a

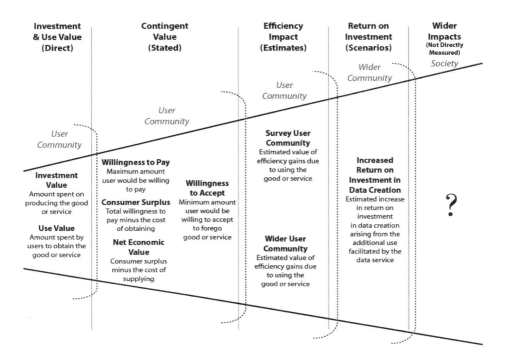

Figure 7. Methods exploring the value and impacts of research data services (based on Beagrie, Houghton, Palaiologk, & Williams, 2012).

marketed good or service. In a nonmarket context, all the willingness to pay is consumer surplus because there is no market price. In practice, however, some expenditure will be incurred in obtaining the nonmarket good or service (e.g., time spent accessing the data service). In this case, the consumer surplus will be the net gain (i.e., willingness to pay minus the cost of obtaining).

Wider benefits and impacts can be explored by looking at the efficiency gains enjoyed by research data centre users and assigning an economic value to them (e.g., based on time saved as a result of not having to create the data themselves), and by estimating the impacts of the increased data use facilitated by the data service on returns to investment in the data collection/creation (e.g., increased returns deriving from additional use). While not directly measuring the impacts of research data use on the economy or society, these approaches can provide an indication of the economic value of such impacts.

SUMMARY, CONCLUSIONS, AND A LOOK AHEAD

We have described a range of frameworks and criteria the information professional can apply, first to understand the logic of a project and its relation to a wider context. From discussing that context we moved to identifying sources of criteria that help identify what to measure for various activities that might form part of an RDM project or programme. These criteria apply variously to policy development, research data and related "research objects," the capabilities of research institutions to deliver activities and outputs, and benefits arising from these.

Long-term impacts cannot be assessed yet for institutional RDM, but we have described economic impacts from studies of data centres that illustrate how these may arise elsewhere. Experience from studies of the UK Data Services' Economic and Social Data Service (Beagrie et al., 2012), the Archaeology Data Service (Beagrie & Houghton, 2013a), and the British Atmospheric Data Centre (Beagrie & Houghton, 2013b) suggests that some approaches may be more or less applicable in different disciplines and fields of research, and among different research data user communities. These approaches have been successfully applied to a range of research data services and centres, and they are providing grounded estimates of their economic impacts and value for the first time.

There remain challenges even with measuring short-term benefits from institutional change. Infrastructures for RDM have evolved over decades in data-intensive fields such as astronomy, geoscience, and genomics, used to packaging data as a research output, whether for consumption in public policy or future research. For institutions it is a new domain, where compliance requirements exert pressure to apply tight resources to meet fresh demands that have political consequences. Information professionals charged with establishing new roles and responsibilities for RDM will encroach on well-established ones. Researchers have until recently been left to make decisions alone about the data they collect or create. For the most part, their decisions have had little support from institutional services, and some may see it as unwelcome bureaucracy.

Despite funding body pressure toward data preservation and sharing, many researchers remain sceptical about the benefits. So it is critically important that evaluations provide rigorous evidence of costs and benefit, and are well-grounded on an understanding of how the various actors involved frame the problems that RDM addresses, and what outcomes they need from a project or programme.

Near-term changes on the horizon include growing recognition by funding bodies of research data as a "first-class citizen" in research (e.g., Piwowar, 2013, on National Science Foundation policy regarding "research products"). This will be supported through collective action by funders, publishers, data repositories, and institutions to make data more easily publishable and to get credit for doing so (Whyte & Ball, 2013).

Our ability to evaluate RDM will get a boost from the growth of data publication, on the back of data citation and tracking services. Key building blocks to ensure that credit flows to researchers who contribute to the "data commons" include:

- Persistent identifiers for data citation, for example, DataCite (Brase, this volume)
- Researcher identifier registries, for example, ORCID (2013)
- Data repository registries, for example, Databib (n.d.)
- Data collection registries, for example, Research Data Australia (2013)

Counting citations is one way to track relative performance of repositories and data producers, but it is not the only one. Much work is still needed to identify the metrics that matter most. The altmetrics movement is a proving ground for metrics, helping to establish the measures that are fit for purpose by devising a range of them and tracking their take-up (Piwowar, 2011).

Comprehensive evaluation models also are needed because "not everything that can be counted counts." Qualitative judgements about scholarly value of data and trust in the infrastructure are needed, as are frameworks that better link up criteria and methods for making those judgements.

NOTES

1. For different types of measurement scales, see the Wikipedia article on levels of measurement: http://en.wikipedia.org/wiki/Level_of_measurement

2. The figure in Jones, Pryor, and Whyte (2013) is based on an earlier version by Simon Hodson.

REFERENCES

Abrams, S., Cruse, P., Kunze, J., & Mundrane, M. (2012). *Total Cost of Preservation (TCP): Cost modeling for sustainable services*. Retrieved from https://wiki.ucop.edu/download/attachments/163610649/TCP-total-cost-of-preservation.pdf

Beagrie, N., & Houghton, J. W. (2013a). *Impact of the Archaeology Data Service: A study and methods for enhancing sustainability*. Retrieved from http://archaeologydataservice.ac.uk/research/impact

Beagrie, N., & Houghton, J. W. (2013b). *Value and impact of the British Atmospheric Data Centre (BADC)*. Retrieved from http://www.beagrie.com/badc.php

Beagrie, N. (2011). *Benefits from the infrastructure projects in the JISC Managing Research Data Programme*. Bristol, England: JISC. Retrieved from http://www.jisc.ac.uk/whatwedo/programmes/mrd/outputs/benefitsreport.aspx

Beagrie, N., & Pink, C. (2012). *Benefits from research data management in universities for industry and not-for-profit research partners*. Retrieved from http://opus.bath.ac.uk/32509

Beagrie, N., Houghton, J. W., Palaiologk, A., & Williams, P. (2012). *Economic impact evaluation of the economic and social data service*. London: Economic and Social Research Council. Retrieved from http://www.esrc.ac.uk/impacts-and-findings/impact-assessment/economic-impact-evaluation.aspx

Beitz, A. (2013, January). *Growing an institution's research data management capability through strategic investments in infrastructure*. Presentation conducted at the 8th International Digital Curation Conference, Amsterdam, the Netherlands. Retrieved from http://www.dcc.ac.uk/events/idcc13/programme-presentations

Brase, J., Socha, Y., Callaghan, S., Borgman, C. L., Uhlir, P. F., & Carroll, B. (2014). Data citation: Principles and practice. In J. M. Ray (Ed.), *Research data management: Practical strategies for information professionals* (167–186). West Lafayette, IN: Purdue University Press.

CARDIO. (2011). Collaborative assessment of research data infrastructure and objectives. Retrieved from http://www.dcc.ac.uk/projects/cardio

Charles Beagrie Ltd. (2011a). *KRDS/I2S2 digital preservation benefit analysis tools project*. Retrieved from http://beagrie.com/krds-i2s2.php

Charles Beagrie Ltd. (2011b). *User guide for keeping research data safe: Assessing costs/benefits of research data management, preservation and re-use.* Retrieved from http://www.beagrie.com/KeepingResearch DataSafe_UserGuide_v2.pdf

Charles Beagrie Ltd. (2011c). *KRDS benefits framework worksheet.* Retrieved from http://www.beagrie.com/KRDS_BenefitsFramework_ Worksheetv1word_July2011.doc

Cragin, M. H., & Shankar, K. (2006). Scientific data collections and distributed collective practice. *Computer Supported Cooperative Work, 15*(2–3), 185–204. http://dx.doi.org/10.1007/s10606-006-9018-z

Databib. (n.d.). *About Databib.* Retrieved from http://databib.org/about.php

De Roure, D., Bechhofer, S., Goble, C., & Newman, D. (2011, September). Scientific social objects: The social objects and multidimensional network of the myExperiment website. Paper presented at the 1st International Workshop on Social Object Networks (SocialObjects 2011), Boston, MA. Retrieved from http://eprints.soton.ac.uk/272747/

Edwards, P. N. (2010). *A vast machine: Computer models, climate data, and the politics of global warming.* Cambridge, MA: MIT Press.

Glenaffric Ltd. (2007). Six steps to effective evaluation: A handbook for programme and project managers. Bristol, England: JISC. Retrieved from http://www.jisc.ac.uk/whatwedo/programmes/elearningcapital/ evaluation.aspx

Hartswood, M., Procter, R., Taylor, P., Blot, L., Anderson, S., Rouncefield, M., & Slack, R. (2012). Problems of data mobility and reuse in the provision of computer-based training for screening mammography. In *Proceedings of the 2012 ACM annual conference on Human Factors in Computing Systems* (pp. 909–918). New York: ACM. http://dx.doi. org/10.1145/2207676.2208533

Hess, C., & Ostrom, E. (2003). Ideas, artifacts, and facilities: Information as a common-pool resource. *Law and Contemporary Problems, 66*(1–2), 111–146. Retrieved from http://scholarship.law.duke.edu/lcp/vol66/iss1/5

Hess, C., & Ostrom, E. (2005). *A framework for analyzing the knowledge commons: A chapter from* Understanding knowledge as a commons: From theory to practice. Library and Librarians' Publication, Syracuse University. Retrieved from http://surface.syr.edu/sul/21/

Joint Information Systems Committee (JISC). (2012). Evidence gathering: The field guide. *JISC MRD: Evidence Gathering.* Retrieved from http://mrdevidence.jiscinvolve.org/wp/2012/08/30/284/

Joint Information Systems Committee (JISC). (2013). *Managing research data programme 2011–13.* Retrieved from http://www.jisc.ac.uk/whatwe do/programmes/di_researchmanagement/managingresearchdata.aspx

Jones, S., Pryor, G., & Whyte, A. (2013). *How to develop research data management services—A guide for HEIs (DCC How-to Guides).* Edinburgh: Digital Curation Centre. http://www.dcc.ac.uk/resources/how-guides/how-develop-rdm-services

Kenney, A. & McGovern, N. (2005, March). *The three-legged stool: Institutional response to digital preservation.* Presentation conducted at II Convocatoria del Coloquio de marzo, Cuba. Retrieved from http://www.library.cornell.edu/iris/dpo/docs/Cuba-ark-nym_final.ppt

National Health and Medical Research Council (NHMRC). (2007). *Australian code for the responsible conduct of research.* Retrieved from http://www.nhmrc.gov.au/publications/synopses/r39syn.htm

Natural and Environmental Research Council (NERC). (2012). *NERC data value checklist.* Retrieved from http://www.nerc.ac.uk/research/sites/data/documents/data-value-checklist.pdf

ORCID. (2013). *About ORCID.* Retrieved from http://orcid.org/about

PARSE Insight. (2010). *Insight report.* Retrieved from http://www.parse-insight.eu/downloads/PARSE-Insight_D3-6_InsightReport.pdf

Pearce, D., & Özdemiroglu, E. (2002). *Economic valuation with stated preference techniques: Summary guide.* London: Department of Transport, Local Government and the Regions. Retrieved from http://webarchive.nationalarchives.gov.uk/20120919132719/http://www.communities.gov.uk/documents/corporate/pdf/146871.pdf

Piwowar, H. (2011, December). *Data use attribution and impact tracking.* Presentation conducted at the 7th International Digital Curation Conference, Bristol, England. Retrieved from http://www.dcc.ac.uk/sites/default/files/documents/IDCC11/slides/HeatherPiwowar.pdf

Piwowar, H. (2013). Altmetrics: Value all research products. *Nature,* 493(7431), 159. http://dx.doi.org/10.1038/493159a

Pryor, G. (2011). *Managing Research Data.* Brighton, UK: Facet Publishing.

Reilly, B. F., Jr., & Waltz, M. E. (2014). Trustworthy data repositories: The value and benefits of auditing and certification. In J. M. Ray (Ed.), *Research data management: Practical strategies for information professionals* (109–126). West Lafayette, IN: Purdue University Press.

Research Councils UK (2011). RCUK common principles on data policy. Retrieved from http://www.rcuk.ac.uk/research/Pages/DataPolicy.aspx

Research Data Australia. (2013). *About Research Data Australia.* Retrieved from http://researchdata.ands.org.au/

Smith, M. (2014). Data governance: Where technology and policy collide. In J. M. Ray (Ed.), *Research data management: Practical strategies for information professionals* (45–60). West Lafayette, IN: Purdue University Press.

Van den Eynden, V. (2013, January). *Data review at the UK Data Archive.* Session conducted as part of post conference workshop Data publishing, peer review and repository accreditation: Everyone a winner? 8th International Digital Curation Conference, Amsterdam, the Netherlands. Retrieved from http://www.dcc.ac.uk/events/idcc13/workshops

Whyte, A. (2011). Emerging infrastructure and services for research data management and curation in the UK and Europe. In G. Pryor. (Ed.), *Managing Research Data* (205–234). Brighton, UK: Facet Publishing.

Whyte, A., & Ball, A. (2013). *Data publishing, peer review and repository accreditation: Everyone a winner? Workshop Report.* Edinburgh: Digital Curation Centre.

Whyte, A., Job, D., Giles, S., & Lawrie, S. (2008). Meeting curation challenges in a neuroimaging group. *International Journal of Digital Curation, 3*(1), 171–181. http://dx.doi.org/10.2218/ijdc.v3i1.53

Whyte, A., & Wilson, A. (2010) *How to appraise and select research data for curation.* DCC How-to Guides. Edinburgh: Digital Curation Centre. Retrieved from http://www.dcc.ac.uk/resources/how-guides

Wilson, J. A., Martinez-Uribe, L., Fraser, M. A., & Jeffreys, P. (2011). An institutional approach to developing research data management infrastructure. *International Journal of Digital Curation, 6*(2), 274–287. http://dx.doi.org/10.2218/ijdc.v6i2.203

Wuchty, S., Jones, B. F., & Uzzi, B. (2007). The increasing dominance of teams in production of knowledge. *Science, 316*(5827), 1036–1039. http://dx.doi.org/10.1126/science.1136099

Part 6

**BRINGING IT ALL TOGETHER:
CASE STUDIES**

15 | An Institutional Perspective on Data Curation Services

A View from Cornell University

GAIL STEINHART

INTRODUCTION

Interest in and support for cyberinfrastructure (CI) development and data-driven research has grown significantly in the past decade or so. Well-curated and accessible data are the feedstock for CI and data-driven research. As custodians of the scholarly record, research libraries might be presumed to have an important role as curators of research data. Libraries are not entirely new to supporting research data in other capacities, with roles such as geographic information systems and social science data librarians being fairly common.

In spite of this seemingly natural fit, introducing and operating data services is a complicated undertaking. Publishing processes, models, and infrastructure are well established and well understood, despite some tension and change in the transition from print to digital formats as well as experiments in open access and alternative revenue models. Researchers do their work, write and submit papers, participate in the peer review process, and libraries acquire and make available the resulting literature. Research data present would-be custodians with a more complicated set of challenges. The definition of data curation used by the Graduate School of Library and Information Science at the University of Illinois (n.d.) nicely captures some of the complexity:

> Data curation is the active and on-going management of data through its lifecycle of interest and usefulness to scholarly and educational activities across the sciences, social sciences, and

303

the humanities. Data curation activities enable data discovery
and retrieval, maintain data quality, add value, and provide for
re-use over time.

This definition encompasses and implies continuing management
throughout the data life cycle, the need for discipline-specific expertise to
add value and ensure quality, support for discovery and access, and preservation of content and access to it over the long term.

The problems are not merely technical; research data curation involves the interplay between multiple, distributed technological and sociocultural systems. From the perspective of individual researchers, research
funders are moving steadily toward requiring the sharing of research data,
yet researchers are often reluctant to share due to concerns over intellectual property, attribution, improper reuse, and lack of time, resources, and
know-how to get the job done. At the institutional level, there exists considerable uncertainty over custodial roles—who should do what, how, for
how long, and who should pay. There is particular tension as to the roles
and responsibilities of disciplines and institutions such as universities and
their libraries. At the broadest scale, intelligent curation services should
support emerging CI, but the interplay of local versus global as well as or-
ganic and more organized CI developments "challenge simple notions of infrastructure building as a planned, orderly, and mechanical act" (Edwards,
Jackson, Bowker, & Knobel, 2007) and make moving targets of optimal CI
development and data curation strategies.

Addressing this suite of challenges is a tall order. Planning and decision making for research libraries wishing to engage in this area can seem
daunting, particularly as opportunities and needs arise while or even before
planning activities are completed. With the hope that others might learn
from Cornell University Library's (CUL) experiences, I present an overview of planning activities, data services and activities (past, current, and
planned), practical lessons learned, and a few ongoing challenges.

PRECURSORS TO RESEARCH DATA CURATION SERVICES

Cornell's interest in support for research and for digital data dates at least
to the early 1980s, with the start-up of the data archive at the Cornell Institute for Social and Economic Research (CISER), Albert R. Mann Library's
hiring of its first nonbibliographic computerized data files librarian, and

the development at Mann Library of an experimental system called the Interactive Numeric Files Retrieval System (INFeRS) to provide access to numeric files in the agricultural and life sciences (Figure 1). The 1990s saw the hiring of CUL's first metadata librarian at Mann Library, the launch of the USDA Economics, Statistics, and Market Information System (USDA-ESMIS, http://usda.mannlib.cornell.edu/), and the development of the Cornell University Geospatial Information Repository (CUGIR, http://cugir.mannlib.cornell.edu/, one of two geospatial data clearinghouses for New York State). The USDA-ESMIS began with an informal conversation in 1992 as to whether the Mann Library could host files from one of its agencies, the Economic Research Service. Twenty years later, Mann provides free and timely online access to data and reports for five USDA agencies. CUGIR was initially created for the purpose of distributing U.S. Census TIGER/Line data online, and funded with a National Spatial Data Infrastructure Cooperative Agreements Program grant. Since its inception, the CUGIR collection has grown to include over 7,500 datasets from 17 partners, with an average of more than 85,000 downloads per year. More recently, the CUGIR team has been encouraging Cornell researchers to use the repository to publish their GIS datasets.

In the 2000s, CUL assumed responsibility for the physics preprint repository, arXiv.org, and established a Metadata Services Unit within Library Technical Services. Around the same time, Mann Library began to develop VIVO, a research and expertise discovery system based on semantic web technologies (Porciello, Devare, & Corson-Rikert, 2008). VIVO development continued at a multi-institutional scale from 2010–2012 with a grant from the National Institutes of Health (NIH); more recently, VIVO has joined the DuraSpace Organization Incubator Initiative, a move that will ensure continued community support and development.

Cornell's institutional repository, eCommons, was launched by former Dean of the Faculty Robert Cooke in 2002, with funds from the Atlantic Philanthropies. Cooke's intention was to have the project start as a faculty-centric (rather than library-centric) one, and to use the DSpace-based repository to support the open access scholarly publishing prototype, the Internet-First University Press. At the conclusion of the funded project, CUL assumed responsibility for the ongoing operation of the repository and has managed it ever since. Cooke correctly forecast the use of the repository

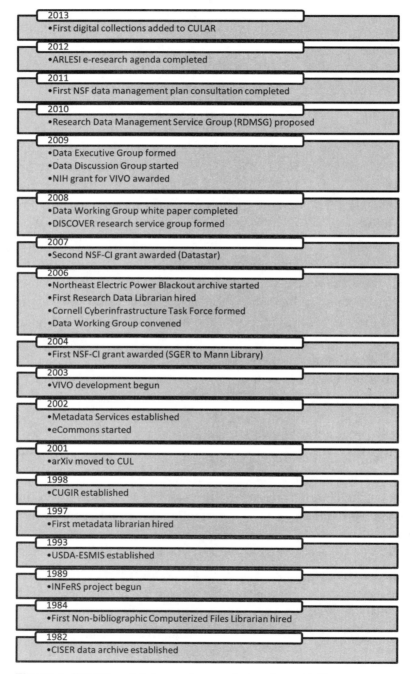

Figure 1. Timeline of data services and planning activities.

for content such as research data, computer code, and other supplementary materials not typically supported at that time by conventional publishers. As of this writing, eCommons contains 86 items classified as datasets. CUL's continued development of an infrastructure for digital preservation led to the CUL Archival Repository (CULAR), a preservation repository intended to support the long-term preservation of CUL's digital collections, including eCommons. The first digital collections to be added to CULAR were processed in February 2013.

While these systems and activities were not focused primarily on the collection, management, and distribution of research data, some have been used in that capacity. Developing these services has helped establish CUL's capacity for supporting data curation with infrastructure and with expertise, positioning the library to work effectively in this arena.

PLANNING FOR DATA SERVICES AT CORNELL UNIVERSITY LIBRARY

Early on, CUL developed relatively specialized data infrastructure and services as opportunities arose. It was not until funders' interest in supporting CI development and data curation became clearer that CUL undertook its first systematic planning initiatives, and since the mid-2000s, planning activities and development of infrastructure and services have proceeded more or less in tandem. Figure 1 provides a timeline view of planning activities and service developments discussed in this chapter.

Data Working Group (2006–2008)

Established in 2006, the Data Working Group was charged with reviewing the current research data curation landscape and with recommending strategic opportunities for CUL. The group included subject area and collection development librarians, Library Technical Services and Information Technology staff, policy experts, and staff from the Weill Cornell Medical College. They reviewed several of the key reports on CI and data curation, and undertook environmental scans of activities within CUL, at Cornell, and beyond. The group also reviewed the current practices and trends of selected disciplines and at other research libraries, educational opportunities for professionals, and selected critical issues related to data curation and sharing.

The Data Working Group made the following recommendations in its final report (Steinhart et al., 2008):

1. *Seek out and cultivate partnerships with other organizations.* This was perhaps the group's most important recommendation, and they suggested that CUL partner with campus units such as the Center for Advanced Computing and Cornell's central Information Technology division.

2. *Provide services to Cornell researchers in several areas.* At the time, the National Science Foundation's (NSF) intention to require data management plans was becoming clear but had not yet gone into effect. The Data Working Group recommended trying to educate Cornell researchers on emerging requirements and helping researchers to meet them. Other opportunities for supporting researchers included providing information on best practices in managing data, referring researchers to appropriate sources of information and expertise, and participating in the formulation of institutional policies on research data retention.

3. *Assess local needs and develop local infrastructure and related policies.* The Data Working Group recommended that CUL work with other stakeholders to identify and articulate researchers' needs for data management infrastructure and participate in its development. The group further recommended the development of selection and appraisal guidelines, an investigation of the role of the library in curating data related to publications, and continued work in the curation of small-scale datasets.

4. *Cultivate a workforce capable of addressing the new challenges posed by data curation and CI development.* This recommendation sought to encourage the identification and development of skills needed and to extend CUL's activities in this area.

5. *Form a Data Curation Executive Group and reorganize the Data Working Group.* The working group recommended the formation of a permanent committee to guide CUL's data curation and CI activities, and a separate group to foster a professional community and development for librarians engaging in this work.

CUL successfully implemented each of these recommendations to some degree, collaborating with other units to explore researchers' needs and to launch new services, experimenting with the development of Datastar (described later in this chapter), developing basic policies for depositing data in the institutional repository, hiring additional librarians with data responsibilities in their job descriptions, and forming the Data Executive Group and the Data Discussion Group.

Association of Research Libraries E-Science Institute (ARLESI, 2010–2011)

With the fall 2010 announcement that the Association of Research Libraries (ARL) and the Digital Library Federation (DLF) would be collaborating to offer the first ever E-Science Institute, a guided series of planning exercises resulting in the development of an agenda for e-research by each participating institution, the time seemed right for CUL to revisit and update its plans with respect to data curation and e-research support in general. A team made up of selected members of the Data Executive Group developed the agenda, which included 21 possible initiatives. CUL's executive leadership group identified several as medium to high priority:

1. *Participate in development of institutional data policies, including Cornell's draft data retention policy.* The Office of the Vice Provost for Research was the original sponsor of the draft data retention policy for Cornell. The original Data Working Group had an opportunity to comment on the original draft policy, but due to changes in leadership and priorities in the Vice Provost's office, the policy has been tabled for the foreseeable future.

2. *Position the Research Data Management Service Group (RDMSG, discussed in greater detail later in this chapter) as a resource throughout the life cycle of a research project.* This objective encompassed working to ensure the continued success of the RDMSG, including ensuring awareness of the RDMSG among researchers, and reviewing information CUL and its partners had already collected to ascertain unmet needs for research support.

3. *Define CUL's role in data preservation in relation to Cornell partners.* The library is generally seen as the natural archive for datasets for the long term, and yet the library lacks the expertise and infrastructure to effectively preserve some of the large and complex types of data being generated by Cornell researchers. This objective prompts CUL to define and articulate its capabilities and role to its partners, so that additional capacity can be developed if needed.

4. *Enhance CUL's metadata services for data.* This activity includes extending VIVO to accommodate basic dataset description (the Datastar project), drafting best practices guidelines for depositing datasets in eCommons, and participating in specific research data projects as the opportunity arises.

5. *Inventory current skills, responsibilities, and positions as they relate to e-research. Identify desired skills that are not present or could be further developed, in order to sustain or improve that balance as positions are revised or created.* This was a priority of the original Data Working Group, and the ARLESI team viewed this as an ongoing need. The library as a whole, as part of its strategic planning process, charged a team with defining a protocol for developing a "competency profile" for all groups of staff positions.

6. *Identify and provide professional development opportunities for existing staff to improve their skills related to e-research support.* CUL staff are encouraged to take advantage of professional development opportunities as they arise. For example, CUL recently sent its life sciences librarian to a workshop on supporting translational and team-based science.

7. *As CUL's staff expertise grows and as opportunities arise, partner with researchers to support discipline-specific support for e-research.* CUL continues to do this on an ongoing basis, participating in the development of proposals to such agencies as the U.S. Environmental Protection Agency, the NSF, the National Endowment for the Humanities, and the New York State Energy Research and Development Authority.

8. *Determine which CUL services are free or fee-based, in order to develop costed and sustainable models and fee structures.* As libraries are asked to provide new services and infrastructure—without an increase in funding or ceasing to provide existing services—it will be necessary to seek sources of revenue in order to provide data curation and e-research services.

Several other recommendations in the strategic agenda were already planned or underway, and so were not included in the priority list above. Among these, the RDMSG was identified as an important component of the library's strategy for supporting researchers. More specifically, we anticipate a need for data management planning outreach and training specific to researchers working with the NIH. Currently, data management plans are only required of NIH projects receiving more than $500,000 of funding in a single year; when the requirement becomes more broadly applicable, the RDMSG will initiate outreach and training activities similar to those undertaken for NSF grant writers. Guidance and training for researchers (including graduate students) in best practices for data management planning and for data management was also identified as important. Cornell is a partner in Purdue University's Data Information Literacy project (http://wiki.lib.purdue.edu/display/ste), which aims to develop data management curricula for graduate students across several disciplines. Cornell's curriculum is offered as a one-credit course for graduate students in natural resources and related fields. Finally, the agenda included a recommendation to examine the options for supporting data deposit in conjunction with articles uploaded to arXiv.org, which is managed by CUL. A small team is currently examining the results of a pilot project that allowed researchers to upload datasets associated with publications in arXiv.org to the DataNet-funded Data Conservancy (http://dataconservancy.org/), as well as the use of arXiv's capability to accept ancillary files as a means for distributing datasets.

Overall, we found the E-Science Institute to be a very productive way to revamp our data and e-research plans. Some team members were somewhat surprised that the exercise did not result in a recommendation to build a new general, campus-wide curation infrastructure, nor did it surface clear needs for other large-scale or overarching activities. Instead, most recommendations focused on matters of policy, staffing, continuing and enhancing existing services, seeking out partnerships, and developing business models. More or different interviews might have surfaced additional opportunities and concerns, but our results might also be what one would expect for institutions already actively providing data services, as well as a reflection of the complex and distributed nature of research and institutions.

Concurrent Campus-Wide Planning Initiatives (2006–2010)

There were two campus-wide efforts in roughly the same time frame as CUL's that were aimed at collaboration and planning for the support of CI and data-driven research: a CI task force formed in 2006, and the Data Intensive Science Organization for Virtual Exploration and Research (DISCOVER) Research Service Group, proposed in 2008. The goal of the CI task force was to assess and make the case for upgrades to Cornell high-performance computing (HPC) facilities in order to make Cornell more competitive for CI grants, and the objective of seeking out CI grants helped shape the 2007 reorganization of Cornell's HPC center. Several library staff participated in the meetings of the CI task force, and while the library played only a minor role in the deliberations and activities of the group, its participation served to make the library's interest in data curation known within Cornell's HPC community.

The DISCOVER Research Service Group was intended to further investigate the needs of Cornell researchers with respect to HPC and data curation, and to explore solutions that might benefit multiple communities. The group consisted primarily of staff and faculty from the Center for Advanced Computing, academic departments, and the library. The Office of the Vice Provost for Research provided two years of funding to support two DISCOVER staff, with the intention that a successful service group would become self-sustaining by obtaining grants or developing fee-based services. DISCOVER staff conducted a dozen in-depth interviews with Cornell researchers and synthesized their concerns into a set of recommendations addressing storage, network, training, and data stewardship, all of which have or are being addressed by the DISCOVER partners. Significantly, it was the set of collaborative relationships established within the DISCOVER Research Service Group that eventually led to the formation of the RDMSG.

IMPLEMENTING DATA SERVICES AT CORNELL UNIVERSITY LIBRARY

Data services at CUL have evolved over time in tandem with changes in research practices and technology, opportunities to pursue specific projects, and the emergence of policies related to research data. Some services and infrastructure have been developed opportunistically, while others have been developed more strategically and as result of the planning exercises described previously.

Early Research Data Curation Efforts at CUL

The mid-2000s saw two separate collaborations with researchers on domain-specific support for curating research materials. In 2004, Mann Library and a faculty member of the College of Human Ecology received a small grant for exploratory research from the NSF to fund work investigating possible collaboration between research scientists and the library. The work focused on two research groups: the Cornell Language Acquisition Laboratory (CLAL) and the Upper Susquehanna River Basin

Agricultural Ecology Program (USAEP). With CLAL, the group developed best practices for digitizing, managing, annotating, and documenting audio recordings collected in the course of childhood language acquisition research. With the USAEP, the group worked to organize, format, document, and publish research datasets of interest to the larger research group and external stakeholders. This early work led Mann Library to apply for another NSF grant, this time to support more generalized services and infrastructure to support data curation. This 2007 award led to the first round of development of an experimental data staging repository (Datastar), discussed in further detail below. Around the same time (2006–2007), CUL's Metadata Services Unit was included in an NSF grant proposal submitted by a member of the faculty of Electrical and Computer Engineering to develop a limited-access archive of data and other materials pertaining to the northeast electric power blackout of August 13, 2003. This archive was developed and maintained on the DSpace platform, but it was eventually discontinued due to lack of funding.

A Staging Repository for Research Data (Datastar)

Datastar was originally envisioned as a platform for user-controlled sharing of research data, the creation of basic metadata (and optionally, more detailed domain-specific metadata, for selected schemas), and a means for publishing datasets to supported external repositories (Khan et al., 2011; Steinhart, 2010). Our goal was to position the library in the research process without requiring interaction with the library if researchers were self-sufficient in using the system. Datastar was built using the Vitro software, the semantic web application and ontology editor that also supports the VIVO application. Datastar required significant additional development to integrate domain-specific metadata schemas, manage complex permissions rules, integrate a Fedora repository, and support the publication of datasets to external repositories. A prototype system with support for CLAL linguistic metadata, selected portions of the Ecological Metadata Language (EML) schema, and metadata for the Data Conservancy and for CUL's eCommons was developed successfully. Proof-of-concept publication workflows to move data and metadata from Datastar to the Data Conservancy, a test instance of eCommons, and a local installation of Metacat (the data and metadata database that supports the Knowledge Network for Biocomplexity (http://knb.ecoinformatics.org/), an ecological data repository) were also developed and tested. While these accomplishments were encouraging, the development of usable interfaces to support creation and editing of metadata for multiple schemas was far too labor-intensive to be scalable and sustainable, and publication workflows could not be developed for some end-point repositories of interest.

With funders' statements that proof of compliance with data-sharing policies would be expected in interim and final reports, the project team turned their attention to supporting basic data registry functions in a simpler, scaled-back version of Datastar. In collaboration with Washington University in St. Louis and supported with funding from the Institute of Museum and Library Services, the team completed a set of Data Curation Profiles (http://datacurationprofiles.org/, which are investigations based on the use of an interview instrument to gather detailed information about the full life cycle of a dataset) to inform the development of Datastar. Using the information gathered in the profiles, and inspired by similar system development at the University of Melbourne in support of the Australian National Data Service, the team is in the process of developing the Datastar software for open-source distribution.

A Campus-Wide Research Data Services Partnership: The Research Data Management Service Group

The RDMSG (http://data.research.cornell.edu) is the most coordinated and current effort to provide research data services to Cornell researchers. With the May 2010 announcement that the NSF would soon require a data management plan (DMP) with every grant proposal, individuals from multiple centers and departments, including the library, began to design a new service group to assist researchers in meeting the NSF requirement. The potential impact for Cornell was significant, with researchers submitting more than 400 proposals to the NSF per year. The NSF had not yet provided specific guidance at the time the group began to plan, but the Interagency Working Group on Digital Data, a group of two dozen federal agencies working to maximize the return on investment from their funded research, had issued a 2009 report that included specific recommendations as to what funding agency DMP policies should include. Using that report as a basis, the Cornell group was able to infer the types of support researchers would likely need to know about to complete a competitive DMP. The group identified the Cornell units with services and expertise to support data management, identified some gaps in services, and proposed a model for a collaborative, virtual organization to support researchers at Cornell (Block et al., 2010).

Jointly sponsored by Senior Vice Provost for Research Robert Buhrman and University Librarian Anne Kenney, the RDMSG is managed by a coordinator and a management council, and it has a faculty advisory board (Figure 2). Management council members represent the main service units and allocate staff to serve as members of implementation teams, some of which are ongoing and some of which are convened to meet specific needs. Ongoing teams include the RDMSG consultants, the web and documentation team, and the outreach and training team. The consultant group includes individuals with disciplinary expertise, technical expertise, and policy expertise, and members come from the library, Cornell's central information technologies unit, Weill Cornell Medical College, CISER, and academic departments.

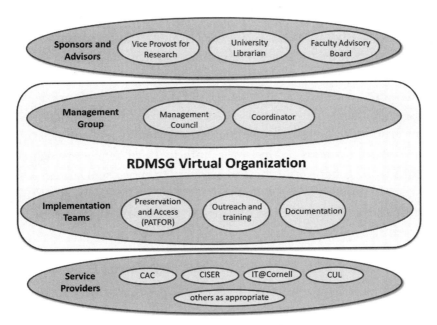

Figure 2. Organization of the Research Data Management Service Group (RDMSG).

Early on, the RDMSG conducted a survey (Steinhart, Chen, Arguillas, Dietrich, & Kramer, 2012) of NSF-funded principal investigators, the results of which showed a need for advisory services for data management planning. Some of the key findings of the survey were that researchers were generally uncertain as to whether their data or metadata conform to standards in their discipline (or even whether such standards exist), and that many do not create metadata to document their datasets. The majority expressed an interest in data management planning assistance. There was moderate interest in guidance on issues of intellectual property and copyright, and (some comments to the contrary notwithstanding) a general willingness to share at least some datasets. Most respondents indicated that they would share relatively small amounts of data (77 percent said they would share 100GB or less), but the diversity of reported types and formats of data was impressive, with respondents listing 77 unique file extensions. These results suggest that service providers can expect to deal with very diverse but generally small datasets, and that researchers will need some assistance in adopting best practices for data management.

The RDMSG has been successful in reaching out to researchers, assisting them with DMPs, and connecting them to data management services on campus. In the first two years, the outreach and training team conducted 30 information sessions on general data management planning or topics for more specific audiences, such as individual academic departments or graduate students, with a total attendance of over 500 individuals. Feedback from session participants was overwhelmingly positive. The RDMSG consultant group also handled more than 100 individual consultations, most of which involved advising on DMPs. Into its third year, outreach efforts will shift from general information sessions to more specialized sessions for targeted audiences, as well as the development of content to support specific curation tasks, such as best practices for depositing research data in the institutional repository.

LOOKING FORWARD: OPPORTUNITIES AND CHALLENGES

CUL's work in data curation has evolved organically over time to consist of three main components: consultation services, core infrastructure, and specialized projects. Specialized projects with individual researchers and research groups who are open to some degree of experimentation have provided an extremely valuable way to explore what data services are possible and practical for the library to offer, and to identify possible improvements to existing services and infrastructure. Learning from these focused efforts, we've been able to develop more general services, while continuing to collaborate selectively on discipline-specific projects. Collaboration across campus units has also been essential, as reflected in the success of the RDMSG.

Some opportunities and challenges remain. These include continuing to improve local services and infrastructure, providing organizational and staff support for data services as they evolve, refining the scope of data services to be provided, and dealing with uncertainty in a rapidly changing research, policy, and technological landscape.

Improving Existing Infrastructure

As noted above, early experience with data services has given us some insight as to how we might improve existing infrastructure. To that end, we recently revisited information gathered in earlier efforts to understand researchers' needs for local data management services and infrastructure. In addition to the RDMSG survey described earlier, these sources included the collection of Data Curation Profiles conducted to support the redevelopment of Datastar, and anecdotal information gathered through the RDMSG consultants' work with researchers. We found that support for a number of repository functions would likely be very helpful to researchers, and some are either already supported or are reasonably attainable with current or planned systems. These include:

- robust linking between datasets and the publications based upon them,
- version management for datasets,
- support for citations, including cut-and-paste citations and/or citation export function for data users, prepublication citation information allowing data owners to cite datasets in manuscripts ahead of the actual availability of data, and the ability to cite a specific version of a dataset,
- ability for data owners to control access to data for groups or individuals,
- policies and technical infrastructure to allow for updates to datasets that change or grow over time,
- record scheduling functions to allow for planned deaccessioning of content (depending on library and university policy developments in this area).

We also know from this exercise that we can expect to be challenged to curate highly diverse materials including less common and proprietary file formats, that quality metadata may be lacking or difficult to come by, and that some data will have privacy and confidentiality issues. Perhaps most significantly, if we decide it is necessary to recover some or all of the costs associated with data curation, we know that researchers are concerned with whether and how those costs will be recovered, particularly for services needed beyond the end of a research grant.

Providing Organizational and Staff Support for Data Services

Deciding where data "fits" in the library is not entirely straightforward. Data services inevitably engage expertise and resources in multiple functional areas, such as public services, information technology, and scholarly communication. The first action many libraries take is to hire a data librarian, often within a public services department, to develop data curation services, and Cornell was no exception. Since that initial appointment, Cornell has incorporated research data services into the job descriptions of additional subject area librarians working in public services, and the university also has refactored a metadata librarian position so that its focus is on science data and metadata. These are promising developments, but elsewhere it remains common for librarians working with research data to find themselves doing so in relative isolation, encountering difficulty in marshaling the resources needed to launch new services and develop infrastructure. When libraries are able to devote resources to develop infrastructure locally, the work is frequently experimental and funded by grants. Some of these projects are more successful than others, but even for successful projects, transitioning from project funding and support to a production-scale service and program can be quite difficult, and many efforts do not progress beyond the proof-of-concept stage.

In addition to staffing to deliver data services and developing infrastructure, it is imperative that data services be a part of a senior administrator's portfolio, in order to ensure meaningful support to set direction and allocate resources for service development. Because research data services are still perceived as new and specialized, they often aren't fully integrated into libraries' organizational structures. At Cornell, primary responsibility for data curation services rests with the Chief Technology Strategist, but because of the cross-functional nature of data curation, the Associate University Librarians for Research and Learning Services and for Digital Scholarship and Preservation Services also play important roles. The ongoing need for effective collaboration and communication across multiple units and functional areas, regardless of the place of data services within the organization, suggests that a cross-functional group such as CUL's Data Executive Group is both useful and necessary.

Regardless of a library's organizational structure, staffing for data services is a significant challenge. Ideally, staff in these roles should possess some combination of research and disciplinary experience, as well as information management and technology skills. Research experience and disciplinary knowledge are particularly important for establishing credibility with researchers and for identifying and understanding their needs. Library and information science programs are offering specializations, certificates, and continuing education programs to train new professionals and to retool practicing librarians for the challenge, and this development holds some promise for rounding out or upgrading staff skill sets. CUL has had good success in attracting qualified applicants for positions with research data responsibilities, and it has used the Data Discussion Group, an informal group with open membership, to attempt to broaden the conversation about data and data services to include more staff.

Refining the Scope for Data Services

Libraries must also define the scope of services they wish to provide. With more traditional publication outputs, it has long been sufficient for libraries to limit their activities to acquiring and managing the finished products of scholarship. Data management, on the other hand, is much more effective when approached from a full research and life cycle perspective, but libraries are not generally viewed as partners in the research process. While this is partly a matter of whether or not library staff have the needed skills, it also represents a fundamental change in the way libraries approach the management of information. It implies a way of working with scholars that is responsive and iterative, and that balances the norms of disciplinary practices with library and information management best practices. Individual data librarians at CUL with sufficient disciplinary expertise have been able to work with research groups at various stages in the research process, but this work requires a great deal of time and specialized knowledge. While this work has resulted in new partnerships and the inclusion of the library in research grants, it is not something we've yet learned how to scale up to serve more than a small number of research groups.

A related issue is whether libraries should direct resources toward generic infrastructure that meets the needs of many researchers in a basic way, or toward more specialized or discipline-specific services, or both. Researchers are often more deeply aligned with their disciplines than their institutions and may prefer domain-based infrastructure to that of their home institution. They also frequently collaborate across institutional boundaries, making it complicated to determine where support is best provided. For the library, the prospect of providing specialized services to selected researchers collides with deeply rooted professional values of equal service and access to information for all. This is a particularly difficult problem if a service does not scale well to meet the needs of all who might wish to use it. The need for disciplinary expertise for some kinds of data services means that library administrators will be forced to decide which disciplines will be served more fully, presuming they are not in the position to staff for data services at the same level they already do for public services and collection development. CUL's approach so far has been to continue to develop and provide basic services and infrastructure that meet most of the basic needs of most researchers (primarily the institutional repository, eCommons, and consultations through the RDMSG, as well as developing the Datastar system), while offering more specialized services on a project-by-project basis, with grant funding or other financial support.

Many research libraries have embraced the work of curating the outputs of "small science" and are relatively comfortable with curating small-scale research data, but few have begun to address the challenges of larger-scale data. So-called "big data," datasets large enough to preclude the use of standard tools and protocols, is sometimes thought of as a solved problem because its curation is frequently inseparable from its collection, management, distribution, and use. Nevertheless, preservation of data once the project or facility that generated it is retired remains an issue. It is also likely that many datasets of more modest scale (but still too large to be handled well by an institutional repository) will require curation and preservation. Preservation is a function that falls fairly clearly within the scope of the library's mission, yet the technical and staff capacity to deal with larger datasets may be found more readily in other units, such as central information technology or high-performance computing. Libraries are quite good at managing digital objects that are small enough to be easily downloaded via HTTP, but medium- to large-scale datasets require other means for access and distribution that most libraries do not currently support. Libraries may be able to ingest larger datasets into repository or archival systems for preservation, but they are not used to provisioning for access at larger scales. If we are to step up to the challenge of hosting larger datasets, we need to develop the capacity to support access as well, or find ways to collaborate with other campus service providers to accomplish this. At Cornell, a review of campus-wide IT support for research is underway, and we expect some useful recommendations to emerge from that exercise.

Dealing With Uncertainty

A final challenge is that of constantly reevaluating the evolving landscape, and there is an ongoing need to assess researchers' requirements for data curation services. Having put significant effort into planning and establishing services, it is worth asking whether funder mandates and the library's response have resulted in an increase in demand for data services, and where we should go from here. So far, beyond the demand for consultative services, we do not yet know how the demand for services will grow. The lags inherent in the review and award process, combined with the average duration of a research grant, mean that we have not yet seen the surge in demand for data curation services we expect to see as the first grant-funded projects subject to DMP requirements draw to a close. At Cornell, we know that the average length of time between proposal submission and notification of an award is 10 months. That means the very first awards with DMPs required in the grant proposals were likely made in the fall of 2011. With 85 percent of Cornell awards lasting three or more years, those first awards will not expire until fall of 2014 (Figure 3). This gives the RDMSG and allied service providers, including the library, a window of opportunity to learn from researchers' expectations, as expressed in the DMPs we have had an opportunity to review, and to plan to fill service gaps that might exist.

More broadly, technology and hardware change rapidly, and modes of scholarly communication and research practice evolve. Librarians with

Figure 3. Timeline of NSF data management plan (DMP) requirement implementation and completion of first affected projects.

liaison responsibilities tend to make an effort to avoid over-contacting faculty to gather information, yet the necessity of doing so to understand faculty needs is ongoing. Library staff are challenged with staying current in developments in information technology, standards, and disciplinary practice. Solutions for data distribution and archival systems may emerge from multiple sectors besides academic libraries; these include major funding agencies, publishers, nonprofit organizations, professional societies, university and library consortia, and community efforts rooted in specific disciplines. It is not clear which of these efforts will emerge as successful and enduring, or whether we should continue to expect to have a whole host of players meeting different needs in different contexts. In spite of that uncertainty, the view at Cornell is that research data are an important part of the scholarly output of the institution, and that it is our responsibility to assume a stewardship role to the very best of our ability.

ACKNOWLEDGMENTS

I thank Anne Kenney, Wendy Kozlowski, and Sarah Wright for their thoughtful comments on an earlier version of this chapter. Without the members of all of the committees, working groups, and project teams described in this chapter, there would be nothing to write about.

REFERENCES

Block, B., Chen, E., Cordes, J., Dietrich, D., Krafft, D., Kramer, S., . . . Steinhart, G. (2010). Meeting funders' data policies: Blueprint for a research data management service group (RDMSG). *eCommons@Cornell*. Retrieved from http://hdl.handle.net/1813/28570

Edwards, P. N., Jackson, S. J., Bowker, G. C., & Knobel, C. P. (2007). Understanding infrastructure: Dynamics, tensions, and design. *Report of the History and Theory of Infrastructure: Lessons for New Scientific Cyberinfrastructures Workshop.* Retrieved from http://hdl.handle.net/2027.42/49353

Graduate School of Library and Information Science. (n.d.). Data curation education program. *University of Illinois.* Retrieved from http://cirss.lis.illinois.edu/CollMeta/dcep.html

Interagency Working Group on Digital Data. (2009). *Harnessing the power of digital data for science and society.* Retrieved from http://www.nitrd.gov/about/harnessing_power_web.pdf

Khan, H., Caruso, B., Corson-Rikert, J., Dietrich, D., Lowe, B., & Steinhart, G. (2011). DataStaR: Using the semantic web approach for data curation. *International Journal of Digital Curation, 6*(2): 209–221. http://dx.doi.org/10.2218/ijdc.v6i2.197

Porciello, J., Devare, M., Corson-Rikert, J. (2008). VIVO: Simplifying research discovery in the life sciences. *Against the Grain, 20*(5): 34–38.

Steinhart, G. (2010, June). DataStaR: A data staging repository to support the sharing and publication of research data. *Proceedings of the 31st Annual IATUL Conference.* West Lafayette, IN. Retrieved from http://docs.lib.purdue.edu/iatul2010/conf/day2/8/

Steinhart, G., Chen, E., Arguillas, F., Dietrich, D., & Kramer, S. (2012). Prepared to plan? A snapshot of researcher readiness to address data management planning requirements. *Journal of eScience Librarianship, 1*(2): 63–78. http://dx.doi.org/10.7191/jeslib.2012.1008

Steinhart, G., Saylor, J., Albert, P., Alpi, K., Baxter, P., Brown, E., . . . Westbrooks, E. L. (2008). Digital research data curation: Overview of issues, current activities, and opportunities for the Cornell University Library. *eCommons@Cornell.* Retrieved from http://hdl.handle.net/1813/10903

16 | Purdue University Research Repository

Collaborations in Data Management

D. SCOTT BRANDT

A lot can be learned about research data by participating in research. It is one way librarians can learn about data life cycle and workflow needs of researchers. The Purdue University Libraries' approach to data management evolved out of investigation of the needs for interdisciplinary research and the ability of librarians to partner and engage in it. The service includes data reference, consulting, planning, and collaboration. It is embedded in interactions across campus and in the Purdue University Research Repository (PURR). PURR is an institutional collaboration that provides help in data management planning, data publishing and discovery, and data preservation.

INTRODUCTION: IDENTIFYING DATA CURATION NEEDS

Purdue Libraries' foray into data management began as a result of an initiative in 2004 to identify how or whether librarians could engage in research by applying library science to interdisciplinary projects. Anecdotes about the difficulty of organizing data, providing access to it, and disseminating it began to emerge. Researchers stated that they lacked the time to organize datasets, needed help describing data for discovery, were not sure how or whether to share data, and asked how the Purdue Libraries could help (Brandt, 2007). A definition of data curation emerging at this time—"managing and promoting the use of data from its point of creation, to ensure it is fit for contemporary purpose, and available for discovery and reuse" (Lord, Macdonald, Lyon, & Giaretta, 2004, p. 1)—served as impetus for many libraries to explore this area to understand it and learn how to help address it.

This was an emerging aspect of the rapidly evolving landscape of research and scholarship. Problems with data curation were not found simply at the end of a research project, "downstream," but also throughout the research life cycle, including at early stages, or "upstream." This meant working with researchers as producers—not consumers—of information. As spelled out in the Report of the National Science Board *Long-Lived Digital Data Collections: Enabling Research and Education in the 21st Century*, there was a "growing realization that intermediate data may be of use to other researchers" (2005, p. 20). This helped the Purdue Libraries identify a focus for exploration: to understand data curation issues that start early in the research life cycle, and how librarians could support needs in this area.

But where to start? Researchers were not used to librarians converging on departments to assess needs related to lab practices and data workflow. Many, if not most, researchers engaged in what has been termed "small science," which often is characterized by a lack of community standards, and because of disparate practices does not lend itself to be assessed easily. For Purdue, this lead to engaging in research: firstly, *with* researchers to understand the context of how they worked, and secondly, *about* researchers and data management practices. The research would lead to developing an e-Data Task Force to determine how to put solutions to practice, and set the stage for the Purdue Libraries to collaborate on a collaborative institutional approach to addressing research data management needs with PURR.

Engaging in Research to Better Understand Data Curation and Management

It was first posited that the Purdue Libraries could learn about data management "from the inside" by working on interdisciplinary research projects that had problems that might be addressed by applying library science knowledge, skills, and tools. Initially, librarians served as co-PIs on projects such as "The Development of a Catalysis Chemistry Discovery Environment: A New Role for Cyberinfrastructure," "Acquisition of a High-speed Petascale Storage System for Data Intensive Science," and "Multidimensional Grammar and Distance Metrics for Analyzing, Accessing and Synthesizing Complex Multimodal Information."

In each case, librarians would work with the researcher to understand how the application of library science could help him or her on the project. It might be helping to design a database that could be used by researchers in multiple disciplines, or to develop a controlled vocabulary that could be used to disseminate information through the web. Librarians scoped a work plan that could address the problem and identified how much of their time would need to be contributed to the project. The problem was that not all grants were funded, and those that were funded were often so different from each other that it was difficult to discern general needs for which a data service could be created. However, it was clear that collaborating with researchers by engaging in research was a new kind of "service" the Purdue Libraries could offer.

In 2006, after learning that the Institute of Museum and Library Services (IMLS) was interested in data curation, the Purdue Libraries sought funding to do a more complete study of "upstream" research data issues. A research project was proposed to IMLS, partnering with the University of Illinois at Urbana-Champaign, which essentially asked the question, "who is willing to share what, with whom, and when?" In 2007, the grant "Investigating Data Curation Profiles Across Multiple Research Disciplines" was funded and the project got underway (Data Curation Profiles, 2010).

Outcomes from the study would ultimately help shape which data services would best help researchers. It was noted that the definition of what was considered data was quite variable; researchers had varying ideas about sharing datasets at different points in the research life cycle; and concerns about getting credit for something shared were very similar across a range of research disciplines (Witt, Carlson, Brandt, & Cragin, 2009). The research demonstrated that data curation services would "need to accommodate a wide range of subdisciplinary data characteristics and sharing practices" (Cragin, Palmer, Carlson, & Witt, 2010, p. 4026). This echoed the findings of others conducting similar research at the time, such as the Digital Curation Centre (DCC), and research that would be done a little later by DataONE (Carlson, 2012).

The research project involved identifying questions and concerns that researchers had, determining commonality among them, and developing an instrument that captured these questions and concerns, which could be used to interview other researchers. This led to creating a structured but flexible format to record and disseminate the information and insights gained in an interview. A profile, in essence, told a "story" about the data in a research project—what the data were, what the researcher was doing with it, and what the researcher wanted to do differently with it. As such, it could identify areas to address data curation and management, and the needs for services could be better understood and identified. Thus, the Data Curation Profiles and its subsequent Toolkit were created.

The Role of the Data Curation Profiles Toolkit at Purdue

A key outcome of the Data Curation Profiles project that would help formulate a data management planning service in the Purdue Libraries was the understanding that data was generated, manipulated, or analyzed at different stages of the life cycle of research. In the Profiles, this was articulated in a "data table" that sought to uncover what the stages were, when there was a change in data workflow, what the outputs were at different points, and the various formats and sizes of files. It was clear that researchers focused on the outcomes and conclusions of their research, and they saw the workflow as a continuum of activity, not possibly sharable outputs. When asked questions about the datasets or collections created at different points in a project, researchers often looked at their data in a new light.

The Data Curation Profile Toolkit enhanced collaboration in research. The original project resulted in several Profiles that could be studied to determine ways to help researchers with data curation issues, problems, or concerns. Later, the Profiles would be used in a variety of ways. To help agronomists with data workflow, the Toolkit was used to interview graduate students who were working on different aspects of the project. The outcome was a set of recommendations for metadata capture and workflow. In an engineering project, the Profiles were used slightly differently to review lab practices and to make recommendations on data management skills training that would enhance the description of data for discovery and dissemination. Additionally, in another project, the Profiles were used to understand the data objects of dance choreography so they could be described, accessed, and preserved.

The Toolkit could help clarify specific research data needs that could be addressed. Many researchers wanted to disseminate research outputs, including datasets, especially since this would help address the broader im-

Data Stage	Output	Typical File Size	Format	Other / Notes
"Raw"	Photos of proteins	Actual file size is small, but the sheer number of files aggregates to TB of data.	.JPEG	Pictures are taken with a CCD camera which can take pictures every millisecond.
"Processed-1"	Video file consisting of strung together photos		.avi (not 100% sure of format)	Pictures are strung together to make videos.
"Processed-2"	Calculations about the Data	Files are very large, though it's unclear as to their specific avg. size	MS Excel	In addition to generating videos of the images, calculations are performed on the data as a part of the processing stage. It's unclear how these calculations are associated with the data, whether they are a part of the video file or not.
"Analyzed"	Metadata		MS Word, or handwritten in lab notebook	Students generate some descriptive metadata during analysis, though it is not uniform or standardized. Metadata are stored in MS Word or are handwritten.
"Published"	Tables or figures within an article		(part of the published article)	Relevant data are extracted, interpreted and represented in a limited fashion through tables and figures in published articles.

Note: The data specifically designated by the scientist to make publicly available are indicated by the rows shaded in gray. Empty cells represent cases in which information was not collected or the scientist could not provide a response.

Figure 1. Data Curation Profiles, data table.

pact of their research. Broader impact, an area to be addressed in a National Science Foundation (NSF) grant proposal, was given greater scrutiny by reviewers after passage of the 2007 America COMPETES Act.

DEFINING A DATA SERVICE

In the fall of 2008, a Purdue Libraries' task force was created to explore and make recommendations on what it would take to develop data services around a repository environment for data collections. The charge of the e-Data Task Force was to investigate issues related to data curation and developing data collections to identify draft policies and procedures related to doing so. The goal was to lead to the development of a data repository and a corresponding set of activities to provide operational data curation services.

The resulting report identified factors to address in developing a viable service, and it made several suggestions regarding policies, roles, infrastructure, and costs. It underscored that services could be developed around a data repository, but that these should extend similar services already delivered in libraries, such as selection and appraisal, acquisition and usage, and preservation and deselection. It averred that these factors likewise extended librarian roles in carrying out such services. It strongly urged that policies be identified to guide and put parameters on these services. And it argued that a sustainable funding model be established to create and support infrastructure and positions to make repository services a viable, production-level service of the Purdue Libraries.

As part of its work, the e-Data Task Force later took part in a prospectus activity that worked through an exercise of detailing responses to the suggestions put forth in their initial report (Witt & Cragin, 2008). It attempted to describe in detail what the service would look like, who would use it, what data would go into the repository, specific features of its capability (e.g., assigning metadata, standards, and identifiers), intellectual property and access control, and specific roles and their responsibilities.

The e-Data Task Force went one step further by developing a proof of concept for such a repository service. An instance of a Fedora repository was created, and datasets were ingested into it. The demonstration of the viability of the infrastructure was secondary to that of how librarians worked with researchers. For each of six datasets, a member of the e-Data Task Force was paired with a liaison librarian and a faculty member from a subject area. In each case, the trio described the data at a collection level, identified how (or whether) it fit within selection policies for that subject area, how the ingest was accomplished, and challenges and issues encountered. Insights gained from this work included identifying positions that would be needed to support such an endeavor (metadata specialist, repository manager, data services specialist) and training that would be needed for librarians to support the service.

As the Purdue Libraries worked in 2010 to prioritize needs to reallocate resources for positions that could support data services, the NSF announced a requirement that data management plans had to accompany all grants. A solution to address the need for data services became an institutional priority. Because of strong relationships built over time, the Dean of Libraries was able to initiate, with the Office of Vice President for Research (OVPR) and the Central Information Officer (CIO) in charge of Information Technology at Purdue (ITaP), callouts to discuss leveraging opportunities at an institutional scale. The outcome was the initiation of a service that combined data management knowledge and expertise from across campus, which came to be called the Purdue University Research Repository.

PURR is the centerpiece of data curation and management, and the service comprises: (1) providing consultation on data curation and management of research projects (e.g., utilizing the Data Curation Profiles Toolkit), (2) facilitating the discovery and dissemination of data collections, and (3) data reference in the form of helping researchers find and use resources, via short data interviews one-on-one.

IMPLEMENTING A DATA MANAGEMENT AND REPOSITORY SERVICE

PURR was developed with the philosophy that, counter to its name, it would not serve one function (that of a data repository), but rather offer several services to Purdue researchers in the areas of data curation, management, and dissemination. It functions as a service point for many of the data services the Purdue Libraries had been developing, integrates with activities of the Sponsored Programs Pre-Award Services, and builds off a scientific research collaboration platform, HUBzero, to develop functionality for publication, discovery, and preservation of datasets. As a service, it leverages relationships to share information, personnel time, technology, and other resources.

Initially, a group of librarians, including archivists, liaisons, and those working in the Purdue Libraries Research and Data Services Department, met with a group of developers from the HUBzero team to scope out work. This became known as the PURR Working Group (WG). Basically, the group's mission was to determine whether and how HUBzero could serve as a platform for data curation and management services. Technical work included determining how the platform could serve as an Open Archival Information System (OAIS), if it could integrate, create, and support identifier systems, and how information packages for submission, discovery, and archiving would be created. The group reported to the Dean of Libraries, Vice President for Research, and CIO, who comprised a PURR Steering Committee.

The group also focused on policies. It was realized that success would require participation from across the Purdue Libraries. Several recommendations were brought to the Planning and Operations Council (POC), a system-wide group responsible for ensuring that strategic planning was integrated throughout the organization, prioritizing needs for resource allocations and so forth. These recommendations included that:

- liaisons would consult on data issues related to research projects in PURR based on their subject areas
- they would serve as gatekeepers for new datasets submitted for publication and/or archiving from associated projects in PURR
- and that they would consult with an archivist on long-term stewardship of datasets, especially when making selection and deselection decisions related to preservation

For example, several members of the PURR WG developed a preservation policy that was reviewed and endorsed by the Purdue Libraries' POC and the PURR Steering Committee. It was deemed crucial that a policy be developed to identify where responsibilities for preservation lay. This is required also by ISO 16363 certification for trustworthiness of digital repositories, which the Purdue Libraries has undertaken (Witt, Kroll, Minor, & Reilly, 2012). This policy identifies what would be considered in scope for PURR to select and how long it would be supported (see https:// purr.purdue.edu/legal/digitalpreservation).

The governance of PURR has evolved and rests heavily on institutional relationships. There is a PURR project director (PD) who has a team of full-time personnel (a repository manager and two systems developers) and part-time assignments of personnel from other parts of the Purdue Libraries (a metadata specialist and digital archivist). The PD works with a HUBzero development team manager (HUBzero employs many developers and programmers). The PD reports to the PURR Steering Committee that provides oversight and advice, and is comprised of representatives from the Purdue Libraries (Associate Deans of Research and for Digital Programs and Information Access), ITaP (Executive Director of Enterprise Applications and the Director of HUBzero), and the OVPR (Managing Director for Launching Centers and Institutes and the Director of Sponsored Programs Pre-Award Services), as well as three faculty members representing a cross section of disciplines on campus. The PURR Steering Committee reports to an Executive Committee (Dean of Libraries, Vice President for Research, and CIO), which approves institutional policy and allocates resources for the repository.

PURR attempts to be what is sometimes referred to as a "cradle-to-grave" service. It provides services for needs all along the research cycle, as were identified in the Data Curation Profiles. It offers consultation in the development of research projects, leveraging the experiences of applying library science to interdisciplinary problems. It also offers consultation in the development and execution of data management planning. It provides publishing functionality to give datasets or collections a data Digital Object Identifier (Purdue University is a member of the international DataCite consortium and one of three institutions in the United States that can "mint" data DOIs), and a discovery environment for finding and accessing them. Additionally, it is developing a preservation environment, where policies will help drive decisions for selecting datasets to be preserved, or as the case may be, deselected.

One of the unique features of the PURR instance of HUBzero is the added functionality of being able to publish data. In this context publishing is defined as:

- selecting elements of a dataset (e.g., data and documentation)
- adding a variety of metadata to the set (e.g., description for discovery and rights for sharing or reuse)
- review of the metadata by the repository specialist and/or a liaison
- addition of a DataCite DOI
- persistence via the DataCite metadata catalog, so the identifier for the dataset can be resolved through time
- creating a suggested citation of the dataset
- uploading the dataset to a website for discovery via Google, Open Archives Initiative Protocol for Metadata Harvesting (OAI-PMH), etc.
- making a commitment to maintain the dataset for ten years, after which a decision will be made for archiving, preserving, or deselecting it

Other facets of PURR include many data curation and management resources for reference, and specialized online reference functionality. Several of the resources are locally developed, such as the Data Management Planning Self-Assessment Questionnaire that was derived from the Data Curation Profiles Toolkit, and there are links to many external sites, such as the DMPTool, an online web form that provides funder-specific fields and help for drafting plans. The Data Reference functionality utilizes Question

Point's widget and routes questions to the Data Education Working Group (DEWG) to answer queries.

LESSONS LEARNED

There have been many lessons learned in the endeavor to build data services at Purdue University. The structure of the organization required several changes to accommodate new services. Those changes have been threefold: reorganizing internally, promoting the librarian as researcher externally, and developing tools and resources to support it all.

Organizational Restructuring

Reorganization happens over many years. An obvious lesson is that sometimes things just take a long time to achieve. This is especially true when the change is perceived as somewhat radical. The Purdue Libraries evolved from what would be considered a traditional organization model in 2004 to something that looked more like an academic unit at Purdue.

As part of an initiative noted above, the position of Interdisciplinary Research Librarian was created in 2004 to explore possible collaboration opportunities. Coincident with that initiative, it was learned that there was a system of college-based associate deans who interfaced with Purdue University administrators and with faculty in their departments. The Purdue Libraries realized that a reorganization that aligned more closely with such college organizations would make them look more like other university units and provide additional access into the education and research enterprise to better understand the "business" of education and research. The decision to create positions of associate deans in the Purdue Libraries to engage further with peers on campus allowed "a place at the table," where policy and large-scale problems were discussed, and further established that members of the Libraries were faculty peers. Positions like the Associate Dean for Research in particular can foster relationships that later help facilitate discussion on research data at many levels—from planning to workflows and storage.

After the position of Associate Dean for Research was created at Purdue, an associated Research Council also was created to support and promote research. Support came in the form of development of policies, clarification of related procedures, and resources and funds to help librarians engage in research.

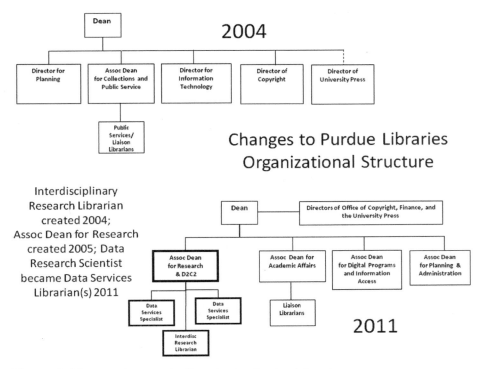

Figure 2. Changes in organization charts, Purdue Libraries.

Reorganization during 2007 resulted in the development of POC, comprised of all the heads of units in the Purdue Libraries, which was designed to drive strategic planning throughout the organization. One of POC's charges was to identify needs across the system, prioritize them, and reallocate resources to fill them. In particular, whenever a position became vacant, POC discussed needs and voted on the most critical to fill. In 2010, when a position came open, the Committee voted to formalize the position of Data Services Specialist, which was filled internally. During another discussion in 2011, further data needs were discussed extensively, and options were raised to add more data-related positions, in particular to either add specialists to each of the three main Purdue Libraries divisions or to create another central position. In the end, a second Data Services Specialist position was created. This position would be more inwardly focused, charged with developing and coordinating a data program, working with liaisons to build resources, tools, skills, and knowledge.

Ongoing Collaborations

When he arrived at the Purdue Libraries in 2004, Dean James L. Mullins pressed the need for the role of librarians to change to meet the evolving environment around them. He spread this message to Purdue University administrators, central IT, deans and department heads, and faculty across the campus. In effect, librarians were asked look beyond the library as their laboratory and to start looking at information needs of faculty in situ—in researchers' laboratories or classrooms. In some cases, this shifted the focus of the Purdue Libraries faculty research similarly. A rare demonstration of early researcher-librarian collaboration is seen in a conference video in which the researcher describes how and why she came to librarians to help her solve problems related to making water quality data from a field station more discoverable (Brouder, Bracke, & Witt, 2008).

One of the biggest lessons learned has been that research collaboration in and of itself is a valued service that reaches across the Purdue Libraries' organization and the University's colleges. Requests for participation continually come to the Purdue Libraries. Usually proposals require looking at problems (e.g., discovery or dissemination of data or information) and devising an approach to solve them, but in different disciplines, with different settings, and with different tools, and so forth. It can be a blessing and a curse that the Purdue Libraries faculty are seen as *the* people to go to with research data problems. Being asked to participate on approximately 20 grants a year has not been a problem so far, since approximately only 20–25 percent are awarded. A sample of such research includes:

- "Integrating Spatial Educational Experiences (ISEE) into Crop, Soil, and Environmental Science Curricula"—5 percent time of Geospatial Information Systems Specialist and Agricultural Sciences Information Specialist
- "Development of an OAI-PMH Interface for nanoHUB.org"—quarter-time graduate student supervised by Interdisciplinary Research Librarian
- "Human Rights Texts for Digital Research: Archiving and Analyzing Amnesty International's Historic Urgent Action Bulletins at Purdue University"—half-time graduate student supervised by Associate Dean for Digital Programs and Information Access
- "Developing Curious and Persistent Continuous Learners: Articulating and Assessing the Role of Information Skills in the First-Year Engineering Cur-

riculum"—10 percent time of Head of the Physical Sciences, Engineering, and Technology Division

- "INTEROP: Developing Community-based DRought Information Network Protocols and Tools for Multidisciplinary Regional Scale Applications (DRInet)"—5 percent time of Data Services Specialist

The Role of Technology

Throughout the building of data services, technology has played an important role. From the start, there were attempts to investigate how technologies could support data, for efficiency and scale of increasing services. Installations of DSpace, Fedora, and Greenstone were explored, but they were not successful as experiments. After an early exploration of building a repository (Brandt & Witt, 2005), the Distributed Data Curation Center (D2C2) was created in 2006. Its primary goal was to explore data in complex settings, and it was meant to be an avenue to leverage collaborations and funding opportunities. Many D2C2 research projects evolved around tools, from working with OAI technology to PURR and Databib, an online bibliography of research data repositories funded by an Institute of Museum and Library Services (IMLS) Sparks! Ignition grant (Witt, 2012). The Purdue Libraries has explored library applications of information technology, from OAI-PMH to OAIS, and from XLST to XML. Often these efforts tended to be project-based, frequently related to interdisciplinary grants, and lacked cohesion to help build a larger data service. A lesson learned is that not every technology can be sustained.

The decision to use HUBzero as the technology upon which PURR is built came with many perks: the team that built the technology resided at Purdue, they provided hosting and programming services for it, and they were interested in expanding the functionality of HUBzero, especially as it related to data. The "grandfather" of all hubs, nanoHUB, was itself a type of repository for software, tools and educational resources. And it was felt that HUBzero provided the greatest opportunity for control over development. That it was a different technology than DSpace or Fedora was a concern, but it was felt that every institution would likely work with whatever best suited their situation, and that by using standards and application program interfaces (APIs), data could be made interoperable as appropriate or as needed.

PURR is a full institutional service, built on institutional understanding, collaboration, and resources.

CHALLENGES AND OPPORTUNITIES GOING FORWARD

As libraries continue to explore how, where, and whether to support researcher data curation and management, they likely will have to continue to evolve the roles librarians can play. In a time where access has truly overcome ownership for most of a library's collection and resources, it will be interesting to see how building new collections of data will be addressed. It is likely that it will have to be done in collaboration with many others—foremost with the institution and its researchers, but likely with other libraries, and possibly with national repositories and publishers. Institutional partnerships, research collaborations, and applications of technology are likely to grow.

Institutional Partnerships

Reorganization can be reactive or proactive. Either way, libraries and librarians realize they must change to keep up with the times. For Purdue, the creation of an organizational structure to parallel academic units on campus was proactive. Initially, it seemed academic units were a little unsure of how this reorganization would affect them. Demonstrating to faculty, as well as to university administration, that librarians wanted to tackle the same problems was key. In doing so, strong relationships can be forged, which can lead to partnerships. Relationships are based on cooperation; partnerships are based on collaboration.

Relationships with university IT units have been well documented, often in the context of institutional changes where the library reports to the CIO (Snyder, 2006). Until recently, partnerships were usually based on leveraging technology, creating efficiencies for printing, storage, and networking through central administration. More and more, one sees collaboration around data services, such as promoting data management planning tools, exploring digital preservation networks, and supporting infrastructure for large interdisciplinary, interinstitutional projects. And in the case of Purdue, collaboration is synonymous with development of the data repository.

Strong relationships between libraries and university research administration were less common before 2010, but they seem to be growing.

Hopefully, the same will be true with partnerships. For Purdue Libraries, a relationship with the OVPR started with the creation of an Associate Dean for Research in the Libraries in 2005, but it was only with the initiation of a research repository that a true partnership was forged.

The OVPR's commitment to this institutional collaboration is a clear sign that it sees the importance of supporting access to research outputs. The OVPR has supported access to people and processes that often are hidden behind the doors of research administration. Working with the Sponsored Programs Pre-Award Services has increased the Purdue Libraries' understanding of how research accounting is handled. Integrating a data management planning link on the pre-proposal worksheet that every researcher must fill out has increased the Purdue Libraries' access and visibility.

The chance to share costs for developing a new paradigm of collection management and access to information is a great opportunity for libraries. For Purdue, the institutional collaboration started with a shared commitment of resources—funds for hosting a HUBzero instance, and cost sharing the people to develop and maintain it. A strong relationship was the foundation upon which a proposal for four years of funding was put forward.

One of the greatest challenges will be to assess the need and demonstrate the benefits of a data repository—this will feed into an evaluation for continued support. Demonstrating need is almost a foregone conclusion for any library going forward. That PURR is useful can be demonstrated by its inclusion in data management plans for grants submitted to funders who require them. There have been over 600. However, it is not easy to gather information that demonstrates PURR has helped grants get awarded. It has been noted that reviews of proposals by funders do not tend to dwell on data management plans. That PURR is popular is partly demonstrated by the range of disciplines represented in published datasets. Subject areas of initial contributors included agronomy, bioinformatics, computer science, engineering education, genomics, and statistics.

Research Collaborations and Consulting

As noted above, research collaboration, especially on data projects, is an opportunity to work closely with faculty and apply library science to solve problems in their research. This is opposed to consultation, which is more likely to be of a shorter term, like an extended reference interview. There are strengths and weaknesses to collaborating. On the one hand, if librarians are welcomed to participate on research proposals across campus, this builds relationships, understanding of research practice, and greater knowledge within a subject area. Even though the majority of the proposals submitted are not awarded (overall acceptance rates are often 10 percent or less), the experience of participating strengthens partnerships and gives librarians a deeper understanding of the "business" of research. But on the other hand, because every proposal is likely to be different, such contributions make it difficult to deduce a specific set of services from the varieties of participation.

As a service in and of itself, collaborating has many challenges. Making initial connections is not easy, as there is often no clear path to working with researchers. Faculty status may help in this regard, where librarians are considered peers, and interdisciplinary research among peers is encouraged. Identifying problems within a project and elaborating a work plan, budget, outcomes, and so forth can be time-consuming, and doing it for project after project can be exceptionally time-consuming. It may not be unusual for a librarian to be on three or four submitted proposals, with the assumption that only one may be awarded funding, but needless to say, there will likely be some hesitancy in doing this. This often will not be the same for consulting, where librarians have more experience and control, scheduling one-on-one reference interviews.

Multidisciplinary collaboration, applying library science to research problems, may be well received at all levels of the university. Purdue Libraries faculty have worked with individual researchers in many disciplines on campus. They have worked at a college department level discussing large-scale problems (e.g., biochemistry's overall data strategy). They have worked as partners with major centers on campus (e.g., Network for Engineering Earthquake Simulation and the Joint Transportation Research Program). They have worked with associate deans to set up workshops and demos for colleges. And they have worked with administrators in the OVPR, the provost and the president, all of whom have recognized the Purdue Libraries' contributions and accomplishments. By engaging in research, librarians contribute to the overall success of the university, and they will be appreciated for it.

Growing out of research collaborations, data services at Purdue were initially based on methodology-led discovery. A research approach to helping a researcher is different than a service approach. The research approach usually involves finding a solution to a specific or unique problem, whereas a service approach often involves referring the researcher and her problem to a set of known resources, tools, and so forth, which she can use. It is the difference between engaging in research and supporting it, of asking, "how can I solve this problem?" versus "how can I help this person solve her problem?" And often the research problem is so unique that the solution doesn't contribute or lead to a set of resources or tools that can be used for a service to solve similar problems in the future. Another challenge is determining how much liaison time and effort to devote. There also may be an opportunity to learn about a range of educational needs in data-related areas.

Technology

Building, borrowing, or buying technology to support new initiatives is often a problem for libraries. For instance, when the NSF DataNet request for proposals was announced in 2007, the Dean of Libraries felt well versed enough in issues to hold a callout to build a team to send a proposal. The Purdue Libraries were able to bring knowledge about data workflow, use, and standards to the table, but relationships and expertise from computer science and technology were needed. However, when the NSF data management planning mandate was announced in 2010, the Purdue Libraries had built relationships, understanding, and expertise that could be brought to bear. As noted above, a unique set of relationships formed between the Purdue Libraries, ITaP, and the OVPR. Together they assessed that HUBzero was an optimal platform to facilitate and fulfill data management needs.

Partnerships also can provide opportunity to develop "street cred" in the eyes of IT or other tech-savvy groups. For instance, because the Interdisciplinary Research Librarian had collaborated with developers at HUBzero, he had a chance to demonstrate that librarians can develop solutions to technical problems. Managers of HUBzero were interested in information technologies popular in the library science field, such as applications of OAI-PMH, Object Reuse and Exchange (ORE), and linked data (Witt & Sivaram, 2011).

However, as librarians have known for some time, it can be a challenge to take manual practices and turn them into technical processes. For instance, whenever someone at Purdue creates a new account on PURR, they are notified through a manual process that consulting services from the Purdue Libraries are available. It would be better to automate this. If someone initiating a proposal chooses to use PURR as part of the project's data management plan, a person from Sponsored Programs Pre-Award Services notifies the repository manager by e-mail, a more or less manual process. The repository manager in turn contacts liaisons by e-mail. Likewise, when a grant associated with a project is awarded, Sponsored Programs Pre-Award Services notifies the repository manager, who notifies a liaison again. The idea behind this process is at the heart of the data service—to ensure researchers and liaisons engage—but it will be much smoother when a technological solution is incorporated.

CONCLUSION

One of the great debates right now is how much should librarians know and practice regarding data curation and management. It has been said that this "territory" is wild and untamed like the Old West. In some ways it is more like the pre-industrial era. The Purdue Libraries as a whole are on the cusp of gaining knowledge and developing tools that will propel us forward in data curation, management, and sharing. It may be helpful to remember that both Watt and Edison had to work on much iteration before they achieved a working steam engine and lightbulb. Once librarians understand what can or should be done with researcher data—and can articulate and demonstrate it—the more likely opportunities for doing so will congeal. This is especially likely in the realm of information literacy, where many librarians have developed skills and expertise.

It has sometimes been noted that as data management deals with organization of information, it is thus something that should come naturally to librarians. Where this is not the case, the obvious approach seems to be to hire new librarians who have "fresh" knowledge and skills, though an abundance of new data curation and management skills do not seem to be prevalent (Mullins, 2012). However, one area where applicable skills are prevalent is in archives, especially with digital archivists, who often have relatable or transferable skills to this area. The Purdue Libraries have utilized several archival specialists in developing PURR, in helping to write policy, address metadata standards, and identify preservations needs. Of course, one has to have the resources to make new hires. The Dean of Libraries at Purdue has partnered with other departments on "cluster" hires, where a need for new university-wide thrusts have been identified (e.g., systems biology), multiple positions have been identified (e.g., a bioinformatician to work in the Purdue Libraries), and the university funds half of the salary of these hires.

It may seem obvious to say that librarians need more training to work hand-in-hand with researchers on their data curation and management. Data consultation with researchers is a gateway entre, given the similarity to an extended reference interview. While specialists in corporate or medical libraries have engaged in extended and collaborative reference for many years, this is new to many academic librarians. This likely will continue to be a challenge going forward.

Data curation and management is integral to the dissemination research; even as scholarship, technology, and attitudes change, it seems there will continue to be a need for librarians to be involved. They will continue to explore and learn how collaborate in this area. This is partly so because automating the research lab is slow going, and there are so many approaches and variations in utilizing technology that it tends to be overwhelming for everyone. Until more applications and technologies come along to better facilitate data curation and management, libraries will stay involved because they know the most about organization and description of data to facilitate discovery and access.

Some may ask if the library is the right place to host data services. If, as current trends seem to indicate, the pressure for data sharing continues to expand, the problems associated with data sharing (time and skill) will continue. It is hard to predict when or how research practice, automation, or commercialization will incorporate or impose ways to make data sharing easier and less time-consuming. DataUp (2012) is an example of a tool that can integrate with workflow, standardize metadata, and push data to a repository, and it may become of primary use for researchers who use Microsoft Excel (which includes a lot of people). But for now there are many different tools used by researchers—Wikipedia (2013) lists 83 under free database management systems and 111 under proprietary database management systems. Librarians are seen as the experts at working through a plethora of resources to find those most useful.

Right now it seems as if there are too many challenges and opportunities. Collaboration will continue, and there is no doubt that libraries' reputations will continue to grow across the university landscape. As is often the case, it takes trust and time to build relationships. Finding the time, balancing activities, and prioritizing involvement always have been challenges for libraries, but libraries always have found a way to step up.

REFERENCES

Brandt, D. S. (2007). Librarians as partners in e-research: Purdue University Libraries promote collaboration. *College & Research Libraries News, 68*(6), 365–396.

Brandt, D. S., & Witt, M. (2005, December 5). *Research data and the distributed institutional repository.* Paper presented at the Fall 2005 Coalition for Networked Information (CNI) Task Force Meeting, Phoenix, AZ.

Brouder, S., Bracke, M. S., & Witt, M. (2008, May). *Purdue scientist/librarian collaborations.* Presentation given at Librarians & E-Science: Focusing Towards 20/20, Committee on Institutional Cooperation, Purdue University, West Lafayette, IN. Retrieved from http://www-s.cic.net/programs/CenterForLibraryInitiatives/Archive/ConferencePresentation/Conference2008/program.shtml

Carlson, J. (2012). Demystifying the data interview: Developing a foundation for reference librarians to talk with researchers about their data. *Reference Services Review, 40*(1), 7–23. http://dx.doi.org/10.1108/00907321211203603

Cragin, M. H., Palmer, C. L., Carlson, J. R., & Witt, M. (2010). Data sharing, small science, and institutional repositories. *Philosophical Transactions of the Royal Society A, 368*(1926), 4023–4038. http://dx.doi.org/10.1098/rsta.2010.0165

Data Curation Profiles Toolkit. (2010). History. *Data Curation Profiles.* Retrieved from http://datacurationprofiles.org/history

DataUp. (2012). About the project. *California Digital Library.* Retrieved from http://dataup.cdlib.org/about_project.html

Lord, P., Macdonald, A., Lyon, L., & Giaretta, D. (2004). *From data deluge to data curation.* Paper presented at the E-Science All Hands Meeting 2004, Nottingham, England. Retrieved from http://www.ukoln.ac.uk/ukoln/staff/e.j.lyon/150.pdf

Mullins, J. L. (2012). Are MLS graduates being prepared for the changing and emerging roles that librarians must now assume within research libraries? *Journal of Library Administration, 52*(1), 124–132. http://dx.doi.org/10.1080/01930826.2011.629966

National Science Board. (2005). *Long-lived digital data collections: Enabling research and education in the 21st century* (NSB-05-40). Retrieved from http://www.nsf.gov/pubs/2005/nsb0540/nsb0540_4.pdf

Snyder, C. A. (2006). CIOs and academic research libraries: A selected review of the literature. *Library Leadership and Management, 20*(2), 72–74.

Wikipedia. (2013). Database management systems by license. Retrieved from http://en.wikipedia.org/wiki/Category:Database_management_systems_by_license

Witt, M. (2012, June). *Databib: An online bibliography of research data repositories.* ACRL Digital Curation Interest Group, ALA Annual Conference, Anaheim, CA.

Witt, M., Carlson, J., Brandt, D. S., & Cragin, M. (2009). Constructing Data Curation Profiles. *International Journal of Digital Curation, 4*(3), 93–103. http://dx.doi.org/10.2218/ijdc.v4i3.117

Witt, M., & Cragin, M. (2008). Introduction to institutional data repositories workshop. Libraries Research Publications, Paper 83. Retrieved from http://docs.lib.purdue.edu/lib_research/83

Witt, M., Kroll, M., Minor, D., & Reilly, B. (2012, July). *ISO 16363: Trustworthy digital repository certification in practice.* Paper presented at the 7th International Conference on Open Repositories, Edinburgh, Scotland. Retrieved from http://docs.lib.purdue.edu/lib_fspres/4/

Witt, M., & Sivaram, A. (2011, April). *Exposing HUB objects for aggregation using OAI-ORE and linked data.* Presentation given at HUBbub 2011: The 2nd HUBzero Workshop, IUPUI, Indianapolis, IN.

17 | Data Curation for the Humanities

Perspectives From Rice University

GENEVA HENRY

At the start of the 21st century, it was uncommon to hear humanities scholars talk about their research in terms of data. By that time, however, some prominent efforts had emerged that allowed scholars to leverage computational resources to discover and present new information.[1] These new approaches would change earlier scholarly analyses and interpretations that were limited by the amount of information a human could manage, both cognitively and physically, with large volumes of printed text. Projects such as the Valley of the Shadow (Ayers, n.d.), the Perseus Digital Library (Crane, n.d.), and The Walt Whitman Archive (Folsom & Price, n.d.) have gained widespread recognition among humanities scholars as reputable, scholarly resources that support research in the humanities. Beyond simply digitizing resources, these projects turned the digitized works into data by adding document markup, optical character recognition (OCR) of text, transcription, geolocation data, and other descriptive elements not normally found in a traditional library catalog record or finding aid for the original works held by libraries, museums, archives, and special collections.

Humanities scholars at Rice University began to realize the benefits of digital scholarship and started working with Rice's Digital Scholarship Services (DSS)[2] team in the Fondren Library to develop digital libraries to serve their research needs and those of their worldwide collaborators. To meet scholars' needs, the DSS team worked with them to understand the ways in which they wanted to use the resources to support their research. The capabilities they requested included the following:

- perform full-text searching, including searches with diacritics and foreign languages (including double-byte character languages)
- search for all names and/or places in a document
- provide scholarly annotations
- visualize the resources on a map as well as along a timeline
- enable geospatial viewing of regions in their historic context (e.g., different boundaries and place names)
- support user tags that reflect the unique vocabulary of their scholarly community
- view transcriptions and translations of texts along with original page images so that any interpretations could be verified by the scholars using the resources
- restrict access to culturally sensitive materials
- create educational resources that contextualize the digitized content so that they could be used in the classroom
- allow digital resources from other online collections to be accessed through a common interface
- enable seamless delivery of audio and video resources without long download times or the need for very high bandwidth networks
- allow multiple digital artifacts to be included when accessing an item; examples include recto and verso images of an artifact, multiple pages of a manuscript, and soundtracks with corresponding programs of musical performances
- allow images to be searched independent of any text from which they originated

The same resources can be used by scholars in different fields, with each approaching them from the context of their own research interests. Their specific needs derive from their own particular objectives for their scholarly contributions. When the resources exist only in physical form in a library, archive, or special collection, the scholars work by gathering the materials together, usually in limited batches at a time and often in restricted locations. This traditional approach to research has a number of limitations. One of the most obvious is that while one scholar is using the resources, they are not available to others who may also need them for their research. But finding the relevant materials is also problematic.

To discover nondigital resources, scholars typically rely on bibliographies created by fellow scholars in their field of study, the descriptive records that a librarian or archivist has created (e.g., library catalog records or finding aids), or the knowledge of the librarians or archivists who manage the collections.[3] The scholar must then discover the additional information within the materials that would enable him or her to create the scholarly contributions he or she wants to make, such as identifying place names for creating map views, noting dates for creating timelines, and deciphering marginalia for interpreting original intent or influences. These discoveries cannot be easily added to the existing catalog records or finding aids for the materials to help others who are seeking this information, since those records are not editable by the scholar. While much of this can be overcome with digital resources, a challenge that librarians and archivists face as curators of these materials is ensuring that the digital materials are not encumbered by scholarly interpretations and additional context that could introduce unintended bias into the original materials.

At Rice University, we have approached digital scholarship with a view toward balancing both the desires of scholars and the concerns of over-contextualizing the resources. The responsibility to curate and manage the digitized or born-digital resources as data while still meeting the research needs of humanities scholars has often meant a separation of the information as data from the enhancements that enable the new forms of scholarship the researchers desire. The various approaches for creating digital data to support humanities scholars impacts the decisions of what must be managed and preserved long-term, and the determination of who the best people are to be involved with the data curation throughout its life cycle. The staffing approaches, infrastructure, and roles and responsibilities are important considerations in discussing digital data curation. Well-documented policies and practices are key to ensuring consistency and continuity in digital content creation and support over time. Documented project profiles for each collection of digital scholarly content will provide an overview of the motivations for creating the collection and the practices used in establishing each digital collection.

The remainder of this chapter describes the approaches Rice University has taken in humanities data curation to address the researchers' needs while serving as trustworthy stewards responsible for managing the resources to ensure their integrity and long-term viability for use by others. Examples of humanities digital projects and collections at Rice are provided to illustrate the challenges and decisions involved throughout the data curation life cycle.

STAFFING, INFRASTRUCTURE, ROLES, AND RESPONSIBILITIES

Decisions about how best to manage digital content are intricately inter-twined with the people and systems available to support the data cura-tion life cycle. When DSS began in 2000, there was a deliberate decision to keep the DSS team small overall and draw other library staff[4] into the digital work. This would allow the library to build skills throughout the organization in working with digital content, since this clearly was an area impacting the overall future direction of the library. The core DSS team that works on managing digital content and supporting faculty research projects is, as of this writing, a small group consisting of the executive director, two programmers, the digital curation coordinator, and sup-port as needed from the two full-time Digital Media Commons (DMC)[5] staff. The DSS position of scholarly communications liaison was created to support the Rice University Open Access Policy; she focuses primarily on archiving published articles of Rice faculty members and copyright is-sues associated with those publications. Staff from the Woodson Research Center Special Collections and Archives work closely with the DSS team, having fully integrated digital activities into their daily workflow. (Digi-tal content created from special collections holdings is made available by Woodson staff on an almost daily basis.) Catalogers in the Technical Ser-vices (TS) group provide metadata for some of the digital collections as their time and expertise permits.

As digitized content from early library-initiated projects began to grow, decisions had to be made about the most appropriate infrastruc-ture to manage our digital content. Files from the early digitization proj-ects were managed in a vendor-supported digital library system, Hyper-ion, which was offered by the library's integrated library systems vendor, SirsiDynix. This system was fine for managing simple files such as PDFs and very simple collection structures, but it could not accommodate more complex collection models or diverse media. It also did not support digi-tal preservation, which is a critical feature for ensuring that the content would be considered as trustworthy and reliable by scholars. It was clear that Rice's digital content would be increasingly diverse, including all forms of multimedia and multiple formats for some complex materials. It also was evident that it would be impossible to maintain multiple systems with a small core team responsible for managing the infrastructure. The content diversity meant that system capabilities would need to be robust, and it was likely that customizations would be needed to support the level of flexibility required for diversity.

After assessing various systems that could support the digital content needs of DSS, the decision was made in 2005 to adopt the DSpace institutional repository platform for managing all of the digital content. As an open-source platform, DSpace afforded the ability to do necessary customizations by having access to the source code. The open-source community around DSpace was becoming well-established, helping to ensure the likelihood of a long-term, sustainable system and the benefit of community contributions to the overall software platform. The architecture that separated the actual digitized objects from their descriptive metadata supported the ability to scale up by adding additional storage as new resources grew while maintaining search performance across the centralized metadata and full-text index. The built-in workflow and interface meant that less programmer time would be needed to bring new collections online quickly; with a very small team (in 2005, DSS had only one programmer), this was a critical consideration. The system also was very easy to use, allowing non-DSS staff to readily work with it to include content and metadata. This aligned with the overall DSS objective of including more library staff in digital projects and making it more a part of their daily workflow in order to support the transition of the library as a whole to working with digital scholarship. The Rice Digital Scholarship Archive (RDSA)[6] is now the primary location for all curated digital resources.

Defining roles and responsibilities has been a much more fluid process. The early plan was that the DSS team would maintain the RDSA, provide technical support that was needed for the digital assets, support the digitization work, manage digital projects to ensure that the many activities that digital projects include would be coordinated, and provide overall strategic direction for the digital projects and priorities. These were all new responsibilities in embarking on digital library activities that did not have clearly identified counterparts in traditional library activities. Other roles—such as digital preservation, providing descriptive information to support discovery, content selection, and serving as faculty liaisons—did have established roles and responsibilities in the existing library organizational structure, so these were viewed as the primary opportunities for drawing in existing staff to support digital projects. As activities proceeded, however, not all of these assumptions were realized for a variety of reasons.

Initially, the concept of digital preservation was believed to align with the traditional role of the library's preservation group. After providing extensive training, however, it became clear that the deeper technical expertise needed to support digital preservation had nothing in common with the skills used in traditional library preservation. The DSS team has, therefore, taken the lead on digital preservation, with support from staff in Woodson, who have demonstrated both interest and technical adeptness in this area.

Providing the descriptive metadata to support the collections has been much more complex than was originally imagined. The cataloging/metadata staff in TS have been the logical group to turn to for this support, but this has had mixed results. Initially, a part-time metadata librarian was hired to help with digital projects, with the other part of this person's time dedicated to traditional cataloging responsibilities. There has been quite a bit of turnover in this position, with each new person having varying levels of metadata expertise. Earlier metadata librarians with strong expertise in metadata standards and digital collection structures were instrumental in defining the appropriate fields and organization for managing the digital collections. More recently, however, the contributions provided by TS staff have been strongest when metadata has aligned more closely with more traditional cataloging work, such as the assignment of Library of Congress Subject Headings (LCSH), descriptions of music performances, and in providing specialized language expertise.

The variety of humanities content and approaches for creating the data needed to support faculty research interests have led to humanities scholars and archivists in Woodson creating or augmenting descriptive metadata. The scholars understand the content through their use of it for their research, while the archivists have worked with much of the material as it resides in their holdings. Technical metadata has been added by DSS and Woodson staff. Online humanities resources not initiated by scholar-driven projects have primarily emanated from Woodson archivists who digitize parts of their holdings as part of their daily workflow. They normally provide the metadata for these resources since they are most familiar with the unique content.

Content selection and liaising with faculty is a function normally associated with subject selectors and subject librarians in a research library. Paradoxically, academic faculty have generally approached DSS staff directly to work with them on digital projects and have not associated their regular librarian liaisons with their research interests in digital activities. The scholars identify the specific content and research they want to do around that content in consultation with DSS staff who can plan next steps and projects to support the research. Some of the Rice subject liaisons have become involved in the digital projects of their faculty, but the level of involvement has generally lessened as the project proceeds. An exception to this has been Mary Brower, the music subject liaison, who maintains a very proactive role with the music faculty and has been very engaged in digital music projects.

The experiences at Rice suggest that a more flexible approach to assigning roles and responsibilities during digital projects will result in higher quality and well-curated collections of scholarly content, especially for humanities content. Collaborations that include the humanities scholars not only result in collections that are described with richer vocabularies, but build a lasting trust that enables further collaborations that endure well beyond the initial digital scholarship projects. Traditional library organizational models do not necessarily enable effective approaches to curating digital collections, but opening digital projects to draw upon pockets of expertise within libraries will allow creative and motivated staff to participate, growing the experiences with digital projects throughout the organization. The library cultural norms and expectations must be adjusted to accept more flexibility and adaptation in supporting digital curation projects without dictating that specific functions and workflows be followed that align with more traditional library roles.

DOCUMENTATION AND PROJECT PROFILES

Rice's Digital Curation Coordinator Monica Rivero and Woodson Archivist Amanda Focke have been diligent in ensuring that the policies, processes, procedures, and information about each of the digital collections is documented so that there is consistency across projects and a history of what was done for each digital collection. The policies and guidelines documentation is maintained in an online wiki (Digital Scholarship

Services, n.d.b). Details are provided for issues related to digitization and project management, guidelines for working with digital resources, quality control of digital assets, file management policies and standards, intellectual property management, metadata guidelines, ingest guidelines, and tips and tools.

Project profiles for most all of the digital collections also are documented and available through the wiki (Digital Scholarship Services, n.d.c). The profiles provide information about the collections, including what type of information is in the collection, scanning standards used, the metadata application profile for the project, the file naming convention that is used, process information about the development of the digital collection (e.g., workflows, content selection process, creation of derivative files, inclusion of master TIFF files in the collection, etc.), and other information that provides useful insights into the digital collection. Profiles of more recent digital collections tend to be more complete, reflecting the changing rigor in the project profile documentation. Because standards evolve over time and technologies change, the project profiles are important for identifying areas in need of attention during digital preservation activities, such as the need for format migrations to support newer software applications for rendering the content.

Documentation regarding Rice's infrastructure for managing digital content and preservation approaches also is maintained in the wiki (Digital Scholarship Services, n.d.a). In addition to maintaining preservation-level metadata, documentation, a robust storage system, and regular local backups of the content, Rice uses multiple external technologies to provide a distributed environment for preserving digital content. MetaArchive (Educopia Institute, 2013) and DuraCloud (DuraSpace, n.d.) are used to keep dark, distributed archives of the RDSA contents. Digital preservation is an area of continued research, with no single solution having emerged as the best approach for providing distributed preservation copies. MetaArchive and DuraCloud provide different architectural approaches to maintaining a distributed dark preservation archive. Each has advantages; thus, both are used to leverage their strengths in the ever-evolving landscape of digital preservation. Rice's websites are archived using the Internet Archive's Archive-It service (Internet Archive, n.d.).

HUMANITIES DATA CURATION CASE STUDIES

The previous sections have addressed the overall approach for providing data curation services for the digital content at Rice. Understanding this general approach allows for a more robust discussion of specific humanities digital data curation activities. This section will provide examples of the creation and curation of some of the humanities digital data, along with the approaches and decisions made throughout the process of developing each collection. The examples will illustrate the ways in which the requests for capabilities made by humanities researchers have been addressed to enable robust digital collections that can be curated by library staff.

The Our Americas Archive Partnership Collection

The Americas collection in the RDSA provides an example of how a variety of features can be enabled through digital data for the humanities. In 2006, the DSS team was approached by a Rice scholar in the humanities, Dr. Caroline Levander, to develop a digital archive that would support her and her colleagues' needs in studying the Americas from a hemispheric perspective. Materials from the various regions in the Americas traditionally have been described by librarians using terminology and classifications that assume a nation-state relationship rather than a hemispheric alignment. This traditional descriptive approach results in the resources being aligned with traditional disciplinary fields such as English, history, Spanish, and so forth. Americas studies scholars, however, are interdisciplinary and use resources across disciplines and nations, with materials written in multiple languages. A proposal for the project, Our Americas Archive Partnership (OAAP), was submitted to the Institute of Museum and Library Services (IMLS) through their National Leadership Grants for Libraries program, and an award was made in the fall of 2007.[7] The following are some of the key capabilities the scholars desired:

- assign terms to the resources that align with the vocabulary of the scholars, not just the standard LCSH
- support full-text searching of documents, including the use of diacritics and searching across languages that include English, Spanish, Portuguese, and French
- view search results on a timeline and on a map that does not show geographic boundaries

- provide translations of non-English texts into English, with the original image of the translated page available for scholars to view
- view transcriptions of documents along with the corresponding page image of the digitized text
- search documents by names of individuals mentioned in the text and place names, including historic place names that may have changed over time
- create research modules that contextualize the content for use in teaching
- allow digital resources from other online locations maintained by other institutions to be accessed and searched through a common interface
- allow multiple digital artifacts to be included when accessing an item (e.g., multiple pages of a manuscript, recto and verso views of an image)
- allow images to be searched independent of any text from which they originated

Some of these needs were beyond the scope of curating the content, so decisions were made about what would be curated and what functionality would be created outside of the actual digitized content. For this collection, more than 25,000 pages and images were digitized, optical character recognition (OCR) was applied to printed texts where possible and/or transcribed by vendors, manuscripts were transcribed by scholars and their students, all materials were marked up using the Text Encoding Initiative (TEI)[8] P5 standard, metadata records were created using both LCSH-controlled vocabulary terms assigned by the library's catalogers and keywords defined by the Americas scholars, location information was marked in texts and added to the metadata records, technical metadata was included for each digitized resource, scholars translated selected materials primarily from Spanish to English (though some of the translated texts included multiple languages that were all translated to English), and an open copyright license[9] was assigned to the digital works. All of these elements are maintained in the curated online collections that are managed through RDSA.

To fully meet the scholars' needs, additional capabilities were also developed, but there is not a commitment to long-term support and curation of these outside features. A website was created to provide added features and functionality, including the ability to search/browse across Rice's collection as well as other relevant online collections housed at institutions outside of Rice, browsing all resources by the vocabulary terms used most frequently by Americas scholars, a timeline widget for viewing search results by time, a geospatial interface to display search results geographically on a map without political boundaries, and links to research modules maintained in a separate repository, Connexions (Rice University, n.d.), which is specially designed to support educational materials.

Through the website, the metadata for the OAAP collection, along with other collections, can be harvested and the text culled to create a full-text search index, thereby allowing searching/browsing across all included materials. An online archive of TEI marked-up text that complements the OAAP collection already existed when the OAAP project began, so Rice collaborated with the Maryland Institute for Technology in the Humanities (MITH) to integrate the Early Americas Digital Archive (EADA) with the OAAP. Standards and protocols to support harvesting both collections, which resided in very different infrastructures, allowed for a seamless merging. A third archive of materials was added after the project began, the Fondo Antiguo Biblioteca Ernesto de la Torre Villar collection from Instituto Mora in Mexico. Due to technology and infrastructure limitations at Instituto Mora, their collection is managed alongside of the OAAP collection in the RDSA, with a commitment for full curation of the resources identical to that provided for Rice's collections. The Americas scholars' specialized vocabulary, referred to as *concepts*, supports browsing of all the resources through a common interface. Figure 1 shows the website interface for the OAAP.

Results of browsing or searching performed through the website's interface can be viewed in a list (Figure 2), along a timeline (Figure 3), or on a map showing geospatially located results (Figure 4). All views allow the user to further refine the search. The resources remain in their contributing repository where they can be curated according to the practices at that institution. Selecting a result will take the user to the contributing online archive, and the appearance may be quite different from the OAAP website. The OAAP collection is managed in the RDSA DSpace repository, which allows the collection to be "themed" to match the look and feel of the website. Research modules, or educational materials, are listed on the website as links to the Connexions repository where the materials are managed.

Separating the special applications and customized presentation from the actual content and its descriptive elements ensures that the curated collections will remain viable long-term, and the data can be used with other technologies and applications as needed for differing purposes. As technologies change over time, the websites may no longer function as planned.

Figure 1. OAAP website interface (http://oaap.rice.edu/).

Figure 2. OAAP results list view (http://oaap.rice.edu/
results.php?mode=advanced&concept=GENDER).

Figure 3. OAAP results timeline view (http://oaap.rice.
edu/results.php?mode=advanced&concept=GENDER
#timeline).

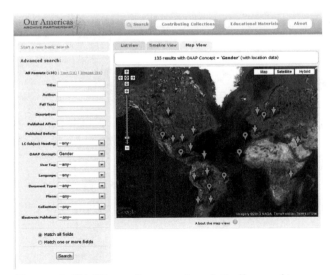

Figure 4. OAAP results map view (http://oaap.rice.
edu/results.php?mode=advanced&concept=GENDER
#satellite).

Committing to long-term preservation of all the applications involved in a sophisticated site to serve scholars' needs can require significant resources that many libraries do not have. By curating the data, however, the content can be presented in flexible ways, allowing newer applications to be used while older technologies are deprecated. As an example, Rice's Travelers in the Middle East Archive (TIMEA)[10] is very similar to the OAAP collection in its intent and presentation. The digital collection is maintained in the RDSA where it is curated along with the other digital collections. A geospatial viewing capability was included in TIMEA's website using the ArcGIS mapping software. When that GIS server was no longer supported, a Google Maps interface was substituted to continue to allow geospatial viewing of the resources, as shown in Figure 5.

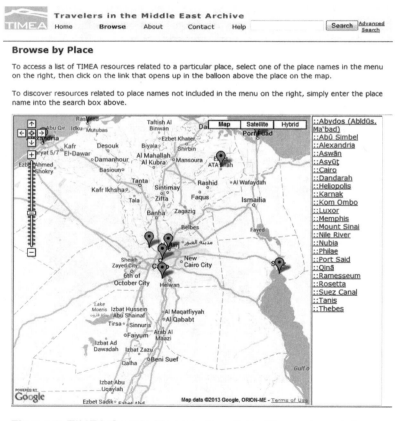

Figure 5. TIMEA Google Map interface (http://timea.rice.edu/browseplace.html).

Transforming the resources into rich data that can be readily mined, searched, displayed with flexibility, and enhanced with scholarly comment requires work. With the OAAP collection, source materials were digitized, texts were OCR'd, transcribed, marked-up, and translated, and metadata was assigned to provide complete descriptions of the resources. All of this is curated and available to users to facilitate the research they want to do. This level of effort for these resources was enabled by grant funds. The documents for the collection were mostly from the nineteenth and early twentieth centuries, so scanning text with OCR did not always work well, especially for non-English materials. Double-key transcription was, therefore, performed on the print documents at a 99.95 percent level of accuracy. There are a number of handwritten manuscripts in the collection, and these were transcribed by scholars and their students working on the project. Where OCR may have missed important diacritics, the transcriptions faithfully captured them, enabling more meaningful searches. The thorough transcription enabled reliable full-text indexing to support robust full-text searching.

Marking up the materials in XML turns unstructured information into data, thus affording a great deal of flexibility. The scholars' desire to view transcribed text along with the digitized pages was realized by marking up the transcriptions with the structural elements of the documents so that line breaks, paragraph breaks, page breaks, headings, and so forth were identified, and the text could be rendered on the screen to match the imaged page. The XML markup followed the TEI P5 standard. Place names and names of individuals were also identified through the markup, enabling better semantic analysis of the materials. TEI also enables scholarly markup of materials, supporting interpretation and enhancements.

The TEI markup was done by numerous groups. The DSS team provided training in TEI to catalogers/metadata specialists, staff in DSS, and humanities scholars and their students. For print materials, the basic structural markup was done by vendors during document transcription. Manuscripts were marked up primarily by the scholars and their students. A quality control process was established for review of the markup independent of those who performed the markup. For the curated collections, the DSS team has been careful to minimize any interpretive annotations, since these resources will be used for differing purposes by scholars in any number of disciplinary fields. For the OAAP collection, scholars were discouraged from including any interpretive markups that imposed a scholar's analysis of the meaning of the text. Annotations were included, however, to provide clarifications of references to places, events, or individuals as well as to regularize vocabulary for improved text search results. Clarifications or notes were included in markup where text, particularly in handwritten manuscripts, was illegible or interpreted based on ill-formed phrases. An example is shown in Figure 6 of the online presentation of a marked-up letter from Joseph E. Johnston to Jefferson Davis (Johnston & Davis, 1862). The underlines indicate annotations made in the markup, primarily to regularize text. These appear as mouse-over pop-ups when viewed online. The XML file for this letter can be viewed online at http://scholarship.rice.edu/bitstream/handle/1911/27262/aa00091.xml?sequence=1.

While XML markup provides rich data, a challenge for curation is ensuring that the markup is aligned with current versions of standards and that the style sheets used to render the markup are updated to support the updated standards. When the OAAP project began, some early resources that were used to prototype the system had been marked up in TEI P4. At the time the project was funded, TEI P5 was the supported standard, so it was necessary to transform the earlier resources to P5. This could not be automated due to the flexibility of the TEI standard. The TIMEA collection was marked up using P4 and has not yet been transitioned to P5. Maintaining multiple versions of standards requires additional curation work to ensure that the materials are reliable as other elements of the online environment evolve.

Translations are included in the collection and are maintained as separate *items* with their own metadata records. An item in RDSA consists of the metadata record and all associated files described by that record. Both the original digital surrogate and the translated documents reference each other. The files for each item in the OAAP collection include all of the digitized page images in JPEG format, a thumbnail of each page, and the transcribed, marked-up text. The master TIFF files for each item are in the process of being included in the item records, but these are not viewable or downloadable by users; this is by design to help manage network bandwidth issues. In the case of translations, the decision was made to include all of the imaged page files with both the original and translated works. The marked-up

Letter from Joseph E. Johnston at Centreville to Jefferson Davis as President, March 3, 1862

[ANNOTATOR'S NOTE: 3
Confederacy]

H^d Q^u Centerville

March 3^d 1862

Mr President,

I respectfully submit three
notes from Major General Jackson, & one
from Brig Leu Hill, for the information
they contain of the enemy.

Your order for Moving can not
be executed now, on account of the condition of
the roads & streams. The removal of public
property goes on with painful slowness – because,
as the officers employed in it report, sufficient
numbers of cars & engines can not be had.
It is evident that a large quantity of it ~~will~~ must
be sacrificed – or your instructions not observed.
Ishall adhere to them as closely as possible.
In convenation with gen, & before the cabinet,
I did not exagerate the difficulties of march-
ing in this region. The suffering & sickness
which would be produced can hardly be exag-
gerated.

    Most respectfully
    Your obt serv
    J.E. Johnston
    General
    His Ex^cy Jefferson Davis
    President

[ANNOTATOR'S NOTE: See over.]

Letter from Jefferson Davis to Col. Abraham Myers, March 3, 1862

Col. Myers, will
read and report
whether any in-
crease can by made
to the number of
cars & engines

    Jefferson Davis
    "

Figure 6. Online presentation of letter from Johnston to Jefferson Davis.

text file for the item is only the one associated with either the original or the translation. This approach to including the imaged pages with the translation items in addition to the original imaged works will maintain the overall integrity of the work and allow scholars to check the translation against the digitized page. Figure 7 shows a page of text that was translated from English into Spanish, along with the digitized image of the page.

Desembocadura del Río Bravo
10 diciembre 1846

Querida Winnie:

Como puedes ver por la fecha de esta carta, he perdido mucho tiempo, que podría haber pasado contigo si hubiera previsto los eventos negativos que han resultado. Pero, vayamos a pensar que todo está en orden para el bien general e instruir a nuestras mentes a actuar como es apropiado para unos colaboradores, de sentir como es apropiado para criaturas unidas por muchas obligaciones de recibir lo que es ofrecido con gratitud, y esperar el resultado que viene con paciencia y confianza.

Por lo tanto, hablo, mi linda esposa, mientras que los vientos azotan las olas y las olas se arrojan [...] y la mayoría de mis maletas a bordo del barco, dejándome esperando en la orilla y ansioso de ascender el Río. Por favor dame crédito por las razones ya mencionadas, bajo tales circunstancias. Es reportado que el General Taylor se está preparando para ir hacia Tampico y que los misisipienses irán con él– se dice que Santa Anna está haciendo alguna demostración de un ataque,

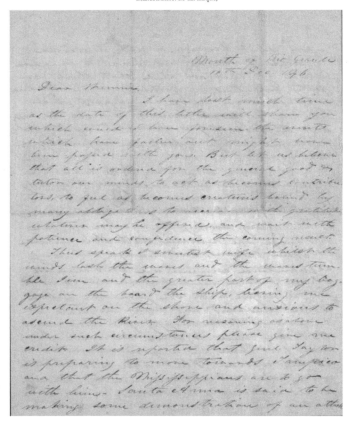

Figure 7. Page from Jefferson Davis letter translated to Spanish.

Another request from the scholars for the OAAP project was the ability to view only images that were included in the larger works. To accommodate this request, JPEG 2000 images were created from the master TIFF files of pages that contained images. They are managed in a separate collection from the texts where they appear, allowing users to more easily browse or search only images in the overall collection. An example of an extracted image is shown in Figure 8.

Figure 8. Co-Co-Pas from "Report on the United States and Mexican Boundary Survey, Volume 1" (http://oaap.rice.edu/view_item.php?id=732&view=list).

The Rice Ephemera Archive

The DSS team has worked with scholars in the Chao Center for Asian Studies to curate their collections of digital ephemera used in their research. Two collections currently are maintained, the Subway Advertisement Archive[11] and the Chinese Commercial Advertisement Archive.[12] In 2009, Dr. Steven Lewis approached the DSS team to discuss archiving the digital images of subway ephemera from Asia that he had been collecting for many years and was the basis of his research. Many of these images were captured with point-and-shoot cameras by his students, thus the images, especially from the earlier years, were captured with rather low resolution. The data, however, cannot be recreated due to the nature of the materials. Ephemera, especially in China, is not preserved for later use since these advertisements are not perceived to have value beyond their brief display.

Requirements from the Chao Center scholars required capturing the Chinese vocabulary in the ads to include in the metadata. Anyone searching by the Chinese characters should be able to discover the content. Since these materials are very nontraditional, the task of creating the metadata has not been done by the catalogers and metadata specialists, but by students of the scholars and one of the programmers on the DSS team, Ying Jin, who has worked closely with the scholars to create the collections. The Chinese Commercial Advertisement Archive has involved a collaboration with the Shanghai Library. These advertisements come from print materials and contain considerably more Chinese metadata than is found in the subway advertisements. Figure 9 shows a public service ad about AIDS in a Beijing subway, along with its metadata record. Maintaining the metadata with both the English descriptions and the Chinese character descriptions is important for supporting the research the scholars are doing.

The Shepherd School of Music Collection

The Rice Shepherd School of Music is renowned for its music performance program. Faculty and student recitals are held throughout the academic year, with many graduates later joining symphonies and other performance groups around the world. The early performances by these musicians are often of interest to those who come to know the artists in their professional careers. Prior to digital recording, the performances were captured on reel-to-reel one-quarter-inch audiotape. As these were beginning to deteriorate, it became important to digitize the works and build an archive where the performances would be available to people around the world to enjoy.

Rice did not have adequate equipment to do the digitization, so the work was outsourced to a company that specialized in transitioning audiotapes to digital files. Recorded on approximately 391 tapes, 340 concerts from 1975–1983, along with the paper programs for each performance, were outsourced for digitization. Rice provided a well-defined METS/MODS XML markup schema for the vendor to follow to provide metadata for all of the digitized work. The XML structure would enable greater flexibility in managing the works and allow them to be organized in multiple ways to provide the greatest range of searching and browsing for works. Each program had

Item Metadata

Show simple item record

dc.coverage.spatial	Beijing
dc.date.accessioned	2011-03-25T20:22:56Z
dc.date.available	2011-03-25T20:22:56Z
dc.date.created	9-1-00 22:17
dc.date.issued	2003
dc.identifier.uri	http://hdl.handle.net/1911/58468
dc.description	This image contains 1 people; 1 male(s); 1 Asian; The origin of the image is Domestic. Watermark Unknown.
dc.format.medium	mix
dc.language.iso	en
dc.publisher	Rice University
dc.subject	People Male Asian Domestic
dc.title	AIDS public notice, AIDS.
dc.type	image
dc.digitization.specifications	Color Mode: 5; Horizontal Resolution: ; Vertical Resolution: ; Creator Mac: ogle;
dc.contributor.creator	Asian Studies, Baker Institute for Public Policy
dc.source.collection	Transnational China Project
dc.identifier.digital	aidshealtha03b
dc.title.subtitle	预防艾滋病是全社会的责任;爱心呵护生命,行动抵御艾滋; [AIDS. It's the entire society's duty to prevent AIDS. Love cares life. Action prevents AIDS. Pu Cunxi, AIDS prevention promoter. PRC Ministry of Health.]
dc.subject.prodtype	Health
dc.subject.prodcat	Public Service Ads
dc.subject.brand	AIDS public notice
dc.identifier.citation	(2003). "AIDS public notice, AIDS.."

This item appears in the following Collection(s)

· Beijing [928 items]

Figure 9. AIDS ad from Beijing subway and metadata record.

performances of multiple pieces written by multiple composers and varying performers of each piece. People searching for specific pieces or composers or performers often will not care which program it was performed in, and multiple performances of the same work, but by different performers on different programs, are not uncommon in the collection.

The audiotapes were migrated to 24-bit/96kHz Broadcast Wave Format (BWF) digital files for preservation. The migration process required that the tapes be "baked," a common practice that is necessary with older tapes to mitigate binder hydrolysis issues ("sticky-shed syndrome"). When audiotapes are baked, there is only one opportunity to digitize the contents; if there are capture errors, it is impossible to try again. After receiving the digitized files, the music went through quality control checking, and a number of problems with the work were found. Some performances came back as empty files; others were captured at the wrong speed. Unfortunately, there was no way to recapture these performances.

The XML markup received from the vendor also was problematic. Keith Chapman, Rice's music catalog librarian, along with members of the DSS staff, spent more than a year performing quality control on the programs and music files, making constant corrections before the collection could be placed online. While outsourcing can be beneficial, our experience with the Shepherd School of Music collection points to the subsequent cost that can be sustained in correcting vendor mistakes.

The performances are maintained in the RDSA in the Shepherd School of Music collection[13] and streamed through streaming servers when a user wishes to listen to them online. One of the challenges with streaming the music is that the formats that are made available for streaming are likely to need to migrate as the server technologies change. With HTML5 (World Wide Web Consortium, 2013), it is now possible to stream using that standard, which would eliminate the need for streaming servers. Because it is new and still evolving, there are performance issues with HTML5, so streaming servers are still preferred for reliable, smooth delivery of audio and video.

The Houston Asian American Archives Oral Histories Collection

Houston, Texas, is home to a diverse international population. Asian Americans form a significant part of the population, and capturing their histories is an important contribution to the city, the state, and the country. Working with the Chao Center for Asian Studies, the library has started building an online collection of the older digitized audio interviews and more current born-digital video and audio interviews. Transcriptions of many of the interviews also are included with the items in the collection, along with any digital photos, résumés, or other materials. This online collection, the Houston Asian American Archives (HAAA) oral histories,[14] provides some interesting examples of data curation issues that other digital collections at Rice had not yet faced. Other Rice digital projects that we worked on already had addressed issues related to managing audio files and transcriptions, but managing the digital video interviews presented some interesting challenges for deciding on formats that could serve as preservation copies and provide well-performing delivery to end users. The need to preserve the consent forms with all of the content for each interview without making it publicly available had to be addressed with this project as well.

When Woodson received the collection for processing, there were several challenges in just handling and organizing the materials. Archivist Amanda Focke realized that the standard archival processing approach would need to be modified to effectively work with this collection. One of the first changes was to establish clear naming conventions for the files so their associations with each interview would be clear. The interviews spanned multiple files, so the processing required that each file be opened and a determination made about whether or not to keep the file and commit to preserving it long-term. With most of the interviews being in Asian languages, partnering with the Chao Center for Asian Studies was key to making these decisions. Students from the Chao Center worked with the Woodson staff to sort through the materials and organize them for use by scholars.

Unlike audio files, the preservation file format for digital video is still not a universally accepted standard. This is an area that continues to evolve, requiring continued attention to the appropriate format and need for migration over time (Blood, 2011; Wright, 2012). The DSS and Woodson staff researched the possibilities for appropriate file formats for the videos, along with consideration of the digital environment at Rice that could support the videos, both now and into the future. Given the large size of uncompressed video files, with each one often being multiple terabytes, storage considerations have factored into the format decisions. Ideally, all uncompressed video will be stored at the highest possible quality for eternity. In practice, however, resources at most universities do not allow this for sizable quantities of digital video. Furthermore, much of the scholarly video capture is not delivered to archives in the highest quality possible, which was the case with the video for the HAAA collection.

After much research and testing of various options, the decision was made to keep the highest resolution of source files that were given to Rice, though most of those are not genuinely high resolution. Those files are then encapsulated in a MOV wrapper for streaming delivery. The DSS staff has spent a great deal of time experimenting with and testing various delivery options. Hinted video (Soundscreen.com, n.d.) is used to provide smooth streaming to users through a streaming server. DSS programmer Ying Jin worked on a formula for converting some of the source video to consistent formats that could be delivered as needed. She also identified a viewer that would enable end-users to have a common, reliable viewing experience with the video. HTML5, while a possibility for streaming, is not being used at this time because it does not provide consistency of delivery, making the viewing experience unpredictable and jerky.

Just as master imaging files for visual resources and imaged text documents are maintained with items in the RDSA, it was desirable to also keep the consent forms of the HAAA interviewees with the rest of the digital archival record so that they, too, would be preserved long-term. While the oral histories are made publicly available, the sensitive information in the consent forms should not be viewable by the general public. The DSS team provided the capability to keep these files hidden from public view, yet included in the full files for the works by the collection submitters so that the digital archival record would be complete. This also is the practice used for retaining master TIFF image files in the repository.

CONCLUSION

Humanities data is some of the richest information available and provides some of the greatest challenges for digital curation. Unlike structured scientific data, humanities data consists of unstructured text, audio, moving images, and visual works that often are not as easy to manage online. From historic manuscripts to ephemera and cultural artifacts of every sort imaginable, humanities scholars are working with source materials that computer scientists are still wrangling with how best to manage, search, and present in online formats. At Rice, we continue to work closely with humanities scholars in curating the digital resources needed to support their research. With each new project, we learn something new and update our curation processes.

As our curation processes change and information becomes more complete for the digital items in newer collections, we realize that the older collections also need to be updated. For example, we now embed all of the metadata for a file in the file itself so that it will be available in the event the file somehow gets separated from its metadata record. Contents in our earlier collections also should benefit from this enhancement, so it is necessary to revisit them to bring the RDSA content to a consistent state. As the technology landscape changes, file formats will need to be migrated so that they continue to be usable. At Rice, the DSS team maintains a current list of the recommended file formats so that everyone who works with the digital content will be aware of the practices currently followed.[15]

The importance of documentation throughout all phases of the data curation process cannot be underestimated, especially for humanities data because of its complexity. The Rice DSS team maintains the documentation in a wiki that is openly available for anyone to view. People working on our digital projects are given access to the wiki so that they, too, can contribute to the documentation and learn from it. Training new staff and students is much easier with the documentation available for them to return to when they need a refresher on how to do something. Staff turnover, though it has been quite low at Rice, is eased by having very well-documented processes, practices, and collection profiles.

Our approach in collaborating with colleagues in other parts of the library and throughout Rice University has proven to be extraordinarily effective in developing rich collections that scholars worldwide find useful. We are happy to provide support to scholars as they use our collections for their research, publications, and various productions. By having a digital curation process that depends on partnerships, we have been able to build digital skills in the library staff and in the humanities scholars who work with the materials. Both undergraduate and graduate humanities students who work on the digital projects are graduating from Rice with digital humanities experience that is shaping their future careers. The early decision not to grow a large DSS group to do all of the digital curation work has had a positive impact in more ways than we could have imagined at the start.

NOTES

1. For a high-level overview of a timeline for digital humanities activities, see What's "Digital Humanities" and How Did It Get Here? (Unsworth, 2012). A more comprehensive account can be found in the *Companion to Digital Humanities* (Schreibman, Siemens, & Unsworth, 2004).

2. The DSS group was formerly known by the titles the Center for Digital Scholarship (CDS, 2008–2012) and the Digital Library Initiative (DLI, 2000–2008). The name was changed to Digital Scholarship Services in 2012, when a library reorganization aligned the Kelley Center for Government Information and Microforms, including the GIS/Data Center, with CDS.

3. Many scholars also point to the serendipitous discovery of resources by browsing the library stacks around a resource they are intentionally retrieving. Though some lament the loss of this serendipitous discovery with the movement of resources to off-site storage facilities or online-only content, it should be noted that serendipitous discovery can also be experienced with online searching and browsing of scholarly digital repositories.

4. The term *staff* is used throughout to refer to librarians, archivists, other professionals, and paraprofessional staff who work in the library. Librarians at Rice do not have faculty status, but they do provide the same services as faculty-designated librarians at other institutions.

5. The DMC was formerly known as the Digital Media Center (2006–2012), the Electronic Resources Center (ERC, 2002–2006), and the Electronic Text and Image Center (ETIC, 1996–2012).

6. See http://scholarship.rice.edu.

7. Our Americas Archive Partnership IMLS National Leadership Grants for Libraries—Advancing Digital Resources, LG-05-07-0041-07.

8. See http://www.tei-c.org/index.xml.

9. All OAAP digital resources are licensed under a Creative Commons Attribution 2.5 License (http://creativecommons.org/licenses/by/2.5/).

10. TIMEA's website is located at http://timea.rice.edu/index.html. The collection is maintained at https://scholarship.rice.edu/handle/123456789/1.

11. See https://scholarship.rice.edu/handle/1911/39098.

12. See https://scholarship.rice.edu/handle/1911/69922.

13. See https://scholarship.rice.edu/handle/1911/43628.

14. See https://scholarship.rice.edu/handle/1911/36136.

15. See https://digitalriceprojects.pbworks.com/w/page/58487493/
Recommended%20file%20formats.

REFERENCES

Ayers, E. L. (n.d.). *The valley of the shadow: Two communities in the American Civil War*. Retrieved from http://valley.lib.virginia.edu/

Blood, G. (2011). Refining conversion contract specifications: Determining suitable digital video formats for medium-term storage. *Library of Congress Strategic Initiatives*. Retrieved from http://www.digitizationguidelines.gov/audio-visual/documents/IntrmMastVid FormatRecs_20111001.pdf

Crane, G. R., Ed. (n.d.). Perseus Digital Library. *Tufts University*. Retrieved from http://www.perseus.tufts.edu/hopper/

Digital Scholarship Services. (n.d.a). *Digital projects for Fondren Library: Digital preservation support*. Retrieved from http://digitalriceprojects. pbworks.com/w/page/44763477/Digital%20Preservation%20Support

Digital Scholarship Services. (n.d.b). *Digital projects for Fondren Library: Documentation*. Retrieved from https://digitalriceprojects.pbworks. com/w/page/17801905/Documentation

Digital Scholarship Services. (n.d.c). *Digital projects for Fondren Library: Projects*. Retrieved from http://digitalriceprojects.pbworks.com/w/ page/41449846/Projects

DuraSpace. (n.d.). *DuraCloud.org*. Retrieved from http://www.duracloud.org/

Educopia Institute. (2013). MetaArchive. *MetaArchive Cooperative*. http:// www.metaarchive.org/

Folsom, E., & Price, K. M., Eds. (n.d.). The Walt Whitman Archive. *Center for Digital Research in the Humanities, University of Nebraska–Lincoln*. Retrieved from http://www.whitmanarchive.org/

Internet Archive. (n.d.). Archive-It. Retrieved from http://www.archive-it.org/

Johnston, J. E., & Davis, J. (1862). [Letter from Joseph E. Johnston at Centreville to Jefferson Davis as president, with note on verso signed by Jefferson Davis, in reply to a March 3, 1862 letter from Joseph E. Johnston]. Jefferson Davis Letters, 1846–1888 (MS 5). Woodson

Research Center, Rice University, Houston, TX. Retrieved from http://hdl.handle.net/1911/27262

Rice University. (n.d.). *Connexions*. Retrieved from http://cnx.org/

Schreibman, S., Siemens, R., & Unsworth, J., Eds. (2004). *Companion to digital humanities* [Electronic version]. Oxford, England: Blackwell Publishing. Retrieved from http://www.digitalhumanities.org/companion/

Soundscreen.com. (n.d.). Compressing and hinting media for streaming. *Soundscreen.com Multimedia Resources*. Retrieved from http://www.soundscreen.com/streaming/compress_hint.html

Unsworth, J. (2012, October 9). What's "digital humanities" and how did it get here? [Web log post]. Retrieved from http://blogs.brandeis.edu/lts/2012/10/09/whats-digital-humanities-and-how-did-it-get-here/

World Wide Web Consortium. (2013). *HTML 5.1 Nightly*. Retrieved from http://www.w3.org/html/wg/drafts/html/master/

Wright, R. (2012). Preserving moving pictures and sound (DPC Technology Watch Report 12–01). *Digital Preservation Coalition*. Retrieved from http://www.dpconline.org/component/docman/doc_download/753-dpctw12-01pdf

18 | Developing Data Management Services for Researchers at the University of Oregon

BRIAN WESTRA

The University of Oregon Libraries, like a growing number of academic libraries, employs a combination of strategies to develop and provide research data management support services. Efforts have included new or reconfigured faculty positions with responsibilities for research data management support; consultations and guidance on data management plans; training for graduate students and faculty in data management; a local institutional repository for preserving and sharing data; and finally, small pilot studies exploring research infrastructure collaborations targeted at data management needs early in the data life cycle. The result of this attention to the data curation needs of the campus is the beginning of an integrated approach to data management at a large research university.

BACKGROUND

The University of Oregon's (UO) core mission is education and research in the liberal arts with a heavy emphasis on the natural and social sciences. The university includes several professional schools in business, law, architecture, journalism, and education. In 2012, the undergraduate enrollment was over 20,800, and just over 3,800 graduate students were enrolled in 77 master's degree programs and 44 doctoral degree offerings. Multidisciplinary and integrative research is a major component of the sciences, including cognitive and decision sciences, ecology and evolutionary biology, biology and the built environment, and materials science. The university has had considerable success in sponsored research despite the fact that it does not have some of the key grant-generating disciplines of engineering and medicine.

Like many other institutions of a similar size, research information technology services at the UO are generally decentralized. The absence of applied computer science/engineering programs and their research and development capacity contributes to the challenges of creating a more robust research cyberinfrastructure. Although some steps toward more centralized services have been taken recently, research computing needs have been generally viewed as the responsibility of the researcher, and by extension, their research team or academic unit. Campus Information Services (IS) provides support in areas such as networks and telecommunications, enterprise administrative applications, and some high-performance computing projects for research. Some colleges and schools are taking an increasing role in research IT, in some cases hiring programmers and other staff specifically for research computing support.

The UO Libraries has a history of positive working relationships with academic and research units across the institution. Collaboration, open lines of communication, and responsiveness to needs have helped the UO Libraries provide useful services in the face of budget constraints, a changing scholarly communications landscape, and the rapid cycle of technological advancements that reframe student and faculty expectations.

The UO Libraries became fully invested in supporting research data management (RDM) with the hiring of a science data services librarian in late 2008. However, there were several antecedents to the creation of that position, which provide context for the current environment.

The UO's social sciences data services lab was established in 1990, and the university has long been a member of the Inter-university Consortium for Political and Social Research (ICPSR). Administratively, the lab is within the College of Arts and Sciences, but it is open to use by all UO students and faculty. The lab supports researchers in acquiring, accessing, and managing on-campus and external datasets. Archiving services for depositing data with ICPSR are also offered but have seen little uptake by research faculty.

By the early 2000s, growing concerns over preservation and access to scholarly output prompted a UO Libraries initiative to investigate and launch an institutional repository. Reports and guidance by the Association of College and Research Libraries (ACRL), the Scholarly Publishing and

Academic Resources Coalition (SPARC), and the Association of Research Libraries (ARL) provided valuable information to the project team. By the end of 2003, the UO Libraries had launched a DSpace-based repository, called Scholars' Bank, which now holds approximately 10,500 items, but very few datasets. Due to the very early adoption of a digital repository, initial submissions were slow, but gradually Scholars' Bank has earned a respected brand on campus.

In 2003, the ARL began to focus on the issues of data management and data curation, and their impact on the research library, shortly after the National Science Foundation (NSF) Blue-Ribbon Advisory Panel issued its report on "Revolutionizing Science and Engineering Through Cyberinfrastructure" (Atkins et al., 2003). Also in 2003, the National Institutes of Health (NIH) implemented a policy requiring a data sharing plan for grant proposals requesting over $500,000 direct costs per year. It was becoming increasingly apparent that data-driven scholarship could have a profound impact on research institutions and the libraries that support them. In succeeding years, a very few institutions quickly moved forward by creating new positions within their libraries to focus on faculty requirements associated with the organization and preservation of research data. In the meantime, other funding agencies were considering the inclusion of data management plans as part of the grant submission process.

Between 2006 and 2008 the UO electronic records archivist began work sponsored by the National Historical Publications and Records Commission (NHPRC) to investigate the research data recordkeeping needs of social scientists. One of the outcomes of that project was a website with guidance structured on established ICPSR training materials. These succinct, user-friendly pages provided basic advice to social science researchers on topics such as recordkeeping planning, managing collected datasets, and preparing data for publication and archiving.

In 2008, in response to a growing awareness of science research data needs, the UO Libraries, with the support of a progressive-minded donor, created a science data services librarian position. An informal team structure provided much of the initial support framework for this new position, which includes some traditional subject specialist responsibilities to the Department of Chemistry and the Science Library. The team consisted of the electronic records archivist, the head of digital library services (now the head of the recently launched Digital Scholarship Center), the map/GIS librarian, the associate university librarian for collections and access, and the science data services librarian. A government documents librarian position, reconfigured to have primary responsibilities for social science data, was added to the group in 2011, and the team was formalized within the UO Libraries as the Data Services Team, in no small part as a response to the demands created by NSF data management plan trainings and consultations.

Since its inception, the team has gone through several organizational iterations, and it is now called the Data Management Advisory Group (DMAG, see Figure 1). It is composed of the science data services librarian, map/GIS librarian, and government documents/social sciences data librarian. This group primarily is responsible for creating services and policies related to access to and preservation of research data, and reports to the Scholarly Communications Team (SCT). The SCT is comprised of the dean of the libraries, the scholarly communications librarian, the head of the digital scholarship center, the open access publishing fund representative, and rotating representation from DMAG, the subject specialist librarians, and an at-large member (librarian).

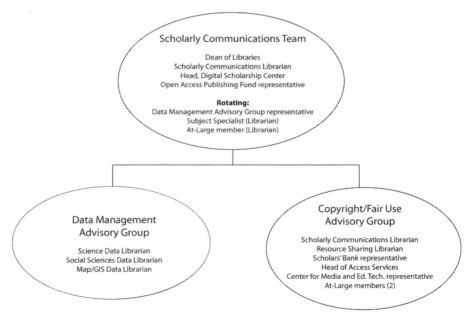

Figure 1. Organization chart of the Scholarly Communications Team, Data Management Advisory Group, and Copyright/Fair Use Advisory Group.

SCIENCE DATA SERVICES NEEDS ASSESSMENT

Library administration drafted a strategic initiative to conduct a science data services needs assessment, and the data librarian finalized the plan and implemented it in the 2009–2010 academic year. The goals of the assessment were to raise awareness of library plans and capacity-building steps, bring insight to the libraries about needs and possible service areas, and identify potential partners for pilot data curation projects (Westra, 2010).

The assessment interview questions were based on materials from the University of Glasgow's Data Asset Framework, and Purdue University Libraries' Data Curation Profiles questions. For the data librarian, the project provided an avenue for developing connections with partners outside the library and with relevant departments within the library. Campus Information Services provided input on the interview questions, as did the electronic records archivist and librarians responsible for scholarly communications and digital services. The vice president for research (VPR) was consulted for support of the project and outreach to research faculty, as were subject specialist librarians, administrators in the College of Arts and Sciences, and the heads of research centers and institutes.

Twenty-five research faculty were interviewed for the study, providing a cross section that was representative of the science departments at the UO. Many of the faculty who participated have since demonstrated their support for the development of library services for RDM. The departments and institutes that participated included: biology; the Center for Advanced Materials Characterization in Oregon; chemistry; computer and information science; geological sciences; human physiology; the Institute for a Sustainable Environment; the Museum of Natural and Cultural History; physics; and psychology.

While much of the literature and popular press focuses on "big data," others have pointed out the volume and importance of smaller datasets in the "long tail" of research data (Heidorn, 2008). A number of faculty noted that their research produced smaller datasets, and their articulation of data management practices and needs frequently grew during the course of the interview. At the time of the needs assessment, relatively few research domains were subject to NSF data sharing requirements, but several faculty noted that if such requirements became widespread, it would likely lead to improved data curation practices.

The most common issues to be identified were the lack of file organization, insufficient storage and backup procedures, and insubstantial and highly variable documentation/metadata that negatively impacted the primary investigator's ability to later find and retrieve data. These challenges in local practice also were reflective of gaps in infrastructure, data management tools, and the absence or lack of adoption of best practices—all issues that have been identified at other institutions. Concerns about data sharing and preservation were subsumed by these issues that more directly impact ongoing research. The assessment provided information and connections with researchers that became a foundation for several other projects that followed.

DATA MANAGEMENT TOOLS IN THE RESEARCH ENVIRONMENT

In the needs assessment and in conversations since then, faculty in natural sciences have expressed a strong interest in applications and resources that could facilitate data management early in the research process. One of the ways in which the UO Libraries supported this work was through a small internal grant toward costs for a pilot study examining one or more tools directed at this part of the data life cycle. The project was a collaboration between the UO Libraries, the College of Arts and Sciences Information Technology group (CAS IT), and several research labs in the Department of Biology. The data services librarian identified several options with low investment thresholds that were reviewed for their applicability to laboratory research data needs and fitness for the existing infrastructure.

After a review of several tools, Open Microscopy Environment's OMERO system for managing image data was selected for the pilot study (Open Microscopy Environment, n.d.). Numerous research groups in biology generate image and video data, and since OMERO is an open-source application with a fairly broad user base, a successful pilot has the potential for a significant impact on data management practices while staying within a limited budget. The pilot study provided useful information about important considerations, such as integration with research workflows, technology considerations, and usability. A follow-up review will be completed in 2013, and CAS IT is working with one research team to explore integration of OMERO with other data management tools under development.

In another example of tools employed in the research setting, faculty in the Department of Chemistry and others have expressed interest in electronic lab notebooks (ELNs). There are a number of compelling reasons for making the transition from paper notebooks to digital systems. Electronic lab notebooks have the potential to significantly improve organization and documentation of data, automate the capture of workflows and provenance, provide search and discovery, and support collaboration and review within research teams. Some ELNs now have the capacity to publish data directly to external repositories.

A small group of faculty and graduate students in chemistry participated with the data services librarian in an informal review of several representative ELNs. The process revealed some of the features that are valued by chemistry researchers. This introduction and demonstration of ELNs highlighted the broad spectrum of functionality that might be useful to a department with research interests ranging from synthetic chemistry to nanotechnology and materials science. Costs of implementation and maintenance were considered the most significant barrier.

The informal process provided a useful introduction to the issues for all involved, but a deeper and more systematic review is necessary before making the sizable investments in technology, training, and integration with research practices that most systems would require. As with nearly any information technology, there is a fairly continuous cycle of change in the ELN landscape, from platform and system design to vendor turnover. Lack of standardization in how the systems handle metadata is also troublesome. Establishing a sustainable funding model will very likely be a prerequisite before the department revisits this issue. The ELN review process employed by the University of Wisconsin-Madison is instructive and provides a good model for other academic institutions to follow (University of Wisconsin-Madison, 2012). There is widespread interest among academic institutions, including libraries, in ELN systems as part of a larger data curation framework, so this will likely continue to be a prime area for investigation and collaboration. The UO Libraries have plans to work with several labs on ELN implementations in the near future.

DATA MANAGEMENT PLAN REQUIREMENTS, CONSULTATIONS, AND TRAINING

The NSF requirement in 2011 that all new grant proposals include a data management plan (DMP) created greater urgency to address RDM services among research faculty, academic institutions, and libraries. In preparation for the NSF requirements, the UO Libraries convened a meeting of representatives of the VPR, research institutes, and IS and academic IT groups in the fall of 2010 to discuss the services, policies, and infrastructure necessary for robust and realistic DMPs. Research faculty at the UO looked to the Libraries to take a leadership role in educating and supporting scientists who would be formulating their DMPs.

The primary outcome of the meeting was an initiative to develop a guidance website and provide consultations and training on RDM. In combination with materials by peer institutions, the content of the website was developed by a team comprised of the data services librarian, electronic records archivist, head of digital library services, and representatives from the VPR (now called the Office for Research, Innovation and Graduate Education, or RIGE), IS, CAS IT, Technology Transfer, and Research Compliance Services. The materials were brought together in short order to provide guidance to research faculty before the NSF requirement went into effect. The diversity of the team yielded materials that covered the topics in sufficient detail with support of their respective units, and incorporated referring links from their own websites to the guidance pages. The site has undergone several revisions since then, streamlining information and improving usability.

In tandem with the website, a consultation service was created through which the data librarian, archivist, digital services librarian, and an IS consultant could respond to requests for information by research faculty and other grant proposal authors. Various outreach channels were utilized to raise awareness at the UO about the NSF requirement and availability of guidance and consultations. The VPR highlighted the NSF requirements and the UO Libraries' data management services in a newsletter to faculty. Several workshops were provided for faculty on the NSF requirements by the UO Libraries team. Presentations were made to departmental grant administrators (DGAs), who, along with Sponsored Projects Services (SPS) pre-award staff, assist faculty in the process of writing and submitting grant proposals. Within SPS, pre-award and faculty development staff and the DGAs have provided a number of referrals, and several DGAs have followed up to ask for reviews of DMPs from the faculty they support. Consultations and reviews have been provided for approximately 60 data management plans out of approximately 310 proposals submitted by UO researchers to the NSF since the inception of the DMP requirement. While this figure may seem to be fairly small, it is important to consider that guidance provided to one researcher is frequently shared with peers who are submitting proposals to the same NSF program or directorate. The data librarians have worked with faculty from a broad range of academic units, including: anthropology, biology, chemistry, education, geology, law, physics, political science, and psychology.

A holistic review of DMPs submitted to the NSF by UO researchers is envisioned for 2013. With the support of SPS, the data librarians plan to review all plans submitted for grant proposals and collect and aggregate information on needs, gaps, resource commitments, and other metrics. This information will help improve training and consultation services to target common weaknesses in plans, and identify areas where infrastructure may need to be bolstered. A systematic review may improve resource planning and allocation to the degree that service providers can use DMPs to forecast trends and issues that are underscored in the plans.

INSTITUTIONAL REPOSITORY

Scholars' Bank is available for deposit and sharing of research datasets, though researchers are encouraged to make use of domain-specific repositories if sustainable and well-managed options are available. Data management guidance for UO researchers highlights select data centers that are judged to meet basic criteria for discoverability, open access, and sustainability, and the Databib.org directory of data repositories provides a good starting point. The UO Libraries are partnering with Oregon State University Libraries in maintenance and support of the two institutions' DSpace systems, and exploring other repository architectures that may be more robust for research data deposits.

In support of data deposit in institutional repositories, the UO Libraries initiated a collaboration with the University of Washington, Oregon State University, Oregon Health and Science University, and Washington State University to use a consortial approach for paying for the DataCite/EZID service agreement. DataCite provides registration for datasets, creating persistent unique digital object identifiers (DOIs) that can be used for citing data. The decision to use DataCite to register deposited datasets was driven in part by the belief that DOIs will be used to create data citation indexes, much like article citation indexes. Data citation metrics have the potential to become another indicator of scholarly impact, and anecdotal evidence suggests that this could be a significant incentive for research faculty to share and deposit their data. It is too early to tell, but indications are that commercial citation indexes, such as the Thomson Reuters Data Citation Index product, will expand to incorporate all DataCite-registered datasets.

RESEARCH DATA MANAGEMENT TRAINING

The UO data librarians have taken several approaches to providing training to faculty and graduate students on RDM. Sessions specifically about DMPs have been provided in stand-alone workshops for faculty, and the UO Libraries plan to offer more training in association with grant-writing workshops offered each fall by SPS. As might be expected, attendee feedback at workshops has placed a high value on discipline-specific examples and resources. However, it is challenging to achieve much domain specificity in a one-size-fits-all session. With that in mind, several other educational interventions have been developed to provide training targeted at subject-specific needs and interests.

One example of this kind of instruction is the integration of data management topics into responsible conduct of research (RCR) seminars. At the UO, this opportunity is a direct outgrowth of relationships built with Research Compliance Services (RCS) during the development of the data management website. The RCS staff are responsible for institutional review board (IRB) reviews for human subjects research, and help departments meet NIH and NSF RCR requirements. With the support of RCS, it has become more commonplace for science departments to include the data librarians in teaching RDM as part of their RCR seminars. Graduate students in these seminars are typically highly engaged in the topics at hand, and it has been a rewarding experience for the data librarians to present RDM best practices and resources in these settings.

On a different front, the UO Libraries are participating with Purdue University (lead institution), the University of Minnesota, and Cornell University in an Institute of Museum and Library Services (IMLS)-funded project to investigate data information literacy (DIL) needs of graduate students in science, technology, engineering, and mathematics (STEM) disciplines. At the UO, the project team has worked with an ecology research team to investigate their RDM practices, and develop and present resources and training to improve individual and team data management competencies (Carlson, Johnston, Westra, & Nichols, 2013). This approach has prompted interest from others in biology and the Department of Chemistry, where the same methods are being applied to several research teams. Research faculty and graduate students alike are interested in improving data management practices, particularly if they perceive that the skills and tools will help them meet funder requirements for data sharing, increase the capacity to preserve research outcomes, reduce the risk of data loss, and improve the competitiveness of grant proposals. The DIL interviews of graduate students also have provided research faculty with a better understanding of their team's practices and needs, which they might not otherwise have obtained.

Finally, in 2013 the UO Libraries offered a for-credit course as an experimental investigation into course-based instruction aimed at master's degree students who are about to begin research projects. The course was headed by the social science data librarian, and included invited speakers from the UO Libraries on metadata, archives and preservation, data management planning, and data sharing.

PROFESSIONAL AND ORGANIZATIONAL DEVELOPMENT

Research libraries cannot provide RDM services alone, and it is essential to be proactive in working with the full range of stakeholders and interested parties. Of course, a supportive environment within the libraries is also essential. An organizational structure and professional and organizational development opportunities are critical components to launching and sustaining new services. The data librarians have participated in workshops, such as those provided through the ICPSR and the DigCCurr Institute at UNC at Chapel Hill, which imparted useful information and facilitated the establishment of support networks and collaborations with colleagues in similar roles at other institutions. The past few years have witnessed a dramatic expansion in the number of special interest groups, e-mail discussion lists, workshops, web resources, and conferences or conference tracks devoted to research data curation issues.

Institutional participation in regional and national associations and consortia can yield synergies that are difficult to achieve by individual staff.

As noted above, the ARL has a history of promoting and supporting the role of libraries in data curation. In 2011, the UO Libraries, with approximately 70 other institutions, participated in the first ARL/Digital Library Federation (DLF) E-Science Institute. Each institution conducted an environmental scan and interviewed key faculty and administrative positions, which generated a useful analysis of library services in the context of the collaborations that science research support necessitates. Under the leadership of the dean of the libraries, the outcome of the institute was a strategic agenda for cyberinfrastructure and data management to help shape UO Libraries planning. Many of the items in the agenda have already been accomplished or are currently underway.

The strategic agenda also provides a useful communication tool and discussion point for work with campus partners. Similarly, there may be other opportunities for data librarians to engage in research support collaborations that will open doors and develop and refine their skills. This has included participation in an institutional data storage needs assessment, initiating and hosting campus meetings on research data and cyberinfrastructure, and working with the Department of Chemistry to develop a symposium on research tools and services for chemistry.

CHALLENGES AND OPPORTUNITIES

The UO Libraries have made significant progress in establishing RDM services to support research faculty and graduate students. To succeed and thrive in supporting scientists who work in increasingly digital research ecosystems, libraries may need to reframe organizational structures, explore new service models, staffing, and technology, and pursue and sustain deeper integration with other units in the academic research institution. Some of the considerations for institutions like the UO are outlined below.

Service Models

Data librarians, or positions combining data and subject specialist responsibilities, are becoming a more common model in academic libraries. Where these positions are placed on the spectrum of "embeddedness" in relation to research teams may be a point of departure for most libraries that are stretched thin by budget restrictions. Because services can be offered in closer context to needs, embedded approaches have the potential for more immediate impact on researchers' data management practices. Embedded staff typically must work with a narrower disciplinary focus and greater domain expertise, and will be able to accommodate fewer researchers. For many libraries, these scalability restrictions may outweigh the benefits that enhanced, targeted services might provide. Some lessons may be learned from clinical medicine informationist positions, which have similar characteristic challenges, barriers, and success factors because much of what they do is "work in context" (Rankin, Grefsheim, & Canto, 2008).

Incorporating data management responsibilities into subject specialist roles may help meet more researcher needs, but it is highly dependent on librarian skills and interests, and how other responsibilities are modified to free up the necessary time. Data librarians must often develop some level of science research expertise, familiarity with research and data analysis tools, as well as metadata, and curation and preservation workflows.

In some respects, data curation is analogous to other collection development activities. The degree to which academic institutions should develop and host their own data repositories is an ongoing topic of discussion. In instances where the infrastructure can be implemented and supported in response to needs for local collections, this is a useful investment. For instance, the UO Libraries hope to increase utilization of the institutional repository for theses and dissertation data by working with the Graduate School, which oversees the dissertation submission process. If there are sustainably funded external data repositories integrated with other aspects of scholarly communication for a given domain, those systems are probably better suited to the task. The UO Libraries have for the present chosen to emphasize disciplinary repositories as the primary option for data sharing, with Scholars' Bank as a secondary choice, should no sustainable domain repository exist.

Co-development partnerships with other institutions may lower the barrier enough to implement more robust repository systems that could not be achieved in isolation. Perhaps as more institutions encounter similar infrastructure needs there will be opportunities to develop and manage resources at consortial levels, much like the integrated library system project for the Orbis Cascade Alliance.

Also of interest is the degree to which self-submission systems for data deposit in these external data centers will proliferate. Dryad for ecology data, ChemSpider SyntheticPages for chemical synthesis data, and the Integrated Earth Data Applications (IEDA) suite of data collections all represent self-submission models that may also include some degree of curation responsibilities assumed by the data repository. If this becomes the predominant model across research domains, metadata and curation support services will increasingly become the provenance of national repositories, rather than supported by the originating academic institutions.

Organizational Structures

At the institutional level, RDM services are highly dependent on healthy partnerships between libraries, information technology, research support, and faculty and graduate students. Vertical integration of RDM services within libraries is an important first step. Engagement with the larger institution is also critical in order to couple operational activities and goals with budgeting, higher-level strategic planning, and prioritization. In the UO Libraries, the dean of the libraries and the associate university librarian for collections and access have taken a proactive approach to supporting RDM, and their continued attention will be required if these services are to be sustained and evolve.

Operational awareness gained through collaborative activities establishes a foundation for interdepartmental efforts such as consistent messaging, consultation referrals, shared resource development, and building institutional capacity. The development of the data management webpages at the UO is a good example of a narrowly focused interdepartmental collaboration that efficiently met a critical need. The UO Libraries have maintained a strong working relationship with SPS and RIGE, and are deepening ties with IS and academic and research IT units. These positive outcomes are due in part to proactive efforts to share information, facilitate meetings and activities, and a willingness to engage in collaborative solutions that can move all parties forward in support of the academic research enterprise. A stronger integration of data services into the campus framework will better serve the institution, and this is a priority for the UO DMAG.

One example of such a collaborative effort is the development of institutional policies for research data stewardship. The university does not currently have a policy for research data stewardship, but there is strong interest in developing a framework that reflects local needs and capacities, and can support the selection and use of secure and curation-friendly services and applications. A campus-wide partnership will be needed to create such a structure, with research faculty input, and enabled by training, tools, and other infrastructure. Absent the infrastructure, policies are at risk of becoming another "unfunded mandate" that does not generate the desired outcomes.

Funding Agency Mandates and Partnerships

Research data management services are highly influenced by funding agency requirements, regional and national infrastructure, and the constellation of other stakeholders that surround the research enterprise. More federal agencies will soon require DMPs as a result of the memorandum from the Office of Science and Technology Policy (Holdren, 2013). Several researchers have commented that the process of writing a DMP has forced them, even if reluctantly, to examine and improve their practices. It has certainly raised the level of awareness of needs for RDM services and infrastructure across the institution. The competition for grant funding provides an inherent incentive for faculty to create well-written, executable DMPs to accompany their proposals. Thus far, DMPs have not received the same level of scrutiny and detailed comments that are directed at other components of proposals in the NSF review process. Until detailed feedback is consistently generated in the review process, their impact on proposal competitiveness will be unknown. It is hoped that the NSF and other agencies will collaborate with the data curation community and research scientists to transparently identify and establish best practices in support of data curation.

Assessment

Other types of feedback and assessment will also help libraries and partners refine and improve activities and programs. Consultations, trainings, and in-context services can provide a mix of anecdotal and quantifiable information. As the UO Libraries work to improve the data information literacy of graduate students, there will be a continued need to assess the outcomes, whether through pre- and post-course testing, or observed and documented changes in practice.

Intentional and directed assessments have the potential to yield a more comprehensive view of attitudes, needs, and outcomes. The data services needs assessment and a more recent campus-wide storage needs survey provided actionable information that continues to influence the direction of services by the UO Libraries, IS, and RIGE.

A mechanism for "early detection" of the data curation needs of funded research projects would facilitate more accurate strategic planning for institutional repository tools and resource utilization. Data management plans do not always convey all the relevant details for infrastructure planning. In fact, the type and amount of data may change significantly during the course of a research project. In some larger proposals, the award is contingent on an explicit commitment by the institution toward the necessary infrastructure. Perhaps it is worth exploring a stronger linkage between grant award notifications and strategic planning to ensure that robust services are, or will be, in place. A research infrastructure that can provide a sustainable baseline of services to all researchers is a desirable outcome, and it may require a significant budgetary commitment from higher levels within the institution.

Data-dependent research practices will very likely continue to evolve at a rapid pace, in parallel with changing research technologies. The UO Libraries is looking forward to continuing on a proactive path of evolution and collaboration with local, regional, and national partners in order to provide the services that will meet these demands.

ACKNOWLEDGMENTS

I would like to thank Deb Carver, Cara List, Margaret Bean, and Victoria Mitchell for their comments and suggestions on this chapter.

REFERENCES

Atkins, D. E., Droegemeier, K. K., Feldman, S. I., Garcia-Molina, H., Klein, M. L., Messerschmitt, D. G., . . . Wright, M. H. (2003). *Revolutionizing science and engineering through cyberinfrastructure: Report of the National Science Foundation Blue-Ribbon Advisory Panel on Cyber-infrastructure*. Arlington, TX: National Science Foundation. Retrieved from http://www.nsf.gov/od/oci/reports/atkins.pdf

Carlson, J., Johnston, L., Westra, B., & Nichols, M. (2013). Developing an approach for data management education: A report from the Data Information Literacy Project. *International Journal of Digital Curation*, 8(1), 204–217. http://dx.doi.org/10.2218/ijdc.v8i1.254

Heidorn, P. B. (2008). Shedding light on the dark data in the long tail of science. *Library Trends*, 57(2), 280–299. http://dx.doi.org/10.1353/lib.0.0036

Holdren, J. P. (2013). Memorandum for the heads of executive departments and agencies. RE: *Increasing access to the results of federally funded scientific research*. Washington, DC: Executive Office of the President, Office of Science and Technology Policy. Retrieved from http://www.whitehouse.gov/sites/default/files/microsites/ostp/ostp_public_access_memo_2013.pdf

Open Microscopy Environment. (n.d.). About OMERO. *University of Dundee*. Retrieved from http://www.openmicroscopy.org/site/products/omero/omero-platform-v4#analyse

Rankin, J. A., Grefsheim, S. F., & Canto, C. C. (2008). The emerging informationist specialty: A systematic review of the literature. *Journal of the Medical Library Association*, 96(3), 194–206. http://dx.doi.org/10.3163/1536-5050.96.3.005

University of Wisconsin-Madison. (2012). *Electronic lab notebook pilot at the University of Wisconsin-Madison: Study findings*. Madison: University of Wisconsin-Madison. Retrieved from https://academictech.doit.wisc.edu/files/ELN_pilot_report_UWMadison.pdf

Westra, B. (2010). Data services for the sciences: A needs assessment. *Ariadne, 64*. Retrieved from http://www.ariadne.ac.uk/issue64/westra/

Closing Reflections

LOOKING AHEAD

19 | The Next Generation of Challenges in the Curation of Scholarly Data

CLIFFORD LYNCH

INTRODUCTION

Requirements for data curation are now well established across a wide range of scholarly disciplines, but particularly in the sciences and some social sciences, through a series of funder requirements for data management plans and policies mandating public access to large classes of research data. Institutional policies and journal editorial policies surrounding the management and availability of research data support and complement the funder-driven initiatives. The need for effective and affordable research data management services will only grow over the next decade.

The previous chapters of this book have covered the evolution of the policy environment and discussed some of the technical issues surrounding data curation. One of the most important and unusual contributions of the book is a series of case studies of pioneer and early adopter experiences in responding to the data curation challenges; in the next few years, we will see many more institutions following in the footsteps described in these leadership case studies, and designing services informed by the experiences documented here. The overarching priorities for the next few years will be to help faculty to develop credible data management plans, to appropriately document the datasets that they share and preserve, and to help them find platforms (either locally developed, through consortia or disciplinary centers, or even via commercial services) to share data and to prepurchase assured bit preservation for periods on the order of five to ten years. Until these three groups of services are in place and operating effectively and at scale, many other challenges will have to wait or will be dealt with only on an ad-hoc basis when absolutely unavoidable.

And there is also a *new* group of challenges waiting in the wings, appearing as a result of the initial success in meeting these first three most urgent and most basic needs.

My purpose in this concluding chapter is to sketch a number of what I believe will be the key next-generation challenges. These are challenges that will ultimately need systematic engagement, and generally better sooner than later. Most of these are not very well understood at this point, and experience with them is very limited; however, it is certainly not too soon to put them on the strategic planning agenda for data curation work, to begin thinking about how to approach them, and in some cases, to start building experimental or prototype services. As with so many aspects of data curation, pure research is of limited value; it is necessary to actually build and deploy attempts at genuine operational services, working with real research data and real researchers, in order to make meaningful progress.

While some of my examples and specifics have been drawn almost exclusively from the United States, I believe that we will see very similar issues emerge in other national settings. Perhaps the area of greatest variation will be in the conflicts surrounding data that involves human subjects, where divergent national policies involving health care delivery—and thus health care records, privacy, and similar issues—may result in quite different outcomes from nation to nation (and thus, perhaps, even more formidable obstacles for sharing and reuse of such data *across* national borders).

MOTIVATIONS AND DRIVERS FOR THE DEPLOYMENT OF DATA CURATION SERVICES

Before looking at these new challenges, it is useful to summarize the forces that are driving the various players—funders, scholars, the institutions that host these scholars, and journal editors—in their current actions related to research data. In general, these players are not calling for data curation, preservation, and sharing because it is abstractly the right thing to do as part of the creation, dissemination, and stewardship of knowledge; their motivations are much more specific and pragmatic. I do not believe that this array of driving forces will change significantly, at least over the next ten years, so understanding them is essential to situating both current developments and the next generation of challenges.

Funders, and particularly public funders, are under great pressure to show how their funding contributes to broad economic growth, how it addresses the needs of society, and to demonstrate that the requirements that they impose on the work they fund makes discovery ever more rapid, extensive, and cost-effective. From this perspective, they are not interested in data preservation or even data sharing other than as a necessary precondition to data reuse; they are interested in conformance to their data management and sharing policies because it is the only way they can create the preconditions for data reuse. They are hungry for examples of how data reuse has improved the processes of scholarship and discovery, or contributed to economic growth, job creation, control of health care costs, or public policy.

While research libraries and other memory organizations do, I believe, have a deep and genuine mission in data stewardship as part of their commitment to managing the intellectual and cultural record and its underlying evidentiary base for the long term, at the broader level of research universities institutionally, the greatest pragmatic and operational interest is in ensuring conformance to funder requirements and managing institutional risk and liability. They certainly will provide some funding support for the long-term stewardship work of their memory organizations. They welcome improvements in the processes of research and scholarship, but usually they rely on the faculty to drive such improvements.

The vast majority of faculty will, at least in the near term, see little real benefit from making their data available for sharing. Despite work on data citation practices and on changing evaluation criteria for researchers, it will take a long time for faculty contributions of data for potential community reuse to make a compelling and widespread difference in tenure and promotion cases; the inertia and conservatism in this system is enormous. So developing and subsequently implementing data management plans will most often be viewed as just one more burden imposed by the funding agencies; faculty will want to satisfy these new requirements in the most time-efficient and easiest fashion. Some faculty (we don't know how many, or in what disciplines) will be very creative in exploiting the growing amounts of data available for reuse and will find their own scholarly work advanced. There will, of course, be some high-profile cases where faculty who obtain important new results through data reuse gain important recognition (keep in mind that the funders are eager to identify, encourage, and recognize these scholars). Even researchers who provide data that is subsequently reused to significant effect may find their contributions honored—but there's a sizeable luck factor here, as it is not so much that they make data available for possible reuse as it is that they were lucky enough to have someone actually reuse it and then make an important discovery.

In a significant number of scientific disciplines, there is a growing crisis of reproducibility. With increasing frequency, papers report results that cannot be reproduced by other researchers. This is not new, and there are many reasons for it, not all of them sinister: inadequately documented methodologies; honest errors, sloppy work, or simply an incomplete understanding of new phenomena that are being reported and their causes (often compounded by a rush to publish); unavailability of data, tools, and/or materials to other researchers seeking to reproduce the work; and outright fraud and fabrication of data. As funding continues to decline and the number of researchers competing for funding (and tenure and promotion) continues to grow, this establishes a hypercompetitive environment that puts greater pressure on reproducibility. This is of great concern to all players—scholars, journals (doing more agressive and adversarial refereeing in response to a growing number of deceptive submissions and retractions), institutions, and funders. This crisis of reproducibility is starting to surface more frequently in political settings and broad public fora, and carries with it a very real risk of eroding public support for science and for scientific research. One easily can see a future where funders and institutions, assisted by journals and many individual scholars, introduce increasingly heavy-handed policies to root out irreproducible research; the retention of data and the sharing of data (perhaps as part of the refereeing process, but certainly effective as of publication) will be important elements here.

A final point on reproducibility: in most cases, it is a fairly short-term problem. Other researchers will try to reproduce results soon after their publication, and much of the practical thinking about reproducibility focuses on a relatively short time window, say five years or so. It is both very costly and very difficult (due to changes in experimental technology and methodology) to think in terms of reproducing a 50-year-old result, particularly without some fundamental rethinking about exactly what one is trying to reproduce.

THE NEW DATA CURATION CHALLENGES

Software

In a substantial number of cases, the interpretation and analysis of data is deeply intertwined with the availability of specialized software. Both the level of interdependence between software and data and the level of complexity of the software vary greatly. There is at least some reason to believe that software "decays" more rapidly than data, and it will require more frequent and more costly interventions to ensure that it continues to be useable over time (though there are promising developments in areas such as virtualization and emulation that offer some hope here, but these are certainly not a panacea).

Software is also vital when trying to reproduce published results. The good news here is the fairly short time horizon means that the software needs to be saved and made available for sharing, but it probably can be successfully maintained across the necessary time period.

It is clear that funders are going to have to develop a more holistic view of data management, and specifically address software as well as data in management plans; some of the major science funding agencies, at least in the United States, are already starting to think about this.

We will need to be able to offer researchers services that can preserve complex collections of interconnected data and software (and documentation), or simply preserve more general purpose software independent of specific datasets. In both cases, it will be essential to be clear about what it actually means to "preserve" the software in question and to understand the cost implications of various choices, particularly over a range of timescales. For example, there is a great difference between a preservation program that ensures that a given set of software is always ready to run on the most popular platform or platforms of the day, and a preservation program that simply makes it possible to launch an effort to resurrect a given set of software in future with a fairly high likelihood of success (given enough time and money). At the more demanding levels of software curation and preservation, the availability and development of the necessary skills and expertise in the workforce will be a serious problem.

Conformance: Auditing the Promises in Data Management Plans

Today, short of a decision by a funder (or an institution) to audit conformance to a data management plan, which is most likely going to be specific to an individual contract or grant, or perhaps to the set of contracts and grants given to a specific institution, there is no way to track conformance to the promises made in a data management plan. Either such mechanisms will need to be developed or there will be reliance on occasional spot audits by funders, probably accompanied by increasingly draconian punishments in order to encourage compliance. This could shift the compliance monitoring burden at least in part to institutions (as is the case with many other funder requirements), but the problems of mechanisms and scale are conserved. Institutions will need to think very carefully about where to situate responsibility for audit and enforcement organizationally: if mishandled, it could easily poison the development of what everyone hopes will be collaborative and constructive relationships between institutional data curators and faculty researchers.

There are a few specific points in surrounding conformance that merit comment. In terms of data sharing for replication of results or reuse, there are two possible approaches. One is to say that data must be shared *upon request*, and to rely mainly on complaints from frustrated requestors to identify compliance problems. The other is to insist that data is placed in a transparent and public repository; it is then possible to just check that the data has been deposited and that the repository is being operated according to good practices. Clearly the second situation is much more tractable from the point of view of checking compliance, but if there are constraints on the data (for example, privacy constraints or a requirement that those who want to reuse the data contractually agree they will not attempt to deanonymize it) then considerations of control, accountability, and liability become complex. There are many implications here for how, why, and under what criteria we certify repositories.

A second issue is how often, and for how long, compliance needs to be verified, and what to do if there is a problem. Suppose that a data management plan promises to keep a dataset for 50 years. Is it enough to confirm that it has been deposited into a "reputable" repository that promises to keep it for 50 years, or do we have to periodically check that it is still there? Who certifies reputable repositories, and what happens if they fall upon hard times or fail recertification? If there is a problem, who is responsible for dealing with it (particularly given that data can outlive the investigator who created it)? Implicit here is that the balance of responsibility between faculty investigators and host institutions in meeting commitments to funders, and how this balance may be shifted by time and circumstance, is going to be mapped out as part of the ongoing focus on compliance.

Implications of Term-Limited Data Preservation Strategies: Managing Reassessment

One of the striking—and in my view overall very positive—changes in thinking about research data stewardship (and many other areas of digital preservation) over the past few years has been the move away from talking about taking a single decision and set of actions aimed at preserving data "forever" (or at least for a very long and indeterminate period of time). Instead, a stewardship organization makes a commitment to take care of a collection of data for a specific period of time—something on the order of 10 or 20 years, perhaps—after which it makes no further promises except that it will see that the collection receives a review and that it will ensure that if some other organization wants to accept responsibility for an additional period of time, it will cooperate actively in an orderly and well-thought-out transfer of the collection that will make every effort to preserve data integrity. This kind of thinking is prominent in the 2010 report of the *Blue Ribbon Task Force on Sustainable Digital Preservation and Access*, for example. This shift is driven in part by the recognition that we still have very limited experience in assessing the relative merits of various preservation choices about research data under constrained resources that say we cannot save everything (indeed, while discarding at this level is familiar to archivists in some other settings, it is relatively unfamiliar to research libraries operating as a system). Another motivation is a recognition that the uncertainties involved in very long-term commitments are not just technical; they are financial (in the sense of rates of return on funds) and organizational.

The upshot of this shift is that for data that does not fit into a disciplinary repository, it is increasingly common to find proposals to guarantee to preserve datasets (at the bit level) and make them publically accessible for a period of five or ten years (with the costs prefunded as part of the grant budget). At least by implication, and sometimes explicitly, there is a reassessment process that will be conducted at the end of this period; if the data is viewed as of sufficient continued value, funding will be found for someone to sustain the data for an additional term (after which the process presumably repeats). Experience with the levels and purposes of data reuse during the earlier periods will help to inform the choices about whether to renew the data. This is perfectly reasonable—but there are no mechanisms in place to support this kind of periodic review and reassessment, or to gather funding other than individual institutional budgets to support ongoing stewardship.

Developing these mechanisms is going to become increasingly urgent over the next decade, and there are some very complex organizational challenges implicit in any successful approach. One is simply scale. Another is the way to balance the views of different disciplines, since the relevance and importance of a data collection to various disciplines may well shift over time. A third deals with tension between decisions that are local to a given institution and allocate institutional funds, and the need to think about research data as a shared asset and shared record that is held by the entire research and education community, nationally and internationally. A fourth challenge is to define the mechanisms and level of participation by funding agencies in the longer-term stewardship of research data. Addressing the challenges here will require both action at the institutional level, by frontline data curators and their institutional leadership, and also policy development and implementation of collaborative mechanisms and frameworks at the national and international levels.

Understanding What Is Worth Preserving

Current trends suggest to me that over the next five or ten years we will collectively retain much more research data than we have the past. Some of this will be driven by the demands for reproducibility, but as already discussed, reproducibility typically supports only fairly short-term retention. Hopes that data will be reused are another driver, but beyond hope, we know very little in general about likelihood of reuse, or the time horizons within which that reuse is likely to occur, if it does occur. There are some classes of data where reuse is quite likely: data that is directly comparable to other data, which can be aggregated into some kind of time series or larger aggregate (for example, a set of medical records that can be combined for greater statistical resolution of rare effects). A lot of this kind of data already goes into disciplinary databases or data repositories. Indeed, one of the powerful catalysts that funders can use to encourage data sharing and reuse is the identification of such classes of data and then the creation of databases or data repositories to facilitate aggregation and normalization.

Beyond reproducibility demands and hopes for near-term reuse, it will fall to our established stewardship organizations to allocate resources for the longer-term preservation and management of selected research data resources. The opportunities will doubtless vastly exceed available resources. The first round of these decisions will come quickly, more quickly than I think that many organizations realize, as short-term commitments funded through data management plans and associated grants expire. Institutions (individually and collectively) come to these decisions with a weak analytic framework to assist in decision making. Among the factors to be considered, and somehow balanced against each other, are: the very difficult to assess hope of reuse in future, perhaps in disciplines very distant from those that originally generated the data; the quality of the data and its documentation; the irreplaceability of many classes of observational (as opposed to experimental) data; the economic or ethical costs of regenerating experimental data (clinical trials, the use of animals, the cost of recreating experimental apparatus); and, of course, estimates of the cost of preserving specific collections of data. We will need good models, best practices, thoughtful analysis of experiences with case studies, and staff development opportunities to help with these critical decisions.

Data Involving Human Subjects

There is an enormous emerging collision between the desires to share and reuse data, with all the benefits these practices can offer, and the very complex institutions and policies that have been established to protect the safety, privacy, and dignity of human beings who provide data to the research process. The landscape here is enormously complicated and problematic—there are very complex regulations from the Department of Health and Human Services in the United States (plus a massive set of revisions currently under review and discussion), inconsistent and sometimes idiosyncratic implementations of these regulations through local campus institutional review boards (IRBs), and a dearth of mechanisms for facilitating multicampus research collaborations (much less international collaborations). The jurisdiction of the IRBs goes far beyond research related to medical and psychological experiments into social science surveys, and, on some campuses, oral history and other interview-based data collection.

One cornerstone concept in protecting human subjects is informed consent; this includes ensuring that potential subjects understand what data is being collected about them, how long it will be retained, who gets to use it, and an understanding of the specific uses to which it will be put (including the risks of those uses). Even if the potential subjects were willing to sign very general release forms that would facilitate sharing and reuse of data, the use of such consent forms would likely be rejected by the local IRB; at best, some specific and constrained kinds of data reuse, such as a meta-analysis, might be included in an acceptable consent agreement.

Another very problematic area here is the anonymization of data involving human subjects. For some kinds of reuse, an anonymized version of a data collection, which breaks the links between data and the individuals that provided it, is sufficient (though, of course, many other reuse scenarios will require the full data). But researchers in many fields and many contexts, from genomics to information science (query logs), have discovered that it is incredibly difficult to irrevocably anonymize data, particularly if data from multiple sources are merged together. So now we see researchers who want to reuse data being asked to certify that they will not attempt to deanonymize it; even more problematically, there may be some attempt to "qualify" the potential reusers and reuses as "legitimate" in some fashion, which quickly runs contrary to the goals of promoting broad and creative reuses, and engaging industry and the broad general public, not just the research community, in the reuse of data (and particularly data produced with public funding).

A broad and constructive conversation on the conflicts between the protection of human subjects and the advancement of scholarly work has been very difficult to advance; many scholars across the spectrum of disciplines conduct their research at the pleasure of the largely unaccountable IRB system, and thus, they are reluctant to challenge this system. There have been some recent promising beginnings, such as the National Research Council project titled "Revisions to the Common Rule for the Protection of Human Subjects in Research in the Behavioral and Social Sciences" (http://www8.

nationalacademies.org/cp/projectview.aspx?key=49500), which has recently issued a workshop report titled *Proposed Revisions to the Common Rule: Perspectives of Social and Behavioral Scientists* (http://www.nap.edu/catalog.php?record_id=18383). Additionally, there have been some very creative developments in the biomedical area (see the work of the Sage Bioinformatics Forum, http://sagebase.org, or the work of John Wilbanks on the Portable Legal Consent Framework, http://weconsent.us).

This creates many challenges for frontline data curation, beginning with the development of data management plans. Data management plans need to be synchronized with negotiations between investigators and IRBs about experimental protocols and the handling of data collected through these protocols, and often these negotiations will continue far into the actual conduct of the research funded under a given grant. As conformance is tracked more seriously, it may be necessary to develop ways to evolve and amend data management plans in light of these ongoing negotiations with IRBs. While there is often some form of support, education, and training available to investigators in meeting IRB requirements, there will be a need to provide these investigators with information and advice on how to *balance* IRB demands with the demands of funders to facilitate sharing and reuse of data. A good deal of the burden here is likely to fall on the institutional data curation staff, who will need to develop considerable expertise in these complex areas. There will also be a demand for flexible data publishing and curation platforms that can meet the IT security requirements imposed by IRBs and by other regulations such as the *Health Insurance Portability and Accountability Act* (HIPAA).

Really Long-Term (Semantic) Preservation

Almost all of the practical research data management preservation work I am aware of has been about preserving bits across time, and ensuring that these bits are documented with sufficient metadata and other explanatory material that then can be understood and reused, today or tomorrow, by people other than those who created it. (In truth, while it may be possible to reuse data without communicating with the creator of the data, it can be perilous, particularly when there is not an active community already working with the data; access to the creator is often a great boon.) At least conceptually, bit-level preservation is fairly straightforward.

There are ideas about higher levels of preservation driven mostly by changing information technology practices and standards (e.g., moving from a proprietary format to an open standard as software evolves; updating ASCII or EBCDIC data to UNICODE; migrating from an older image format like JPEG to a newer one like JPEG 2000; converting from SGML to XML). These conversions will be much less frequent than migrating from one storage system or medium to a newer one and copying the bits over; they can be substantially more complex, however, and involve sometimes very subtle curatorial choices. Yet over extended periods of time, they are important in keeping materials meaningfully useable and interpretable. We have some experience with these types of conversions, though limited.

As we think about preserving research data across really long periods of time, however, it is clear that matters get very complex indeed. The underlying experimental methods or observational tools change as technology changes; understanding of the contexts surrounding data shift as new disciplinary paradigms emerge, and agreement on what data is actually significant and what characterizes objects or processes also changes. We have almost no experience in this area, or only very unsatisfactory partial analogies (trying to understand alchemical texts from the perspective of modern chemistry, for example). Understanding the limits of our ability to preserve, and our ability to reuse across long periods of time and the massive evolution of knowledge will be very important in making decisions about where to invest and what promises we can responsibly make to the present and the future. At the very least, it is important for our frontline data curators to inject a note of humility and caution about confidence in very long-term preservation.

CONCLUSION

We are at the early stages of a genuine systemic and systematic response to the data stewardship challenges framed by the emergence of e-research, and to seizing the opportunities promised by more effective, broadscale data sharing and reuse. Key players in the system—notably the funders and policymakers—have made a clear commitment to addressing the issues and to forcing other players to do so as well.

Today intensive frontline institutional research data curation efforts are underway to respond rapidly to the most basic needs: documenting data management plans, setting up data documentation, bit preservation, and data publishing services. Some leadership institutions now have relatively advanced, robust, and comprehensive services in place; many others are following, with initial services either deployed or in the advanced planning stages.

I have not devoted much attention here to these three basic services, which are extensively covered elsewhere in this volume; however, it is important to emphasize that while they are reasonably clear conceptually, as the scale and depth of experience increases, some very critical operational issues are going to emerge. For example, data repositories are going to emerge as very attractive, high-value targets on an increasingly hostile Internet. Further, the security problems that we tend to emphasize here (because of incidents in other contexts) are data breaches: some attacker obtains access to data that was not intended to be generally available. But probably of greater concern in the data curation context is outright destruction or, even worse, deliberate corruption (perhaps quiet, unannounced, and subtle) of research data, potentially calling results and reputations into question through problems with replication, or leading to chains of erroneous conclusions or pointless investigations as data is reused and the corruption propigates.

Another area of great concern is ensuring that research data is appropriately documented to permit and facilitate reuse (which also implies discovery and assessment, but goes beyond these activities). It is easy to be glib about this, and to appeal to library and/or archival descriptive practices, which are by and large entirely insufficient to support the full cycle of reuse. We can certainly point to some real successes in documenting for reuse, ranging from social science survey data to remote sensing and geospatial data, clinical trials, or gene sequences, but this is often data that is collected with reuse in mind, and often comes out of fairly large-scale data acquisition projects. In other settings there is very little experience with data reuse; today's attempts at documentation are mostly best guesses and assumptions, unproven in actual reuse situations. And the documentation—and particularly automatic documentation (of parameters and readings from various kinds of experimental apparatus, data provenance, or computational workflows)—is still a very active research area. As we gain more experience with reuse in different domains and contexts, we will learn what documentation practices work and what is needed to support the goal of reuse. It is essential that we feed this back into data curation best practices on a continuing basis, and that the curators and investigators who work together to document new data continually absorb these lessons.

The stewardship challenges do not stop with the three fundamental services, and there are specific and complex barriers that conflict with the goals of greatly expanded sharing and reuse. These are related to, but are not precisely the same as, stewardship challenges, and these are easy for curators to overlook unless they keep the mandate to facilitate reuse and not just preservation firmly in focus. Finally, it is clear that an enormous imbalance exists between the resources currently available to fund these efforts and the potentially almost infinite demands of a fully realized data stewardship program; a key strategy in managing this imbalance is the effective use of the *specific* policy goals, such as data reuse, as shaping and prioritizing mechanisms in shaping an overall stewardship effort.

It is my hope that this article has provided a better understanding of these emerging issues and the way they are likely to unfold over the next decade or two, and identified many of the key next-generation research challenges that are going to require attention in the not-very-distant future.

About the Contributors

Suzie Allard is associate professor and associate director in the School of Information Sciences at the University of Tennessee. Her work focuses on how scientists and engineers use and communicate information. Current projects center on science information and science data curation. She is a member of the DataONE Leadership Team and the Board of Directors for the Networked Digital Library of Theses and Dissertations. She is PI or co-PI on grants funded by the National Science Foundation, the Institute of Museum and Libraries Services, the Alfred P. Sloan Foundation, IEEE, and others. Allard has published numerous papers in peer-reviewed journals, spoken at venues around the world, and published several book chapters focused on data curation and data science. Allard received a bachelor's degree in economics from California State University at Northridge, an MS in library and information sciences, and a PhD in communication from the University of Kentucky.

George Alter is director of the Inter-university Consortium for Political and Social Research (ICPSR), a professor of history at the University of Michigan, and a research professor in the Population Studies Center, Institute of Social Research, also at the University of Michigan. Alter's research grows out of interests in the history of the family, demography, and economic history. He is particularly interested in methods for reconstructing and analyzing life histories from longitudinal data, and he has recently participated in two cross-national comparative projects. The "Eurasia Project" examines demographic responses to economic stress in five societies in Europe and East Asia. The "Early Life Conditions" project asks whether experiences in childhood have long-run effects on health in old age.

Neil Beagrie is a director of Charles Beagrie Ltd., an independent management consultancy company specializing in the digital archive, library, science, and research sectors. Beagrie was PI for the Keeping Research Data Safe (KRDS) projects and co-investigator with John Houghton on the Impact of the Archaeology Data Service studies, the British Atmospheric Data Centre, and the Economic and Social Science Data Service. His previous career spans a range of senior information management roles, including programme director for digital preservation at the UK Joint Information Systems Committee, assistant director of the Arts and Humanities Data Service, and head of the Archaeological Archives and Library at the Royal Commission on the Historical Monuments of England. He is a fellow of the Royal Society for the Encouragement of Arts, Manufactures and Commerce, and he has published extensively on research data management issues. Further information, including published articles, is available from www.beagrie.com.

Christine L. Borgman is professor and presidential chair in information studies at the University of California, Los Angeles, where she conducts research in data practices and policy. She is the author of three books from MIT Press: *Scholarship in the Digital Age: Information, Infrastructure, and the Internet* (2007), *From Gutenberg to the Global Information Infrastructure: Access to Information in a Networked World* (2000), and the forthcoming (2014) *Big Data, Little Data, No Data*. She is a cochair of the Committee on Data for Science and Technology/International Council for Scientific and Technical Information (CODATA/ICSTI) Task Group on Data Citation and has served on the U.S. National Academy Board on Research Data and Information (BRDI) and CODATA.

D. Scott Brandt is associate dean for research and professor of library science in the Purdue University Libraries. He is the acting director of the Distributed Data Curation Center, home of the award-winning Data Curation Profiles Toolkit. He interfaces with research administration throughout

Purdue, is responsible for helping to build data services, and helps promote research in library science, which has included many interdisciplinary collaborations and a strong record of extramural funding. Brandt received his BA degree in English literature and his MLIS from Indiana University. He worked previously as associate head in the MIT Libraries, and he is author of two books: *Teaching Technology* (Neal-Schuman, 2002) and *Unix and Libraries* (Meckler, 1991).

Jan Brase has a degree in mathematics and a PhD in computer science from the University of Hannover. He was head of the Digital Object Identifier (DOI) registration agency of the German National Library of Science and Technology and has been executive director of DataCite since its founding in 2009. He is vice president of the International Council for Scientific and Technical Information (ICSTI), cochair of the International DOI Foundation (IDF), and a cochair of the CODATA-ICSTI Task Group on Data Citation. Brase's ORCID ID is 0000-0002-8250-6253.

Sarah Callaghan has a BSc in physics and music from Cardiff University, and a PhD in radiocommunications from the University of Portsmouth, UK. She is a senior researcher and project manager within the British Atmospheric Data Centre (BADC), where she project managed and provided technical input into the EU Framework 7-funded Common Metadata for Climate Modeling Digital Repositories (METAFOR) project, the JISC-funded Overlay journal infrastructure for Meteorological Sciences (OJIMS) and Peer REview for Publication & Accreditation of Research Data in the Earth sciences (PREPARDE) projects, and the United Kingdom's Natural Environment Research Council (NERC) data citation and publication project. Her main research interest is data citation and publication, and she also is a cochair of the CODATA-ICSTI Task Group on Data Citation. She is an associate editor for the Wiley-Blackwell and Royal Meteorological Society's *Geoscience Data Journal*.

Jake Carlson is an associate professor of library science and a data services specialist at the Purdue University Libraries. In this role, he explores the application of the theories, principles, and practices of library science beyond the domain of traditional "library work." In particular, Carlson seeks to increase the Purdue Libraries' capabilities and opportunities to work in data-related research. Much of his work is done through direct collaborations and partnerships with research faculty. Carlson is one of the architects of the Data Curation Profiles Toolkit (http://datacurationprofiles.org) developed by Purdue and the University of Illinois at Urbana-Champaign, and the PI of the Data Information Literacy project (http://datainfolit.org).

Bonnie Carroll is founder and CEO of Information International Associates, Inc. (IIa), a company providing information management and technology services to government and industry. Carroll is on the CODATA Executive Committee and is liaison to the CODATA/ICSTI Task Group on Data Citation. She was cochair of the Task Group from 2010–2013. She also is a member of the U.S. National Academy BRDI and executive director of the U.S. Federal Scientific and Technical Information Managers interagency group known as CENDI.

Ann Green is an independent research consultant focusing on the digital life cycle of scholarly resources. She brings an extensive background in digital curation, research data management, user-driven support services, and the development and promotion of standards for metadata and digital preservation. Green has played a key role in the conceptualization and evaluation of digital infrastructure, policies, systems, and services for the creation, access, and preservation of digital assets. From 2008 to 2011, she served as a digital information strategic analyst for the Office of Digital Assets and Infrastructure at Yale University. She is the former director of the Social Science Research Services and Statistical Laboratory at Yale, and previously held the position of data archivist at the University of California, Berkeley, and at the Cornell Institute for Social and Economic Research. She is past president of IASSIST and former chair of the Executive Council of the ICPSR. She also has served as a consultant for numerous digital preservation initiatives, including the Center for Research Libraries' (CRL) Certification and Assessment of Digital Repositories.

Geneva Henry is the university librarian and vice provost for libraries at the George Washington University in Washington, DC. Prior to assuming this position on July 1, 2013, she was the executive director of the Digital Scholarship Services (DSS) at Rice University's Fondren Library. She joined Rice in 2000 to start the university's digital library initiative, which has grown to include many projects, both grant-funded and internally sponsored. She collaborated closely with faculty at Rice to support their research and teaching, with many efforts focused on digital humanities. She is active in professional organizations and serves as a board member for several organizations and projects. Prior to joining Rice, Henry was a senior IT architect and program manager with IBM, where she was involved with several complex systems programs for government agencies, universities, and museums worldwide. Her earlier career involved applied research in artificial intelligence at TRW and the Rand Corporation.

John Houghton is a professorial fellow at Victoria University's Centre for Strategic Economic Studies (CSES) and director of the Centre's Information Technologies and the Information Economy Program. He has published and spoken widely on information technology, industry, and science and technology policy issues, and he has been a regular consultant to national and international agencies, including the Organisation for Economic Co-operation and Development. Houghton's research is at the interface of theory and practice with a strong focus on the policy application of economic and social theory, and of leading-edge research in various relevant fields. Consequently, his contribution tends to be in bringing knowledge and research methods to bear on policy issues in an effort to raise the level of policy debate and improve policy outcomes. In 1998, Houghton was awarded a National Australia Day Council's Australia Day Achievement Medallion for his contribution to IT industry policy development.

Michele Kimpton is CEO of DuraSpace and one of the founders of the organization. DuraSpace is an independent 501(c)(3) nonprofit organization committed to the management and preservation of our shared scholarly, scientific, and cultural record. The DuraSpace community includes more than 1,500 worldwide institutions that use DSpace or Fedora open-source repository software, two projects that are stewarded by DuraSpace, to provide durable access to documents, imagery, and media. DuraSpace also offers a number of managed services—such as DuraCloud and DSpacedirect—to better enable institutions with limited technical support or resources to manage their digital content. Kimpton recently was named a Digital Preservation Pioneer by the Library of Congress's National Digital Information Infrastructure and Preservation Program (NDIPP). Previously, Kimpton was the founder of the DSpace Foundation, a nonprofit organization set up to provide leadership and support to the community of users of the DSpace open-source software platform, and before that she was director of the Internet Archive. She is one of the founding members of the International Internet Preservation Consortium.

Ardys Kozbial is the collections and outreach librarian at the Harvard University Graduate School of Design. In her previous position as technology outreach librarian in the University of California-San Diego Library, much of her work focused on digital preservation, especially in collaboration with the San Diego Supercomputer Center (SDSC). Additionally, she worked on technology-based grant projects, from grant writing to project management, depending on the needs of a particular project. Before working at the University of California-San Diego, Kozbial spent 12 years working in architecture collections at Harvard University, the University of California, Berkeley, the University of Texas at Austin, and Payette Associates (a Boston-based architecture firm) as a librarian and archivist. She received a BA from the University of Michigan and an MS in library and information science from Simmons College.

Sherry Lake is the senior data consultant in the Data Management Consulting Group at the University of Virginia (UVa) Library. Lake provides expertise, support, and training in the areas of data management, metadata production, data organization, and preservation. She was instrumental in the creation of the National Science Foundation (NSF) data management plan templates, which were used locally at UVa and which later were used as the source of guidelines for the DMPTool, an online service used at over 500 U.S. institutions that helps researchers create data management plans. Lake has held several positions at the UVa Library supporting various digital projects within and outside the library. She has expertise in a variety of metadata standards across different disciplines, including geospatial and statistical data collections. She earned a MS in information sciences from the University of Tennessee, Knoxville, and a BS in computer science from the University of Virginia's School of Engineering and Applied Science.

Melissa Levine is lead copyright officer at the University of Michigan Library. With over 20 years of experience in museums, libraries, and educational institutions working on policy, business affairs, and intellectual property, she provides guidance on copyright policy and practice in the university context. Previously, Levine handled business affairs at the Smithsonian Institution and cutting-edge digital library issues as assistant general counsel and legal advisor at the Library of Congress's National Digital Library Project. Levine has a longstanding interest in museums, with experience as acting director of the Frost Art Museum at Florida International University; associate director for finance and administration at the Wolfsonian Museum; and acting curator of the World Bank Art Program. She is a graduate of the University of Miami School of Law and Emory University, a member of the Virginia bar, and chair of the American Bar Association's Copyright Policy Committee. She teaches in the Johns Hopkins University museum studies program and the University of Michigan School of Information.

Jared Lyle is director of Curation Services at the Inter-university Consortium for Political and Social Research (ICPSR), part of the Institute for Social Research at the University of Michigan. His work includes developing and maintaining a comprehensive approach to data management and digital preservation policy at ICPSR. Lyle has been with ICPSR since 2004, where he has processed and archived data, managed acquisitions, and coordinated research projects on digital preservation and data sharing, including the Data Preservation Alliance for the Social Sciences (DataPASS), a partnership of social science repositories that archives, catalogs, and preserves at-risk data collections. Lyle also helps lead a workshop in the ICPSR Summer Program titled "Curating and Managing Research Data for Re-Use."

Clifford Lynch has led the Coalition for Networked Information (CNI) since 1997. CNI's wide-ranging agenda includes work in digital preservation, data-intensive scholarship, teaching, learning and technology, and infrastructure and standards development. Prior to joining CNI, Lynch spent 18 years at the University of California Office of the President, the last 10 as director of Library Automation. He is both a past president and recipient of the Award of Merit of the American Society for Information Science, and a fellow of the American Association for the Advancement of Science and the National Information Standards Organization. In 2011, he was appointed cochair of the National Academies Board on Research Data and Information; he serves on numerous advisory boards and visiting committees. His work has been recognized by the American Library Association's Lippincott Award, the EDUCAUSE Leadership Award in Public Policy and Practice, and the American Society for Engineering Education's Homer Bernhardt Distinguished Service Award. He holds a PhD in computer science from the University of California, Berkeley, and is an adjunct professor at Berkeley's School of Information.

David Minor is director of Digital Preservation Initiatives at the University of California-San Diego (UCSD). In this role, he helps define current and future work needed for the preservation of vital resources. He also is the program manager of Chronopolis, a national-scale digital preservation network. In addition to his digital preservation duties, he is lead for the Curation Services Program in the Research Cyberinfrastructure Initiative on the UCSD campus.

Laura Molloy is a researcher at the Humanities Advanced Technology and Information Institute (HATII) at the University of Glasgow, working in the areas of digital curation and research data management. She has experience in design and delivery of training and skills development for researchers and support professionals, including work with Digital Curation Centre and on the JISC-funded projects Incremental and Data Management Skills Support Initiative (DaMSSI). Molloy has gathered and analyzed evidence of benefits arising from the JISC Managing Research Data Programme. Her European Commission-funded experience includes delivery of outreach and training events for the Planets project, online outreach materials for Digital Preservation Europe (DPE), and development of a curriculum framework for digital curation in the cultural heritage sector for the DigCurV project. She is a regular speaker on digital curation and research data management, particularly in relation to nonscience research.

Carol Minton Morris (Terrizzi) is director of marketing and communications for the DuraSpace Organization, a position she has held since 2009. She joined the National Science Digital Library (NSDL) team at Cornell University as a research assistant in 2000 and served as communications director for NSDL initiatives from 2000–2009. She also served as the communications director for the Fedora Commons organization from 2007–2009. In her current role, she leads strategic editorial content and materials planning, development, and distribution focused on sustaining open-source projects (DSpace, Fedora) and marketing services (DuraCloud, DSpaceDirect). She is chair of the annual International Open Repositories Conference Steering Committee and serves as cochair of the National Digital Stewardship Alliance (NDSA) Outreach Working Group. She reports on digital library and repository-related meetings and conferences in *Dlib Magazine*.

James L. (Jim) Mullins is dean of libraries and Esther Ellis Norton Professor at Purdue University. He has been in his current position since 2004, with over 40 years of library experience. Before his appointment at Purdue, he was associate director for administration at MIT Libraries and earlier held administrative/faculty positions at Villanova University and Indiana University. Mullins received his BA and MALS degrees from the University of Iowa, and his PhD from Indiana University. He has been active professionally within the Association of College and Research Libraries (ACRL), Association of Research Libraries (ARL), the International Federation of Library Associations (IFLA), and the International Association of Scientific and Technological University Libraries (IATUL). He has been recognized as a leader in advancing research libraries and their roles within e-science, scholarly communication, and space use, along with redefining how the work of a librarian must change and evolve within the research university environment.

Joyce M. Ray is currently a visiting professor in the Berlin School of Library and Information Science at Humboldt University. From 1997 to 2011, she was associate deputy director for library services at the Institute of Museum and Library Services, where she directed grant programs for research and development of best practices in libraries and development of educational programs in graduate schools of library and information science, among other programs to improve U.S. library services. She formerly held positions at the National Archives and Records Administration. She has been on the faculty of the Johns Hopkins University since 2011, where she has helped to develop a graduate certificate program in digital curation in the museum studies graduate program. She has a master's degree in library and information science and a PhD in history, both from the University of Texas at Austin, and she has published on topics in digital preservation and curation in libraries, archives, and museums.

Bernard F. Reilly, Jr., is president of the CRL, a partnership of 270 U.S. and Canadian university, college, and independent research libraries. At CRL, Reilly has led several major digital preservation projects funded by the Andrew W. Mellon Foundation, the NSF, and the John D. and Catherine T. MacArthur: Foundation: the Political Communications Web Archiving Investigation (2002–2004); Auditing and Certification of Digital Archives (2005–2007); Case Studies of Long-Lived Digital Collections (2008–2010); and Electronic Evidence and Human Rights (2009–2010). Prior to joining CRL, Reilly was director of research and access at the Chicago History Museum (1997–2001), where he directed the administration, digitization, and dissemination of the CHM library, archives, and architecture, audio, television, and pictorial collections. Reilly was head of the Curatorial Section of the Prints and Photographs Division of the Library of Congress (1987–1997), which provided curatorial and policy support for the early development of the National Digital Library.

Jenn Riley is the head of the Carolina Digital Library and Archives at the University of North Carolina (UNC) at Chapel Hill. She leads a service-focused department that combines digital technologies with library and archival collections to support the work of scholars, students, and librarians at UNC and beyond. In this role, she also works to enhance faculty digital research and scholarship, builds partnerships to advance the state of the art in digital libraries, and develops sustainable and streamlined workflows for the publication of digital content. She holds an MLS from Indiana University, an MA in musicology from Indiana University, and a BM in music education from the University of Miami. Prior to arriving at UNC in 2010, she was the metadata librarian with the Indiana University Digital Library Program.

Andrew Sallans is head of Strategic Data Initiatives and the Data Management Consulting Group at the University of Virginia Library. His group works with researchers and other support units across the institution on issues of research data management. His group also is the primary institutional support unit for emerging data management planning requirements, such as the 2011 NSF data management plan mandate. He serves as the coleader of the DMPTool project, chair of the DataONE Users Group, the PI on a citizen science crowdsourcing project, and is presently involved in an initiative to advance data-intensive research support services across the UVa Libraries. He earned an MS in the management of information technology from the McIntire School of Commerce at the University of Virginia, an MS in library and information studies from Florida State University, and a BA in archaeology, history, and art history from the University of Virginia.

Brian E. C. Schottlaender is the Audrey Geisel University Librarian at the University of California, San Diego. The UCSD Library was the first in southern California to partner with Google on its global book digitization project. Long a proponent of cooperation between and amongst libraries and related organizations, Schottlaender chairs the HathiTrust Board of Governors. He also is a member of the Boards of Trustees of the Digital Preservation Network and of OCLC, and serves as an elected member of the Governing Council of the ALA. In 2010, Schottlaender was named the Melvil Dewey Medal winner by the ALA in recognition of "creative leadership of a high order." Schottlaender, who held positions at the California Digital Library, UCLA, the University of Arizona, and Indiana University before joining UCSD, is also the recipient of the ALA's Ross Atkinson Lifetime Achievement Award (2007) and Margaret Mann Citation (2001).

MacKenzie Smith is University Librarian at the University of California, Davis, and is an academic research library leader specializing in information technology and digital knowledge management. Prior to joining UC Davis in 2012, she was Associate Director for Technology and Research Director at the MIT Libraries, where she oversaw their technology strategy, operations, research, and development. Her research has focused on information technology applications in research libraries, such as semantic web-based scholarly communication platforms and digital research data curation including long-term preservation and archiving. She was the project director for MIT's collaboration with Hewlett-Packard to build DSpace, the open-source digital archive platform now in worldwide use, and has led many other research projects that advanced the international digital library agenda. She was a research fellow at the Creative Commons for science and data governance policy, and has consulted widely in the library field. Prior to MIT, Smith managed the Harvard University Library's Digital Library Program and held library IT positions at Harvard and the University of Chicago.

Yvonne Socha holds a degree in journalism and a master's degree in education and information science. She is an assistant professor and medical librarian at the University of Tennessee Health Science Center in Memphis. Her research interests include health informatics and bibliometrics. While a graduate student at the University of Tennessee, she completed a practicum with International Information Associates, in which she conducted an inventory of existing literature, data citation, and attribution initiatives for the CODATA/ICSTI Task Group on Data Citation. This research was compiled into a bibliography and utilized by the Task Group. She later rejoined the group as an independent consultant and editor of the project report.

Gail Steinhart is Head of Research Services at Cornell University's Albert R. Mann Library. She oversees the development and delivery of innovative research support services and projects, including those related to research data, geographic information systems, and services that help researchers meet research funding requirements. She also serves as the research services subject specialist for environmental sciences and the library liaison for environmental science activities at Cornell. She is a member of the Cornell University Library's Data Executive Group and Cornell University's Research Data Management Service Group, which seek to advance the library's and Cornell's capabilities in the areas of data curation and data-driven research, respectively. She holds MS degrees in library and information science (Syracuse University) and ecology and evolutionary biology (Cornell University), and worked for nearly 15 years in environmental research before becoming a librarian.

Paul F. Uhlir is director of the Board on Research Data and Information and of the U.S. CODATA at the National Academy of Sciences in Washington, DC. He works on topics at the interface of science, technology, and law, with a focus on digital research. He holds a JD and MA in international relations from the University of San Diego, and a BA in world history from the University of Oregon.

Tyler Walters is dean of the university libraries and a professor at Virginia Tech. He is a 2010 ARL Research Libraries Leadership Fellow. Walters serves on many professional bodies such as: the Coordinating Committee of the National Digital Stewardship Alliance (Library of Congress); the Steering Committee of the Coalition for Networked Information; the Board of Directors and Executive Committee of DuraSpace; the Board of Directors of the National Information Standards Organization; the Executive and Steering Committees of the Library Publishing Coalition; and the Editorial Board of the *International Journal of Digital Curation*. Walters is a founding member of the MetaArchive Cooperative, a digital preservation federation, and he serves on the board of its management organization, the Educopia Institute. He is the lead author of the 2011 ARL report, "New Roles for New Times: Digital Curation for Preservation" (http://www.arl.org/bm~doc/nrnt_digital_curation17mar11.pdf). Walters is a PhD candidate at Simmons College and focuses on knowledge creation and production in research universities, organizational trust development, and authentic and transformational leadership.

Marie E. Waltz has worked as a special projects librarian at the CRL since 2002. During this time, she has worked on CRL projects related to digital and print repositories. She currently is responsible for managing CRL's Audit and Certification of Digital Repositories services and has participated on all CRL audits. In addition, she is a member of the working group establishing the ISO standards for auditing digital repositories. Besides digital preservation, Waltz is on CRL's PAPR registry development team. The PAPR registry discloses information about print archiving programs and their holdings. Prior to working at CRL, Waltz worked as an information analyst at PepsiCo and as head of Access Services at the San Diego County Public Law Library. She received her MLS from Indiana University in Bloomington, Indiana.

Brian Westra is the Lorry I. Lokey Science Data Services Librarian at the University of Oregon (UO). He provides consultation support for faculty with their NSF data management plans, teaches research data management to graduate students and faculty, and supports data curation and cyberinfrastructure initiatives in the sciences. Westra also is the liaison to the UO Department of Chemistry. He has an MS in environmental science (Western Washington University) and an MSI in library and information services (University of Michigan).

Angus Whyte is a senior institutional support officer in the Digital Curation Centre. He works alongside partners in United Kingdom universities to improve services that support researchers and other stakeholders in data management. Whyte has authored guidelines and articles on a range of data issues, including case studies of researchers' data practices. He has a PhD in information science from the University of Strathclyde, and before joining DCC, he was for 10 years a postdoc researcher in the social informatics field, working on requirements discovery and evaluation of information systems to support engagement in policymaking.

Index